# The Gatekeepers

The Global Media Battle
to Control Australia's
Pay TV

Mark Westfield

jointly published

Pluto
Press

CM

SYDNEY · LONDON

For my dear late father, Ray,
and mother, Audrey

First published in 2000 by
Pluto Press Australia Limited
Locked Bag 199, Annandale NSW 2038
Website:media.socialchange.net.au/pluto

in association with

Comerford & Miller
36 Grosvenor Rd, West Wickham, Kent BR4 9PY UK

UK and Ireland distributers:
Central Books
99 Wallis Rd, London E11 5LN UK

Cover design by Mark Brooks

Cover photos of Rupert Murdoch and Kerry Packer supplied courtesy
of Newspix.

Edited by Bruce Pollock

Index by Neale Towart

Design and typesetting by DOCUPRO

Printed and bound by McPherson's Printing Group

Australian Cataloguing in Publication Data

Westfield, Mark.
The gatekeepers: The global media battle to control Australia's pay TV.

Includes index.
ISBN 1 86403 102 6.

1. Subscription television—Australia. 2. Television broadcasting—Economic
aspects—Australia. 3. Television broadcasting policy—Australia. I. Title.

384.5550994

UK Cataloguing in Publication Data

UK ISBN 1 871204 19 4

A catalogue record for this book is available at the British Library

# Contents

# Chronology

*1972*

November: John Elliott, Peter Scanlon, Richard Wiesener and Bob Cowper buy jam maker Henry Jones for $35 million and find it owns a television and radio station whose manager, Ray Gamble, is ambitious to begin a pay TV business in Australia; later identifies two US cable operators, but Elliott is persuaded by Communications Minister Tony Staley to wait until pay TV legalised in Australia.

*1979*

Fraser Government establishes Aussat to order and launch a national satellite.

*1982*

Australian Broadcasting Tribunal recommends that pay TV be introduced to Australia "as soon as practicable".

*1983*

After Labor victory, Elliott realises pay TV doomed in short term and orders Gamble to sell Henry Jones' media assets; Gamble begins work on management buyout with help of merchant bankers John Gerahty and Robin Crawford. Gamble introduces them to his old friends Wiesener and Scanlon; Broadcast and Communications (Broadcom) lists in late 1983.

*1984*

Steve Cosser buys Riviera 104 and has chance meeting in Monaco with Richard Wiesener, who introduces Cosser to Ray Gamble and his backers.

*1985*

September: Cosser hires merchant banker Wayne Burt.
November: Seven Network's Ron Casey makes low offer of $2.7 million for 1986 VFL rights; Cosser offers more than the $3.5 million the VFL received in 1985, plus chance to earn more if Broadcom on-sells the rights for a profit; VFL awards rights to Broadcom.

*1986*

Seven's ratings plunge in 1986 football season; Casey offers Cosser $9 million to win back VFL rights.
September: Labor Communications Minister Michael Duffy announces four-year moratorium on pay TV to help commercial networks adjust to equalisation and aggregation policy.
November: Duffy announces cross media ownership rule.
December: News Limited bids $1.8 billion for Herald & Weekly Times group.

*1987*

January: Alan Bond offers Kerry Packer $1 billion for Nine's Sydney and Melbourne stations; Rupert Murdoch sells Ten network to Frank Lowy for $842 million.
February: Murdoch sells HSV-7 in Melbourne acquired with HWT takeover to John Fairfax for $320 million; Warwick Fairfax jnr buys 1 per cent of John Fairfax.
July: John Fairfax forced to sell Seven Network to Christopher Skase's Qintex group after Labor wins election.
August: Warwick Fairfax launches $2.25 billion takeover bid for John Fairfax.
October: stockmarket falls 20 per cent.

*1988*

Reserve Bank begins lifting interest rates after NSW State election in April; federal bureaucracy begins review of broadcasting and telecommunications policies.

*1989*

September: Steve Cosser buys control of Ten Network from Frank Lowy for outlay of $22 million lent by Lowy.

November: Qintex goes into receivership.

*1990*

March: Hawke Labor Government wins fourth term; Bob Hawke appoints Kim Beazley Communications Minister.

July: Kerry Packer regains control of Nine Network from troubled Alan Bond.

September: Labor national conference approves Beazley plan to merge Telecom and OTC to form "Megacom"; Beazley extends moratorium on pay TV another 12 months; Westpac puts receivers into Ten Network.

*1991*

Cosser identifies MDS technology as a way of transmitting hi-fi audio to households.

November: Beazley releases draft Broadcasting Services Bill; Cosser's Broadcom applies for one MDS licence to narrowcast video and audio direct to corporate customers in Sydney; Optus consortium wins second national telephone carrier's licence with bid of $800 million.

December: Paul Keating wins Labor leadership in party room vote; Conrad Black's Tourang consortium buys John Fairfax for $1.4 billion using complex ownership structure.

*1992*

January: Keating appoints Graham Richardson Communications Minister; Bob Mansfield appointed chief executive of Optus; Telecom board appoints American Frank Blount as chief executive.

March: Steve Cosser starts MDS service to small number of corporate clients.

May: Richardson forced to resign over Marshall Islands affair.

June: Broadcasting Services Bill, minus pay TV section, goes to Parliament; Broadcom applies for 12 new MDS licences days before issue of licences closed off.

October: Keating sets digital technology standard for satellite pay TV; government to issue three pay TV licences.

November: Part 7 of *Broadcasting Services Act* passes through

Parliament, legalising pay TV; Packer buys 9.7 per cent of Westpac in sharemarket raid.

December: CanWest buys Ten Network from receiver for $245 million using complex ownership structure; Communications Minister Bob Collins announces auction for 200 MDS licences; Optus satellite destroyed with crash of Long March rocket.

*1993*

January: Packer walks out of Westpac board meeting, rejecting offer of board seat; Cosser raises $2.5 million from investors for Australis; Collins announces auction of two commercial satellite licences; MDS auction cancelled at last minute after heavy network lobbying on Keating.

February: Rodney Price becomes chairman of Australis Media, as Broadcom now known; Cosser runs anti-Government ads criticising decision to cancel MDS auction in lead-up to March election.

March: Keating wins "unwinnable election"; Kerry Packer hires Brian Powers as his chief executive; Packer invites News and Telstra to form consortium to bid for satellite licence.

April: Wayne Burt raises further $8 million for Australis; Paul Keating addresses News Corp conference on Hamilton Island; Albert Hadid and Hi Vision group bid $177 million and $212 million respectively to win satellite licences; Time Warner disqualified on technicality; Telstra board votes to buy 10 per cent of Seven Network, joining News, which would take 15 per cent.

July: first satellite bids fail to attract backers, and cascade down to next price level.

August: Hadid persuades Lenfest Communications to back his final bids for A and B licences.

September: Australis lists on stock exchange; Telstra begins trials using cable-based multi-channel service in Sydney.

October: Cosser hires Neil Gamble as Australis chief executive; Telstra calls for tenders to build cable network offering 64 channels.

November: Lenfest buys B licence from Hadid and on-sells it to Australis.

*1994*

February: PMT consortium launches legal action against satellite licence holders alleging collusion; Rod Price persuades

Communications Minister Michael Lee to instruct Telstra to drop action.

March: CTS consortium announces it will offer multi-channel service using Telstra cable.

April: Kerry Packer takes option to buy 15 per cent of Optus for $318 million; Telstra board agrees to start limited cable roll-out to 1.1 million homes in suburbs; Optus and Continental Cablevision announce joint venture to build cable network.

May: Australis raises $175.5 million from Australian and overseas investors; Lee draws up lengthy anti-siphoning list preserving rights to most major sports for commercial networks and ABC.

June: Kerry Packer announces merger of Australian Consolidated Press and Nine Network; News buys 1.5 per cent of John Fairfax.

July: MDS auctions begin and PMT does not bid; Australis picks up most licences, some at high cost because of bidding by Albert Hadid; Burt and Hadid reach agreement to stop Hadid bidding, but the two later disagree on terms of deal; Rupert Murdoch agrees to build film studio in Sydney; Optus and Continental Cablevision announce plans for multi-billion dollar cable network passing two million homes to deliver telephone and pay TV services; Telstra lifts roll-out target to 1.7 million homes.

August: Australis opens negotiations with both Optus and Telstra to run Australis's 10-channel program package on either Optus or Telstra cable.

September: PMT agrees to dissolve; launch of Optus Vision adding Nine and Seven networks to Optus-Continental Cablevision consortium and lifting cable roll out target to pass three million homes at cost of $3 billion; Optus courts News to try to get it into Optus Vision.

October: News agrees, joins Optus Vision, then withdraws; Australis and Optus Vision sign up, between them, all Hollywood studios except Fox.

November: News announces joint venture with Telstra and cable rollout to cost $3.5 billion; Seven quits Optus Vision after Lee says Government will not allow cable groups to have regional monopolies.

December: Sam Chisholm negotiates program supply deal with Australis to supply News-Telstra alliance.

*1995*

January: Australis launches its Galaxy service on Australia Day, broadcasting its Premier Sports channel using MDS; Australis says will broadcast Australia v West Indies Test in the Caribbean but stopped by anti-siphoning rule and Nine's refusal to use its rights to cover series.

February: Ken Cowley asks Australian Rugby League for pay TV rights to the game and proposes 12-team competition; Kerry Packer tells ARL he has all rights to the ARL; Michael Lee persuades Ten network to broadcast cricket Test series to allow Australis also to show it; Packer raises his stake in John Fairfax after Rupert Murdoch is reported saying he would like to buy more shares; Packer endorses John Howard as Prime Minister in interview on his Nine network; Keating attacks Packer, accusing him of "scam" over cable roll-out.

March: News-Telstra launch their pay TV venture, calling it Foxtel.

April: Geoff Cousins starts as head of Optus Vision the day News reveals it bought clubs and players to start 12-team Super League competition; Kerry Stokes raids market for Seven Network shares; Cousins wins Seven back into Optus Vision with offer of $10 million sign-on fee.

May: Stokes becomes chairman of Seven after buying 20 per cent of the company; Australis raises $US175 million in a "junk" bond raising in the US; ABC's Australian Information Media consortium collapses after it fails to persuade Australis, Foxtel or Optus Vision to take its news and current affairs channels; News signs southern hemisphere rugby unions to 10-year pay TV rights deal.

July: Australis approaches Foxtel with merger proposal as Optus Vision prepares to start price war with cheap connection fees and monthly subscriptions.

August: Bob Mansfield resigns from Optus Communications to take managing director's job at John Fairfax; Australis announces $122 million loss for the year to June 30.

September: Optus Vision announces $29.95 connection and $25 a month subscription; News and ARL begin their actions against each other in the Federal Court.

November: Murdoch and Packer agree to reshuffle their media interests with News taking a stake in Nine and Packer selling his 17 per cent Fairfax stake to News.

*1996*

February: Australian Competition and Consumer Commission blocks proposed Australis-Foxtel merger; Justice Burchett finds against Super League and in favour of ARL; Lachlan Murdoch offers Super League to Kerry and James Packer, which they refuse; Rodney Price approaches TCI for funds to keep Australis afloat.

March: News wins stay to appeal against Justice Burchett's decision; Price and Australis finance director Geoff Kleeman meet TCI's Fred Vierra in London hoping to sign funding agreement, but told TCI and News want to buy Australis's program supply agreement to Foxtel instead.

April: Neil Gamble approaches Kerry Packer who agrees to guarantee short-term loan of $US125 million by Australis; Packer takes first and last right of refusal over Australis assets.

May: Gamble approached to take job as head of Sydney casino.

June: new Prime Minister John Howard launches Optus Vision's local call service.

July: draft prospectus for fresh bond raising in US by Australis reveals that loan funds from previous rescue would be exhausted by July 31.

August: Australis announces joint venture with Optus Vision to share control of Australis's satellite licence and assets; Gamble resigns.

September: Cousins resigns; Australis attempts to make another bond issue in the US to repay loan guaranteed by Packer; Australis announces loss of $251.7 million for year to June 30.

October: Federal Court full bench overturns Burchett decision and backs Super League; Packer and Lenfest take up $US75 million of the Australis bond issue when it attracts little interest in US; Optus Vision commits $160 million over five years to ARL; Seven sues Optus Vision partners alleging they had breached shareholder agreement.

*1997*

March: Optus Communications buys out Optus Vision partners to end row.

April: Ken Cowley retires as News Limited chairman to be replaced by Lachlan Murdoch.

May: NSW Supreme Court rules declares Australis-Optus Vision satellite joint venture breaches Australis's agreement with Foxtel.

June: Ziggy Switkowski sacked as Optus chief executive; News and PBL agree to "equalise" their pay TV interests; Australis and Foxtel reignite merger discussions.

July: Cable & Wireless buys Bell South out of Optus Communications; Australis and Foxtel announce merger plans.

September: Rupert Murdoch meets C&W head Dick Brown to reach "understanding" between pay TV groups in Australia; Australis reports loss for year to June 30 of $297 million; Foxtel loses $212 million for the year and Optus Vision $388 million.

October: ACCC wins injunction stopping Australis-Foxtel merger; Telstra and Optus stop cable roll-out well short of initial targets.

November: Australis and Foxtel call off merger; Lachlan Murdoch re-negotiates movie supply deal with Hollywood studios in Vancouver; Telstra seeks winding up orders against Australis.

*1998*

May: bond holders appoint receiver to Australis; Telstra wins winding up order against Australis; Australis fails to make payment to Movie Partnership; studios switch supply agreement to Foxtel; Australis loses program feed; Foxtel moves to dominant position in pay TV.

# The cast

*(In alphabetical order)*

Ken Arthurson: chairman of the Australian Rugby League, which bitterly opposed the establishment of a rival Super League by Rupert Murdoch's News Limited.

Peter Barron: former journalist and adviser to Labor Prime Minister Bob Hawke, was Kerry Packer's main lobbyist in Canberra.

Kim Beazley: Labor Communications Minister who presided over auction for second telecommunications carrier and sale of Aussat satellites.

Frank Blount: chief executive of Telstra.

Mark Booth: chief executive of News-Telstra pay TV joint venture Foxtel.

Ron Brierley: New Zealand-born investor who tried to broker sale by Steve Cosser of his MDS licences to Kerry Packer.

Neil Brown: former Liberal Communications Minister who held crucial bid in satellite licence auction.

Wayne Burt: merchant banker and adviser to Albert Hadid, Lenfest Communications and Australis; devised Project Midsummer strategy to win satellite licence for Australis.

Mark Burrows: merchant banker who advised News Ltd in its efforts to take investment in Seven Network.

Peter Burrows: stockbroker who underwrote Australis Media float.

Bob Campbell: chief executive of Seven Network who tried to resist attempts by News to put together group of like-minded investors in the network's float.

Ron Casey: former chief executive of Seven Network station HSV-7, which lost rights to Victorian Football League to Steve Cosser at a critical time for the station.

Sam Chisholm: chief executive of UK BSkyB satellite service, who played main role in negotiating Telstra-News Corporation agreement through which Australis would supply its program package to Foxtel.

Malcolm Colless: executive in charge of business development at News.

Bob Collins: Minister for Communications who enacted Broadcasting Services Act and then cancelled MDS auction in controversial circumstances.

Margaret Combes: head of Americana cable group in the US who introduced Albert Hadid to Gerry Lenfest.

Steve Cosser: entrepreneur who briefly had control of Ten Network and then established Australis Media.

Geoff Cousins: chief executive of Optus Vision consortium which embarked on $3 billion cable roll-out to offer pay TV and telephone services in competition with Telstra.

Ken Cowley: chairman of News Limited, the Australian arm of the global News Corporation; close confidant of Rupert Murdoch and key player in establishing Super League.

Bob Cowper: colleague of John Elliott in takeover of Henry Jones, which owned media assets in Riverina; later attempted to have pay TV legalised in Australia.

Ivan Deveson: chairman of Seven Network who, with Bob Campbell, resisted News's attempt to win control of Seven; later dumped as chairman by Kerry Stokes.

Michael Duffy: Communications Minister who announced cross-media ownership rule which led to major changes in media ownership in Australia.

John Elliott: entrepreneur who orchestrated takeover of Henry Jones; lobbied Liberal ministers in 1970s to have pay TV legalised.

Warwick Fairfax: son of Sir Warwick Fairfax who launched ultimately disastrous $2.25 billion takeover bid for John Fairfax group in 1987 after sale by Fairfax of its Seven Network to Christopher Skase.

Nick Falloon: finance director of Kerry Packer's Publishing and Broadcasting Ltd (PBL) who was a key negotiator in the April 1996 refinancing of Australis.

Allan Fels: competition regulator who twice blocked attempted mergers by Australis and Foxtel.

Chaim Fortgang: US lawyer acting for investors who bought $US175 million in Australis bonds in 1995.

Peter Frame: Time Warner's representative in Australia; failed to negotiate position in satellite licences after having bid disallowed on technicality.

Stuart Fowler: chief executive of Westpac, which placed Ten Network into receivership while it was under the control of Steve Cosser.

Simon Gadir: technician who performed most of the financial modelling for Albert Hadid in lead-up to their UCOM Pty Ltd lodging winning bid for satellite A licence in April 1993; estimated licences were worth far more than believed by other bidders.

Neil Gamble: chief executive of Australis Media; hired from Wormald International where he had worked with Bob Mansfield.

Ray Gamble: (no relation) manager of TV and radio stations at Griffith bought by John Elliott in Henry Jones takeover.

John Gerahty: former merchant banker who was chairman of Steve Cosser's Broadcom.

Christine Goode: senior Department of Communications bureaucrat who was made scapegoat for MDS licence debacle.

David Gonski: merchant banker who helped devise complex ownership structures which enabled foreigners to have control of John Fairfax and Ten Network.

Ross Grant: merchant banker who advised Kerry Stokes on his ambitions to buy into Seven Network; also wrote experts' report which was never published into first merger between Australis and Foxtel.

Leo Gray: barrister associated with Hi Vision consortium which won first bid for satellite B licence with $212 million offer; claimed to have jointly devised with Albert Hadid the cascading bid mechanism which allowed UCOM and Hi Vision to control satellite bidding process for seven months.

Peter Gray: stockbroker who worked with Peter Burrows on Australis float.

Albert Hadid: won first round of satellite auction with offer of $177 million for A licence; later got control of both licences as bids cascaded down and onsold them to Lenfest for $13 million.

Don Hagans: Australian head of US cable group United International Holdings, which was an Australis franchisee in regional areas.

Martin Hannes: Australian head of US cable group Continental Cablevision, which joined Optus Communications to form Optus Vision.

Bob Hawke: Labor Prime Minister ousted by Paul Keating just before Federal Government considered new legislation to legalise pay TV.

Don Heller: head of development at Lenfest Communications, sent to Australia to establish satellite pay TV business; bought out Albert Hadid and on-sold licence to Australis, with Lenfest taking controlling interest.

David Hill: managing director of the ABC, which fought hard for two channels for pay TV.

Paul Keating: Labor Prime Minister after beating Bob Hawke in party room vote; the main power in government behind media law changes through the 1980s and in devising a formula for the satellite licences.

Mark Johnson: director of Macquarie Bank who advised John Fairfax in disastrous purchase of HSV-7; later deputy chairman of Australis.

Geoff Kleeman: finance director of Australis during difficult negotiations to make fresh bond issue in 1996.

David Leckie: chief executive of Nine Network and influential in drawing up of controversial "anti-siphoning" list locking up important broadcasting rights for commercial networks.

Gerry Lenfest: chairman of Lenfest Communications who committed the US cable group to joint venture with Albert Hadid in August 1993.

Frank Lowy: wealthy shopping centre developer who sold Ten Network to Steve Cosser.

Ross McCreath: finance director and later in project development for Australis; long-term employee and colleague of Cosser.

Bruce McWilliam: UK-based lawyer and friend of Sam Chisholm who helped negotiate program supply deal for Foxtel with Australis.

John Malone: chairman of TeleCommunications Inc, which owned 50 per cent of Lenfest Communications; offered then later withdrew crucial rescue funds for Australis.

Robert Mangioni: Australis lawyer.

Bob Mansfield: chief executive of Wormald International, then Optus Communications before quitting to run John Fairfax.

Neville Miles: adviser and stockbroker to Kerry Packer and also to Ivan Deveson at Seven Network.

Tom Mockridge: former press secretary to Paul Keating; later chief executive of Foxtel.

Rupert Murdoch: chairman and chief executive of News Corporation.

Lachlan Murdoch: Rupert's son; sent to Australia to "learn the ropes" and became enmeshed in Super League battle; renegotiated program supply arrangement with Hollywood studios for Foxtel.

Simon Murray: chief executive of Hutchison Whampoa who insisted that his group would not be a bidder for the second telecommunications licence unless the Aussat satellites could be used for pay TV.

Chris North: senior Department of Communications bureaucrat.

Wayne Nowland: designer of Aussat satellites in the 1980s; foresaw their use eventually for pay TV and installed the necessary transponders.

Cass O'Connor: media analyst who worked with Malcolm Turnbull; drew up controversial "Turnbull Report" which predicted inevitable demise of Australis.

Sean O'Halloran: legal counsel for Seven Network and later the last chief executive of Australis.

Kerry Packer: Australia's richest man through his 45 per cent controlling interest in media and entertainment group Publishing and Broadcasting Ltd; strong proponent of need for a dominant pay TV player.

Steve Plant: banker hired by Don Heller to help protect Lenfest Communications' $10.7 million deposit on satellite licences.

Brian Powers: American chief executive of Kerry Packer's PBL.

Rodney Price: chairman of Australis and company's chief dealmaker; involved in negotiations with Hollywood studios and with Sam Chisholm and Bruce McWilliam on Australis program supply arrangement with Foxtel.

Graham Richardson: Labor Communications Minister appointed by Paul Keating; forced to resign before he could win passage of new broadcasting law legalising pay TV.

Don Russell: chief adviser to Paul Keating; closely involved in cancellation of MDS licence auction and in devising structure of satellite licences.

Peter Scanlon: partner of John Elliott in Henry Jones takeover; later investor in Broadcom and chairman of the company.

Christopher Skase: brash young entrepreneur who bought Seven Network cheaply from John Fairfax and won back control of football broadcasting rights from Steve Cosser at high cost.

Basil Sellers: early backer of Cosser; sold Belgravia mansion to Rodney Price.

Greg Solomon: partner of Cosser in music business and in Monaco radio station.

Julie Steiner: head of ABC's news and current affairs channel for pay TV, but failed to find a buyer for the service.

Kerry Stokes: wealthy Perth-based developer and media tycoon blocked by Ivan Deveson from joining News in Seven Network float, but later raided Seven register and won control of the network.

Zigmunt "Ziggy" Switkowski: Polish-born nuclear physicist who took over as managing director of Optus Communications at turbulent time for the group after resignation of Bob Mansfield.

Lynton Taylor: long-time executive with Kerry Packer; helped start World Series Cricket, then after leaving Packer formed short-lived consortium to supply programs to Telstra cable.

Iain Thompson: senior Westpac executive who managed the Ten Network receivership and eventual sale to Canadian Izzy Asper; rebuffed approach by Ken Cowley to get Ten sale process reopened.

Malcolm Turnbull: merchant banker and adviser to News in its dealings with Australis; also approached Chaim Fortgang with offer to buy out US bond holders.

Gary Weiss: colleague of Ron Brierley; offered to invest in first Australis fund raising.

Richard Wiesener: partner of John Elliott in Henry Jones takeover; later a close backer and business partner of Steve Cosser in dealings with potential buyers of Australis.

Murray Williams: public relations consultant for Australis; later convicted over inside trading in Australis shares.

# Introduction

The new millennium opened with the two largest takeovers in history. The Internet service provider America On Line (AOL) offered $US350 billion worth of its shares for the world's largest media and entertainment company, Time Warner, and UK mobile phone group Vodafone AirTouch won the German wireless communications and engineering conglomerate Mannesmann AG for Euro 181 billion, also in shares.

These mergers sparked a buying frenzy of media and telecommunications shares in Europe, the US, and on Asia-Pacific stock exchanges as investors placed their bets on which would be the next target, or predator.

Vodafone's victory over Mannesmann after the Germans made the first move on the UK company represented a grab for market share and customer numbers in the fast-growing mobile telephone business. It also gave Vodafone the muscle to negotiate alliances with content providers in the even more rapidly growing Internet e-commerce industry.

AOL's takeover of Time Warner, announced just 11 days into the 21st century, sent shockwaves through the telecommunications, media and entertainment industries because it was such a powerful demonstration of the stockmarket's ability to deliver enormous pricing power to new-age information technology businesses. In the new economy the protagonists are companies like AOL and Microsoft with stock valuations counted in the tens or even hundreds of billions of dollars, yet these companies often possess negligible tangible assets.

In the heated climate of the stockmarket boom of the late 1990s, investors cast aside traditional valuations of companies based on profit and dividend yield to focus on expectations of revenue growth that might flow to businesses like AOL or Yahoo from their exploitation of the Internet. Investors were taking a gamble that the stock prices of these new-age companies would simply keep rising. In AOL's case, the shares had been driven up to the point where it had a capitalisation 30 per cent greater than its much larger merger partner. AOL had one-sixth Time Warner's staff and one-fifth of its revenues before the merger.

In succumbing to AOL, Time Warner acknowledged that this re-ordering of priorities had made its established cable and entertainment operations less important than AOL's ability to bring to the partnership 24 million customers in 15 countries. AOL could combine its huge customer base from its core Internet access business with online content and electronic business alliances with dozens of retailers and service companies without massive investment in equipment and bricks and mortar. It is a virtual corporation. Unusually, too, for an Internet-based company, it actually made money. Still, it was an enormous gamble by Time Warner and its chairman Gerald Levin and pivotal shareholder Ted Turner. What if the information technology bubble created on global stock exchanges should burst? What has become crystal clear, however, is that in the so-called new age the traditional company is coming under threat of being taken over or, worse, marginalised.

Amid the rising tide of mergers, stockmarket floats, and hype surrounding the Internet which spilled over from 1999 into 2000, two media proprietors in particular were acutely aware of the vulnerability of their own corporations to a similar takeover from an opportunistic technology group. One was the Australian-born, but US-based, Rupert Murdoch, whose News Corporation—with its film and television interests in the US, satellite pay TV in Asia, South America and the UK, and newspapers in the UK and Australia—was nearly as large as Time Warner. The other was Kerry Packer, whose ownership of the dominant television network and largest magazine group in Australia made him a powerful operator and formidable foe on his home ground. Globally, however, he was relatively small and perhaps better known as one of the world's "whale" gamblers with a reputation for breathtaking wins and losses in the casinos of Las Vegas and London.

Apart from their exposure to possible takeover, or having an alliance proposal imposed on them on unfavourable terms, Murdoch and Packer realised it would be increasingly difficult for them to do deals without possessing high-priced share currency to acquire businesses priced in similarly over-priced stock. It was a game, but unless the players went along with it, they could be swallowed or pushed to the periphery.

Murdoch and Packer floated off divisions likely to find favour among investors greedy for technology stocks with their promise of an ever-increasing price. Recognising this trend early, Murdoch first floated part of his BSkyB satellite pay TV venture in the UK in the mid-1990s. Then, in the wake of the AOL-Time Warner merger, which raised the stakes so high and encouraged even greater risks, Murdoch moved to list his US, Asian and South American satellite businesses, his digital encryption system and News's quarter share of his Australian pay TV venture, Foxtel. The new company would contain assets worth $US50 billion in the bloated valuations of the day.

Packer printed his high-priced Internet currency by floating just 20 per cent of a company called ecorp, which held a ticketing business, a joint venture with Microsoft in Australia known as ninemsn, and the eBay Internet auction franchise for Australia.

As a result, the share prices of their core companies soared too, making them harder to take over and strengthening their hand in any future deal. It also made them considerably richer. The Murdoch family's 30 per cent of News Corp was worth $US17 billion in the wake of the AOL-Time Warner deal, and Packer's 45 per cent of his listed operating group, Publishing and Broadcasting Ltd, $US3.5 billion.

The two men had built their empires from relatively modest beginnings in comparison with the wealth they would later achieve. Murdoch inherited a struggling afternoon newspaper, *The News*, in the Australian city of Adelaide in 1953, and Packer, two television stations and a handful of magazines on the death of his father, Sir Frank, in 1974. The Murdoch inheritance had a value perhaps in the single-digit millions given that the newspaper was under pressure from a larger rival too close altogether, and Packer's television and magazine interests were valued at the time at about $100 million.

Murdoch and Packer are not friends, but have worked together in the past for their mutual benefit, in particular in carving up the US newspaper insert market between them in the 1980s and rationalising it. They have a healthy respect for each other and rarely compete directly.

But there is one, spectacular, exception to this unwritten code between the two media tycoons. In the early 1990s, when the Australian economy had become largely deregulated, the stand-out industry which remained tightly governed by a web of rules and law was media.

Ownership of the newspaper group John Fairfax Holdings had been restricted by a number of legal and administrative rules and law changes over the years as it came under takeover threat from a number of entrepreneurs in the 1980s and more serious moves by first Packer, then Murdoch.

Governments used the media laws to reward tycoons in favour in the Australian capital Canberra, or punish those it distrusted. The two media proprietors would woo governments with promises of support in return for decisions favourable to their corporations. Friendships were formed and then destroyed when corporate interest clashed with political reality. For years, governments had been too scared to allow a fourth commercial television licence in Australia for fear of retribution from Packer's media interests.

They had also shied away from allowing direct-to-the-home cable or satellite subscription television, also as a result of Packer's lobbying. Cable TV began in the US in 1948 and by the 1980s cable or satellite pay TV had been introduced to all industrialised countries and many Third World nations, but was illegal still in Australia more than 40 years after it started in the US. Packer had been able to convince successive governments that pay TV was unnecessary. The country had three commercial and two government-owned networks which Packer and his lobbyists asserted had served Australia well.

By the early 1990s, however, this argument was becoming tired. It was obvious, too, to the politicians that Packer was more worried about protecting his Nine network from further competition than any concern for the national interest.

But deregulation of Australia's telecommunications industry combined with the early stirrings of the global merger activity which culminated in the huge Vodafone and AOL takeovers a decade later would send events spinning out of Packer's control and put him on a collision course not only with his rival and occasional business partner, Rupert Murdoch, but also the government of the day. It would be the greatest and most costly set-piece confrontation ever to shake the corporate landscape of Australia.

# 1
# Out of the frying pan

Neil Gamble clambered out of a taxi and hurried across the busy lunchtime footpath towards the foyer of an anonymous 13-storey building on the southern fringe of Sydney's central business district.

Just 20 minutes earlier he had been having a sandwich in his office when he received a phone call he thought would never come. 'Would you like to talk?' the caller asked. 'Yes,' Gamble replied, a little eagerly.

Within minutes he was in the taxi, nursing his bulging briefcase. Gamble was anxious – no, desperate – to hear what his caller had to say. It may lead to a last-minute financial lifeline being extended to his company, Australis Media, Australia's first pay television company. Only 15 months earlier it had started broadcasting its multi-channel service under the Galaxy brand name amid plenty of media hype and fanfare. Now, on this autumn afternoon on April 16, 1996, the company was days at most from being forced into receivership.

Creditors owed money for the expensive set-top decoder boxes and other equipment were demanding immediate payment of the $76 million owed to them. Gamble might have been able to rustle up $5 million, at best. Australis was losing money heavily and would bleed more than $8 million that week. It was projected to lose a further $11 million the week after.

Australis was being shot to pieces in the crossfire between its two cable-based rivals, Foxtel and Optus Vision, which had moved into the industry after Australis and were engaged in a mighty set-piece battle on behalf of the two phone companies behind them. Not only were they spending a combined $7 billion on new cable networks, they were also discounting their subscriptions and connection fees to win maximum customer numbers. The losses would be huge in this war of attrition. Foxtel and Optus were fighting for market share of a telephone business worth $5 billion a year in revenues. Pay TV for them was a sideshow. It was the sizzle. Phones were the sausage.

In this hostile environment, Australis was heavily out-gunned by the cable networks, yet it was forced to offer the same uncommercial rates as its rivals. As a result, income from the company's 108,000 subscribers could not cover its installation and programming costs, not to mention its mounting debt interest bill. If Australis failed, investors in Australia and the United States owed more than $500 million stood to lose the lot.

Gamble – a tall, sandy-haired South African with a keen sense of humour – had resigned himself to the inevitable: the humiliation of corporate collapse and perhaps years fighting creditors in the courts. He reflected as he walked towards the security desk that it would take a miracle now to save the company. Australis needed at least $100 million, maybe closer to $200 million, to buy the time to get its business back on track and to meet the heavy repayments due to American fund managers in four years time. Four years! If he could get it through the next four weeks he would be doing well.

Australis had been offered another way out, but Gamble believed it would only delay the collapse by a few months at best. Unless he came up with something else, and quickly, he would have no choice in the coming days but to sell the company's main asset, a 25-year contract to supply Foxtel with Hollywood movies.

Australis had beaten Foxtel 18 months earlier to sign up some of the best movie product from Hollywood. But the prize came at great cost, because Gamble and his fellow negotiators were no match for the greedy studio chiefs and their lawyers. Foxtel had to go cap in hand immediately after to buy the movies from Australis at an even higher price.

Now the negotiating power had changed hands. The Foxtel partners, Rupert Murdoch's News Corporation and Telstra, Australia's dominant telecommunications group, wanted to buy back the contract as part of a 'rescue package' for the stricken Australis. Gamble was between a rock and a hard place: as Australis was losing money on its own pay TV service, the current deal to supply movies to Foxtel represented its main revenue for the future.

The two sides were still haggling over the price, but with time running out quickly for Australis, the issue could be resolved with one phone call. Fortunately for Gamble, News Corp lawyer Ian Phillip was still doing some last-minute work on the sale contract. Had the document been ready that day, as expected, then Australis would have been forced to take the price on offer and sign, then and there.

Australia's Corporations Law has strict penalties for directors of companies trading while insolvent. Australis was gone. It was living in the breathing space of a technicality. News Corp's lawyer had given Gamble a window of opportunity, perhaps 24 hours. He was now in the office of News Corp's main commercial rival to see what alternatives, if any, might be on offer.

As he signed the visitors book at the security desk, Gamble quickly ran his eye over the names above his, to see who had been there before him. This was one of corporate Australia's more interesting visitor records.

The lift to the third floor was slow and gave Gamble a few moments to reflect on the traumas of the last few months which had taken such a toll on him and his colleagues. There had been phone calls at all hours of the night, meeting after meeting with bankers, lawyers, and investors large and small across the United States, in Britain and Australia. Plenty of people had kicked the tyres, had a look, but walked away. There was no-one left now but News Corp and Telstra and they were dictating the terms. He had to be realistic. Even if this potential investor wanted to put in some money, he would need some time to think about it. This would be another disappointment.

He suddenly froze. What if he had been spotted walking into the building? Sydney is a small town. If word got to News Corp or to Telstra headquarters less than a block away that he had been seen, the Foxtel partners would not wait a minute longer and move immediately to enforce the sale agreement they dearly wanted. Foxtel was bleeding money on this expensive programming arrangement. And what was worse for News Corp and Telstra was that the deal required them to reveal a contingent liability in their annual accounts for the total amount of the expected payments to Australis over the 25 years of the contract: a whopping $4.5 billion. It looked terrible and spooked investors.

The lift finally reached the third floor and Gamble stepped into a reception area dominated by a large timber desk covered with magazines. He walked past some photographs of the early days of television and a 1950s studio camera towards a tall reception desk guarding the suite of executive offices behind it. The woman behind the desk rang through to announce that Gamble had arrived.

As Gamble waited, his eyes were forced to wander around the reception area, which looked as if it had been undisturbed for 20 years. The wait seemed much longer, but about 10 minutes later, a cheery bespectacled man emerged from around a corner. 'Good to see you Neil,' said Nick Falloon as he extended his hand. 'And you too,' replied Gamble as he took it.

Falloon was a New Zealander in his early 40s who had graduated from Waikato College with a business management degree. After crossing the Tasman in the early 1980s to try his luck, he landed a job as divisional accountant at Australian Consolidated Press, the media company controlled by Kerry Packer. Falloon's fortunes expanded with Packer's. By early 1996 he was chief financial officer of a far larger corporation, Publishing and Broadcasting Ltd, which owned Australia's dominant Nine television network and the country's largest magazine empire.

Falloon was a dependable type with good analytical skills, the sort of person needed at PBL to offset the restless energies of Packer, who had also carved out an international reputation as one of the world's most feared gamblers, regularly winning or losing tens of millions of dollars at casinos in Las Vegas and London. Despite his reckless gambling, Packer was well known as a corporate miser, never willing to pay more than 50 cents for a dollar's worth of assets. His skill in squeezing a good deal at the expense of business associates and rivals alike was legendary.

The two barely had time to exchange pleasantries. Gamble was expecting to get perhaps half an hour to explain to Falloon Australis's pressing financial problems. But as Falloon led his guest through a door just off the reception area, he moved to one side of the long, narrow office they were entering. Behind the large desk to the left bathed in sunshine from the window next to it sat Kerry Packer, in shirtsleeves, smoking a cigarette. In front of the desk, also seated, were Packer's son James and Brian Powers, a fast-talking, Coca Cola-sipping American who resigned his partnership with San Francisco-based investment bank Hellman and Friedman three years earlier to manage Kerry Packer's sprawling media fiefdom and extensive private interests, estimated to be worth more than $3 billion. On the wall behind the heavy-framed Packer was a large print of an African bull elephant in full charge.

The three men were all staring intently at Gamble, who was startled at being ushered into such a high-powered group so quickly. They said nothing until Kerry Packer took another draw of his cigarette and broke the tension: 'What's the story,' he demanded.

Gamble was used to making pitches to prospective investors over the previous few weeks. But he was not prepared for this. If he made a mess of what he had to say over the next few minutes, there would be no second chances. He'd be out on the footpath with nothing. He immediately gushed out a rundown on Australis's assets, its satellite licence and 80 microwave multipoint distribution licences around the country, its 108,000 subscribers, future potential and, of course, its 25-year contract to supply key movie programs to Rupert Murdoch's Foxtel.

It was an enthusiastic presentation which lasted a good 15 minutes. Kerry and James Packer, Nick Falloon and Brian Powers listened patiently. When Gamble finally stopped, Packer said, 'That all sounds fine, but what do you want?'

'I've got no cash,' Gamble replied.

'Son, that's a hell of a way to start a conversation with me,' Packer bellowed back.

Gamble gathered himself. He knew he had about 30 seconds to win Packer over, or he would be walking out with nothing. 'I understand that, but by the end of the week, and I expect to be signing an agreement as early as tomorrow or the day after, and then it will be all over. I'm sure you guys must be interested in some of that. By putting some money into Australis you'd put your foot on the long-term contract to supply movies to Foxtel.'

Packer accepted that there was some urgency. But he wasn't going to be rushed either. 'OK, we'll leave it at that for the moment.'

Gamble and Falloon left the room and walked back across the reception area into the company's boardroom. It was a windowless room with old political cartoons from the group's *The Bulletin* magazine around the walls. The two talked for another 20 minutes or so about Australis's predicament and the pressure the company was under to sign away the Foxtel program contract. Falloon said he'd think about what Gamble had said and would call back. Falloon rejoined the Packers and Brian Powers in Kerry Packer's office.

The Australis chief stepped out into the warm autumn sunshine and walked up Park Street to hail a cab to take him to Australis's large new office building, looking oddly out of place with its roof covered in satellite dishes in the run-down city edge district of Pyrmont. The building was wedged up against a busy new overpass feeding traffic to and from Sydney's north-western suburbs.

As he walked heavily up the 10 or so steps leading off Pyrmont Bridge Road into the Australis office foyer, and past a wall of monitors showing each of Galaxy's 16 channels, Gamble had no idea whether the Packer people would extend a lifeline, or not. Even if they decided to do something, he asked himself, what could they do in such a short time?

He pushed open his office door and noticed a number of phone messages on his desk. Two stood out. One was to call Malcolm Turnbull, a merchant banker retained by News Corp. The other was from Sam Chisholm, the London-based head of Rupert Murdoch's UK satellite pay TV operation, BSkyB.

Perhaps more than any person in Australian corporate circles, Malcolm Turnbull's name inevitably provokes reaction. He can be courteous, charming and flattering one minute, and bursting with dark volcanic rage the next, depending on whether or not he is getting his way in negotiations. A Rhodes Scholar and barrister, he defended the aging former 'spycatcher', Peter Wright, in the famous 1986 trial against the power and influence of the Thatcher Government which used all legal avenues to try to prevent publication of Wright's book, *Spycatcher*. Turnbull beat the system for Wright with brilliant advocacy.

In 1987, Turnbull turned his hand to merchant banking with Nicholas Whitlam, the tall, silver-haired son of the former Labor Prime Minister, Gough Whitlam. The pair boasted they had access to any boardroom in Australia. Turnbull and Whitlam were both possessed of powerful egos and it surprised no-one when they later fell out acrimoniously.

Gamble picked up the phone nervously to call the merchant banker. Turnbull had been retained by Chisholm two months earlier after a proposed merger between Australis and Foxtel had been contentiously rejected by the doctrinaire chairman of Australia's Competition and Consumer Commission, Allan Fels. In the wake of Fels' decision to stop the merger, Australis went to News Corp for money and, on Chisholm's advice, News retained Turnbull and his boutique investment bank, Turnbull and Partners, to analyse Australis to determine whether it was worth saving.

As the weeks ticked by and it became apparent that Turnbull and his associate Cass O'Connor – who crunched the numbers on the satellite broadcaster – were pessimistic about Australis's chances, News Corp decided that rather than pumping in more money, it wanted to buy an asset. With Australis up against the wall financially, and News now calling the tune, the movie supply contract was the obvious and most convenient asset to purchase.

When Gamble was put through to Turnbull, the merchant banker wanted to talk about arrangements to manage Australis's creditors once News had purchased the movie supply contract, a deal which, for all Turnbull knew, was imminent.

Gamble was enormously relieved. At least Turnbull, with all his contacts around town, hadn't heard anything of the meeting just held in Kerry Packer's office. But the conversation reminded him that the clock was ticking quickly, and the window of opportunity he may have been hoping to jump through several hours earlier was closing fast.

What Samuel Hewlings Chisholm lacked in height he more than compensated for in intelligence, guile and aggression. A former floor wax salesman for S.G. Johnson in New Zealand, Chisholm was promoted by the company to State sales manager for Victoria, in Melbourne. Then after answering an ad in the Melbourne *Sun News Pictorial* for a salesman at GTV-9 in Melbourne, he was hired by Wilf Barker in 1967 before starting a remarkable rise through the ranks of the Packer family's Nine television group. After Sir Frank Packer's death in 1974, his son Kerry asked Chisholm to take over TCN-9 in Sydney, which was struggling in the ratings at the time and was little more than a branch operation taking programming from the Melbourne station. By the turn of the decade, Chisholm had put Nine in front in the ratings in Sydney, a lead it would never lose, with programs like the *Mike Walsh Show*, Mike Willesee's *A Current Affair*, *60 Minutes*, *Sunday* and the *Today Show* all produced in Sydney. He carved out a formidable reputation for toughness and free-spending at Nine, where he thrived in the climate of creative tension he generated among the network's highly paid personalities.

Chisholm survived an attempt by Alan Bond to sack him immediately after Packer sold the two-station network in January 1987 to the Western Australian entrepreneur for what was regarded as a stunning price at the time, $1.05 billion. Bond had wanted to put in a friend, David Aspinall, but Packer insisted Chisholm stay, believing that he would eventually buy back the network at half the price Bond agreed to pay. Although the billion-dollar price tag sounded impressive, Bond paid Packer only $800 million and issued Packer $200 million worth of preference shares, which Bond was due to buy three years later in a form of delayed settlement. Packer told Bond that so long as he had an interest in the network, Chisholm had to stay.

Bond knew Packer would make life very uncomfortable for him if he persisted in trying to sack the network boss, so Chisholm stayed. Chisholm went on a spending spree, upgrading the Sydney studio complex and investing heavily in executives and television talent. After all, it was Bond's money now.

As time ticked by and Bond Corporation began sinking under the weight of its $10 billion debt, Packer sensed that Bond would not be able to pay him the $200 million. In December 1989, advised by his friend, the merchant banker Malcolm Turnbull, Packer launched a bid for Bond Media, the Bond Corp subsidiary which held the Nine Network. By July 1990, he had won 51.5 per cent of the company, effectively for the cost of the $200 million Bond owed him.

Chisholm had knocked back a number of offers from Rupert Murdoch to go to the UK to work for his struggling satellite pay TV company, Sky TV. But soon after Packer regained control of Nine and started to hack into network spending, Chisholm accepted Murdoch's offer. When Chisholm left Nine he was at the peak of his standing and Nine was unassailable as the dominant Australian commercial network. At Sky he was confronted with a business bleeding cash at a rate of about $7 million a week,[1] an outflow so profuse it nearly brought down the whole News Corp empire in December 1990. One of Chisholm's first tasks was to negotiate a merger with the rival BSB pay TV consortium and emerge as boss of the joined entity, BSkyB, which quickly began to make money. The turnaround of the satellite pay TV business in the UK effectively saved News Corp.

He then used his monopoly buying power in the UK to renegotiate the movie supply contracts with the Hollywood studios. Now that the studios weren't able to play off two UK pay TV bidders for their movies, they were forced to take heavy price cuts. Chisholm reduced dramatically the long-term payments to the studios by about $2 billion. The studio chiefs would never forgive him.

Chisholm's final coup was to win the exclusive rights to Britain's Premier League football for what seemed the huge price of £670 million in 1992. It gave BSkyB the surge in subscriptions it needed to add revenue to the cost savings Chisholm had achieved through the merger and the Hollywood movie supply contracts. It made both Chisholm and News vitally aware of the importance of good sports programming in pay TV.

Chisholm was a person used to getting his way. He had powerful instincts both as a businessman and negotiator, but also a strong sense of when a deal might be going off the rails.

Murdoch brought in Chisholm and his legal adviser and friend, Bruce McWilliam, to negotiate the so-called Telstra-News Corporation (TNC) agreement with Australis in late December 1994. Sixteen months later, they were negotiating to buy it back and had upped their offer on April 11 to $250 million. McWilliam imposed a seven-day deadline – of Friday April 19 – for Australis to sign the sale contract.

On the Monday, April 15, London-based McWilliam received a faxed letter from Gamble and Australis's lawyer, Robert Mangioni, seeking $300 million for the TNC agreement. In the letter, Gamble wrote, 'The $250 million consideration needs to be increased to $300 million (which) would more fairly reflect the value of the assets being sold.' Gamble added that he would also 'strongly encourage News/Telstra to give the Foxtel merger a final go'. He said it might be possible to overcome the concerns of the competition watchdog.

The letter gave Chisholm and McWilliam every reason to believe that it was now only a matter of meeting Australis half way to seal the deal. Gamble rang McWilliam that Monday evening to reiterate the request for the $300 million, adding that Australis's directors were deeply concerned about the solvency of the company.

At the time he sent the letter, Gamble was preparing to phone Nick Falloon to try to excite the Packer group's interest in a rival proposal. There was a distant chance at best of something coming from PBL, so Gamble wanted to keep the Foxtel deal alive. After all, it was the only firm proposal on the table and Australis had run out of money and time. This wasn't the first time the much smaller Australis would try to play off the far richer camps of the two telephone groups, nor the last.

Although a deal appeared to be close, in London Chisholm sensed that the urgency had suddenly gone from the Australis side. He was unaware, too, that News's lawyer, Ian Phillip, from the firm Allen Allen and Hemsley, was taking his time over the documentation for the proposed transaction.

At 7am London time on Tuesday, Chisholm put in a call to Gamble to make his final offer and hurry things along. Gamble's secretary, Anne Bailey, told Chisholm that Gamble was in a meeting. She would tell Gamble that Chisholm had called. Chisholm then tried to call the London-based chairman of Australis, Rodney Price, at his Belgravia home. Price wasn't there. He tried to call Australis's lawyer, Robert Mangioni, at his office at the Sydney law firm, Tress Cocks and Maddocks. Mangioni was 'in meetings' and unavailable. Chisholm left a message to say News was ready to sign the sale contract. Suddenly he started to feel very uneasy.

After talking to Turnbull on the phone for a few minutes, Gamble decided to have an early night. He would call Nick Falloon first thing in the morning.

Gamble left his home overlooking Sydney's Balmoral Beach early on Wednesday, April 17 for the 25-minute drive to Pyrmont. He had barely left his driveway to join the stream of traffic bound for Sydney's city centre when his car phone rang. It was Rodney Price, who was calling from New Zealand, where he was about to go into a board meeting of the investment company Brierley Investments Ltd, of which he was a director.

Price wanted to know what was happening. He had initially opposed Gamble making the approach to the Packer camp because he believed Packer and Murdoch would cooperate to squeeze Australis out of the pay TV industry. If Gamble started talking to the Packer people, Price said they would alert Murdoch. Gamble said this did not appear to be the case this time. Packer and Murdoch were at war anyway over the pay TV rights to the Australian Rugby League competition and probably weren't talking. He was right. Packer was ready to do a deal with Australis, and he wasn't about to tell his erstwhile friend and now declared enemy, Rupert Murdoch.

Price wished Gamble luck and said he would be flying over that afternoon to Sydney. Could he meet him at the airport? Gamble agreed, but wasn't sure whether negotiations would continue or not with the Packer people that day, and even where he might be.

It was about 7.30 am when Gamble walked into his office. He waited a few minutes, then tried Nick Falloon's direct line. Falloon answered. Gamble asked Falloon whether it was worthwhile for the two sides to continue their discussions. Falloon said yes, the door was open, and his people wanted to talk.

Gamble walked quickly over to a nearby office and grabbed his finance director, Geoff Kleeman, a short, wiry accountant with greying hair. Kleeman had worked with Rodney Price since their early days in Adelaide in 1983 at the dairy group Southern Farmers. The pair had moved on to the feared 1980s stockmarket raider Industrial Equity Ltd after it snapped up Southern Farmers in the 1980s takeover frenzy, and then on to building materials group Pioneer International when Price won the plumb job there as managing director. Kleeman was part of a small network of people whose paths had criss-crossed over the years and finally led to Australis.

Before Gamble left work the previous night he had asked Kleeman to come in early the next morning, just in case. The two took a cab back through the busy early morning traffic to Park Street.

Falloon had called in a regular adviser to the Packer group, Geoff Levy, a lawyer-turned-merchant banker with the advisory firm Wentworth Associates, whose principal was David Gonski, another South African and a close confidante to Kerry Packer. Gonski's capacity for lateral thinking would make him one of the most sought-after advisers in Australia, particularly when it came to devising complex corporate structures to get clients around Australia's ridiculous and politically motivated media ownership rules. Levy was joined by lawyer Gina Cass-Gottlieb, a partner with the specialist media law firm of Gilbert and Tobin. Australis lawyer Mangioni, a partner with the firm Tress Cocks and Maddox, joined Gamble and Kleeman at Park Street.

After their discussion with Gamble the previous afternoon, Kerry and James Packer, Brian Powers and Nick Falloon had re-gathered in Kerry Packer's office to consider whether or not the group should put money into Australis to keep it alive. Kerry Packer said he wasn't keen on pay TV and reiterated his view that only one pay TV operator could survive in Australia's small market. His main interest consistently over the years had been the Nine television network, owned by the listed company Publishing and Broadcasting Ltd, of which he owned 45 per cent. At this moment, Packer was being driven by motives other than the search for value. He had been engaged in a bitter war of words with Rupert Murdoch. The two had fallen out heavily over rugby league's pay

TV rights and the rivalry had become personal. Packer wasn't averse to taking a bet when the odds were good. Even if he couldn't touch the TNC agreement with the Murdoch-Telstra joint venture, Australis's satellite and microwave distribution licences were worth something.

Powers, a quick-thinking, hyperactive person, cautioned that any rescue would be very risky. The company was clearly in deep trouble, and there was no way of knowing in the tight time frame in which they were working how bad the position was. But he liked the 25-year arrangement to supply Foxtel with programs. It was an arrangement that appeared to be legally watertight and binding on News Corp and Telstra, even if PBL took an interest in Australis. Powers said the Foxtel partners were desperate to buy the contract and cancel it, thus wiping out the $4.5 billion contingency in their accounts. It would be great to get control of that contract and hold it over Murdoch as a bargaining chip. Powers told his colleagues that to reduce the risk they should seek a first and last right of refusal over all of Australis's assets as a condition of PBL's participation in any rescue.

When Gamble and Kleeman arrived at Park Street, they went straight to the boardroom to meet Powers, Falloon and the PBL advisers. Gamble opened the talks by asking the PBL people to put in $US50 million in exchange for shares in Australis. He had asked for a US dollar amount because the bulk of Australis's commitments – payments to the Hollywood studios – were made in the US currency. All of its financing was priced in greenbacks. The Australis team said that if the Packer interests went in, it would attract other investors.

Powers responded quickly, saying that PBL wasn't prepared to put in that much and that $US25 million was as far as it would go. He said he wanted the risk spread more widely. Other investors would have to be found.

Gamble said he was confident that Lenfest Communications group, a US cable television company which owned 50 per cent of Australis, would pitch in $US25 million. He phoned Lenfest vice president Don Heller at his home in Springfield, a suburb of Philadelphia, to tell him what was happening and sound him out as a possible participant in the rescue. Heller said Lenfest probably would be, despite the fact that the group had lent Australis $US19.24 million only three months earlier to pay the Hollywood studios. Heller said that this loan would need to be repaid in any larger fund raising.

Gamble also called Gary Weiss, an Australis director who ran the UK-listed investment group GPG Plc for veteran New Zealand investor Sir Ron Brierley, a friend of Kerry Packer's. In the ring-around, Gamble also called Don Hagans, the head of the Australian affiliate of United International Holdings, the US pay TV group which was Australis's largest franchisee in Australia. It was very much in UIH's interests to see Australis survive, because it was the source of UIH's programming. Also on his list was J.P. Morgan, the US bank whose funds management arm in Australia was an early investor in Australis.

Falloon rang Ziggy Switkowski, chief executive of Telstra's main phone rival, Optus Communications, and asked him if Optus was prepared to invest.

As the day dragged on and the negotiators had emptied the Coke and mineral water from the bar fridge in the large sideboard in the boardroom, it was becoming apparent that Australis would have trouble raising the amount of cash it needed – somewhere between $US75 million and $US100 million, or roughly $125 million to $166 million in Australian dollars.

Switkowski rang back to say his shareholders weren't keen to invest in Australis. Optus was already in the throes of spending $3 billion on a national roll-out of cable through the Optus Vision consortium, of which it owned 47.5 per cent. Falloon's argument that it would potentially allow Optus to control the supply of movie programs to its rival's pay TV venture wasn't sweet enough to tempt the nervous Optus shareholders. The others were prepared to invest money, but nothing like the amounts required.

Right through sometimes intense negotiations, Powers and Falloon questioned whether PBL should be involved in the deal. A number of times, they said later, they were tempted to pull out. This would have killed the rescue immediately.

Around lunchtime Gamble left the room to call Rodney Price, just as the Australis chairman was about to get on a plane for Sydney. He gave him a rundown on the progress of the discussions. By now, Price had had some time to think about a link with the Packer camp and was a convert to the idea. He urged Gamble to try to get more from PBL, to ask again for the $US50 million. Price complained that Sam Chisholm was trying to 'screw' him and Australis on the movie programming sale to News.

Back in the boardroom, Gamble put the case again for the higher amount. Powers asked if he and Falloon could be excused, and they went in to see Kerry Packer. About 45 minutes later they returned. Powers was firm that PBL wouldn't put in any more than $US25 million. At this point, the American raised the issue of PBL's desire to have the comfort of a first and last right of refusal over Australis's assets in the event the 'rescue' failed and the company collapsed. Gamble's attempt to get more out of PBL had only resulted in Kerry Packer toughening the conditions even more.

Gamble and Kleeman didn't like this at all, and argued strongly against it, saying it might breach the terms of an earlier bond raising in the US. It would certainly restrict Australis's ability in the future to raise money. Powers was firm. Gamble and Kleeman knew they had absolutely no negotiating power. If these talks led to nothing, then they were at the mercy of News and Telstra. 'We had no choice,' Gamble said later. 'Life was better than death.'

About 5pm Gamble took a car to the airport to meet Price, then drove him back to Park Street. Price, an imposing man, snappily dressed and with prematurely grey hair, went in to meet Kerry Packer. The two knew each other from the 1980s when Price was managing director of Industrial Equity Ltd. IEL and Packer made a tactical takeover bid together for Robert Holmes a Court's BHP takeover vehicle Bell Resources in 1988, but as a strategy to wring some money out of Holmes a Court it failed. Packer was a good friend, through their mutual love of cricket, of Sir Ron Brierley, founder of Brierley Investments Ltd, which in turn owned 51 per cent of IEL. After chatting for about an hour, Price had to go to another meeting, and left.

Gamble and Kleeman continued the discussions with the PBL team, now led by Falloon, until about 8pm, when the meeting broke up. By this stage, Falloon and Brian Powers had effectively knocked on the head any chance of PBL putting hard cash into Australis. Instead, the discussion evolved into a plan for Australis to take out a short-term loan which would be guaranteed by PBL and other investors.

They agreed to meet back at Park Street at 8am the next morning. Falloon wanted to know everything about Australis – its cash flows, debt, assets, business plan, and all details of programming deals – before he would commit his company to taking an exposure.

Gamble headed straight home to Mosman and Kleeman to his house at St Ives.


The more than usual activity at 54 Park Street that day had started to attract attention. Long white cars and taxis pulling up outside the building and depositing and collecting men and women holding briefcases had been noticed, and word reached News Corp's Australian headquarters, about a kilometre further south in the heart of Sydney's rag trade district, Surry Hills.

That Wednesday evening, Ken Cowley, chairman of News Corp's Australian subsidiary, News Limited, called Sam Chisholm at BSkyB's offices at Isleworth, west of London, and said he thought something was afoot. Could the Australis people be talking to Packer?

Cowley couldn't – as he might have done in the past – put a call in to Packer or Brian Powers to find out what was happening. The normally cordial relations between News and PBL had chilled since Rupert Murdoch publicly accused Kerry Packer of 'welshing' on a deal the two struck in London the previous November, part of which involved Packer attempting to broker a settlement of the fierce war over rugby league broadcasting rights for pay TV. The rivalry between Packer and Murdoch was more than matched at the next step down in their organisations. Brian Powers and Murdoch's executive chairman in Australia, Ken Cowley, had grown to despise each other.

Murdoch and Packer had experienced fallings-out from time to time in the past, but came together to cooperate when it suited them. In April 1996, Packer was still smarting from Murdoch's accusation and he had just been presented with a way of getting some revenge.

Cowley's call confirmed Chisholm's mounting suspicions. He grabbed the phone. Price, with whom he had a prickly but ongoing dialogue because both men lived in London, still could not be found. If Chisholm had known he was in Packer's office at that very moment, he would have exploded.

Gamble was 'in a meeting', as was Mangioni. Chisholm was fuming with frustration and inquisitiveness. What was happening here?

When the two teams regrouped in the PBL boardroom the next morning, the pace of negotiations lifted. Falloon was pushing for the best deal possible for PBL and gradually, hour by hour, put in place a deal in which Lenfest's banker, Toronto Dominion, would extend a six-month loan to Australis with repayment guaranteed by PBL and three other backers: Brierley's GPG Plc, the franchisee UIH and funds manager J.P. Morgan.

This would give Australis the breathing space to arrange long-term financing of $US200 million-plus with a placement of bonds or convertible notes in the US, where investors such as Merrill Lynch, Smith Barney and Oppenheimer knew and better understood pay TV. PBL's risk was minimal, yet it emerged with its controversial first and last right of refusal over Australis's assets. Price, Gamble and Kleeman realised that without PBL's participation, the deal simply would not happen. They could not say no to Powers and Falloon.

Around 8pm that night, with the talks grinding on, Mangioni checked with his office for messages. Although it was early morning in London, there were already two calls from Chisholm asking the lawyer to phone him urgently. Instead, Mangioni rang Gamble's wife Jean, and suggested she take the phone off the hook. The Australis people believed they were so close to sealing a deal with PBL and the other investors that they could risk offending Chisholm now and allowing the Foxtel rescue proposal to lapse.

Despite the main elements of the rescue package having been agreed to, the negotiations lasted until 4.30am the next day. PBL had 5 per cent of the rival Optus Vision pay TV consortium and one of its main incentives for doing a deal with Australis was to strike a deal which would allow Optus to use Australis's satellite rights to broadcast the Optus Vision channels. Although Optus Vision's controlling shareholder, Optus Communications, owned all four satellites in orbit over Australia, Australis had the only licence and it also had rights to the IREDETO digital transmission technology.

No-one else, not even Optus, could use the satellite to transmit a multi-channel signal. Falloon, Gamble, Kleeman, Geoff Levy and Mangioni were drained and exhausted. Gamble was aware that Rod Price may be trying to ring him, so about 4.45am he switched on his mobile phone. Almost immediately, it rang. 'Rod?' Gamble asked. 'No,' replied the voice. 'It's Sam Chisholm here. I've been trying to ring you at home, but your phone's been engaged.'

Chisholm was having dinner in the West End restaurant Ondine with Dominic Morris, an adviser to British Prime Minister John Major. His mind wasn't on the food, or particularly on Morris, whom he was trying to recruit to work at BSkyB. Instead, he excused himself every 15 minutes or so to step out on to the footpath to try to call Gamble, Price or Mangioni on his mobile phone. It was 8.45pm in London and Chisholm had been ringing all day. He was impatient for answers.

Finally, he had Gamble on the line. 'It's very early for you to be up,' Chisholm quipped. 'I've been walking the dog,' Gamble replied nervously as he looked around the room, his eyes finally meeting those of Falloon, who was sitting next to him. 'I'll increase the offer $25 million,' Chisholm said. 'Thank you Sam,' replied Gamble. 'I'll put that to the board. We're meeting in a few hours.'

Gamble pressed the 'hang-up' button on his Ericsson mobile. He looked at Falloon again, and the PBL man – who had lingering doubts as to whether News and Chisholm really were putting the squeeze on Australis – realised then the pressure Australis was under to sign with Foxtel. Chisholm's call confirmed in Falloon's mind that PBL was doing the right thing. Before Gamble could say anything, Falloon said, 'We have a deal.'

About 10am – after all the documentation had been drawn up by Cass-Gottleib and Mangioni – Price, Gamble and Weiss met again in the PBL boardroom with Powers, Falloon and Kerry and James Packer to gather letters of intent from the parties agreeing to support the interim loan by Australis. The fax machine was humming as letters came in from UIH in Denver, Tony Pearce at J.P. Morgan in Melbourne and Don Heller of Lenfest in Philadelphia.

For the first time in more than 24 hours, during which time they had virtually been prisoners on the third floor of 54 Park Street, Gamble and Kleeman walked out into the daylight and hailed a taxi back to Pyrmont. Rod Price arrived soon after for a meeting of the Australis board later that morning to endorse the rescue deal and walked into Gamble's office. Gamble asked Price, 'How are we going to deal with Sam?'

Price picked up the phone on Gamble's desk and dialled Chisholm's number at his apartment in Hyde Park Square. The phone rang for a while because it was about 4am in London and Chisholm was asleep. Time zones meant nothing in this business, with the players accustomed to phone calls coming out of the night from Britain, the west or east coasts of the US, or Australia at any time without warning.

When the BSkyB chief executive picked up the receiver he was alert, and asked who was calling. 'Rod Price,' Price said cheerily. 'Have we got a deal?' Chisholm asked.

'We have a deal, but not the one you're expecting.' Price said. 'Thank you for your fresh offer, but we are unable to accept.'

Said Chisholm, 'So what are you going to do?' Price: 'You'll see.'

At 4pm eastern Australian time, as trading on the Australian Stock Exchange was closing for the day, Australis announced the refinancing package. In London, Chisholm was prepared for the worst after receiving the early morning call from Price. Chisholm had just received a fax relating Australis's announcement when he called McWilliam about 7.15am.

Both Chisholm and McWilliam knew now that Foxtel's best interests lay in the collapse of Australis, which would shake loose the movie supply contracts Australis had negotiated with the Hollywood studios. The numbers put together by Cass O'Connor of Turnbull and Partners suggested it was only a matter of time before Australis's long-term debt repayment commitments to US bondholders would trip up the company, notwithstanding the short-term relief extended by Kerry Packer and his friends. What News Corp and Telstra needed now was for the full extent of Australis's financial vulnerability to come to light.

By snatching Australis and its valuable program supply agreement from under Rupert Murdoch's nose, Packer took his revenge for Murdoch's 'welsher' taunt. News Corp responded immediately by suing Lenfest for allegedly breaching a verbal agreement made a few days earlier to buy the Foxtel movie supply agreement.

Australia's pay TV industry was little more than a year old, but it had already become a fiery battlefield where even the winners would sustain heavy damage. For the inevitable losers, the corporate equivalent of oblivion awaited.

### THE GATEKEEPERS

In hindsight, you try to anticipate what the environment is going to be like after you make investment decisions and just about everything that could go wrong, did go wrong. To play that game you had to be a player with monstrous pockets because they were really strategic battles. They weren't just battles with a short-term objective, it was really people judging how things were going to be in 10 or 15 years and therefore they dug in for the battle. In hindsight too, every battle that could possibly be fought along that road was fought.

– Bob Mansfield, former chief executive of Optus Communications,
August 7, 1998.

Bob Mansfield wasn't talking about World War I and the battles of Verdun and the Somme. He was reflecting on Australia's greatest and most costly corporate engagement, a toe-to-toe contest between two phone companies, fought mostly with money, and very large amounts of it.

In their quest to become the gatekeeper to Australia's six million homes, the two companies, Telstra and Optus Communications, committed a total of $7 billion to lay down separate cable networks to offer an array of new applications starting to emerge on the Internet. Home shopping, home gambling, home banking and electronic commerce would be among the offerings, but the biggest prizes for the two players would come from telephony. The ultimate objective, of course, was to make money by tapping into the growing level of discretionary spending households were directing into these so-called on-line services.

To the ultimate winner potentially would go billions of dollars in additional revenues. The contest dragged in the country's most powerful business tycoons – Rupert Murdoch, Kerry Packer and Kerry Stokes – and their commercial empires. It was complicated by erratic government policy in response to the rapid developments in technology, and the strategy and force employed by the combatants.

Being the smaller of the two contestants, Optus elected to use speed and surprise to try to out-manoeuvre its ponderous and heavily-armoured rival.

The gurus of the new information age, such as Microsoft's Bill Gates, were painting compelling scenarios of telephones converging with computer terminals and television screens to free households to explore new ways to communicate and do business. New technology such as digital compression would allow high fidelity sound and broadcast quality video to be downloaded from the Internet or sent down a cable from a service provider. The opportunities appeared to be limitless for the corporations and individuals nimble enough to get in first.

The theme was adopted quickly by Rupert Murdoch, the executive chairman of News Corporation, with its film, television and newspaper interests in Britain, North America, Australia and Asia. Optus and Telstra, like phone companies everywhere, were fully aware of the impending changes. They accepted that these developments were inevitable, and that they were unfolding very quickly. How should they respond? What would happen if they didn't? To add to their uncertainty during this period of rapid change in the early and mid-1990s, Australia was heading towards deregulation of its tightly controlled telecommunications industry on July 1, 1997. This would usher in a flood of new entrants into the business. For the established duopoly, there wasn't much time to prepare for the changes ahead.

The environment demanded spontaneous and sometimes high-risk decision making. Although Telstra was in the process of privatising, government still wanted to use it as an arm of social policy to provide cheap communications to sparsely populated remote areas of Australia, while at the same time demanding multi-billion-dollar dividends to finance fistsful of dollars election bribes. In 1997 alone, the Howard Government sucked more than $4 billion in dividends out of Telstra, including a special, one-off payment of $3 billion for which Telstra had to borrow.

Sensing that this could become an enormously costly struggle which might prove fatal for the loser, Optus moved first and committed $3 billion, then Telstra $4 billion, to roll out cable networks to give them the capacity to offer the array of new media applications they believed their customers would want. This would be Australia's second-largest infrastructure project after the $11 billion North West Shelf oil and gas project. While the investment would be a big call on Telstra's funds, Optus was promising to spend an amount that was more than double its net worth at the time.

No other country had allowed two full-service cable networks like this to roll out nationally. The economics of such bold undertakings would be questionable in a country like Australia, which is the size of mainland United States but has one-fifteenth the population. Also, the US has more than 100 pay TV cable companies, many of which were struggling.

For all the pledged outlays on cable networks, the combatants knew too that their bold plans to create information superhighways would fail unless they had one or more products that would attract customers to their rather more prosaic phone systems. Otherwise, their cable with its 500-channel capacity would be like an eight-lane freeway without cars.

Both companies reached the same conclusion separately, that they needed a 'killer' application. This product needed to have widespread appeal to a mass market. In keeping with the high level of technology both companies envisaged would be contained in their new systems, this irresistible offering had to be something that was not previously available and therefore especially attractive.

Optus and Telstra decided to offer multi-channel subscription television, or pay TV. No longer would television viewers have to wait two years to watch Hollywood movies, or be deprived of live sporting action because a cricket Test clashed with a particular network's high-rating soap opera. This would be the service to attract customers to their telephony systems or, in Telstra's case, discourage them from switching to the competition.

The other high-margin products such as home shopping, gambling and banking would come later, after Optus or Telstra had first won their way into the household, and established their set-top decoder box on the television monitor. At this point, they would no longer be mere phone companies, but gatekeepers to the home for a world of entertainment and business products.

Unfortunately, these well-laid plans were forced off course almost at the beginning. By the time Optus and Telstra had announced their ambitious plans for their national cable networks, within a few weeks of each other in late 1994, they had already been beaten to the best movie and sports programs.

A specialist pay TV company, an upstart from outside the established media and telecommunications fraternity, was preparing to offer a 10-channel package delivered by satellite and microwave by January 1995. Australis Media was also very close to signing up the best Hollywood studios and valuable sports programming rights, threatening to leave the phone companies high and dry without the necessary movies and sport for their expensive new cable systems.

About to square up to each other, Optus and Telstra realised they would have to deal with a third player, or destroy it, in a contest where there were no established rules. Telstra would rely on the tried and tested law of 'might is right', but suddenly it was being dramatically out-manoeuvred by its smaller and more nimble opponents. This was going to be a game of catch up and stay ahead. Of pressing the flesh in Canberra, of stroking potential investors. Of feeding a niggling competition watchdog a few bones, and winning the hearts and minds of a cynical public.

All three players realised early on that at least one of them would pay the ultimate price and fail. Of the survivors, one would be forced to submit to the stronger of the two. It was a matter of corporate life and death. It was a one-off, a gladiatorial contest the likes of which Australia had never seen before and, perhaps, will never see again.

# 2

# Setting the stage

Just weeks after he turned 32 years of age, John Elliott bought control of the staid Tasmanian food processing company, Henry Jones (IXL). It was November 1972, and the strategy of buying asset-rich but poorly performing corporations cheaply and either breaking them up or resuscitating their business was not as commonplace as it was to become more than a decade later in the 1980s.

Elliott had been careful to cultivate the support of the Melbourne establishment figure Ian McLennan and the blue chip life insurance group National Mutual in his bid for control of Henry Jones. His consortium, a company called General Management Holdings,[1] named after the initials of Australia's largest car maker, General Motors-Holden, won control of Henry Jones for $35 million in a raid considered bold and imaginative at that time.

During this hostile takeover bid, Elliott brought onto his team a Sydney-based former McKinsey and Co colleague, Richard Wiesener; an Adelaide stockbroker from the firm Guest and Bell, Bob Cowper; and a former marketing director at H.J. Heinz, Peter Scanlon. As the trio sifted through the Henry Jones records to get a better idea of what they had bought, they found a subsidiary company called Murrumbidgee Television Ltd which had a television and radio station in Griffith, NSW, and 30 per cent of radio station 7HT in Hobart. The three men in all their research into

Henry Jones before the takeover had never heard of this component of the company.

Murrumbidgee Television was run from Griffith by one of the TV industry's most experienced practitioners, Ray Gamble (no relation to Australis's Neil Gamble, who was working as a chartered accountant in South Africa at this time). Ray Gamble had started in broadcasting with Amalgamated Wireless of Australia (AWA) in 1951. After joining Henry Jones in Sydney in 1959, he applied for the TV licence in Griffith, where Henry Jones sourced much of its fruit for processing and had a significant presence in the Murrumbidgee irrigation area. In the wake of Elliott's 1972 takeover, Bob Cowper elected to take charge of Henry Jones' investments, including the newly discovered media business. He phoned Gamble and asked him to come to Melbourne to talk about the business.

'I was talking to Cowper and Elliott, and they asked, "What do you believe will be the future of the industry?",' Gamble said later. 'I said cable television. That is what is going ahead in the US.' Gamble obviously impressed the two men and he was given the go-ahead to travel to the US to study the industry. Cable television was started in the US in the late 1940s by an enterprising television shop owner trying to sell his product in a town in the shadow of a mountain which interfered with the signals from the three commercial networks of the time. The retailer ran a cable from a transmitter he erected at the top of the mountain to his shop, where the town's residents were amazed at the clarity of the picture. They all wanted it too.

A tall man, heavily built with steel-grey hair, Gamble persuaded Elliott in 1975 to invest in two US regional cable operators that Gamble had identified.

Elliott was becoming increasingly involved in Liberal Party politics in the lead-up to and after the 1975 federal election. With the win by Malcolm Fraser's Liberals in December 1975, the new Minister for Communications, Tony Staley, assured Elliott that the Government would allow pay TV in Australia. Staley urged Elliott not to spend Henry Jones' money in the US, but to wait instead for pay television to start in Australia.

Although Gamble was keen to press on with the pay TV project, it was a fair way down Elliott's list of priorities. Gamble continued to run Henry Jones' modest media interests, but kept up the pressure in the meantime on Elliott to get Canberra focused on the issue. Staley eventually agreed after being lobbied by Elliott to commission in 1980 a report from the Australian Broadcasting

Tribunal (ABT). This report in 1982 recommended that cable and radiated subscription services be introduced 'as soon as practicable'.

One of the submissions to the ABT inquiry strongly in favour of subscription television was by a young business executive, Martin Hannes, managing director of the family owned Hanimex photographic and film printing company. The Hannes family, wealthy from the earnings of Hanimex, had been founding shareholders of 2 MMM, one of the array of bright new frequency modulation (FM) radio stations which sprung up around Australia in 1980 when the Government released new spectrum for this clearer and significantly superior sound to the tired AM radio signal. Hannes' interest in pay TV had been kindled while he was studying for his master's of business administration at Harvard and he was able to interest one of his fellow shareholders in 2 MMM, radio identity Rod Muir, in trying to establish a pay TV business in Australia.

Hannes told Muir that if they were going to be serious, they would have to bring in a US cable company as a partner to give them access to programming, subscriber management skills, and knowledge of cable technology. He travelled to the US and visited cable groups in Los Angeles and San Francisco, but it wasn't until he met Bill Schleyer and Tim Neher, at Continental CableVision in Boston, that he found an enthusiastic backer. Armed with the knowledge that the third-largest US cable group was an eager potential player in Australia, Hannes was able to present a far more compelling submission to the ABT.

In the early 1980s, potential players like Hannes and Ray Gamble considered cable to be the most likely delivery system, although the Fraser Government had come under pressure from the owner of the Nine television network, Kerry Packer, to consider satellite. In 1977, as Packer was putting together World Series Cricket, he saw how the US networks used satellite extensively for live broadcasts, and he wanted one for Australia. There was a strong element of self-interest in his proposal. Packer didn't want the satellite to broadcast direct to the home. It would be an alternative to Telecom's ground-based microwave network, used to back-haul programs within the Melbourne-Sydney network and also to move programming between his network's affiliate stations around the country. It would allow his Nine Network, and the other networks, too, if they chose, to offer national networking.

Packer commissioned a report from an American technician, Donald Bond, who predictably gave a glowing recommendation for satellite. These arguments fell on fertile ground in Canberra. By the end of 1979, Fraser's Cabinet approved the formation of a special purpose company, Aussat, to manage the process of ordering and eventually launching a satellite. But it would be another six years before Australia's first satellite was launched from the US space shuttle. The legislation governing Aussat specifically forbade it from transmitting signals direct to the home, thus ruling it out of any role for the foreseeable future in pay TV.

Satellite, therefore, was not an option, nor was it even considered by Gamble and Cowper, who by 1978 had identified the Gold Coast as an area to trial a cable pay TV service.

The planning at Henry Jones on pay TV dragged on, but Elliott and his key people were becoming increasingly absorbed with their ambitious plans to expand the company through takeovers. In 1979, Elliott and his three colleagues swung their energies into another corporate target, Queensland's Provincial Traders – maker of the fast food Chiko Roll; followed by malt extract producer Barrett Burston; and then the Adelaide establishment company Elder Smith Goldsbrough Mort. After this last acquisition in 1981, Elliott renamed his group Elders IXL, which had become a substantial corporation. Media and pay television were fast fading as matters of importance for Elliott and Elders.

First Staley, then in 1982 his successor, Neil Brown, failed to deliver legislation legalising subscription television, and after the defeat of the Fraser Government in March 1983, Elliott decided it was not worth the wait. The incoming Labor Government of Bob Hawke had a Cabinet full of people opposed to pay TV, fearing an electoral backlash among the party's blue-collar constituency if key sports programming rights were lost to subscription television. The free-to-air culture in Australia – with its three commercial networks, the Australian Broadcasting Corporation and the ethnic SBS TV – was probably stronger than in any Western society. Pay TV was always going to be a hard concept to sell.

Martin Hannes shelved his plans for cable, too. He phoned Schleyer soon after Labor's election win to tell him that pay TV in Australia would be on the backburner for a while. The two agreed to keep in touch.

The commercial networks, particularly Packer's Nine Network, had become highly influential in Canberra by the early 1980s. Although he had yet to achieve the power and influence that came with his greatly enlarged wealth by the end of the decade,

Packer was a formidable force in the government lobbies. He maintained a large house in Canberra's Mugga Way, where he entertained key politicians, and was a deft lobbyist personally and through the veteran journalist, Alan Reid. Although he was frail with failing health by the time Labor regained power, eight years after John Kerr sacked the Whitlam Government, Reid's mind was razor sharp. He had been able to maintain contacts at the highest ministerial levels right through the Whitlam, Fraser and Hawke administrations. Reid had virtually open access to the senior Labor ministers, in particular Michael Duffy, the Communications Minister, and Hawke himself. When Hawke and his ministers spoke to Reid, they believed they were speaking to Packer . . . and they were right. Reid was one of the few employees whom Packer treated with respect and deference.

During the mid 1980s, when Reid's health deteriorated, the lobbying was taken over by wine merchant and journalist Richard Farmer and, after 1986, by Peter Barron, a former journalist and adviser to Hawke and to NSW Premier Neville Wran. Their brief to keep the lid on pay TV was a simple one. The line Barron used with great effect through this period with Victorian ministers such as John Button (Industry and Commerce), Duffy and Senator Robert Ray (Defence) was, 'How would Victorians take it if they had to pay to see their football on television?'

According to the powerful former chief executive of Nine during this period, Sam Chisholm, 'Packer was the principal driver against it. His argument was that pay TV was completely unnecessary. Australia already had a free television service. There was nothing else required. He resisted it with brilliant success.'

Elliott decided that if he could not get his way in developing cable television in the foreseeable future, then Henry Jones should quit the media business. The Labor victory also encouraged Wiesener and Cowper to leave the country to take up residence in Monaco, where they established a consultancy advising companies on exotic tax avoidance schemes, using tax havens like Monaco. In Australia, where deregulation of financial markets was imminent and with a corporate landscape littered with potential targets, Elliott had more important matters to attend to. Within weeks of the Liberal loss in the March 1983 election, he told Ray Gamble to start selling the media businesses. He had already found a willing buyer for the Tasmanian radio station 7HT in the brash and outspoken Launceston newspaper proprietor Edmund Rouse, who was later jailed for attempting to bribe a Tasmanian politician.

Gamble decided he would try to buy the Griffith businesses. He travelled to Sydney to start putting together a management buyout of the Griffith TV and radio station. He had heard of Hill Samuel, which was probably the best-known merchant bank of the time, and headed for its offices in the Stock Exchange building in Sydney's Bond Street. The first door he knocked on was that of Robin Crawford, a middle-ranking executive in the corporate advisory division. Gamble wanted funding to buy the stations, then float the company on the stockmarket, all of which Crawford said he was able to do. He also needed a chairman. Crawford suggested his boss, John Gerahty, a pale, bespectacled man who was about to leave the bank to pursue his own business interests.

Crawford and Gerahty introduced Gamble to a remarkable group of people who, like Elliott, were just beginning to explore the possibilities flowing out of a deregulating market and the flood of bank credit that was starting to stimulate the corporate sector for takeovers and buyouts of this sort. Unlike Elliott, who ran the company making the moves, the people in Gerahty's circle were the facilitators to the deals, the advisers. In the early 1980s Hill Samuel was among a small group of merchant banks which advised on the biggest and most daring deals. Others included Baring Brothers Halkerston, Lloyds Corporate Finance, Schroders, and Bankers Trust. The bright, highly-paid bankers who ran these small advisory houses did not know it at the time, but they were on the brink of the most breathtaking period of corporate activity Australia had ever experienced.

Gerahty and Hill Samuel were gaining a reputation for clever deals that gave their clients enormous leverage with minimal outlays of cash or borrowed funds. Another feature of the transactions was their complexity – devices such as put and call options over share parcels; issuing partly paid shares with full dividend entitlements; gaining control of corporate targets with stakes of 20 per cent or less; setting up offshore entities and the like; often all combined in one deal. They didn't play by the old rules, but made them up as they went along. In the eyes of the corporate establishment buffeted by their tactics, these men represented the crass, fast, new money which proliferated in the 1980s.

Through Crawford and Gerahty, Ray Gamble bought the stations, then packaged them to float on the stockmarket at a time when shares were starting to take off as the Australian economy recovered from the 1981–82 recession. Among the investors who bought shares in the float were Gerahty, and some friends of Ray Gamble's from Elders, Peter Scanlon and Richard Wiesener, along with an emerging entrepreneurial client of Crawford's, Basil Sellers. Wiesener knew Gerahty from their days at Columbia University in New York and the two had worked together briefly at Schroders in the early 1970s, but they hadn't seen each other for years until Gamble reintroduced them.

When Broadcast and Communications listed in late 1983, the 75c shares jumped immediately to $1.50. It was a good start.

At the time of this float, Gerahty and Crawford were working on an even more ambitious acquisition and subsequent listing. Basil Sellers had earlier quit his job as a stockbroker with the Adelaide firm Day Cutten and had turned his hand to property development and speculative home building after buying a company called Devon Homes. Devon was caught badly by the 1982 recession and was overextended and near collapse when Sellers flew to Sydney to meet Crawford, then working with Schroders. Crawford had been looking for a buyer for a Sydney manufacturer of formwork plywood for cement construction, Ralph Symonds, which had been in receivership for a staggering 13 years. What is more, it was still listed and its shares trading.

Through Crawford, Sellers bid for the company and was able to turn it around quickly, thus staving off the collapse of Devon which would have ended Sellers' budding career. After the success of Ralph Symonds, Crawford, who had moved by this time to Hill Samuel, had found an even bigger deal. Textiles group Bradmill was to close its Hunter Valley denim manufacturing business, National Textiles. It was losing money and the company reckoned it would be cheaper to import the fabric. Crawford persuaded Sellers to buy it and, because he promised not to sack any workers, also won a substantial cash grant from the NSW State Government. Sellers and Crawford bought National Textiles through a company called Linter Corporation, and listed it on the stock exchange.

As the momentum of the stockmarket began to gather through 1984 and into 1985, and Hill Samuel acquired a banking licence and was renamed Macquarie Bank, the coterie of current and past executives with the bank continued to create fresh deals and take the big fee commissions that came with them. Preparing and reconstructing companies to take advantage of the gathering share price boom was the biggest game among the bankers and stockbrokers offices in the Melbourne and Sydney CBDs and, to a lesser extent, in Adelaide and Brisbane. Perth had its own group of dealmakers, such as Alan Bond and Laurie Connell, most of whom were to come unstuck so spectacularly later. The exception was a young former TV repairman from Melbourne who made his fortune in property development in Perth named Kerry Stokes.

Gerahty's next step was to organise a merger between Linter and Broadcast and Communications to combine Linter's steady earnings from its textile business with the potentially high-growth media interests of Gamble's company.

Another deal that was consuming his time was bringing together investors to strengthen a small listed rural property group which John Elliott and Peter Scanlon had acquired, Australian Farming Properties. Macquarie Bank arranged a large placement of shares in AFP Investments, as it was now known in late 1985, as part of a takeover of Linter. As a result of this share shuffle, Sellers and Scanlon emerged as major shareholders and Scanlon was appointed chairman.

AFP Investments rose from these humble beginnings to become a top 20 company with a capitalisation of nearly $2 billion (from just $25 million a year earlier) as its fortunes rose on the back of the sharemarket boom, and in particular the rise in the value of Elders IXL stock through 1986 and 1987. Ray Gamble stayed with the merged company and ran its media arm. It bought radio stations in Dubbo, Parkes and Mudgee, then dabbled in the UK where it took some shareholdings in media companies.

Linter's share price rose with the rest of the market. It seemed as if Macquarie Bank and its alumni such as Gerahty and Crawford could do no wrong. More than that, they believed everything they touched turned to gold.

In August 1984, at the height of the European summer, a young former radio journalist who had turned his hand to selling taped background music to department stores and office buildings in Australia was on holiday in the principality of Monaco. Lying on the beach one hot afternoon, Stephen Cosser and his wife Sue Cameron were listening to a radio sitting on the sand nearby. It was tuned to a music station playing 1960s and 1970s pop, interspersed with a disc jockey's rapid-fire Italian, French and tortured English commentary.

It was rough and ready, but far better than anything else Cosser had heard among Monaco's limited listening offerings. He asked the people with the radio the name of the station. 'Sovereign,' they replied. Cosser made some inquiries that afternoon and found out it was an unlicensed station called Radio Sovereign, broadcasting out of Ventimiglia just over the Italian border.

His background music business – which he had started in 1979 while he was working as the presenter of the Australian Broadcasting Corporation's popular current affairs radio program *AM* – was doing quite well, so he decided to drive to Ventimiglia to have a look at the operation. If radio had any glamour attached to it, there was none here. Sovereign's studio was a collection of electronic junk in a cramped room in a run-down flat in the town.

But he was interested in the business. It broadcast into the wealthy French Riviera region and Monaco and, with a bit of smartening up and a good announcer, it could pull in some good advertising revenues. He asked the station's Italian owners if they wanted to sell. After some haggling, they agreed on a price. Cosser had bought himself a radio station.

Cosser's first customer as he door-knocked shops and businesses around Bondi Junction back in 1979 had been Greg Solomon, the proprietor of a small chain of denim wear shops, Jeans Junction. Solomon agreed to take the taped music, but on the condition that he took a share in the business. The pair later named their enterprise The Music Company. Five years on, Cosser rang Solomon from Monaco to tell him their company had just bought into the radio industry in the Riviera and suggested he fly over and have a look at it.

Cosser and Solomon were discussing a more suitable name for the radio station over dinner in a small Italian restaurant called Pulcinella in Monte Carlo's restaurant district on the eastern side of the town. Neither liked the name Sovereign. Radio Riviera, one suggested, or perhaps Riviera 104, referring to the station's wavelength. While they were talking and eating, Solomon thought he heard an Australian accent at a nearby table.

He got up and walked over to the dark-haired man dining with another person who appeared to be a client. Solomon introduced himself. 'You must be an Australian,' he said to Richard Wiesener. After getting over his initial embarrassment, Wiesener joined Solomon and Cosser at their table for a glass of red wine. Early the next morning, he phoned his old friend Ray Gamble in Griffith. 'Ray,' he said, 'I've just met two young guys who are doing some very interesting things. I think you should meet them when they get back to Sydney.'

This chance meeting in Monaco brought Wiesener and Cosser together and they would form a partnership which would take them through a daring grab for control – albeit briefly – of one of Australia's television networks before it succumbed to receivership in 1990. Then the pair began planning an equally challenging venture, starting a pay television company they would call Australis Media.

When Ray Gamble phoned Cosser on his return to Sydney, the veteran radio and television man would introduce Cosser to a new network of people who would inspire him to realise those ambitions.

The 50 or so guests mingling in AFP Investments' office suite high in the Qantas tower off Jamison Street, Sydney, were toasting Linter's purchase of Broadcast and Communications, which was renamed Broadcom after it acquired 55 per cent of Cosser's The Music Company. Ray Gamble was introducing Cosser to Linter's shareholders and its backers in the investment banking community. One was Peter Burrows, whose stockbroking firm E.L. Davis was half owned by Macquarie Bank. He remembers meeting Cosser for the first time at the party. 'I couldn't believe how young he looked. He was smooth with a mellifluous voice and boyish face which helped him persuade people. He was a brilliant talker, with a lot of charm, a great salesman.'

Cosser, too, was impressed with the people he met. Most of them were starting to make staggering amounts of money dealing with parcels of shares on the stockmarket. *Business Review Weekly* magazine featured Sellers on the cover of its April 16, 1987, edition which told the story of 'How Basil Sellers made $200 million on shares in 36 weeks'. At a party about this time, Crawford boasted that he had made $1 million that day with the increase in value of his AFP shares.

It was a veritable connections factory, according to stockbroker Peter Gray, a friend of Cosser's who worked with Gerahty and Crawford at Macquarie Bank at the time. 'You'd go to a Linter listing party, for instance, and there would be the investors, the bankers and the underwriters. They were all there in that circle. You could have done a deal without leaving the room.'

Cosser had come a long way from humble beginnings as an orphan in London, raised by adoptive parents. His father was a British army sergeant who was on posting to Cyprus when Cosser, in his mid-teens, first tried his hand as a compere for forces radio.

His parents moved to Brisbane when he was 17 and he parlayed his brief experience in Cyprus into a series of disc jockey jobs in the Queensland capital.

At the age of 29, as he moved among the bankers, stockbrokers and entrepreneurial types becoming wealthy beyond the imagination of a young DJ 12 years earlier, Cosser was on the threshold of becoming rich himself. He was hungry enough and determined to succeed. With the backing of Linter and, ultimately, AFP Investments, Cosser and Ray Gamble moved quickly to take Broadcom into new ventures. These included a half-hour *Business Sunday* program for the Nine Network, which he negotiated with Nine boss Sam Chisholm. When Chisholm took the program back in-house after six months, Cosser moved the concept across to Ten, where the network ran it on Sunday nights under the *Business Week* name.

Cosser, who managed the business day-to-day, was also producing a half-hour *Australian Business Report* for US cable TV and he hit a new high when he won the lucrative contract to provide the in-flight entertainment for Qantas.

The business was doing well, but Cosser ran it on a shoe-string. In September 1985, Robin Crawford suggested he hire an assistant to take up some of the workload and nominated a young executive Macquarie Bank had hired a year earlier, a New Zealander named Wayne Burt. Cosser told Crawford he would call him. The next day, Burt took a taxi from Macquarie's Bond Street offices in Sydney's central business district for the 15-minute drive out to Double Bay, where Cosser and Greg Solomon had modest offices above the Roma Arcade in the heart of the village. 'Let's go next door,' Cosser suggested to Burt, 'and we'll have our interview there.' Cosser took Burt to the Sheaf Hotel, where they talked over some Heineken beers. The two hit it off. They were both in their late 20s, and were eager to take advantage of the opportunities abounding in the market.

For Burt – who held a doctorate in economics from Dunedin University and liked to be referred to as 'Doctor' – Broadcom's humble offices above a busy shopping arcade were a bit of a step down from the high-powered environment at Macquarie. But he was only a small player at the bank, and Cosser offered him a chance to get involved in a business which was starting to grow rapidly. Burt would later give Cosser an opportunity to push his business into a league well beyond Broadcom's ambitions of the time. But in late 1985, the opportunities were plentiful. Two months after Burt accepted Cosser's offer, in November 1985, Broadcom stumbled fortuitously onto a deal which would project this suburban video and music production house to national prominence and put it into conflict, not for the last time, with the powerful television networks.

Since television started in Australia in 1956, the Seven Network had held the rights to the Australian rules competition of the Victorian Football League and, from 1990 onwards, the renamed national competition, the Australian Football League. Seven retained the rights because of an unofficial agreement between the two commercial networks (three after 1964, when Rupert Murdoch and Reg Ansett established the Ten Network) not to bid for sports programming held by rivals. It was called Keep Off The Grass (KOG). As Seven had been a long-term holder of Australian rules football, Nine would respect that and never make a serious offer. Typically, it would pull out at the last minute saying it didn't have the facilities. Likewise, Seven and Ten never challenged Nine's rights to the cricket, for which it paid so much in 1977 when Kerry Packer established the breakaway World Series Cricket. Ten disturbed the order when it poached the rights to the mainly Sydney-based rugby league from Nine in 1988, but KOG ensured generally that the networks kept their costs on sports programming to a minimum.

As the 1985 season drew to a close and Seven's rights to the VFL for 1986 and options over the ensuing three years expired, the VFL itself was undergoing dramatic changes. Peter Scanlon had become a VFL commissioner and long-serving general manager Jack Hamilton was in the process of retiring. His successor, Ross Oakley, wasn't due to start until November, more than a month after the end of the season. By the time he took up his position the very important matter of the sale of the television rights was still in limbo.

Knowing that neither Nine nor Ten was making a serious bid and that the VFL was vulnerable while it was changing its administration, the general manager of Melbourne's HSV-7, Ron Casey, finally lodged a bid for $2.7 million for the 1986 season. This was considerably below the annual $3.4 million Seven had paid over the previous three years.

At the VFL commission meeting in November to discuss the television rights, Scanlon said, 'We have a problem. We haven't got bids from Nine or Ten and we can't possibly accept this offer.' He then told the meeting that he knew a company in Sydney called Broadcom which might be interested. 'Why don't you let Broadcom put in an offer?' He challenged his fellow commissioners to be creative and new, and do it a different way. The VFL commissioners were not aware that Scanlon was chairman of Broadcom.

Steve Cosser rang Oakley the following day and asked for a meeting. At first Oakley was a little cynical about the suggestion of an outsider buying the rights because of the long-standing relationship with Seven. Cosser told him the VFL needed a catalyst, another party to come in and break the grip the networks had on sporting rights.

Oakley saw the logic of this. Cosser offered Oakley $3.5 million, or $100,000 above the old Seven figure. He proposed that Broadcom would then on-sell the rights to another network and that any amount raised above this figure Broadcom would share with the VFL, up to $5 million. Above this upper limit, Broadcom would keep everything. Oakley was happy with the deal. The AFL was guaranteed more than it had been receiving and there was a chance of some extra money. He regarded it as next to impossible that Broadcom could achieve more than $5 million. At its next meeting, the VFL approved the Broadcom proposal.

Although the VFL was assured of getting its money, it was taking a risk because Broadcom didn't have a television station, much less a network, to show the sport. For Cosser and Broadcom there was also a chance that they may not be able to on-sell the rights to enough stations to recoup the money they had pledged to the AFL. As a small and relatively unknown business trying to break the grip of the networks on sporting rights, they were unlikely to get very far with the commercial networks.

When the VFL announced that it had sold the rights to Broadcom, all hell broke loose. Seven and Casey were incandescent, although they had pushed their luck by bidding so low in the first place.

A number of football clubs loyal to the old KOG system and to Seven lobbied the AFL commission hard to try to have the decision reversed, but to no avail. Melbourne's newspapers railed against the decision to award the rights to interests outside the main networks and, worse still, to a Sydney company.

Very quickly the fact that Scanlon appeared to have a conflict of interest as a commissioner and a director of Broadcom came to light in the media. Broadcom, Cosser and Scanlon suffered a barrage of criticism, but toughed out the hostile coverage. From the VFL's perspective, it would not be pushed around on rights, particularly on the money it expected to get for them.

Predictably, the three commercial networks shut their doors to Cosser, who had been hoping that their own greed and desire for ratings would overcome any sentimental attachment to KOG. Cosser had walked all over the grass. It just wasn't the way to play the game.

Scanlon wisely stepped into the background during this difficult period. One by one, however, Cosser began to get takers for Broadcom's football rights. First, the Australian Broadcasting Corporation in Melbourne agreed to take the game. In Sydney, the Special Broadcasting Service took it, in Adelaide it was bought by the Ten Network affiliate owned by Robert Holmes a Court, and also Holmes a Court's Seven Network station in Perth. An outsider who had taken plenty of punishment from the media during his three takeover bids for BHP and Co, Holmes a Court did not shy away from encouraging another entrepreneurial type like Cosser to ruffle some establishment feathers.

Another taker was SportsPlay, a direct subscription sports service for pubs owned by a group of Melbourne businessmen, which later merged with Holmes a Court's Club Superstation and Nine Network's Sky Channel to form Sky TV.

Cosser had achieved the remarkable feat of cobbling together his own 'network' to win almost national coverage of Australian rules football. Those stations brave enough to breach KOG were rewarded with record ratings, even the ABC and SBS. But Cosser's first foray into mainstream media was a costly one. Payments from his hotch-potch network of stations fell $1 million short of Broadcom's commitments to the VFL.

Most of Cosser's backers – Scanlon, Gerahty and Sellers – were making so much money on the stockmarket at this stage this amount was hardly noticed. Broadcom's successful grab for football rights hardly mattered to Nine and Ten, either. They'd never had the programming in the past. It shook up Seven though, far more than Cosser could ever have imagined. Seven's ratings plunged without the VFL. Casey realised he would have to get the football back, at all costs, for 1987. So before the end of the 1986 season he went to Cosser to try to negotiate the rights back.

Cosser was nursing his losses from 1986, but he knew he had something that Seven desperately wanted. He was certainly most unimpressed with the way the established networks, and Seven in particular, had handled this challenge to their privileged position. Perhaps, and he believed it highly unlikely, one day he might own one of them. That day may come sooner than he would expect.

On November 27, 1986, Labor Communications Minister Michael Duffy posted a short statement on the noticeboard of the parliamentary press gallery. In effect, it stated that from that day onwards, owners of newspapers could not own or control television interests in the same city, and vice versa. This policy would stop media owners from having an 'exaggerated influence' over local affairs. Existing positions where proprietors owned a newspaper and television station in the same city as permitted under the prevailing two-station rule would be protected.

Duffy's statement would have a profound impact on Australia's media industry, setting in train a series of takeovers and acquisitions which would see all three commercial networks change hands. It would lead to the dismemberment of Australia's largest newspaper group, the Herald and Weekly Times, and receivership for the second largest, John Fairfax.

The commercial networks were about to enter a period of tumultuous upheaval. Duffy's short statement represented the outcome of a protracted and sometimes bitter debate within the Government on a replacement for the old two-station rule which had been introduced by the Menzies Government in 1964. As a media ownership control mechanism, the two-station rule – which limited proprietors to ownership of two television stations – had come under intense pressure during the late 1970s and early 1980s because of the trend by television proprietors like Kerry Packer and Rupert Murdoch to network their programming to affiliate stations in the other capitals. In regional areas, however, towns usually had only one commercial station (as well as the ABC), which would be able to cherry pick the best programs from the three networks. Despite being able to have this choice, with some exceptions the program quality of the country stations was invariably woeful. Labor also saw many of these small stations as hotbeds of National Party influence, often being owned by families of National Party figures such as former Deputy Prime Minister Doug Anthony in Murwillumbah. The Labor figure intent on using policy to break up these cosy monopolies was not the Communications Minister Michael Duffy, but the Treasurer, Paul Keating.

His contempt for the conservative, rural-based National Party was not unusual in the Labor Party, but Keating's determination and capacity to punish his political opponents set him apart from his colleagues. His policy changes were all eminently justifiable on the grounds of rational economics, but like a laser-guided bomb there was often a precision about the changes he initiated which would have unfortunate consequences for his enemies.

In the course of his energetic pursuit of reforms to the financial system and taxation, Keating kept an eye out for opportunities to become involved in policy areas of interest, such as media. Keating had grown up in the working class Sydney suburb of Bankstown, the son of boilermaker Matt Keating.[2] He was active in Labor politics from a young age, and had developed a very strong view that his party was on the outer with the mainstream media. Labor's long period in Opposition from 1949 to 1972 and the fall of the Whitlam Labor Government in 1975 had been a product partly of anti-Labor bias by the media, the newspapers in particular. He believed from his early days in politics after being elected to the seat of Blaxland in October 1969 that Labor's future hopes rested with greater ownership diversity in media.

After Labor regained office in March 1983, Duffy had been toying with a concept devised by his department of issuing regional television stations with two supplementary licences to allow them to provide a service that would be comparable to the three channels available to metropolitan audiences. Labor Prime Minister Bob Hawke wasn't happy with the proposal, and he asked Keating and the Industry and Commerce Minister, John Button, to consider the reforms to regional broadcasting as a committee. Keating thought the supplementary licence plan was a terrible idea and would only entrench National Party interests. The discussions between the ministers coincided with a push, mostly from Packer's Nine Network, for the metropolitan stations to have greater control over stations in other capital cities for networking purposes.

The two-station rule meant that the proprietors owned their two stations in the most populous markets of Melbourne and Sydney, which was the case for Nine and Ten. John Fairfax owned the Seven Network stations in Sydney and Brisbane and, because its audience reach was much lower than Nine and Ten's, it was also able to own the Seven station in Canberra. After it bought 15 per cent of the Herald and Weekly Times in 1979 to help defend the Melbourne-based group from a looming takeover attempt by Rupert Murdoch, Fairfax was forced to sell Canberra because its audience reach was added to H&WT's Seven franchise in Melbourne.

In short, Packer wanted to be able to buy more stations to give him greater control to realise his networking ambitions. He was also troubled by the fact that the independent regional operators could pick and choose between the three networks for programs. It meant that the networks earned nothing from the sale of programs to the regions and also eliminated networking opportunities in the bush. This element of the Packer lobbying struck a chord with Keating, who saw it as an opportunity to strike against the National Party interests in the country. He suggested delineating large regions embracing at least three country stations and force each station to align themselves with one of the three networks. This would make every country station hostage eventually to the networks, but it could be sold politically by the Government as bringing metropolitan viewing to the country.

They would no longer be able to play off the networks to get the best deals on programming, which represented a substantial boost for Packer and the other networks. After being approached by Sydney businessman Paul Ramsay – who planned to use the coming changes to acquire a number of stations in country NSW to form a regional franchise to deal with one of the networks – Keating could see that this process would create a number of similar corporate regional franchises. This would break the National Party's hold on the country stations forever. The Government selected the Canberra region as the first of these aggregated areas. Nine would transmit its service into this area from its Wollongong affiliate, WIN-4. Paul Ramsay's Prime group decided to link up with Seven and he would start a new service for Canberra. This forced Fairfax's old Capital 7 to change its signal to 10.

This concept of equalisation and aggregation sounded fine on the hustings for the very long 1984 election campaign, but as it started to come into effect over the ensuing years, it caused enormous disruption as the old family proprietors were forced to surrender their station ownership in the face of an onslaught from new corporate owners of the wider network franchise groups. Tasmania and Western Australia, the smallest and largest States, would remain out of the policy loop for some years because their small and scattered populations meant that only two stations were commercially viable.

The transition to equalisation in the wealthy Canberra market was difficult, but elsewhere it was a mess. The most extravagant manifestation of this policy occurred in northern Queensland, where the Telecasters North Queensland group had long been close to Nine. It was to become a fully-fledged affiliate of the Nine Network under the policy, but when Labor's aggregation policy reached this region in 1991, Packer's Nine put the squeeze on TNQ. It told the company that it wanted 25 per cent of its gross revenues in return for providing vital movie and sports programming. This would have more than trebled its programming costs and probably sent the regional affiliate broke. It was a take-it-or-leave-it offer, which TNQ had to refuse in the end. TNQ was forced to switch its program sourcing from Nine to the lower-rating Ten.

Nine then sold its north Queensland affiliation to WIN-4, which was owned by Bruce Gordon, a reclusive businessman who lived in Bermuda. Gordon started his working life as a magician and with the help of Kerry Packer and long-time Nine Network director Bruce Gyngell, secured a job in program sales at the old Desilu studios, later taken over by Paramount. Over the years he became very rich and his WIN-4 station was frequently rumoured to be a potential buyer of Packer's Nine Network when fresh talk surfaced about Packer's intentions on the John Fairfax newspaper group in the early 1990s.

As far as the three networks were concerned, though, the difficulties of implementing aggregation and equalisation meant that the networks were able to persuade Michael Duffy to impose a four-year moratorium on pay TV from September 1986. Duffy didn't need much convincing to slap a ban on pay TV for a few years. As a fanatical supporter of the VFL club Essendon, Duffy was appalled at the thought of people having to pay to watch football and cricket. Although the Australian Broadcasting Tribunal had recommended an early start to cable-provided pay TV in 1982, it was hardly an issue for Duffy or the viewing public.

He had already been lobbied soon after Labor's election win in March 1983 by a senior Telecom executive, Bill Pollock, who urged the Government to postpone any development of cable pay TV until 1990 at least. By then, Telecom argued, fibre optic technology was expected to be developed to the stage where it could be used to deliver a range of services, pay TV being one, all the way to the home. Telecom had already begun linking the main metropolitan centres with high-capacity fibre optic cable to carry the heavy voice and data (facsimile machines were growing in popularity) between the cities. Its next stage was to put down fibre optic cable within the cities where phone and data traffic was also over-loading the old twisted copper wire network. Telecom envisaged from the early 1980s that when it was ready to start rolling out cable, revenue earned from a popular application like pay TV would help pay for the investment. Pollock made the point to Duffy that when the government finally lifted the ban on pay TV, Telecom wanted to be part of it. Telecom's lobbying of government in these early years proved to be effective and perceptive.

Although by the early 1980s cable pay TV was a mature industry in the US, and Ray Gamble at Henry Jones IXL had been ready to establish a cable network on the Gold Coast, Duffy's own prejudices combined with the Telecom advice and the continuing pressure from Nine provided him with the justification to ban it.

But Duffy did allow a form of pay TV at this stage. The *Radio-communications Act* passed by Labor in 1983 made allowance for video and audio entertainment services and, after the 1984 election, he announced that these multi-channel services could be provided to pubs and clubs. Three operators stepped forward to provide these services: SportsPlay, formed by a consortium of Melbourne businessmen; Robert Holmes a Court's Club Superstation; and Sky TV, owned by Kerry Packer. These would be the first commercial customers of Australia's A series satellite which had been launched from the US space shuttle that year.

Apart from this token concession to pay TV for pub and club patrons, the government maintained the moratorium on subscription services to households until September 1990. The latest pretext for continuing the ban was the difficult transition process for equalisation.

But cracks were starting to appear in the facade of resistance by the networks. The surge in popularity of the limited multi-channel services for sports narrowcasting to pubs and clubs of the three satellite operators started to give some viewers at least a taste of what pay TV might offer. Also, yet another parliamentary committee in 1989 recommended to the government that it make an immediate in-principle decision to introduce pay TV in Australia. This committee, chaired by Labor backbencher and former Telecom union organiser John Saunderson, recommended that cable and microwave (MDS) be the two favoured technologies for a subscription service.

By the end of the decade, the original three sports program providers who set up in 1985 to use the AUSSAT satellite had shrunk to one. Alan Bond, during his brief stewardship of the Sky

TV business, mopped up his two rivals. In the case of Club Super-station, Holmes a Court sold the loss-making business to Bond for just $1.

Despite the early difficulties caused by equalisation and aggregation, its implementation made it inevitable that the old two-station rule would have to go. It was redundant now. Full national networking by the television proprietors was achievable and necessary for their commercial interests, but the old rule stopped this. The challenge for the Government was to devise an alternative policy.

After having put together the new regional broadcasting policy, there was no stopping Keating now. He harked back to an old private member's bill he unsuccessfully put to Parliament in 1976 when the concentration of media ownership was a burning issue for him. The thrust of his bill was to keep the ownership of television stations separate from that of newspapers. Ten years later, and despite the distractions of a troubled economy and a plunging currency, he pressed very strongly in Cabinet for a development of his old policy. Although audience reach had been an issue for the two-station rule, Keating wanted no limits on television ownership. The main restriction was that a television proprietor could not own more than 15 per cent – the accepted threshold for control – of a newspaper in the same city.

Although Duffy had to accept the bare bones of the Keating policy because the Treasurer brought most of the Cabinet and caucus in behind him, the Communications Minister insisted on an audience reach limit. He wanted the 43 per cent enjoyed by Nine and Ten at that time to become the limit for the new policy.[3] This was never realistic, because under the cross-media rule, the television proprietors were likely to buy more stations. While Keating wanted no limit, his Cabinet colleagues felt some restriction was necessary and settled on 75 per cent. Keating had once again hijacked Duffy's policy and put up very little resistance to this one variation.

One point which made Keating's task of selling his policy to colleagues easier was his expectation that the Herald and Weekly Times group would probably be taken over. Corporate raiders Robert Holmes a Court and Ron Brierley had bought into the share register, sensing a takeover battle for the lumbering, under-performing group. The dogs were barking. Melbourne's *Herald* had conducted an emotional and effective campaign against Labor's asset test on pensions during 1985. Although the government introduced the asset test, the *Herald*'s campaign nearly ruined the political career of the Social Security Minister Brian Howe. Keating also sounded out some corporate confidantes before putting the proposal to Cabinet. He asked one of them, Ken Cowley at News Limited, whether the group still harboured ambitions to control H&WT. Cowley told him News did.

Murdoch owned the Melbourne and Sydney Ten stations. His newspaper empire at this stage was relatively modest compared with the scale it would achieve later. It consisted of the national *The Australian*, the *Daily Telegraph* and *Daily Mirror* in Sydney, the *News* in Adelaide and the Sunday *Western Mail* in Perth. Australia's largest newspaper publisher, H&WT, owned or controlled the country's biggest circulation newspapers, the *Sun News-Pictorial* and *Herald* in Melbourne, plus the *Courier Mail* in Brisbane and the *Advertiser* in Adelaide. It also owned HSV-7 in Melbourne. The Sydney-based John Fairfax and Sons had Seven Network stations in Sydney and Brisbane, plus its newspaper titles which included *The Age* in Melbourne, *The Sydney Morning Herald*, the Sydney afternoon tabloid, *The Sun*, and the national business paper *The Australian Financial Review*.

Although existing cross-media interests were allowed to continue, the new rule forbade any further acquisitions which would breach the rule. After he prevailed in Cabinet on the issue, Treasurer Keating proudly boasted in one of his typical one-liners that media proprietors could be 'a queen of the screen' or 'a prince of print'. They could not be both.

Keating briefed Murdoch at a dinner in New York about the impending changes,[4] and also let Packer know what was about to happen. Within weeks of this announcement, News Limited launched a $1.8 billion takeover bid for H&WT. Rupert Murdoch had chosen to be a prince of print. Because this was a new acquisition, he would be forced to sell his two Ten Network stations. With share and property investors making money hand over fist in the boom economy of the time, he didn't have to wait long before the wealthy shopping centre developer Frank Lowy stepped forward for the network.

Lowy bought Ten for $842 million through a company he controlled called Northern Star Holdings, which owned a collection of small newspapers on the north coast of NSW. In a classic 1980s corporate structure, Northern Star was owned by an investment company called Westfield Capital Corporation (WCC), which in turn was controlled by Lowy's main operating company, Westfield Holdings Ltd.

Lowy had set up WCC to exploit the investment opportunities of the rising share market. Lowy hired the prominent corporate lawyer, David Gonski, to run the company. South African Gonski, still only 30 years of age, was perhaps Sydney's most brilliant corporate legal technician who used his skills to move WCC into the media industry with the acquisition of Northern Star. Gonski's subsequent purchase of Ten for Lowy was typically complex, as was the final structure in which Ten would eventually come to rest. In early 1987, Northern Star's prospects were bright. With Ten, however, it had bought big trouble.

As News was mopping up H&WT in late January 1987, Kerry Packer was offered $1.05 billion for his Nine Network stations from another property developer, Alan Bond, on the day Bond lost the right to defend the America's Cup sailing challenge off Fremantle. Another Perth entrepreneur, Kevin Parry, was backing the 12-metre yacht *Kookaburra*, which beat Bond's *Australia IV* and went on to lose the Cup to American Dennis Connor.

Not only was Murdoch required to sell his two Ten Network stations, but as H&WT had two high circulation newspapers in Melbourne, he would have to sell H&WT's HSV-7 in that city as well. The station was in the middle of a ratings slide after having lost the Australian rules football rights in 1986, but after Ron Casey negotiated a sub-contract for the football from Broadcom for 1987, HSV-7 had hopes the ratings would recover. Casey would have been sorely regretting that he tried to be smart with the VFL by this stage. Cosser knew he had Casey and Seven over a barrel, and he was able to extract from Seven a staggering $9 million for the 1987 broadcast rights, nearly three times what Seven had last paid in 1985. Of this, Broadcom kept everything above $5 million. It was also entitled, as part of its agreement with the AFL, to half of any amount it received for the rights over $3.5 million and under $5 million. Broadcom would take a total of $4.75 million from Seven for the 1987 rights alone. Casey may have got his beloved football back, but at very high cost. After all this, Broadcom still held the master rights.

Still, HSV-7 was suffering at the time Murdoch would be obliged to sell it. To his great surprise, he was rushed by an eager buyer for the station. John Fairfax, advised by Macquarie Bank director Mark Johnson, offered him the enormous sum of

$320 million for the station. Even in this time of high asset infla-
tion and easy credit, no other potential bidder, including Holmes
a Court, was prepared to offer anything like this amount. What
amazed Murdoch was that Fairfax owned *The Age* in Melbourne
and was buying the station in defiance of the new cross-media
ownership rule. Unless there was a change of government at the
election due later in the year, or Labor failed to get its changes
through the Senate, Fairfax would have to sell it again at a loss. It
was a huge risk. Sensing that Labor might be vulnerable in the
Senate, Fairfax executives Greg Gardiner, Max Suich and Fred
Brenchley paid a visit to Keating straight after the HSV-7 purchase.
Gardiner put it to Keating that the legislation might be blocked by
the Senate if Fairfax were to conduct a campaign against the new
rule. Further, he suggested to Keating that if he were to make an
exception and allow Fairfax to keep the Melbourne station, the
group's newspapers would remain quiet on the issue. Keating was
horrified at what he regarded as a blackmail threat and rejected the
overture. 'If I give you a break I'll have to give Rupert and Kerry
breaks as well. You'll have to sell the station,' he told the Fairfax
men, who left Canberra empty-handed. The tense meeting marked
a distinct souring of relations between Keating and the Fairfax
press.

In the meantime, Murdoch was happy to take an amount for
HSV-7 at least $100 million more than he believed it was worth. In
one move, he greatly reduced his takeover costs and threw his main
newspaper rival into disarray to an extent that even Murdoch could
never have imagined.

When Fairfax took over the station it moved quickly to try to
revive its ratings. It sacked some of its well-known newsreaders,
including Mal Walden, reshuffled the program line-up, and allowed
Casey to retire. It proved to be a disaster. Ratings for its once-
popular news plunged into single figures. The changes were
portrayed in the parochial Melbourne media, now owned by
Murdoch, as meddling from Sydney, where Fairfax was based.

In the midst of this very public display of management inepti-
tude, young Warwick Fairfax flew to Sydney from the US, where
he had been studying at Harvard, for the funeral of his father, Sir
Warwick. He was appalled at what he read. On February 17, he
bought 1.5 million shares, or about 1 per cent of the company, with
$35 million he had borrowed from Midland Bank.[5] He had taken a
seat at the table and started to hatch plans to buy back the company
for his family.

After Labor retained power at the July 1987 election, Fairfax realised it would have to sell HSV-7. It had paid so much that it knew it could never recoup the money. Fairfax would have to sell the whole network to disguise the loss it would crystallise on the sale of the one station. Had it stayed out of the breathtaking media ownership changes of early that year, it would have been in the enviable position of being able to keep its Sydney-Brisbane Seven Network and its newspapers. Its late entry into the feeding frenzy when it feared it might miss out cost it hundreds of millions of dollars. It was one of the most costly and ill-considered blunders of the decade.

It sold the three stations to a rising investment company, Qintex Australia, controlled by a boyish-looking entrepreneur named Christopher Skase. Although the announced price was $750 million, Skase extracted very favourable time payment terms from Fairfax for his purchase, which meant he paid far less when the payment was reduced to a net present-value dollar figure. Seven was still comfortably the second rating network, and Skase in effect paid less to Fairfax than Lowy had outlaid for the lower-rating Tens from News Limited. Fairfax was out-manoeuvred at every point.

After winning control of Seven, the first thing Skase did was to repair the network's damaged image in Melbourne which resulted from Fairfax's brief stewardship of HSV-7. His priority was to secure full control of the VFL rights after learning that Seven had only got them back under a sub-contract from Broadcom. When Skase called Cosser to start negotiations he knew he had little or no bargaining power, but he was prepared to pay well for the exclusive rights because of the favourable publicity he would get for the network in Melbourne. Cosser once again extracted a hefty multi-million dollar sum for selling the unencumbered contract to Seven. Broadcom kept the lot.

The torment continued for Fairfax after it sold the network to Skase. For young Warwick, the sale was the last straw. He could see the publishing empire built by generations of his family being frittered away. On August 31, advised by the aggressive Western Australian merchant banker Laurie Connell, Warwick Fairfax launched a $2.25 billion cash bid for the company.

He held the offer price after the October 22–23 stockmarket crash in Australia and he was rushed with acceptances, even from his own family, whom he hoped would keep their holdings. The takeover ended up costing Warwick $2.55 billion and was financed entirely by borrowings. Despite the strong earnings of the group's newspapers the takeover proved to be a disaster for the company. John Fairfax Group, as Warwick renamed it, struggled to meet the punishing interest payments on the debt. The once-rich, family-controlled empire fell into receivership in December 1990.

At the time Warwick Fairfax launched his bid to buy his inheritance, the Australian sharemarket was looking very 'toppy' – over priced and ready to take a fall. The excesses of the 1980s were reaching a fountainhead of lavish spending, waste and extravagance in corporate and stockbroking circles. AFP Investments, for instance, had call options which would oblige it to buy shares totalling 17 per cent of Elders IXL from Goodman Fielder and SA Brewing early in 1988 at prices which assumed that the Elders share price would keep rising indefinitely.

Robert Holmes a Court was sitting on 30 per cent of BHP, 16.6 per cent of Pioneer Concrete and numerous other leveraged investments. Warwick Fairfax was planning his debt-driven bid for John Fairfax. Entrepreneur John Spalvins, who had warned the market late in 1986 that he was selling because prices had soared well above fundamental valuations, had returned to the market to buy bank shares.

Steadier heads among the market players were preparing for a correction, possibly a big one. But most market participants were oblivious to the gathering storm clouds.

Yet another pair of ex-Macquarie Bank executives who had struck out to make their fortunes in the rising sharemarket, Phillip Cave and John Willson, had formed a small investment company called Reil Corporation. It was a meaningless name, but in an era when companies were being formed and liquidated by the hundreds almost daily, coming up with fresh names had become a challenge. Cave was playing around with words with a pen and paper . . . real . . . riel . . . reil . . . that's it!

Like John Elliott 10 years earlier, the objective of people like Cave and Willson was to buy companies with well-known brands but which, through poor management, were underperforming and whose shares were trading at low levels. They would bid and win control cheaply, cut costs by retrenching staff and closing unproductive factories, sell un-needed assets, then float the company back on the sharemarket and reap a huge profit. Reil was one of dozens of small 'vulture' funds which preyed on sick companies. Although Cave and Willson had worked with Gerahty and Crawford at Macquarie and moved in the same circles, Reil was very much on the fringe of the aura surrounding AFP. By mid-1987, AFP's spectacular share price rise on the back of Elders' vaulting stock had made its main shareholders hundreds of millions of dollars in paper profits in a matter of months.

Cave and Willson's first target was a maker of plastic cups and containers, Lilypak. Reil then started to move into the mainstream by acquiring some of Australia's best-known brands, with the purchase of Sunbeam Victa from the troubled Allegheny Corporation of the US. They scored quite a coup when they were able to lure the managing director of McDonald's in Australia, Bob Mansfield, to run their emerging operation.

Mansfield, short and fit with a cheery countenance, had joined sugar producer CSR as a cadet after leaving Barker College in 1969. Six months before he completed his Bachelor of Commerce degree at the University of NSW, he quit CSR and joined McDonald's as an assistant accountant. His enthusiasm and willingness to get his job done earmarked him within the organisation for a rapid rise. Within 12 years of joining he was managing director.

Mansfield, now 46, says of his decision to quit a well-paid job in a multinational corporation to chance his luck with a couple of hopefuls in the market, 'I had a fantastic time at McDonald's, but I started asking myself did I want to spend the next 25 years without trying something else. There was really only one answer, and that was no.'

In early October, Cave and Willson were drawn to the crisis engulfing the security and fire protection group, Wormald International. The company had repelled hostile bids from Alan Bond and John Spalvins, only to fall victim to the Singaporean investor Lee Ming Tee, who had built up a stake of 19 per cent and began stripping the company of cash. Wormald was a classic opportunity for people like Cave and Willson.

After a few days of negotiations, Reil agreed to pay Lee $3.14 a share for his holding. This would give Reil effective control of the group. On the night of Friday, October 19, Cave, Willson and Mansfield gathered in their modest offices at 231 Miller Street, North Sydney, and broke open the champagne. They would begin the work of turning around this once-great group, which was the world's largest fire protection company at the time, on Monday.

Mansfield woke up on the Saturday morning to the 8am news on his clock radio. The New York Stock Exchange's Dow Jones index had fallen 5 per cent on what would be dubbed 'Black Friday'. The Australian market would probably fall on Monday in sympathy, he thought, but the correction didn't appear to be enough to cause too much concern. The three began to develop their plans for Wormald. True enough, the Australian sharemarket was rattled by the sharp plunge in New York on Friday, and fell a similar amount. It had been slipping since late September and more and more investors took advantage of the giddy prices at which stocks were changing hands to sell at what looked to be the top of the market.

The following day, however, the market was hit by a wave of panic selling. Overnight, the Dow Jones had fallen a whopping 20 per cent, wiping hundreds of billions of dollars from the New York market's capitalisation. Soon after the Australian market opened at 10am, Cave, Willson and Mansfield were watching the Reuters screen in Willson's office. To their horror the Wormald share price plunged that morning from over $3 to below $1. Reil had borrowed $90 million just three days earlier to buy its stake in Wormald. Now two-thirds of its investment had been wiped out. That evening, Cave got the first phone call from his young company's worried bankers.

The sharemarket crash also had a catastrophic effect on the high-flying AFP Investments. During 1987, as AFP was trading ever more deeply in Elders shares, Peter Scanlon had negotiated separately to buy the Elders stock owned by food group Goodman Fielder Ltd and Adelaide-based brewer SA Brewing Holdings. The two parcels represented a total of 318.6 million shares, or 16.85 per cent of Elders. Typically, the proposed purchases were complex and involved options by Goodman Fielder and SA Brewing to 'put' the shares to AFP over a period of time and at a range of prices, from $3.80 a share up to $5.45. It is not strictly correct to simply add up the number of shares at the proposed exercise price because the purchases would be staggered. But the raw total was a figure of $1.4 billion. Elders shares were sold down heavily in the October crash, from $4.08 to a low of $1.53 at one stage, before recovering to $2.20. If Goodman Fielder and SA Brewing were to exercise their options, they would drive AFP to the wall.

Scanlon persuaded the two companies to surrender their put options and proposed a different arrangement in which the shares would all be placed into a company called Petitio Ltd. Goodman Fielder's New Zealand executive chairman, Pat Goodman, even agreed to lend Petitio $200 million to cover the shortfall between the dividends it would receive from its Elders shares and the interest it would pay on the money this special-purpose company borrowed to buy the shares from Goodman and SA Brewing.

It was a classic example of AFP creativity, but it relied on the extreme generosity of Pat Goodman and SA Brewing chief executive Ross Wilson. The deal saved AFP from ruin, although the October crash effectively signalled the end of AFP as a force in the market. From then on, it staged a slow retreat as a player. Its investments in Linter and indirectly in Broadcom were sold or dealt with in a series of corporate restructures. Ray Gamble returned to Griffith, and Steve Cosser won back control of Broadcom, although Scanlon, Gerahty, Richard Wiesener and Basil Sellers remained as private investors in his company.

For Bob Mansfield, the next four years were very tough as he shouldered most of the burden of trying to rescue Wormald and stave off collapse for Wormald's main shareholder, Reil Corp. One of his first tasks was to hire a finance director to deal with Wormald's anxious banks. Mansfield retained Andrew Banks of the firm Morgan and Banks. One of the first people he sought out was a young South African accountant who had been working with Wang Laboratories for the past seven years. Neil Gamble was keen to move on, too. When he arrived at Wormald's head office in Sydney's Crows Nest on his first day at work, there were three bankers waiting outside for him.

Neil Gamble was able to keep the banks at bay by persuading them that he and Mansfield were the best people to conduct the program of asset sales to repay the debt of $550 million. He and Mansfield decided the best way to do this was to sell one of its core businesses, the security division. This was resisted by the Wormald board, chaired by the volatile former managing director of the AGC finance group, Rob Robson. The argument was so bitter, Mansfield quit.

Gamble took over as acting chief executive and was able to find a buyer for the business in the UK Chubb group, which was offering $138 million, far higher than Wormald believed it would get. This sale took most of the pressure off the group financially, but Wormald's torment was not over. After being tossed about by a variety of 1980s predators and having just suffered a near-death experience, it had come to the notice of yet another entrepreneurial group looking for an opportunity in the post-crash market.

The New Zealand property developer Chase Corporation identified the point of weakness at Wormald as its main shareholder, Reil. Chase bought Reil from Cave and Willson and, through it, the 19 per cent interest in Wormald. In a classic scenario of a small fish being eaten by a larger fish, which is swallowed in turn by an even bigger fish, Chase fell prey to high interest rates and the 1989 property market crash. It became a target. Rather than taking out a collapsing property group with some dubious assets, Peter Scanlon and AFP exploited Chase's desperation and bought the New Zealand group's most attractive interests, 19 per cent of Wormald and a controlling stake in film and photo processing company Hanimex.

Scanlon wanted Mansfield back in charge and offered him his job back. Mansfield and Gamble were back as a team.

Their resuscitation of Wormald culminated in September 1990 when they were able to announce a modest profit of $23 million (after several years of heavy losses) and the sale of the business to the US fire protection company, Tyco Laboratories. Wormald's long-suffering shareholders were offered $1.90 a share in cash plus stock in an Australian listed company called Tyco Investments, which in turn held 16 per cent of the US group. The sale ended six years of torment for Wormald. In the early to mid 1980s it had been one of Australia's best-known international companies before it became the target of the corporate raiders: in turn, John Spalvins, Alan Bond and finally Lee Ming Tee.

It joined a host of Australian companies such as packaging conglomerate ACI International, Herald and Weekly Times, brewer Tooth and Co, and baker and miller Allied Mills. All were market leaders in their day but paid the ultimate price for their conservative managements' failure to identify the rapid changes fuelled by financial deregulation during the turbulent decade of the 1980s. They were taken over by entrepreneurial opportunists, broken up, and their names expunged.

Mansfield was physically and mentally exhausted after his experience with Wormald. He repaired to his house with his wife and five children in St Ives, in Sydney's verdant upper northern suburbs, to concentrate on his family and his golf for a few months.

He was also an avid newspaper reader, and was drawn to one of the biggest running stories of the day, which was the Federal Labor Government's proposed tender sale of the second national telephone carrier licence.

Although Labor's reformist zeal was starting to run out of steam by this stage, a fresh, and highly potent, factor would start to play a part in the next round of reform: the struggle for the Labor leadership. After having floated the dollar and deregulated the financial system, Labor Treasurer Paul Keating found it inconsistent that broadcasting and telecommunications should remain insulated from competition. His ambitions on the Labor leadership were also getting stronger as the 1980s wore on and he felt he had done all he could in Treasury. Keating was keen to start putting his mark on areas outside his portfolio. Prime Minister Bob Hawke had been well aware of Keating's intentions as early as 1985, when the Treasurer pressed him to make a verbal agreement that he would succeed Hawke after the next election. Labor won government again in July 1987, and then its historic fourth term in March 1990, by which time Keating's leadership ambitions were becoming increasingly overt. But Hawke believed he should continue and, anyway, favoured his fellow Western Australian and Rhodes scholar, Kim Beazley, as his eventual successor.

The leadership contest would be fought on many fronts before it was finally resolved. One of the most spectacular clashes would be brought on by Labor's decision to set in train parallel reviews of broadcasting and telecommunications policies.

The three commercial networks had been extraordinarily effective in delaying the introduction of pay TV over the years. Potential pay TV operators like Ray Gamble may have come and gone, but the three commercial networks were a constant and resourceful lobby group determined to block or delay pay TV for as long as possible. The inexorable rise in cable subscribers in the US at the expense of the four television networks only increased their determination to delay the introduction of pay TV. Between 1989 and 1991, the market share of viewing hours held by the four US networks fell from 78.4 per cent to 71.2 per cent and cable rose from 21.6 per cent to 28.8 per cent, with cable revenues over this period rising from around $US10 billion to more than $US25 billion.[6] If this trend was replicated in Australia, it would cut deeply into the networks' revenues.

The ownership shake-out at the networks in the wake of Paul Keating's new media ownership rules left the three of them financially troubled. Their new owners had little idea of how to manage these complex businesses and their difficulties were compounded by the sharply rising interest rates of the time. By early 1990 Seven was in receivership after the collapse of Skase's Qintex group, Ten was losing money heavily and tottering, and Nine was in the process of another change of ownership.

All three were so preoccupied with their own problems that they lost touch with developments in Canberra, which would eventually produce policies permitting the introduction of pay TV. Had they not experienced this period of turmoil, the network masters arguably would have continued their relentless pressure on politicians to delay pay TV's start indefinitely. In the overworked words used by fallen entrepreneur Skase to explain his demise, they took their eye off the ball.

Bond's empire started to collapse in December 1989 when the National Australia Bank moved to take possession of his brewing group after the bank detected numerous breaches of loan covenants relating to the breweries. Packer took advantage of Bond's financial troubles to launch a takeover bid for Bond Media Ltd, the company that held the television network. After some legal manoeuvrings, Packer won back control in July 1990. Seven, as part of Skase's Qintex group of companies, was in the hands of a receiver from November 1989 onwards. Ten, too, would also go into receivership, but not yet.

Lowy had the financial capacity to weather the interest rate storm, but he sensed that the property market was about to suffer a correction. He did not need a bleeding television network exacerbating the situation. In mid-1989 he decided to sell his network before it threatened his core business: shopping centre development and management. As the decade of greed was closing, Lowy handed over Ten to a brash intruder into the mainstream media industry, Broadcom Ltd, whose principal, an impish looking 34-year-old, Steve Cosser, engineered a remarkable deal to take control of the network's Brisbane, Melbourne and Sydney stations from Lowy without paying him any money.

As part of the deal, Lowy and Westfield also sold their Adelaide, Canberra and Perth stations for $185 million to Sydney businessman Charles Curran, a former stockbroker and accountant who was the architect of the Curran tax avoidance scheme. Curran, in fact, put up no money either. The three stations came across to him with $130 million in bank debt, which the businesses would have to support. There was another component of mezzanine funding to the tune of $45 million, plus $10 million in equity credited to Curran by Lowy.

These side-by-side transactions valued the equity in the Ten Network at just $109 million. Lowy's Westfield Capital Corporation, through its subsidiary Northern Star, had paid News Corporation $842 million for the Melbourne and Sydney stations in February 1987, using $430 million in cash and borrowing the rest. In the ensuing two years, Northern Star bought another four stations in the other capitals, and by mid-1989 it had spent $1.3 billion building the network.

When Westpac Bank lent Northern Star the initial $415 million to buy Ten, the bank's head of corporate banking, Iain Thompson, reckoned that with a $430 million equity cushion he was as comfortable with the loan as he had been with any deal in his long career. Then, Lowy, a post-war refugee from Czechoslovakia, had described Ten as the 'worst house in a good street'. The property analogy gave an indication as to how he saw the investment. By spending some money on a few renovations, he would tart up the network then on-sell it for a profit.

Yet two years after the acquisition, when Westfield Holdings' finance director Stephen Johns, and the group's adviser, Macquarie Bank managing director Tony Berg, came to see Iain Thompson in his office at Westpac's Martin Place headquarters, they presented to the banker as a *fait accompli* the deal in which most of WCC's equity had been wiped out by the sale to Broadcom.

Ten came to Cosser through the people network he joined when he sold The Music Company to Ray Gamble four years earlier to form Broadcom. One of Broadcom's backers and a director of the company, John Gerahty, became a director of WCC in 1986. At a WCC board meeting in July 1989, David Gonski mentioned to Gerahty that Lowy was becoming disenchanted with Ten, as it was losing so much money. There seemed no end in sight to the rise in interest rates. Gerahty suggested to Gonski that he talk to Steve Cosser. Broadcom might be interested in taking a role. Cosser had made no secret of his ultimate ambition, to control a network, but until the industry became so traumatised by the dramatic ownership changes of the previous two years, networks were a little too expensive for small players like Cosser.

Cosser had learned a lot from people like Peter Scanlon, Richard Wiesener and Gerahty about applying small shareholdings to gain enormous leverage to take control of companies. When Gonski called him to talk about Ten, Cosser realised this could be the biggest deal of his life. He rang Ross Grant, another former Macquarie Bank executive who set up the boutique investment bank Grant Samuel and Associates in 1988 with Melbourne's highest-profile merchant banker, Graeme Samuel.

Lowy's keenness to sell, mixed with his ability to take a substantial loss and his desire to negotiate an exit which he could announce to the market as a completed deal, presented Cosser and Grant with enormous leverage. In their initial discussions with Frank Lowy and Gonksi, Cosser and Grant indicated they were mainly interested in the regional stations that Charles Curran eventually got. But as the talks progressed in Westfield Holdings' office tower in William Street, a short walk from seedy Kings Cross, it became evident that Lowy was prepared to sell the network very cheaply. Lowy reasoned that he wanted to give the new owner the breathing space to make a go of the network.

Cosser then set his sights on the program-generating metropolitan stations in Sydney, Melbourne and Brisbane. Learning from Scanlon and Wiesener, he said Broadcom only wanted enough of Northern Star to give it control, that is, 19.9 per cent. Northern Star was carrying more than $600 million in debt, which it could not service from its deteriorating revenues.

Lowy and Gonski agreed to buy the main studio complexes at North Ryde in Sydney and Nunawading in Melbourne's southeast at inflated prices to enable this debt to be reduced to around $400 million. After all the calculations were netted out for the assets and debt, the parties worked out that Broadcom would acquire its interest in Northern Star for 43c a share, or about 30 per cent less than the price at which the stock was trading in the market at the time. The rest of WCC's 31 per cent interest Northern Star would be sold to a number of institutions, including AMP and Bankers Trust, at the same price.

Even at this low price, the parcel of shares Broadcom would take was worth $22 million, which would normally have been a big bite for Cosser. The real leverage came from the fact that Lowy loaned Broadcom the money to buy the share parcel with five years to repay without any recourse back to Broadcom. If Cosser had wanted to walk away at any time, he could have. This appeared to give Cosser ample time to turn the network around and make enough money to pay Lowy out at the end of the five-year period.

In the negotiations, Lowy gave, then gave more. Cosser took, then took again.

When news that the deal was being negotiated at such a low price broke in a story in *The Sydney Morning Herald* on August 30, Cosser and Grant panicked. Surely, another potential buyer would come in and out-bid them now everyone knew how cheaply Lowy was prepared to sell control of the network. Two days later, on a Saturday morning, Cosser called a press conference in Broadcom's main studio in Bay Street, Ultimo. It would be the new headquarters of the Ten Network. Cosser could hardly restrain his glee as he sat behind a long trestle table flanked by Ross Grant and David Gonski to announce the transaction. The 80-odd journalists, lawyers and merchant bankers who crowded into the studio were still amazed at the low price at which Cosser had negotiated control of Ten.

In the wash-up, Lowy and WCC lost about $350 million on their Ten investment. In late July 1989, at which time Lowy had decided to sell out of Ten with the realisation that he would lose heavily, he accepted a standing offer from his friend, the Melbourne businessman Solomon Lew, to buy WCC's 7.8 per cent holding in retailer Coles Myer for $366 million. The profit on the Coles Myer exit would be offset for tax purposes against the Northern Star loss. This cloud had a silver lining for Lowy. In fact, Lowy did well to get out when he did. As events unfolded at Ten, it is more than likely that he would have lost far more had he stayed in.

At the time Cosser took control of Northern Star, it appeared to be the deal of the 1980s, perhaps the century. Cosser had surpassed his teachers. Suddenly, he was being mentioned in the same breath as Packer and Murdoch. Of course, Scanlon, Wiesener and Gerahty were there to share the potential spoils as shareholders in Broadcom. Ray Gamble had moved on during the traumatic shake-out suffered by Linter after the crash and had decided to focus his efforts running his Griffith television and radio stations.

Cosser had suddenly realised his long-held dream. He sold his house in Wolaroi Road in Woollahra and bought a large two-storey home in the even more upmarket Wentworth Road in Sydney's seriously rich belt of Vaucluse. The former radio announcer had travelled a long way from his days driving his battered Honda Accord in 1981 to deliver muzak tapes to clients in his spare time. Cosser ordered a new Jaguar, driven by a uniformed chauffeur.

His ego was well and truly stroked now. If he was to be a proprietor, he would live like one. He could look his mentors Scanlon, Wiesener and Gerahty in the eye, but he faced enormous problems in trying to bring Ten's losses under control.

# 3

# Bush track to the superhighway

When Kim Beazley arrived for the 8am meeting with two of Hong Kong's most powerful businessmen, he and his travelling party were hot and heavily jetlagged. The party had flown in late the previous night from a whistle-stop tour of the United States. There was much at stake at the Hong Kong meeting, not the least being the fate of Beazley's proposed telecommunications reforms, which he had fought through Cabinet the previous year against the bitter opposition of Treasurer Paul Keating. If the plan fell apart now he would be humiliated and Keating would have the last laugh.

It was October 2, 1991 and in four weeks bids were due to close for the government's auction of the second national carrier's licence to compete against Telecom. Under the Beazley plan, the tender for the licence would include the purchase of the government company Aussat Pty Ltd, which owned two satellites and was in the process of ordering two more. These satellites were being used for international telephone link-ups out of Australia, for aviation control and defence, as well as remote broadcasting by the ABC.

Time was running out now to find a buyer for these satellites as part of the sale of the second carrier licence. Beazley was having trouble exciting much interest from the large overseas phone companies he had lobbied. Unless he could interest a big US or UK phone company in buying Aussat as part of the licence to compete with Telecom in Australia, his big plan would fall in a heap.

Beazley and his party had just spent a week doing a four-cities-in-four-days tour of the United States, seeing the chief executives of three of the country's biggest phone companies: AT&T, Ameritech, Bell Atlantic and Bell South. He had not been encouraged by the response from the Americans. Although they all professed a keen interest in the Asia-Pacific region, he came away doubting that any of them would be a bidder. They were more interested in picking the eyes out of the market rather than setting up as a full national carrier to take on Telecom across the range of services, as Beazley wanted.

The objective observer couldn't blame them. Beazley's plan to merge Telecom with the Government's Overseas Telecommunications Corporation (OTC), as a prelude to inviting a second carrier to take on this monolith, tilted the playing field heavily in favour of the local player. He was now in Hong Kong about to meet Richard Li, son of Li Ka-Shing, the controlling shareholder of Hutchison Whampoa, and the managing director of the property and communications conglomerate, Simon Murray.

Although it was still early in the day and mid-autumn, the heat was already beginning to build in downtown Central where Hutchison Whampoa's office tower rose high among the district's skyscrapers. Beazley had with him his two advisers, Patrick Walters and John O'Callaghan, and a senior departmental officer, Mike Hutchinson. They were joined in Hong Kong by a banker with Credit Suisse First Boston, Mike Fitzpatrick, the former Carlton ruckman who had been advising Beazley on the sale of the licence and the satellite.

This was the last throw of the dice for Beazley. Unless he could be sure that Li and Murray were firm bidders, the auction he was trying to arrange would be a farce. There was only one other bidder, a consortium called Optus Communications.

Hutchison Telecoms, the communications division of Hutchison Whampoa, had formed a consortium with retailer Coles Myer and Telecom New Zealand to bid for the licence. The syndicate was called Kalori, which is an Aboriginal message stick.

Murray met Beazley as he and his entourage stepped out of the lift. The Hutchison boss then walked with them up a flight of about 20 stairs to the company boardroom with its large windows and breathtaking view of Hong Kong harbour below.

Murray was at least half a metre shorter than Beazley, who is a tall, overweight and slightly dishevelled man. The Australian was struck by the strength of Murray's handshake and the force of his gaze. Like so many senior executives with the large Hong Kong 'hongs', Murray was a Scotsman. As a former French Legionnaire, he was a tough, nuggetty person who gave the overwhelming impression he would take no nonsense from his staff or from people with whom he did business.

The men and their staffs sat around the large table in the elaborately decorated boardroom with its large prints of Hong Kong scenes arranged around the walls. Beazley began the discussions by telling the Hutchison men that he hoped they would take up the opportunity offered by the tender for Australia's second licence. He stressed the need for a powerful competitor in Australia's telecommunications market to compete with Telecom, now enlarged after its merger that year with OTC.

Murray replied that Hutchison's main interest would be in catering for corporate business and mobile phones. He didn't see much point in trying to duplicate Telecom's national telephone network. Li, who spoke with a Canadian accent, didn't say much at all, and when he did it was usually fairly hostile, questioning whether Hutchison needed to invest in Australia. This is not what Beazley wanted to hear. As the conversation continued, it became obvious he was on a different wavelength to the Hutchison pair.

When the discussion got to the satellite, Murray got straight to the point: 'Unless you allow the satellite to be the exclusive carrier for pay television in Australia, we will not bid.' Beazley was taken aback. Not only was pay TV illegal in Australia, he and most of his Cabinet colleagues didn't want it. It was usually dismissed fairly quickly whenever the issue arose in Cabinet because of the ingrained opposition of many ministers to the notion of viewers paying for sports broadcasting. It would be a blow to Labor's sports-loving, blue-collar constituency. Conveniently, this was also the very strong argument being put in Canberra for many years by the three commercial networks, Kerry Packer's Nine in particular.

But if Hutchison pulled out, the tender would be reduced to a one-horse race. Beazley could see tens of millions of dollars potentially being stripped off the value of the licence.

The rival Optus Communications group was interested in the satellites only for use in long distance, international and mobile phone telephony. None of the partners had any television experience and it was not mentioned in the extensive business plan submitted as part of their bid for the second carrier's licence. This group was made up of Australian transport and security group Mayne Nickless, Britain's Cable and Wireless, and Bell South of the US. They were backed by three Australian institutions: the AMP Society, National Mutual Life and the Government's Australian Industry Development Corporation.

An important selling point for Optus in the lead-up to the Government's decision on the successful bidder was the fact that it was 51 per cent owned by Australian interests. The consortium ran a series of full page advertisements in major newspapers extolling its Australian-ness, although it was clear to anyone who knew anything about telephone operations that the people really running the show would be the UK and American phone companies, which held the balance of 49 per cent between them.

Despite Optus's focus purely on its proposed telephone business, Beazley didn't have to exercise much brainpower to realise that he was going to have to persuade his colleagues to change their minds on pay TV, or see his precious second bidder back away. He was forced to agree with Murray that, yes, the satellite would be allowed to be used to transmit a multi-channel pay TV service.

Fortunately for Beazley, the future generation satellites were designed perfectly for such a task. Due to the foresight of the satellite designers at Aussat, the new generation B series satellites, when they were designed in 1987, were equipped with high performance beams on seven of their 15 transponders. This made them ideal for broadcast-quality multi-channel pay television. At the time these features were designed into the new satellites, pay TV was subject to a moratorium to September 1990, which would be extended for a further 12 months. There was no guarantee it would ever be lifted, given the lobbying power of the commercial networks.

According to Wayne Nowland, chief of business operations at Aussat, who designed both the A and B series satellites for the government instrumentality,

> We recognised that the satellites were going to be out there for 14 to 15 years and it was obvious to us that pay TV would happen. You only get one shot at it. Once the satellites are launched you can't bring them back and re-design them. If we didn't equip the satellites to carry pay TV we could never be a player in the business in the future.

Kim Beazley was Defence Minister at the time Nowland designed the new generation satellites in 1988. The Labor minister would never have known that Nowland's perceptive thinking would one day save his auction for a second carrier's licence. From the day of

Beakley's meeting with the Hutchison bosses, pay television became inevitable in Australia.

In the wake of Labor's fourth term win in March 1990, Prime Minister Bob Hawke overlooked the claim of the ambitious Senator Graham Richardson for the plumb portfolio of Transport and Communications and gave it instead to his fellow Western Australian and supporter, Kim Beazley. Richardson was given the Social Security portfolio, a post he did not want.

Had Richardson won the role as 'minister for mates' (as this combined portfolio had become known, because it invariably meant dealing with media proprietors Rupert Murdoch and Kerry Packer, and Hawke's friend, the head of transport group TNT Ltd, Sir Peter Abeles) events probably would have unfolded entirely differently. By denying Richardson the portfolio he wanted, the Prime Minister pushed Richardson into the camp supporting Paul Keating's ambitions to the leadership.[1]

Beazley inherited a very hot ministry in the post-election environment. First, Hawke had pledged during the election campaign that Labor would move to introduce greater competition in telecommunications, dominated in Australia by the Government's wholly-owned telephone company, Telecom. Once Labor had floated the dollar and deregulated the financial system in the mid-1980s, it became glaringly obvious that it could not keep important activities like telecommunications tightly bound by regulation. Also, the industry was on the verge of major technological changes with satellite, fibre optic cable and the development of digital signals and digital compression promising to dramatically alter the way people communicated and received pictures and information on their television sets and computer screens.

Labor's review of telecommunications policy, which started in 1988 under two senior bureaucrats, Michael Hutchinson and Tony Shaw, had produced some early reforms such as the formation of a regulatory body, Austel. Telecommunications would present enormous challenges for the new minister, given the very strong influence of the powerful Telecom trade unions on Labor nationally and in Victoria. Second, Beazley's predecessor, Ralph Willis, had initiated a review of broadcasting policy, also in 1988, and the following year received a report entitled *Future Directions for Pay Television in Australia*, written primarily by a senior departmental adviser, Chris North. The paper did not make any recommendations, rather it canvassed the strengths and weaknesses of the various means of delivery for pay TV: by satellite, microwave distribution (MDS), cable, and by telephone line by means of a technology known as asymmetric digital subscriber line (ADSL).

Beazley's task of tackling broadcasting and telecommunications would be complicated because it was inevitable that the two issues would converge once the Government was forced to nominate the satellite as a pay TV transmitter. His Government had the power to make and break the various delivery systems through legislation. Although the satellite effectively became the Government's preferred technology, because it was linked to the sale of Aussat, private sector supporters of cable and MDS exerted intense pressure on politicians on both sides of politics to give equal or at least neutral treatment to their systems.

Labor's ability to cope with the divisions in its own party in the face of this industry pressure would become increasingly strained and erratic as the issues moved closer to final resolution. Not surprisingly, the Government wasn't prepared to tackle such contentious issues as telecommunications and broadcasting and risk offending the networks and/or the unions in the lead-up to an election. After the election and with another three-year term ahead of it, Labor and Beazley could begin to take on the twin issues.

Hawke wrote a long letter to Beazley on April 8, 1990 nominating the policy areas that he wanted the new Communications Minister to address. These included telecommunications, broadcasting, aviation, rail, and the waterfront.[2] It was a formidable agenda. Any changes to the role of Telecom and the government-owned airlines Qantas and Australian would also require changes in formal Labor Party policy, either at its regular biennial conference or at a special conference called for the purpose of making these specific changes. On top of the commercial and economic considerations that would influence reforms of these industries would be the far more unpredictable and volatile factors of party and union politics.

Paul Keating also was anxious that reforms of the telecommunications industry be done in an economically rational way and that the changes not be corrupted by political considerations. Keating was still seething over some of the Government's decisions in the lead-up to the 1990 election, in particular Bob Hawke's decision to overturn Cabinet's majority vote to allow resumption of gold and uranium mining at Coronation Hill in the Northern Territory, and the promise of a $50 million subsidy to the Kodak

Australia film manufacturing plant in Hawke's electorate in Melbourne's northern suburbs. Keating warned Hawke during 1989 that if he was to make some politically soft decisions ahead of the 1990 election, he should not interfere with the bedrock of economic policy. After the election, it was essential that the Government return to the task of micro-economic reform.

The Kodak executive who negotiated the subsidy with Hawke was Zigmunt 'Ziggy' Switkowski, a Polish-born immigrant raised and educated in Australia with qualifications in nuclear physics. He would later move across to the telecommunications industry, to become a prominent figure.

Beazley's department had already done a lot of work on telecommunications and broadcasting policy, but his office opted to concentrate on the more pressing matter of what to do with Telecom. Although his department had put to him an options paper with six scenarios in which government could create competition in the market, Beazley had been strongly influenced by a proposal put to him by Telecom's managing director, Mel Ward, with the backing of the Telecom unions. Their plan was for Telecom to acquire the Government's international carrier, the Overseas Telecommunications Corporation (OTC), to form an unstoppable communications group. Beazley wanted to bring in a full second national carrier to compete against Megacom, as he called it, although this part of the Beazley plan was opposed by the unions.

Beazley had looked at telephone companies around the globe and didn't like any of them. The UK experience, however, was the closest to his preferred model. Margaret Thatcher had set up British Telecom as a large and impregnable phone company, privatised it partially, then invited tenders for a rival to create a duopoly. The Mercury consortium stepped forward to take on the might of BT. Six years later, as Beazley pondered his options for Australia, Mercury had hardly made a dent on BT's grip on the UK market. According to one of his closest advisers, Patrick Walters:

> Kim was keen on this model and everybody agreed in his office that this was the right way to go. He was looking at the big picture, at where the industry was looking globally. British Telecom was heading in that direction. Most other carriers we looked at were wholly government-owned with a separate international arm, like Australia and Japan. The US looked a mess with its seven regional carriers. Kim wanted something simple, and strategically good for the country. It came almost instinctively as the way to go.

To give the second carrier a chance against Megacom, Beazley proposed to include Aussat as part of the tender process for the second telecommunications licence. Ward and Telecom had suggested it to the minister, knowing full well that Aussat was a heavy loss maker needing a large injection of capital.

Aussat had two A series satellites already in geostationary orbit and another two B series satellites on the drawing board. Beazley dressed up the sale of the satellite as a boost for the potential competitor. In fact, Aussat was heavily restricted in what it could do. It couldn't compete against Telecom in offering phone services, for example. It was restricted even further from entering any field in which the monopoly carrier was a player after Telecom took a 25 per cent interest in the company in 1985. Aussat's main income, which reached $100 million a year by the end of the decade, was derived from providing back-haul services for the commercial networks and the ABC. By 1990, Aussat had debt totalling $600 million from the cost of its satellite launches and construction of ground stations. Most of its income went into servicing its debt. The Government had refused to inject any more money to put it on a sounder financial footing. The only option, and one pushed by Aussat staff, was to sell the business to a private sector operator.

Compared with Labor's approach to financial deregulation, where the market was thrown open virtually to all comers, Beazley's prescription for telecommunications reform was far more cautious. His primary goal, according to another adviser, John O'Callaghan, was to introduce competition in a way which would be politically achievable in a strongly pro-union Labor parliamentary party. Any reforms would also require approval to change party policy at a special national conference of mostly union delegates. The road to telecommunications reform was pitted with political potholes and obstacles.

Beazley's main opposition to his proposal came from within the party, from Treasurer Paul Keating and his Treasury department. Keating and Treasury were scathing of the Beazley plan, regarding it as a recipe for entrenching the Telecom monopoly or, at best, creating another cosy duopoly. It would also encourage union featherbedding. Rather than promoting increased competition, it would discourage it. Treasury suggested selling OTC and allowing it to become the basis for the second carrier, probably in partnership with a large overseas phone company such as AT&T of the US or even Telecom New Zealand. Regulations requiring Telecom to be subject to price caps and untimed local calls, would be stripped away. The market would then be open to all comers. Keating scoffed at the idea of selling Aussat, which he described as 'space junk', to the second carrier. Colleagues of Keating's and members of Beazley's staff said Keating became obsessive and very personal in the way he pressed his case.[3]

OTC senior executives, led by their managing director Steve Burdon, also lobbied hard against the Beazley model, urging that the Government adopt the Keating proposal. Unusually for a government enterprise, OTC also lobbied the media to push its preferred course. Its main fear was being smothered by the huge Telecom bureaucracy, with more than 86,000 employees.

Burdon said OTC was worth more to the Government as a separate entity, and argued that it was leaner and more efficient than Telecom. The earnings history of the two businesses supported Burdon's argument. In its last full year as an independent business, in 1991, OTC made a net profit of $276 million on revenue of $1.7 billion. Its return on equity was 49 per cent, impressive on any commercial measure. By contrast, the much larger Telecom had revenues in 1991 of $9.5 billion, earned a net profit of $1.6 billion and made a return on the Government's equity in the business of 10.8 per cent.

Keating's very public argument with Beazley on this issue was one of the most spectacular conflicts over policy in Labor's 13 years in government. At the crucial Cabinet meeting on September 10, 1990, however, Keating suffered one of his few defeats. Beazley won with the support of most of his Cabinet colleagues, but in particular that of Hawke, who revelled in Keating's discomfort.

After the vote was taken, an angry Keating threw his pencil onto the Cabinet table and got up to leave. 'I didn't think I'd see the time when the Commonwealth of Australia, the Cabinet, would be cajoled into a second rate decision by a bunch of second rate union officials and the centre left in South Australia,' he lectured his colleagues through gritted teeth. 'If you're happy to live with that, you can count me out.'

The subsequent special conference of the Labor Party on September 24, 1990 approved the change of policy to permit competition for Telecom. Over the ensuing two years, Telecom merged with OTC to form an unstoppable telecommunications monopoly. It carried the cumbersome name of Australian Overseas Telecommunications Corporation until 1993, when it was renamed Telstra.

After winning Cabinet approval for his telecommunications reform, Beazley realised it would be a year at least before he would be in a position to deal with the next of his reform tasks, broadcasting law. Michael Duffy's September 30, 1990 deadline for the moratorium on pay TV was approaching, so Beazley extended it yet again for 12 months.

Three days after Beazley's Cabinet win on telecommunications policy on September 10, 1990, Westpac bank rocked the television industry by moving to sack Steve Cosser and terminate Broadcom's 10-year management contract with the Ten Network. The bank's decision to call in receivers James Millar and Robert Dunn had been brewing for two months or more. Ten had been throwing out plenty of signals that it was in deep trouble, so the bank's move came more as a shock than a surprise.

Westpac itself was having problems at this stage, with a growing number of its clients experiencing trouble servicing their debt as commercial interest rates climbed to a peak of over 20 per cent in January 1990. Northern Star was paying about 16 per cent interest on its debt, which had blown out to $455 million by this stage. It was losing between $1.5 million and $2 million a week on its operations. This was *before* its interest commitments of a further $1.4 million a week. Westpac and the other two banks to the company, Commonwealth and Citibank, were financing these losses by increasing their lending to Northern Star. Westpac had been watching the situation closely and from March 1990 started to take a more active role in the management of the network.

When the notice of demand from Westpac's lawyers Allen Allen and Hemsley for repayment of the syndicate's loan was served on Broadcom's lawyers, Freehill Hollingdale and Page, on Monday September 10, it came also as a shock to Cosser. The previous week he had enjoyed a relaxed lunch with Westpac's managing director, Stuart Fowler, in the bank's 28th floor dining room. The issue of Northern Star's borrowings was barely raised, at Fowler's insistence. It would be a social occasion. But Fowler had been urged twice by the bank's deputy managing director, Frank Conroy, not to proceed with the lunch. It could send Cosser the wrong signal. Westpac was moving closer to a decision to appoint a receiver and any indication from the bank that all was well could be interpreted by Cosser that the bank was, in fact, happy with the exposure. This was far from the case. Westpac already had Millar and Dunn on standby and it required only a board decision to set in train the formal legal process.

Cosser had sought the meeting with Fowler to try to get an indication of the bank's attitude towards Northern Star and Broadcom. He had heard all the theories and believed that Westpac was set on winding up Northern Star and removing Broadcom as manager of the Ten Network as part of a Packer-inspired conspiracy.

Cosser had gone to see Conroy two days before his lunch with Fowler, and left none the wiser as to Westpac's intentions. Conroy gave away nothing, but at least he listened to Cosser. It was a tense meeting, but Cosser felt that Westpac didn't hold any animosity towards him.

Fowler was quite the opposite. He was expansive, completely ignoring the advice of his subordinates to put Cosser at arm's length at this sensitive time. Northern Star was a major client of the bank, he told Conroy, so it was fitting that he meet the company's controlling shareholder. The stark contrast in the mood of the two senior bankers reflected the deep divisions within Westpac over the Northern Star account.

The Broadcom boss came away thinking that, perhaps, everything was OK. After all, Fowler was supposed to be bank's most senior executive.

When Cosser took over Ten almost exactly a year earlier, it was losing money, but he believed the $200 million reduction in debt from the sale of the studio complexes at North Ryde and Nunawading had placed Northern Star and the network on a reasonably sound footing. Its finances had been completely restructured in the course of the sale and it was therefore a different business.

He moved Ten into Broadcom's more modest premises in Bay Street, Ultimo and Broadcom's offices to a run-down rented building in Castlereagh Street. The windows of this building looked into a multi-storey concrete carpark across the road. It was awaiting redevelopment and in very poor condition, but it was cheap. Cosser would keep Broadcom and its background music business just ticking over while he dealt with Ten.

At the network, he sacked the high-profile (in Australia at least) American managing director Bob Shanks who had been hired by Lowy with much fanfare only a few months earlier. Cosser took over the chief executive's role himself. Cosser found the network was paying far more for its sporting and movie supply arrangements than it could afford. Revenue was getting harder to come by as the

Australian economy started to stagger under the weight of high interest rates.

As it was the lowest rating of the three commercial networks, Ten was losing revenue as advertisers concentrated on the higher rating Seven and Nine. Its interest payments did not reduce in sympathy. As Northern Star found it was unable to meet its interest commitments, the banks rolled up its interest, and by March 1990 Northern Star's debt had climbed to $455 million. Of this, Westpac was owed $255 million, and the rest was divided between Commonwealth Bank and Citibank.

This loan was not secured at the time Broadcom took over. Rather, the syndicate had lent the money to Northern Star on a negative pledge basis. This was a popular style of lending in the 1980s, particularly to investment companies like Lowy's Westfield Capital Corporation, which often didn't have the hard assets to offer as security. Negative pledge lending was more flexible than the traditional form of securing loans. It enabled companies to borrow up to certain limits providing the borrower stayed within certain ratios, such as debt to equity. After Paul Keating admitted 16 foreign banks into Australia in 1985 and financial deregulation fired up the staid State government-owned banks around the country, there was no shortage of lenders by the late 1980s prepared to write big, high-risk facilities.

While Westpac may have been happy to agree to a negative pledge arrangement for a company in Frank Lowy's group, it was not so accommodating for a small operator like Broadcom. It insisted that its money be secured against the network's assets. By the time the security arrangements were formalised in March 1990, however, Ten's losses were accelerating and the banks needed to increase their exposure to cover the unpaid interest. The loan was extended for six months, to September 30. Westpac at this stage believed Broadcom had a chance of turning the network around.

At this stage too, the banking syndicate called in Peter Ferris and Brian Schwartz, of Ernst and Young Corporate Finance, to do an independent examination of Northern Star's finances, rather than rely on the assurances of Broadcom.

Cosser knew he was running fast just to stay still. He was cutting costs where he could to offset the falling advertising revenues and punishing interest payments. By the time the banks and their retainers were starting to intervene in mid-year, Cosser had already taken more than $60 million in costs out of the business. But rather than stemming the losses, the network was bleeding more. By July, its losses had grown to $2 million a week before interest payments. The Ten Network was haemorrhaging at a rate of about $175 million a year.

Ten's binding programming agreements with Hollywood studios MCA and Fox, plus the high cost of its rugby league broadcasting rights, which Cosser inherited, were also draining the network. After Lowy bought Ten in 1987, he broke the 'keep off the grass' rule with the other networks and jumped on a plane to Los Angeles to bid for program material from the Hollywood studios. He was dealing with studios which would later openly boast that they had written contracts with the UK's BSB satellite pay TV group which would ensure that BSB would go broke, which it was close to doing before it merged with Rupert Murdoch's rival Sky TV. No doubt they said the same thing among themselves about Ten, after Lowy left Hollywood.

The arrangement with MCA was particularly disadvantageous. It was a so-called 'output deal' where Ten was obliged to take whatever the studio gave it. Some of the programs were unusable. But Ten had to continue making high payments to the studio, no matter what the quality of the content.

Ten added to its burgeoning cost base with an expensive foray into current affairs, spending $17 million on the program *Front Page* in its first and only year. Lowy also offered a staggering $47 million over three years for the rights to the Australian Rugby League games, traditionally the preserve of Nine. By throwing money at program suppliers in a desperate bid to lift the network's sagging ratings, Lowy succeeded only in pushing up his own programming costs dramatically without any significant offsetting increase in ratings and sales revenue as recession started to close in.

After Schwartz and Ferris reported to Conroy and the bank's head of corporate banking, Iain Thompson, in August, the bankers realised they had a serious problem on their hands. Westpac retained Malcolm Turnbull and Cass O'Connor to advise the bank how best to deal with Cosser. Thompson picked Turnbull rather than another specialist media adviser, Gresham Partners, which was also bidding for the work, because he believed the situation might get nasty. If people started suing each other, Thompson wanted Turnbull's legal skills on his side.

Thompson also wanted Turnbull and O'Connor to draw up a strategy for the network which would see it return to profit. Until he was appointed in August, Turnbull had been advising Packer on the recapture of Nine and had just been appointed to the board of

Nine Network, as it was now known, after the takeover of Bond Media. Turnbull resigned from the Nine board when Westpac retained him on the Ten matter. His long-term association with Packer as a friend and business adviser immediately raised suspicions in the Broadcom camp that he was a stalking horse for Packer in his dealings with Ten. Turnbull vehemently denied any continuing connection. But when Turnbull took on Gary Rice as a consultant after Rice parted company with Nine in Packer's August shake-up at the network, Cosser's suspicions grew.

Turnbull also enlisted as a consultant a retired Westpac corporate banker, Doug Ferdinands, who did the credit analysis for the proposed reconstruction of Ten. The Turnbull team decided the best way forward for Ten was to cut costs dramatically by sharing facilities and running cheap, bought-in programs. Ratings would fall under this strategy to about half the prevailing levels, but the Turnbull plan estimated Ten could return to profit by the following year.

Members of the Broadcom camp lobbied the media intensely at this stage, hinting that this was a grand conspiracy by Westpac, Turnbull and ultimately Packer to destroy the network and hand part of its audience and advertising revenues to Nine. The conspiracy theorists were further encouraged by the fact that Turnbull was also advising the Hudson Conway property group – controlled by two of Kerry Packer's friends, Lloyd Williams and Ron Walker – in its attempts to buy the Seven Network from the Qintex receiver.

Armed with Turnbull's business plan, the Ernst and Young analysis and with the belief that Northern Star would be unable to service its interest without continuing bank support, Westpac's lawyers Allen Allen and Hemsley sent Northern Star's solicitors Freehill Hollingdale and Page the notice of demand. This gave Northern Star 24 hours to demonstrate that the company could refinance its $455 million in borrowings by the September 30 due date for repayment.

Northern Star declined to reply within 24 hours, so Allens served the company with a notice of default the next evening. Media headlines were dominated the following morning by what appeared to be an imminent move on Northern Star. 'Bank to pull plug on Ten' screamed *The Australian's* front page banner headline. The next day, receivership became a formality.

Cosser had one good card up his sleeve, a legally watertight, 10-year management agreement with Northern Star to run the network. If Westpac wanted to force him out, it would have to go to court, which would only exacerbate the network's financial problems.

In a day of frantic negotiations at the Bay Street studios of Ten, on Friday September 14, Cosser persuaded the receiver to retain him as chief executive in exchange for Broadcom dissolving the contract. When Cosser was driven back across town in his Jaguar to Broadcom's offices in Castlereagh Street, a reception committee of about 10 photographers and cameramen were waiting for him. Cosser had always been the man behind the news, not making it.

Westpac was fighting bushfires on many fronts by September 1990. Its loan book was deteriorating sharply and 20 months later in May 1992 the bank was forced to announce a shock loss for the six months to March 31 of $1.66 billion, mostly on loans to property developers. Frank Lowy's fear about the effect of rising interest rates on his industry had been correct. His decision to quit Ten, despite the losses he took on the sale, proved highly perceptive.

Another factor which prompted Westpac to move sooner rather than later on Northern Star was a growing concern, shared by the other commercial networks, that a new and potent competitor could be up and running in Australia in about a year. It was pay TV.

Steve Cosser's 12 months as a network proprietor was ending in humiliation. He remained briefly in token control as managing director, but every decision he made was vetted by the receivers, James Millar and Robert Dunn, and the banks. Less than a month after Millar and Dunn moved in, they sacked Cosser and appointed Gary Rice as managing director.

Broadcom was in deep trouble now. Its fee income from its management agreement now cut, it was also attempting to recover some of the $13 million it had invested in the Ultimo studio, which Broadcom leased, to fulfil its obligations under the management contract. Millar told Cosser to walk away and hand over the lease to the receiver.

Cosser couldn't do that because it would ruin him. He moved to another restored warehouse building over the road, and started negotiations with Millar to recover some of the money. Without any leverage in these crucial talks, Cosser had little hope of getting any money from the receiver. Help came from an unexpected quarter. One of his directors on the Northern Star board was Max Walsh, a veteran financial and political journalist and television commentator, who hosted a program for the network called the *Walsh Report*. Walsh had worked for many years in Canberra and knew Paul Keating well. He was well respected in the media industry and gave Cosser and Broadcom significantly more credibility than they would have had without him. As the weeks dragged by, Cosser became increasingly desperate as he made no headway with the receiver.

In December, Walsh suggested to Cosser that he might approach the Treasurer to see whether his old friend might be able to do something. Walsh sought out Keating in Sydney just after Christmas and explained what had happened with Broadcom and the network. Broadcom's existence was under threat now because the receiver had refused to reimburse Broadcom for the money it had spent on the studio. Keating told Walsh he would think about it.

A day or two later, Keating called Fowler and asked him whether he was aware that the studio and its assets belonged to Broadcom. Fowler said he believed the bank was aware of this. Keating left the conversation at that. The overseer of policy controlling the banking system had made his point to the head of a bank which valued the Treasurer's continuing good will.

Remarkably, Cosser was able to make a dramatic breakthrough almost immediately. Within days, the receiver agreed to pay Broadcom $7 million. Keating's subtle pressure had saved Cosser and Broadcom.

During this period of crisis for both Broadcom and for Ten, the receiver agreed initially to continue to pay for the expensive rugby league rights which were costing Ten more than $15 million a year. Millar told the Australian Rugby League he would renegotiate the contract for 1991 at the end of the 1990 season. Millar then changed his mind and told the ARL the contract was too expensive. In the ensuing negotiations over price, the rights lapsed.

The ARL put the 1991 broadcast rights back out to tender. Ten did not bid and, with Seven observing the KOG rule, Nine won back the league for the next season for just $5.6 million.

Worried that they might lose ratings, Rice and Millar then agreed to pay Nine $7 million for the rights to the popular *Friday Night Football*, which Cosser had initiated the previous season, and the regular home-and-away games. Seven bought the rights to international matches for $1 million. Nine kept the high-rating

State of Origin games and the grand final. Ten's handling of the rugby league rights seemed a shambles, and only fuelled the conspiracy theories that Kerry Packer was pulling the strings in the background. Nine had certainly done very well in taking back the league rights for no net cost. Rather, it made a profit of over $2 million.

Cosser retreated to Broadcom's dilapidated offices at 303 Castlereagh Street, financially bruised and his ego severely shaken. The poor state of the building with its leaking roof and noisy plumbing made the sharp descent to reality for Cosser a difficult transition. He was glad at least that he hadn't been tempted to take more ostentatious quarters at the height of his ascendancy at Ten, just a few months earlier. There was no shortage of opulent office accommodation starting to come on to the Sydney market. His music business would keep his suddenly reduced interests afloat until he came up with his next plan. In the year before he bought Ten, his sound and video businesses made a net profit of $690,000.[4]

One of Cosser's longer-term aims was to move overseas to live, probably to France. He began discussing it openly with trusted colleagues like Ross McCreath, a fresh-faced accountant who was just 23 when Cosser hired him in late 1987. Cosser had made mistakes and had clearly underestimated the task of managing a troubled network. He had also made powerful enemies – in Westpac, with Kerry Packer and in the Labor Government, who would make life difficult for him if he stayed in Australia.

But Cosser wasn't ready to leave town yet. Despite his recent humbling experience, by mid-1991 he was already working on his next plan to make money in the media. He and McCreath had been following the noisy debate in Canberra over broadcasting and telecommunications reform with great interest, because they could see an opportunity to put together a pay TV business. McCreath had become a jack of all trades in the Broadcom organisation. By the time it took control of Ten, he had moved on from being a humble accountant to take charge of project development. In particular, he demonstrated skill in finding new ways to transmit Broadcom's music programs across the city to customers. Working with a former Telecom engineer, David Jupp, hired by Cosser in 1986, McCreath initially developed the use of the FM sub-carrier either side of the main FM frequencies to send out their prepared music to commercial clients.

Jupp and McCreath then trialed a technology called digital music express, which was capable of transmitting up to 60 channels of high fidelity audio into households. It would require a special descrambler box in the home to accept the signal. It was a big step up from background muzak. More importantly, it was intended to be a product for direct broadcast to homes, rather than the narrowcasting of a direct signal to customers in their more established, corporate, business. This was a major departure for Broadcom and would prepare the way for Cosser's next step.

Although he was running Broadcom on a shoestring, Cosser had enough seed money to move on to his next venture, thanks to Paul Keating's phone call. Kim Beazley's deliberations over the rewriting of broadcasting services and the introduction of pay television would give him one more opportunity to make money. He knew from personal experience that the three commercial networks were still suffering after a tumultuous four years in the industry. This once-powerful source of opposition to pay TV would not be the force it was.

Cosser, McCreath and Jupp never proceeded with digital musical express, although it was undoubtedly a good idea. Instead, they decided to move straight on to pay television. They identified from their extensive research that the multipoint microwave distribution system (MDS), used widely in the US and Europe, was the best method of delivering a multi-channel service. It had its limitations, because it operated at higher frequencies than UHF and was thus vulnerable to black spots behind buildings and hills. As it was a line-of-sight technology, it required repeater facilities to reach obstructed areas, particularly in hilly cities like Sydney. An MDS transmitter had a range of 50 kilometres, so it could cover most Australian cities that were flat.

Another attraction of MDS for Cosser and McCreath was that it was available. Free-to-air television, radio and the digital and analogue mobile phone networks occupied most of the available spectrum. McCreath needed only one phone call to Beazley's department to establish that high frequency MDS licences were literally available over the counter.

The department didn't advertise it, but McCreath learned that there were five categories of MDS licence: those that could be used to transmit data; still pictures; sound; narrowcast of video and audio; and, finally, full broadcast. The fifth category, direct-to-the-home pay television, was illegal, thanks to the lobbying power of the commercial networks and the very strong belief among Labor ministers that subscription television represented a threat to their election prospects. Also, Paul Keating wanted to delay the introduction of the new medium until the latest digital technology was available. He told colleagues Australia had done the correct thing by waiting for the PAL-D technology for colour television, and he didn't want the pay TV industry to rush in and adopt analogue technology which would be superseded in a year or two.

Within days of Beazley releasing his draft Broadcasting Services Bill in November 1991, McCreath lodged an application for its first licence. Broadcom wanted to start a news service for its corporate clients. As the law stood, it could beam out a narrowcast service to particular clients, but it could not broadcast a service directly to homes in the suburbs. That was the exclusive preserve of the commercial networks.

The Department of Transport and Communications informed Cosser by mail in January 1992 that Broadcom had been awarded a microwave licence at a cost of $23,000. Cosser started putting together his Newsvision service. There was no competition in those days, so Cosser had little trouble negotiating non-exclusive arrangements with CNN and the NBC network of the US, the BBC, ITN and Financial Times TV of the UK, plus local news from the Seven Network and SBS. Cosser didn't waste money on a presenter. His service required only one operator to cut the feeds from these providers and re-broadcast them over the MDS link to the hotels and corporate clients which took the transmission. Newsvision began narrowcasting a no-frills service out of Broadcom's dilapidated Castlereagh Street offices in March 1992.

Cosser and McCreath had read Beazley's draft Broadcasting Services Bill from back to front and knew that there was nothing in it to stop a pay TV service based on MDS. They decided to buy more licences to provide them with additional channels in Sydney, Melbourne and Canberra. Ultimately, they planned to sell the business they were putting together or, alternatively, they might float it on the stockmarket. The future looked very promising indeed. Other pay TV mediums such as cable and satellite looked to be several years away at the earliest.

Cosser could see a window of opportunity opening for him. This could be his biggest corporate kill yet.

On November 19, 1991, Kim Beazley announced Optus, with its offer of $800 million as the winner of the second national carrier's licence to compete against Telecom. The Government had recouped all of the costs and accumulated losses incurred by the Aussat satellites. It was an excellent deal for taxpayers.

In the end, ironically, Hutchison did not bid. The Kalori consortium had been preparing to make an offer of $720 million. Simon Murray found his plan to bid for the second licence was being undermined by Richard Li, who urged his father, Li Ka-Shing, not to proceed and instead look for opportunities in telecommunications in the UK. When it became apparent over the next four weeks that Hutchison would not be bidding, Beazley's office went to great lengths to try to persuade the company to change Li's mind, fearing that the auction and the potential price for the licence and satellite could collapse. According to one former Labor adviser, 'It was a frantic effort to keep them in and, when they pulled out, to keep it quiet.'

Murray resigned from Hutchison a short time later. Optus, too, would have been mightily upset if it had realised it had paid so much when it was bidding alone at the end of this auction. After realising later that it had paid full price, Optus was determined to extract maximum value from its new satellites.

Beazley's announcement that the licence and satellite had been sold also legally bound the Government to legalising and proceeding fairly quickly with pay TV. It was a black day for the commercial networks. The networks' most pressing challenge from now on would be to try to control the process through which pay TV would be introduced to Australia, and preferably to own any pay TV licence issued by the Government. To date, Kim Beazley had not been the most cooperative of ministers, from the networks' point of view.

With telecommunications on the path to reform, Beazley a week later released an exposure draft of the Broadcasting Services Bill, along with an explanatory document prepared by his department, for public comment. Beazley's outline for the broadcasting law changes was the culmination of a three-year review of broadcasting policy by the department. On pay TV, the draft bill proposed, as expected, that Aussat satellites would be the primary carriers for any future pay TV service. Beazley's information paper did not close off other forms of pay TV delivery, such as cable and multipoint microwave distribution (MDS). The regime would be 'technology neutral', stated the department's paper.

Satellite would have an enormous advantage over rival technologies in delivering pay TV. Not the least of these advantages was the fact that it could instantly reach more than 90 per cent of the Australian population and be highly attractive to any program suppliers because of this large potential market. It turned pay TV into a national enterprise rather than the regional operations that Ray Gamble and Martin Hannes had in mind for their cable businesses. To cable the country would cost anything between $7 billion and $10 billion.

At this stage, the issue of whether the satellite would transmit analogue or digital signals was not on the agenda within the department or the Government. Nor was there any thought about interactivity; that is, the ability of the householder to send signals back to the broadcaster. This would emerge later as an important factor which would swing the industry's sights back towards cable delivery of pay TV, despite the high cost. Interactivity was critical for the phone companies, Telstra and Optus, which would want to use cable for telephony as well as a range of services such as home shopping, banking and gambling. For them, the satellite was of interest only as a way of delivering one of these services, pay TV.

With the state of technology in 1991, however, cable appeared to be out of the question on the grounds of cost and the time it would take to roll out through the suburbs. MDS had limited range, was a line-of-sight technology and would therefore have trouble providing a service to much more than 60 per cent of a hilly city like Sydney. But it did have one major advantage over the rival systems. MDS was far cheaper than the alternatives and the technology allowed it to be put in place within a few months. Even if it lacked penetration because of its line-of-sight limitation, it would be a very effective technology to 'skim' a 10 per cent or 15 per cent share of homes and make it very hard for the more extensive satellite or cable to come in later.

As Beazley prepared to publish his draft broadcasting legislation for comment in November 1991, simmering leadership tensions in the Labor Party began to break out in public. Within four weeks, Hawke would no longer be Prime Minister and Beazley would be replaced as Transport and Communications Minister. After losing a vote of the parliamentary Labor Party in June, Keating had the numbers this time. The waverers, who had kept Hawke in the leadership since that vote, started to move across to Keating as party powerbroker Graham Richardson set the groundwork for a second challenge at year's end. Keating won the next round in the Government party room on December 19, 1991, by 56-51. It was not decisive, but it was enough. Keating would have time to consolidate his leadership in time for the next election, anything up to 18 months away.

In January, the new Prime Minister appointed Richardson to the portfolio he had hankered after since Labor's 1990 election win, Transport and Communications. He would become the next 'minister for mates'. One of Richardson's good mates was Kerry Packer, the Nine Network proprietor, who was watching the unfolding developments in pay TV with increasing anxiety.

Optus's purchase of the Aussat satellite along with the second carrier's licence prompted another call by Martin Hannes to Bill Schleyer in Boston. 'It looks like things are heating up again,' Hannes told Schleyer. 'If you're still interested, perhaps it might be a good idea to come over here.'

Hannes' call in early December 1991 caught Schleyer and Continental Cablevision at an opportune time. The group had expanded aggressively in the US through the 1980s, buying up regional clusters in the east and the mid-west. It was now on the look-out for international opportunities. Schleyer told Hannes: 'We are still interested, and we'll be over to have a look.'

Bob Mansfield had been following the tender process for the satellite and the second carrier's licence in the newspapers, although it was only of academic interest to him. But within days of the announcement of Optus winning the licence, he received a call at his home from a friend, Kerry McInnes, a partner in the search firm Spencer Stuart. 'I've got the job of finding a managing director for Optus,' he told Mansfield. 'Would you consider it?'

Mansfield had been out of a job for six months. He didn't know a thing about running a telephone company, but he knew a lot about marketing. This was a serious job and definitely worth a go, he thought.

He wasn't at all nervous when he walked into the foyer of the Aussat building in Sydney's Wynyard Square for the interview before the full Optus board, because he believed he didn't have a chance of getting the job. As he entered the boardroom, overlooking the rich carpet of trees in Wynyard Park below, Mansfield was confronted by the faces of silver-haired chairman Brian Inglis, a former Ford Australia chief executive; American Charlie Coe from Bell South; Ian Webber, the head of Mayne Nickless; and the

Cable and Wireless nominee, Geoff Phillips. Mansfield put on an impressive display of salesmanship. He had learned managerial skills the hard way when pulling Reil Corp back from the edge of oblivion and restructuring a large industrial group in Wormald. What Mansfield was best at was marketing, courtesy of his 12 years at McDonald's.

Most of the men sitting around the board table were American or English. As they listened to this quintessential Australian who was good on his feet and knew a lot about management, they realised their task of winning business in a country like Australia would be much harder if they chose one of their own for the job.

They opted for Mansfield against candidates from Bell South and Cable and Wireless. Almost immediately after, they realised the wisdom of their choice when Telstra appointed an American chief executive, Frank Blount, a long-time executive from AT&T. It was an ironic situation. A largely foreign-owned company, Optus, using Mansfield's Australian-ness as a powerful marketing tool against the wholly Australian-owned Telstra, with its American boss.

Mansfield would say later, 'I saw myself as the conductor of the orchestra. I couldn't play the instruments nearly as well as the players who did, but I played the role of directing the people dynamics.'


Bill Schleyer arrived in Sydney in a late-January heatwave. Blinking in the bright summer light after the long flight from the US east coast winter, Schleyer was met at Kingsford Smith Airport by Martin Hannes. Schleyer brought with him no less a figure than Amos Hostetter, the chairman and chief executive of Continental Cablevision. The Americans were serious indeed.

On the drive across the city to Hannes's North Sydney office, the Australian explained that Paul Keating had just ousted Bob Hawke as Prime Minister and that the person they would be dealing with on the pay TV issue would be the newly-appointed Communications Minister, Graham Richardson. The sale of Aussat to Optus two months earlier meant too that satellite would be the most likely delivery system for pay TV in Australia because it made the scope of the business national. Cable, as the Americans well knew, was better suited to regional roll-outs which characterised the industry in the US.

Hannes knew that Schleyer and Hostetter would not be discouraged by satellite. Continental Cablevision had a 15 per cent interest with a number of other cable groups in the Primestar satellite pay TV business in the US and was familiar with the technology.

Hannes had arranged for the Americans to see Richardson the next day. First, the Continental Cablevision people needed to talk to Hannes about their desire to appoint an Asia-Pacific chief executive, to be based in Sydney.

# 4

# The game gets serious

Graham Richardson threw himself into the Transport and Communications job with eagerness and enthusiasm after he was appointed in January 1992. It was a portfolio he had hankered after since Labor's 1990 election win. Although it contained a wide spread of responsibilities, his energies were devoted almost entirely to the Broadcasting Services Bill and, more precisely, to Part 7, the section which dealt with pay TV.

Like Michael Duffy, Richardson was an opponent from the start of subscription television, fearing a voter backlash in Labor's blue-collar heartland if coverage of popular sports such as cricket and football migrated across to pay television. A short, plump, ruddy-faced man with blow-dried, grey curly hair, Richardson was a likeable person with a knockabout personality and a dry sense of humour. Behind the engaging veneer, however, was a ruthless streak. A fiercely ambitious man, Richardson had spent 20 years rising through the ranks of the Labor Party machine as an administrator and politician, stepping over the heads of those who got in his way. He was feared and respected in the party. Apart from his ability to manoeuvre himself into the right position at the right time for further advancement, he had a good nose for political danger and opportunity.

Richardson also actively cultivated the company of powerful businessmen, who he could lean on at the appropriate time for donations to the party and could also support his own ambitions.

One of these businessmen was Kerry Packer. Richardson never shied away from his association with Packer and at times openly flaunted it, reminding ministerial colleagues that 'Packer won't like that'. In drawing on Packer's commercial clout to enhance his reputation as a political power-broker, 'Richo' in turn openly pushed Packer's causes in Canberra.

Having inherited a situation from Kim Beazley in which pay TV was inevitable, Richardson did not want the new medium to damage the commercial networks which he believed had served Australia well. In meetings with Nine chief executive David Leckie, his counterpart at Seven, Bob Campbell, and Gary Rice, who had been hired by Malcolm Turnbull at Ten, he told the networks he would not only be sympathetic to their requests, but wanted them to have a role in the new industry. After all, the networks had the programming, the expertise and the money to make pay TV work – on their terms, of course.

As far as the networks were concerned, their first choice was to stop pay TV altogether. If they couldn't do that, then they wanted to control it. Kim Beazley had pushed the pay TV agenda too far now for it to be stopped. Richardson was given some comfort in this position by Martin Hannes, who was in the process of accepting Amos Hostetter's offer of the position as head of Asia Pacific for Continental Cablevision. Hannes told Richardson that his group had no objection to involvement by the networks. Experience overseas had shown that bringing in new players for pay TV did not work.

Early in 1992, both Seven and Ten were still being managed by their banks. It would be 18 months before Seven was floated, with Murdoch's News Limited and Telecom coming in as core shareholders. Ten would be sold by Westpac in December that year for just $242 million to a consortium controlled by Israel Asper's CanWest Global Communications Corp.

All three networks were willing participants in the push to delay pay TV, but their capacity to put up money as part of a serious campaign at this stage was limited. So the campaign to delay pay TV, hobble it with unreasonable conditions or, alternatively, control the licence, was conducted mostly by Nine's David Leckie, and Kerry Packer's adviser and lobbyist, Peter Barron.

First, Richardson needed to familiarise himself with the industry. Six weeks after he was appointed by Keating, he took an entourage of staff and advisers on a two-week tour of the US, the UK and France to see pay TV in operation. If he was going to re-write the legislation as it applied to pay TV, Richardson needed to learn a bit more about it, what it was capable of, and where technology was taking the industry. It was a grand tour which included his senior adviser Helen O'Neill, two departmental advisers, Christine Goode and Chris North, and a journalist with the *Sydney Morning Herald*, Fred Brenchley, who had been keenly following developments in pay TV.

One issue which Richardson would have to learn more about and which had started to emerge for the Government was the evolution of digital technology and whether it would replace analogue in the near future. Would the Government allow the marketplace to decide whether to use analogue or digital, or would the politicians enforce one technology or the other? The networks had raised the subject of making digital mandatory because with compression techniques it would be possible to have many more channels than with the established analogue technology. Even the high performance transponders on the Aussat satellites would allow for only one channel per transponder. With digital compression, each transponder could carry between six and 10 channels, depending on the complexity of the picture. With digital transmission, the information of a conventional television signal is coded into complex combinations of zeros and ones which are unscrambled by a decoder box back into pictures on the viewer's television monitor.

While digital technology allows for great flexibility, it is not significantly superior to analogue until smart technology known as compression is used with it. Compression works by transmitting only changes in pictures and not the whole picture, as is the case with analogue. As a result, it uses up far less capacity in terms of megabits. An analogue television signal might require 140 megabits of information a second. The same picture using digital compression uses only eight. In early 1992, however, the technology was still untried and appeared to be a long way from commercial application.

First stop on Richardson's tour after the 14-hour flight, first class, across the Pacific was Los Angeles. Richardson and his party arrived on a Saturday and were due to be briefed the following Monday by studio chiefs at News Corporation's 20th Century Fox studio. On Sunday, however, Richardson was Rupert Murdoch's lunch guest at his house in the Hollywood Hills. After lunch with Murdoch and his daughter Elisabeth, the News chief invited Richardson to his study where the two men talked for nearly three hours on global developments in subscription television. Murdoch stopped to scan through the 50 or so channels on the local cable network on a television in his study. Richardson questioned him on technology and which delivery system would eventually prevail. 'Cable,' Murdoch answered without hesitating. With all the emphasis on satellite in Canberra, this was the first time that anyone in the industry had mentioned cable to Richardson as a serious option.

At the Fox studio the next day, Richardson and his staff were briefed on how the studio's movies were faring in the marketplace. The executives who gave the briefing were particularly enthusiastic about the prospects of *Home Alone 2* after the success of the first version. *Toys*, starring Robin Williams, which turned out to be a flop, was being made at the time. During the briefing, Murdoch walked in. When the studio executives saw the News Corp chairman greet Richardson warmly they realised they had not been dealing with another routine visitor to the lot. 'They all stiffened their backs a little when they saw Rupert and Richo exchanging pleasantries with such familiarity,' according to one of Richardson's people.

At a briefing the next day at the studio for Richardson and his staff, Murdoch expressed enthusiasm for satellite despite his prediction the previous day that cable would eventually be the dominant technology. As he walked to his office with Richardson and staff in tow he hinted that News might invest in satellite delivery in the US. News Corp's BSkyB service in the UK was starting to enjoy the benefits of the savings from the merger between his Sky Television and the rival BSB consortium in November 1990. In the month he saw Richardson, the merged BSkyB made its first operating profit, of just £100,000.[1] The merged business's biggest saving was in its much-reduced payments to the Hollywood studios, Fox being one of them. After a period of cut-throat competition between the two UK satellite operators, in which losses were catastrophic for both, some commercial sanity had been restored to the UK pay TV business. Importantly for Murdoch, News Corp and his energetic pay TV chief Sam Chisholm emerged in firm control of the combined business.

When Richardson asked Murdoch about the timing for commercial introduction of digital broadcasting, the News chairman said, 'It's four or five years away, at least.' BSkyB was broadcasting an analogue signal in 1992. It didn't move across to digital until September 1998.

Next stop for the Richardson party was Denver, Colorado, where he spoke to senior executives from John Malone's

TeleCommunications Inc, and then to Atlanta, Georgia, where he talked to the people from Turner International. Both groups were keen at that time to invest in pay TV in Australia. 'Everyone seemed to want a piece of pay TV in Australia,' Richardson recalled later.[2] But what Richardson really wanted to do in Atlanta had nothing to do with pay television. Kerry Packer and Greg Norman had arranged for him to play a round of golf at the magnificent Augusta course. This was probably the highlight of the trip, he would tell friends later.

Then it was on to Washington, to visit the company Data International, which was at the leading edge of the development of digital technology. The company was optimistic that digital television would be viable within a year or two. Unfortunately, the demonstration for the Australian Minister showed that development probably had a little further to go. The picture broke up into black squares occasionally and the engineers were unable to properly 'anchor' the screen.

Richardson's party next took the short hop to New York, where he was due to meet some of the senior executives of the Time Warner group, the world's largest media company, with its studio, magazine and cable interests in the US. It was the second largest cable operator in the US with 7.5 million subscribers, behind the giant TeleCommunications Inc (TCI) of John Malone, with nearly 13 million cable subscribers. Time Warner had a strong programming relationship with Kerry Packer's Nine Network and had been closely following the Australian Government's proposals for broadcasting law changes. It was about to move one of its senior cable executives out to Australia to ensure the group would be well positioned to be a serious player. The Sydney office of Time Warner had arranged with Richardson's office before he left Australia to visit this man, Peter Frame, along with some even more senior Time Warner people in New York.

Richardson and his entourage checked into the Grand Hyatt Central Station, with Richardson occupying the presidential suite, thanks to an arrangement he had with the Hyatt group. Early the next morning, Richardson and party waited in the lift foyer for the Time Warner party to arrive. As the lift doors opened, the Australians took a collective step back. Six men in long black overcoats walked from the lift, led by an Al Pacino lookalike, Michael Fuchs. His black hair was slicked back, and he had a long white silk scarf and a long scar down the left-hand side of his face. Fuchs was president of Home Box Office, Time Warner's specialist movie channel, and was regarded at the time as the fast-rising star of the organisation. He was accompanied by Stephen Rosenberg, a senior vice president of HBO International; Lee de Boer, vice president, new business, of Time Warner Cable; Peter Frame; and two heavily-built bodyguards. The only thing missing, the Australians thought, were the violin cases. Richo was impressed.

Frame's bosses looked fairly imposing, but Frame himself struck Richardson as someone who looked after himself: nuggetty by not overweight, a keen tennis player aged about 50 with fair, receding hair.

The Time Warner men sat down with Richardson in a lounge area of the large hotel suite and asked the minister questions about the level of foreign ownership, whether a foreign player like Time Warner would be able to team up with one of the Australian networks and whether in fact the networks would be able to participate. Richardson assured them they would. One of the Time Warner people mentioned Nine and Packer. At this point, Richardson suggested they move into another room, leaving staff outside. The conversation was getting a little too sensitive.

After half an hour or so, Richardson and the Time Warner men emerged and the whole group took the lifts to the ground floor where two stretch limousines waited to drive them out to Long Island, the location of Time Warner's HBO satellite uplink facility which broadcasts the movie service to central and south America. Although Time Warner was primarily a cable operator, Richardson's hosts told him, it was starting to fully appreciate the advantages of satellite.

Driving through Queens on the way back to Manhattan that afternoon, the two cars carrying Richardson's party and the Time Warner people suddenly pulled over next to a seedy baseball stadium. Richo was hungry and he had spotted a chilli hotdog stall and insisted they stop to have one. That night, Rosenberg and another Time Warner executive, Carl Rosetti, who was vice president, new business, of Time Warner Cable, shouted Richardson a meal of his favourite food, Chinese, at the fashionable Shun Lee West restaurant, followed by the latest hit musical in town, *Miss Saigon*.

After the culinary and cultural delights of New York, Richardson's courtesy call to Sam Chisholm at BSkyB in London and a visit to the operations of Canal+ in Paris were uneventful and mundane.

On returning to Australia late in March 1992, Richardson's department put together a summary of conclusions from the trip. The first was that pay TV over time would have some impact on the commercial networks, but not nearly as much as the networks were claiming. Second, compressed digital on satellite was a 1996-97 technology at the earliest. Despite the department's conclusion, which was to prove fairly close to the mark, Richardson was confronted on his return by the commercial networks, who were becoming increasingly edgy about the legislation soon to go into Parliament, which would legally unshackle the development of pay TV.

In early April, the networks invited Richardson to a meeting at the offices of their powerful lobby group, the Federation of Australian Commercial Television Stations (FACTS), in Avenue Road, Mosman. The FACTS building is a nondescript 1980s concrete and glass structure wedged behind an old sandstone cottage and masked by an adjoining BP service station in Sydney's suburban lower north shore. It is almost invisible. A passer-by could walk past it and not see it. Yet, with the backing of the Packer organisation, it houses the most powerful lobby group in Australia.

As Richardson walked into the FACTS boardroom with departmental officer Christine Goode for the afternoon meeting, he had little time to savour the soothing view over a small park surrounded by a clump of large trees at the rear of the building. In the room were David Leckie, Bob Campbell and the Seven network's legal counsel, Sean O'Halloran, Ten chief executive Gary Rice and FACTS' executive director Tony Branigan. Campbell was also chairman of FACTS, a position which rotated among the network bosses. The meeting turned into a haggling session more at home in a Marrakech *souk*.

Despite the fact that Seven and Ten were still in the hands of their banks, Seven's Campbell led the charge with Nine's David Leckie in putting the networks' demands to Richardson. The networks had the programming and the expertise to run pay TV, so why not give it to them? Leckie and Campbell argued that they were entitled to the action at least as much as foreign interests. They were well briefed and knew that Richardson had been impressed by the Time Warners and the TCIs, which he wanted involved in pay TV in Australia. By being in a position to bid for both free-to-air and pay TV rights from the Hollywood studios, the commercial networks could block out any pay TV licence holder, they claimed. This final threat was pure bluff. But Campbell and

Leckie were in a position to exploit the numerous unresolved issues still hanging over pay TV to try to ram home their wish-list.

Although he was unashamedly sympathetic to the networks, Richardson had some tough calls to make on how to allocate the limited number of satellite channels in the face of so many demands from potential players both local and overseas. Technology would become a major issue, and then he had to get his proposals through his party, large sections of which were antipathetic to his leanings and deeply suspicious of the networks and the proprietors who stood behind them.

Right now, he had three very vocal and demanding network chiefs to deal with, and he knew that if he didn't give them a lot of what they wanted, Kerry Packer would be most unhappy. The networks' most pressing concern – the protection of their advertising revenues and viewing audiences – exposed a glaring inconsistency in their argument. While insisting on tough controls to hobble pay TV's ability to 'siphon' off sports programming, and to ban advertising on pay TV, they also wanted to control it.

The pressure on Richardson was all the more intense because Optus was required to provide only six channels on one of its satellites for pay TV. Although the new B series satellites had 15 transponders, only seven were equipped with the high-performance beam, and Optus needed one for its own purposes. Each transponder could carry only one analogue channel, so trying to satisfy all the demands from only six channels would prove an impossible task. The first of the B series satellites was due to be launched in August by a Long March rocket from the Xichang launch site in western China.

At the time of his April meeting with the networks, Richardson and his advisers had opted to sell one licence covering four channels then, a year later, two separate single-channel services. This became known as the 4+1+1 model. This was not unreasonable, given that the only successful satellite pay TV operation was Rupert Murdoch's BSkyB in the UK, which was running a four-channel analogue service.

Not surprisingly, the networks wanted control of the four-channel service proposed by Richardson. Leckie and Campbell pressed for the networks to own up to 25 per cent each of the licence, or 75 per cent potentially between the three. Richardson urged them to be reasonable. What they wanted was out of the question politically. 'I can't give you the lot,' he said. Then the bargaining started. Finally, Richardson agreed to argue for a cap of up to 15 per cent per network but with a combined limit of 45 per cent. He would need to get this formula through Cabinet and the Labor Party Caucus, where he knew the hard-heads in his party would have difficulty accepting even this reduced level. A combined 45 per cent interest in a licence would still give the networks effective control if they bid together.

Labor's left and centre-left groupings, who accounted for more than half the numbers in the Caucus, regarded the introduction of pay TV as an opportunity to encourage some new players into Australia's media industry. This was also the view of Richardson's department which, according to Richardson, had a political agenda to limit established players as much as possible in the new medium.

To add to Richardson's difficulties, the Democrats, who controlled the balance of power in the Senate, were insisting on a role for the ABC in pay TV. Richardson didn't want the public broadcaster in the business because it would cost taxpayers a lot of money. ABC managing director David Hill, his general manager of pay TV Kim Williams, and a partner in the finance group Australian Mezzanine Investments, Joe Skryzinkzi – who estimated he could raise $40 million to finance a commercial ABC pay TV service – were finding willing pro-ABC listeners among the Democrats, Labor's left and centre factions and even the Liberal Party.

Although Richardson was able to persuade his Cabinet colleagues to accept a condition that no television station could own more than 15 per cent of a pay TV licence (the true intent of this clause being that at least one, and perhaps two, commercial networks could own *up to* 15 per cent) the Labor Caucus would not agree.

Led by centre-left leaders Chris Schacht, a senator from South Australia, and John Langmore, a left-wing Lower House member from the Australian Capital Territory, Caucus ganged up on Richardson and told him the networks could own one of the two single-channel services, but only 5 per cent each of the four-channel licence. This would give them a total of 15 per cent only, not nearly enough to control the licence. Richardson's main problem was that too many players were chasing a very limited transponder capacity on the satellite.

Packer was furious when he found out that Richardson could not deliver control over pay TV to the commercial networks. After spending Easter at Coolum on Queensland's Sunshine Coast, Richardson drove back to Sydney via the picturesque New England

Highway, stopping at Packer's large Hunter Valley property, Eller-ston, near Scone, for the night before the final four-hour drive into Sydney. Packer flew up by helicopter the next morning to have lunch with Richardson before he completed the road journey. It was not a pleasant meal.

Packer and Richardson argued heatedly. Packer wanted the networks to own most, if not all, of the main licence and made the point that if the US program makers got control they would use the licence to siphon money back to Hollywood. Richardson wanted a studio or a large US program house to have a pivotal interest and argued back that a Time Warner or CNN would bring expertise as well as programming to the licence. The US partner could work with the Australian networks. Richardson didn't say it, but his hands were tied by the insistence of the overwhelming num-bers on Labor's backbench to keep the commercial networks in a minority position. When he drove off, Packer was still angry with him. Richardson had not convinced him at all that a strong foreign investor would be good for the main licence. Packer could only see the potential damage that pay TV would eventually inflict on his core business, the Nine Network. As a trade protectionist, Packer was deeply suspicious of any foreign involvement in an industry which would depend heavily on foreign program content.

Out of the blue, however, Richardson was to get an answer to the seemingly insoluble problem of how to carve up the limited satellite transponder capacity among the many interests who wanted a share. In early May, Optus chief executive Bob Mansfield wrote to Richardson seeking a meeting to clarify an important aspect of the proposed 4+1+1 plan. Mansfield brought with him to Canberra Ian Boatman, the Optus chief operating officer who had been seconded to Optus from one of its main shareholders, UK phone group Cable and Wireless.

When the pair were ushered in to see Richardson, Mansfield asked the Minister: Was Optus obliged to supply six transponders, or six channels? Digital compression was coming, and it would enable each transponder to carry up to eight channels, or a total of 48. It would be a waste of raw transponder capacity if Optus was obliged to give over six transponders to the pay TV licence hold-ers who might later be able to use digitalisation to enormously expand their service without having paid for it. The technology would probably become available some time in 1994, or less than two years away. Optus had paid the Government $800 million for the second carrier's licence and the satellites, and it was entitled to be able to exploit the satellite's capacity to its full extent.

Suddenly, Richardson could see a way out of the squeeze he found himself in. He was well aware of digital technology, but had received varying estimates of when it might be ready for commercial use. Here was the chief executive of the new owner of the Australian satellites saying the technology was well advanced. What was more, it would give the Government sufficient channels to satisfy the Packers, the Murdochs and anyone else who wanted a piece of the action, maybe even the ABC.

Unfortunately, Richardson would never get the chance to distribute his new-found bounty. At that moment, he was heavily preoccupied with another, more pressing issue. During his meeting with the Optus executives, the division bells rang in Parliament and Richardson had to excuse himself to go to the Senate chamber to face a confident Opposition which could smell blood – his.


Graham Richardson climbed on board the Mystere VIP jet at Canberra's Fairbairn Airport on April 28, 1992 for the one-hour flight to Melbourne for a meeting with the union leader, Laurie Ferguson. Richardson was putting the final touches to his submission to Cabinet on the Broadcasting Services Bill that he had inherited three months earlier from Kim Beazley.

Ferguson was among a number of unionists who had been lobbying the Government for last-minute changes to the Bill to satisfy their concerns over freedom of speech and protection of journalists' sources in this landmark legislation, which would dictate the direction and behaviour of the electronic media for years to come.

As Richardson stepped through the door into the small passenger area, he sat down next to one of his principal communications advisers, Chris North, who was reading *The Australian* newspaper. 'What's this?' North inquired, showing Richardson an article headed 'Richardson accused of heavy tactics to get mate off charges', written by Peter Alford and displayed prominently on the front page. The report stated that a Victorian MP had claimed in State Parliament 12 days earlier (it had obviously been missed by the media at the time) that Richardson had pressured the government of the Marshall Islands to drop serious passport charges against an Australian businessman. The man was Greg Symons, a relative by marriage of Richardson. Symons was carrying a letter of introduction from the Australian Minister when he was arrested and later charged over his involvement in a multi-million-dollar passport scheme to enable wealthy Chinese businessmen to gain quick entry into the United States by taking advantage of the Marshall Islands as a former US protectorate. Richardson was quoted in the article as having no knowledge of Symons' business affairs and that he was 'stunned by the charges'. Symons was sentenced later to three months jail for forgery and conspiracy.

Richardson suspected it was only a matter of time before the story became public. Symons was arrested on April 2 after getting off a plane in the Marshall Islands capital, Majuro. Later that day, Richardson received an urgent phone call from Symons' lawyer in Majuro, asking the Australian Minister to telephone the President of the Marshall Islands to persuade him to give Symons back his passport.[3]

Despite his alarm at seeing the Marshall Islands story in print that day, Richardson flew on to Melbourne to have his meeting with Ferguson in a private lounge at Tullamarine Airport. Although nothing Ferguson told him encouraged Richardson to change his legislation, criticism of the proposed changes from Ferguson and the rest of the union movement quietened considerably after the meeting.

From the day *The Australian* story broke, the Liberal Opposition knew they were on very fertile ground. Over the next two weeks they bored in relentlessly at Richardson, who in the past had inflicted so much embarrassment and pain on them, and who they loathed more than any Labor figure, apart from Paul Keating.

In the Lower House, Opposition Leader John Hewson rained blow after blow on Richardson, as well as his Prime Minister for supporting his Minister. In the Senate, senior Liberals Robert Hill and Richard Alston meted out similar treatment to Richardson directly. Day after day the Opposition assailed Labor with more and more revelations. On top of Richo's Marshall Islands involvement, his use of stockbroker Rene Rivkin's apartment and Rolls Royce in London during two visits to the city were thrown in. Not only was Richardson being shredded by the Opposition's irresistible assaults, but their attacks started to draw in other Labor Ministers, including Foreign Minister Gareth Evans and Speaker Kerry Sibraa, unwitting collateral players in Richardson's foolish act of loyalty to a distant relative.

By mid-May, Keating's patience was exhausted. He gave Richardson three days to provide a full explanation. His Government appeared to be in disarray. With an election less than 12 months away, the electorate was hearing of nothing else but the Marshall Islands, Graham Richardson and a sleazy business deal gone wrong. Government was paralysed.

Richardson resigned on the night of May 18. A full report demanded by Keating from Richardson on his knowledge of Symons' business affairs showed that Richardson had been fully briefed about the passport scheme in a letter Symons wrote to him in September 1991. This was a spectacular coup for the Hewson Opposition, which was in a state of exultation. For Keating and Labor it was a massive blow. Only five months after achieving his long-held dream of leading the Labor Party, Paul Keating, his Government, and his grandiose plans to educate and civilise the Australian people, appeared to be in political ruins.

The next few days represented the lowest ebb for Labor since it won government in March 1983, and a crisis for Keating. He could either seize the initiative and lead his party out of the political black hole into which Richardson had dragged it or, if he failed, lurch on to annihilation at the next election.

Keating showed remarkable resilience in this time of despair. He took the opportunity of Richardson's resignation to announce a reshuffle of his ministry on May 26. The most important move was to bring in as the new Minister for Transport and Communications Bob Collins, a rotund, popular Northern Territory senator who was good on his feet in debate on the floor of Parliament. Collins was a tough, no-nonsense type with a dry sense of humour. But he would prove to be well out of his depth and unable to handle the intense politics of this challenging portfolio. His main credentials for the job were that he was close to both Keating and Richardson and was known jokingly as 'the northern-most member of the NSW Right'.

Perhaps Collins' lack of grasp of the issues suited Keating. Five days after he appointed Collins, and before the new Minister could begin to come to grips with the complex issues of pay TV, which would dominate his short tenure, Keating accepted a standing invitation to appear on the Nine Network's *Sunday* program on May 31.

In an extraordinary political performance, Keating announced major reforms in airlines, pay TV and education in a rallying call to his party to support him, or face defeat at the next election.

The Prime Minister conceded his Government was looking 'sloppy' over the Marshall Islands affair and went on to spell out a series of initiatives, two of which directly impinged on Collins' portfolio. Keating told his interviewer, Laurie Oakes, that Labor would merge its two airlines, Qantas and Australian Airlines, and privatise 70 per cent of the combined airline in defiance of official party policy, which a few months earlier had capped the sell-down at 49 per cent. Pay TV would be opened up to a range of technologies rather than allowing just one satellite operator with a five-year exclusive licence, as was being proposed.

'I've been quite uncomfortable about the fact that we're about to exclusively nominate satellite television as the only vehicle for pay television between now and 1999,' Keating said. 'There's no particular reason why we ought to make it exclusive. There's no particular reason why Telecom, who has cabled up most of the Australian suburbs at least to the street corner if not the home, that anyone else that wants to be in the pay business shouldn't be able to be in it,' he said.

By suggesting that the Government would open up pay TV to other delivery systems, Keating justified the proposal before the Government to allow the three commercial networks to own up to 45 per cent of a satellite licence, but limiting individual networks to a maximum of 20 per cent. On the challenge of pay TV to the television networks, Keating said, 'They always tell us how good they are. We'll now see how good they are.'

Keating's broad brush policies needed considerable refinement. But he had broken the inertia that was paralysing his Government and reinvigorated the debate on pay TV. He had also raised for the first time, by a Government minister at least, the prospect of fibre optic cable delivery of pay TV. This medium had been largely disregarded until then as being too expensive, with the industry estimating a cost of about $7 billion to cable up most of the population. Also the process would take years. Telecom had not been doing any fresh lobbying in Canberra and its chief executive at the time, Mel Ward, was as surprised as anyone to hear the carrier's name being bandied around. Keating didn't mention microwave distribution (MDS), but he didn't rule it out either. Steve Cosser and Ross McCreath – whose Broadcom had been awarded a microwave licence in January 1992 – were buoyed by Keating's promise to encourage other technologies.

Satellite was still favoured by the industry because it would deliver a service to more than 90 per cent of the population as soon as the signal was switched on, but transponder capacity limited it to six channels. Although Bob Mansfield and Ian Boatman had raised with Richardson a few weeks earlier the possibility of digital compression providing a far greater number of channels, digital was not yet included in the equation by the man making all the moves in media policy at that point, Paul Keating.

The Cabinet briefing documents prepared initially by Kim Beazley and re-worked by Graham Richardson were now Bob Collins' responsibility. One very significant document provided to Collins in the chaotic initial days in his new portfolio was a briefing paper which outlined in detail the framework for the proposed auction of the satellite licences. It was prepared by the small, hardworking section in the department, headed by deputy secretary Christine Goode, charged with the task of selling the licences. This small group was very highly regarded in the bureaucracy after its successful disposal of Aussat and the second telephone carrier's licence the previous year. The paper was addressed to Graham Richardson, but in the confusion of his resignation and the appointment of the new Minister – the fourth in this portfolio in six months – no-one had time to change the name on the covering sheet.

On reading the document, Collins sensed that the department was very keen to introduce competition to the established media groups and that pay TV would be the way to do this. The bidders needed to pay a deposit of only $500, as opposed to the more normal requirement of a 5 per cent security which, in the case of the satellite licence, could represent an amount of several million dollars. The paper made it clear the Government should not set the hurdle too high for potential new players in the industry or it would discourage them. To ensure that bidders were people of substance, the department would vet them first to confirm they had the backing and credibility to build a pay TV service. Collins agreed entirely with the department's objectives.

The new Broadcasting Services legislation, minus the pay TV section, was due to go to Cabinet the day after Keating's remarkable television performance. It would be the first serious attempt by a post-World War II government to re-write broadcasting rules since the *Broadcasting Act* of 1942. When Collins introduced the Bill to the Senate, he said in relation to the part dealing with pay TV (which would be dealt with separately):

Part 7 provides for a competitive, more market-driven approach to the introduction of these services, colloquially known as pay TV . . . The arrangements will realise greater diversity in ownership and program types and provide a wide choice of services to subscribers. They offer unlimited scope for commercial and technical innovation.

The technological neutrality of the Bill is no more apparent than for subscription broadcasting services. Licensees are encouraged to use whichever delivery mechanism suits their commercial needs. This will contribute to the commercial modernisation of Australia's communications infrastructure.

This, after all, will be the most significant and largest scale new entertainment service that we will see in the next few years.

Collins' speech was written for him by his departmental advisers. In it he painted the scenario favoured by his bureaucrats of an open and competitive pay television market using a variety of technologies. In this environment it would be hard for a dominant player to emerge. The intense lobbying efforts on pliable politicians by potential pay TV players and by the networks to either stop it or own it would ensure that the outcome would be greatly different to the model outlined by Collins in his speech. The new Minister could not have known that the politics of his portfolio would distort his words beyond recognition.

Most of the Bill was passed through both Houses before the end of June 1992, with Part 7 going to a Senate Standing Committee, where the numerous interest groups would have another opportunity to impress their views on the legislation. At least it would be done in an open forum, rather than the backroom deals that had typified the process so far. Collins and his colleagues all knew that further battles would lie ahead when this section was due back in the Parliament in September. Also, there were still powerful elements in the Cabinet and Caucus who were fiercely opposed to pay TV. By hiving it out of the main body of the legislation, ostensibly for further review, Collins realised there was a possibility Part 7 could be killed off altogether.

Once Steve Cosser had got his pay TV business using MDS to narrowcast his Newsvision service to a handful of corporate clients by March 1992, he was able to start planning for a six-channel service to include movies and sport. At this stage, Broadcom had Australia's pay TV industry to itself.

One evening, Cosser, McCreath and Rick Solomon (Greg Solomon's brother, who worked for the music side of the business), were discussing Cosser's ambitions in pay TV. What they needed, Cosser said, was a new corporate name. The three tossed around a few possible names. Rick Solomon suggested 'Australis'.

McCreath was sitting at his desk on Friday, June 3, finishing off applications for 12 MDS licences, six in Melbourne and six in Sydney. Would he post them to the department in Canberra, or fax them? he asked himself. McCreath wanted to get home. He couldn't be bothered sealing them in an envelope, affixing a stamp and posting them, so he decided to fax them instead.

It was a remarkably lucky and timely decision. At 9am the next Monday, after McCreath's faxes had arrived, the department suspended the issuing of any more MDS licences. The Minister was about to table his legislation in the Senate and his department felt it might be unfair to give any single technology an edge over the others while the terms of pay TV delivery were being settled in Parliament.

Cosser and McCreath received their fresh licences four weeks later. They now had 13 licences, at a total cost of just under $300,000. They would need more later to be able to offer six channels in the other capitals, if they wanted to set up a national six-channel service. But Broadcom had got through the gate before it slammed shut. Cosser had a good business idea and enough licences to start looking for potential buyers of the business. He was also close to leaving Australia to live in Paris. First, he wanted to see if he could excite some interest in the business he was starting to put together. He called Malcolm Colless, head of business development at Rupert Murdoch's News Limited in Sydney. 'Malcolm,' Cosser said to the News executive, 'I might have an interesting proposition for you.'


Paul Keating's declaration on the *Sunday* program that he wanted more diversity in the way pay TV was delivered also rang alarm bells at the networks, in particular at Nine and the ABC. Until then virtually all the focus had been on satellite. This was despite the findings of John Saunderson's 1988 parliamentary committee recommending MDS be the preferred technology as an interim delivery system, until fibre optic cable was sufficiently developed (courtesy of strong representations to the committee from Saunderson's former employer, Telecom). This report had been well and truly forgotten by this time, although it was to prove remarkably prescient.

By throwing open the prospect that the Government would entertain MDS and cable, Keating forced potential players in pay TV to re-think their strategy. Within days of Keating's *Sunday* appearance, the new Minister, Bob Collins, received letters from David Leckie at Nine, the ABC's David Hill and Time Warner's newly installed Australian representative, Peter Frame. The letters were all very similar. They all asked for MDS licences. Nine and the ABC suggested they use spectrum devoted to their electronic news gathering networks for MDS subscription services. They were all worried that Steve Cosser may have got the jump on them. When Collins wrote back to tell them that the issue of MDS licences had been closed off until the legislation was passed, they would all be disappointed. They would also become determined opponents of MDS. If they couldn't have it, then no-one else should either.

When the Senate committee finally released its report on September 17, its 22 recommendations were unspecific and lacked focus. Five dealt with the role of the ABC. This was a tribute to the effective lobbying of ABC managing director David Hill, whose efforts to win a pivotal role for the ABC were highly effective in Canberra, but were generating considerable hostility from journalists within his own organisation concerned that pay TV would commercialise the ABC. Unfortunately for Hill, Keating shared the view of ABC journalists and couldn't see much of a role for the public broadcaster either.

The conflicting agendas of the Liberal, Labor and Democrat senators on the committee meant that the final report, along with the two dissenting reports from the non-Government members, was 'a dog's breakfast', according to one industry observer.[4] Keating and Collins were able to ignore the report completely.

The committee had been thrown into some confusion when it received an additional submission from Optus on September 6, three days after its public hearings finished. Optus informed the committee in writing that it would exercise its right as a general carrier to supply compressed digital video satellite channels to licensed operators, rather than 'raw' transponder capacity. It estimated that the new technology would be available in 12 to 15 months, a forecast which proved to be highly optimistic. It was obliged to provide at least six channels for pay TV, but digital compression would allow Optus to supply 24 channels in the satellite's first year of service, rising to 48 in the third year.

A delegation from Optus led by Wayne Nowland briefed the committee for most of the next day. Optus wanted to offer as many channels as possible. Digital compression technology was less than two years away, and would not cause undue delays for any pay TV licence holder, Nowland argued. Any auction process for the licence or licences was several months away at least. After this, it would take another 12 to 18 months to establish the business. More pressing for Optus was the fact that it was planning to launch its second B series satellite, after a number of delays, in December. It had to know precisely the terms and conditions of any pay TV licence so it could configure its satellite accordingly.

The problem was Keating didn't want 24 channels to be available. He wasn't sure now that Optus was insisting on digital what the optimum number of channels would be, but it was certainly less than that. He wanted sufficient channels for Kerry Packer and Rupert Murdoch plus a new entrant, perhaps one of the international groups such as the US cable groups Comcast, Continental Cablevision or Time Warner – which had all let it be known they were potential players – and maybe one for the ABC, to satisfy the pressure from the Caucus.

To have too many operators in a business where the start-up costs would run to about $400 million, plus the cost of the licence, would invite commercial ruin. This was the very strong view being put to Keating and his chief minder, Don Russell, by Peter Barron, Kerry Packer's main Canberra lobbyist. There was no way Packer would be a player in pay TV unless it was as part of a dominant consortium to ensure potential losses were minimised.

Although Keating had no time for the Senate committee's report, he seized on the knowledge that digital technology was Optus's preference, and the new options this offered, to tighten his control of the policy debate in his party. He and his senior private secretary, Russell – a tall, shaven-headed man – worked relentlessly to devise a pay TV structure that would satisfy the media barons on one hand and win acceptance by the Labor Caucus, and perhaps the Democrats in the Senate, on the other.

In the week beginning October 5, Richardson's 4+1+1 model was still on the table, although it was now clearly subject to change as a result of the digital development. Russell spent hours that week negotiating with Bob Collins' department and with Collins' senior adviser, Jack Lake, over possible combinations of licence packages: whether the Government should enforce digital or leave it to the industry; deciding whether or not the networks should be allowed in; what conditions would apply to other delivery systems such as MDS. Keating took at least one phone call from Kerry Packer during this week. Packer urged Keating in this call to legislate for digital and discard analogue, which had had its day, Packer said.

The networks' lobby group, FACTS, chose this highly sensitive time to hold a conference in Canberra on the future of the industry. Nine Network director Bruce Gyngell backed his boss's more direct lobbying efforts by urging the Government to delay pay TV's introduction. 'The introduction of pay TV, far from improving existing channels and choice, will undermine and erode the achievements of the past and weaken the production base,' he told his colleagues and industry observers.[5] 'It will stifle Australian production through lack of money. It will be the start of a decline in standards,' said Gyngell, the first person to appear on television in Australia when he opened Nine's service in 1956 with the words, 'Welcome to television.'

Three days before Caucus was due to be briefed ahead of a full Cabinet discussion the next day, Gyngell publicly urged the Government to delay its decision on pay TV until the new Australian Broadcasting Authority – which had been established with the June passage of most of the *Broadcasting Services Act* – had investigated the use of digital compression technology. He accused supporters of pay TV of being motivated by revenge.

On Monday evening, October 12, Keating ignored Gyngell and unveiled his pay TV proposal to the scheduled Caucus meeting. Keating wanted to enforce a digital signal, which would enable compression techniques to deliver more than six channels. He also insisted that Australia move directly to the next technology and not become committed to analogue, which he regarded as already out of date. He often used the example of the Labor Government's decision in the early 1970s to wait until the PAL-D technology for colour television was commercially available, and asserted that the wait of a year or two was worth it. Digital also provided Keating with the additional channels to give him an ideal licence structure. The Government would auction two licences of four channels each, and give one news and current affairs channel to the ABC. One of the four-channel licences would be for new entrants into the industry, and the second would be for established players. Keating was keen to ensure that the established media players – and he had in mind Kerry Packer in particular – would have some competition, and set the structure to ensure that the second four-channel licence was put out of his reach. He had stamped his foot firmly once again on broadcasting policy. The proposal was entirely his, and Don Russell's.

This package, Keating believed, met most of the demands of his party and the Democrats, on whose votes he would rely in the Senate, particularly in relation to the ABC, which Keating didn't want in pay TV at all. Most of his party members were happy that the ABC was included and Keating also acknowledged he was unlikely to get any legislation through the Senate unless the ABC had a role. But ABC managing director David Hill was still not happy. He wanted at least two channels and accused Keating of trying to 'ghetto-ise' the public broadcaster. 'We don't want the booby prize of being asked to provide only a new channel which is the high-cost, low-revenue channel,' he complained after learning of Keating's latest prescription for the industry.[6]

Even potential pay TV participants thought the Keating model a good one. According to Bruce Wolpe, a lobbyist over the preceding weeks for US cable company Comcast, the Keating plan was 'probably the one that will break the political deadlock'.[7]

Optus's chief operating officer, Ian Boatman, also applauded Keating for insisting on digital. It meant that Australia was 'adopting an evolving technology rather than a dying one'. He conceded, though, that the adoption of digital would delay pay TV for up to a year. The technology was untested commercially. There was no international standard in place. Australia would be the first country to use it.

The commercial stations thought this was an excellent idea, too. Seven chief and FACTS chairman Bob Campbell told Errol Simper of *The Australian* at the time, 'It makes good sense to wait and go with digital.'

Although Keating's decision to opt for digital appeared at first blush to be a forward-thinking policy move, it greatly assisted the commercial networks, whose interests were served by delay. This would give the networks breathing space to organise themselves, lock up programming, and strengthen their dominant position.

Another unforeseen consequence was that it would open a window of opportunity for rival technologies, MDS in particular. Steve Cosser was already using it to narrowcast his Newsvision service to clients. This delay would force a re-think, too, on cable, which the Government and the industry had written off as a most unlikely option until this point. It was too expensive and would take too long to roll out through the suburbs. Now that satellite pay TV delivery was being pushed back into 1994 and perhaps even 1995, MDS looked very attractive, but even cable suddenly looked a possibility.

The intense backroom arm-twisting in Canberra over pay TV over these weeks coincided with the season of corporate annual general meetings in Australia. Rupert Murdoch, in Australia for the News Corporation annual meeting in Adelaide on October 13, the day after Paul Keating outlined the latest pay TV model, told an impromptu press conference after the meeting that News had no plans 'at this stage' to enter pay TV in Australia. 'We haven't got interested in it yet,' Murdoch said. 'I mean it depends on how it turns out.'[8]

A fortnight later, Kerry Packer echoed the contradictions of the attitude of the networks towards pay TV. He told shareholders at Nine Network Ltd, of which he owned 43.5 per cent, that he opposed the introduction of pay TV, but it was inevitable and therefore he wanted to be part of it. 'Government, the Opposition, the Democrats, the media are all clamouring for pay TV,' he said. 'The only people I know of who aren't clamouring for it are the public.'[9] Yet Packer's group would be 'part of a consortium that's in there. We see that as part of the future of the television industry and we have to be there.'

By late October 1992, Ten's receivers were preparing to sell the three-station network to a consortium led by the Canadian broadcaster CanWest Global Communications. CanWest and its eccentric lawyer/proprietor, Israel 'Izzy' Asper, had been casting around the Australian media scene since the start of the year looking for recovery situations. Ten fitted its requirements perfectly.

CanWest was the largest private television operator in Canada, with five television stations and a number of rebroadcasting stations. It also owned 20 per cent of New Zealand's non-government TV3 network.[10] It was an experienced operator with the money to buy Ten. Unfortunately for CanWest, the 15 per cent limit on foreign ownership meant it could not simply buy the network outright. Australian investors would need to own the other 85 per cent. CanWest, not surprisingly, was not prepared to come in as a core shareholder when it could not exercise control, or at least some measure of influence, and 15 per cent was not enough.

A similar situation confronted another Canadian, Conrad Black, 12 months earlier when his Tourang consortium – comprised of his UK-based The Telegraph Plc and US investment house Hellman and Friedman – was attempting to buy John Fairfax. Tourang's lawyers, Geoff Levy and Stephen Chipkin of the firm Freehill Hollingdale and Page, devised a structure which appeared to satisfy Australia's foreign ownership rules. The share ownership was divided into two separate lines of stock. One line was ordinary shares and the other was non-voting debenture stock, which had a so-called economic interest, that is, an entitlement to dividends only. Levy and Chipkin's idea was refined by David Gonski, a former Freehills partner whose boutique advisory firm Wentworth Associates had its offices on one of the floors occupied by Freehills in Sydney's MLC building.

Tourang was forced to come up with this structure very quickly in early December 1991, after its bid for Fairfax was rejected initially by Labor Treasurer John Kerin on foreign investment grounds. It cobbled together the Freehills-Gonski model which gave Black's Telegraph Plc 15 per cent of voting shares in Tourang, and Hellman and Friedman part of the mirror issue of non-voting debentures.

Tourang was fortunate in its timing. The Hawke Labor Government was in the throes of leadership turmoil. Bob Hawke could see Paul Keating starting to move in on him again and, in a bid to head off any potential embarrassment, sacked Kerin the day after he rejected Tourang's application for foreign investment approval to proceed with its bid. Kerin at a press conference was unable to understand an acronym contained in a Treasury briefing for an economic announcement. The Treasurer had to ask one of the journalists present what GOS was. It was gross operating surplus. When Tourang re-submitted its application a few days later to new Treasurer, Ralph Willis, he approved it, just days before bids closed with the adviser to the Fairfax banks, Mark Burrows, later that month.

Nearly 12 months on, Westpac and its partners in the Ten banking syndicate had tried hard to interest potential Australian investors in joining CanWest to buy the network, with little success. The bank's advisers, Malcolm Turnbull and Cass O'Connor, knocked on a lot of doors attempting to excite interest in a cheap network with plenty of potential 'upside', as they say in the merchant banking business. They got mostly brush-offs.

Two of Kerry Packer's friends agreed to invest: property developer Robert Whyte and advertising figure John Singleton. Hungry Jacks hamburger franchise founder, Jack Cowin, was another investor. He was a fellow Canadian living in Australia who recognised a bargain and remembered CanWest's ability to carve out a niche market in Canada. They were joined by Melbourne businessman Isi Leibler and Telecasters North Queensland (TNQ), which took the Ten signal and had an interest in stable ownership of the parent network after two years of uncertainty. TNQ was controlled by an investment company called Suspirium, owned by two former South Africans, Brian Sherman and Laurence Freedman, who were better known for their interest in the funds management group, Equitilink. The group put together to support CanWest were essentially 'bottom feeders' who had come in at a very low price with little risk of losing money.

Although there was widespread suspicion in the industry that Kerry Packer was behind the consortium, the anecdotal evidence at least suggests this was not the case, despite his association with Whyte and Singleton. At one meeting with Turnbull and O'Connor, Asper asked them who Kerry Packer was. Packer had left a number of messages for the Canadian at his hotel asking him to call, but Asper declined. Packer may not have had any influence over the network personally, but he had people sympathetic to him as shareholders.

Westpac had already written off $100 million of its $255 million exposure to Northern Star after it went into receivership in September the previous year. Fifteen months later, Westpac finally accepted an offer of $245 million from the CanWest consortium. Of this amount, CanWest and the other investors paid a total of just $90 million cash, with Westpac leaving in the $155 million in its written down loans to the network.

The CanWest group had bought a three-station network for almost $600 million less than Frank Lowy had paid Rupert Murdoch for just two stations five-and-a-half years earlier. This would turn out to be the bargain of the decade for CanWest and its initially reluctant backers. It would float five years later for nearly $2 billion.

Although CanWest was supposedly not in control of Ten, it was able to exert very significant influence through its ability to appoint the network's chief executive, and through the ownership structure. It was an even more aggressive version of the Freehills-Gonski model put together for Tourang and Fairfax. Geoff Levy was helped by another Freehills partner, now a Supreme Court judge, Kim Santow, to build the CanWest structure. Although the Fairfax shareholding arrangement was designed to give Conrad Black control while holding under 15 per cent, it was also designed to spread the economic benefits to its foundation shareholders before a public float several months later. The CanWest device was designed not only to give CanWest control of the network, but virtually all of the benefits through its ownership of the debentures which paid high dividends.

CanWest held just 6.8 million, or 14.9 per cent, of Ten's 45.5 million ordinary voting shares, but the Canadians owned all of the 45.5 million non-voting debentures. This arrangement of voting and non-voting, but high yield, shares gave CanWest a 57.5 per cent interest in the network's profits and dividends. In any other industry a shareholding of this magnitude, whether it be voting or economic, would constitute clear control, but the fledgling Australian Broadcasting Authority later cleared CanWest of allegations that it controlled Ten, much to the amazement of the industry.

Soon after they took control, Asper and CanWest sacked managing director Gary Rice and replaced him with a former CanWest executive, Peter Viner. CanWest and Izzy Asper pulled the wool over the eyes of the ABA. From then on, the regulator was seen as an easy touch.

When Rupert Murdoch found out that Westpac had sold the network to the CanWest syndicate he was livid, but even more upset by the low price. News had been slow to move in this situation and when it became clear the network was close to a sale, Murdoch asked Ken Cowley to try to get the bidding process reopened so that News could make an offer. It would try to use a structure similar to the Geoff Levy model which allowed Conrad Black to control Fairfax with a shareholding of just 15 per cent. But Cowley was rebuffed by the bank's Iain Thompson. 'A deal has already been done,' Thompson told Cowley.

News would find it difficult to get around the combination of the cross media ownership rules and the 15 per cent foreign ownership limit, but the Government's acceptance of the Fairfax and CanWest structures convinced Murdoch that he could perhaps use a similar contrivance to buy back into Australian television. Although News

Corp was an Australian company, it was treated as foreign because its controlling 32 per cent shareholder, Murdoch, had taken US citizenship in 1985 so he could establish the fourth television network there.

Despite the setback of failing to re-acquire his old network, Murdoch was determined to get back into television in Australia. If CanWest could pull off such a huge and apparently easy victory over a gullible regulator, then so could he. His News Corporation would 'do a CanWest'. After all, there was another network still in receivership.

Three days after Westpac and CanWest jointly announced the sale of Ten on October 16, Murdoch was due to give a speech at the Asia Pacific Business and Investment Congress at the Park Grand Hotel (now the Sheraton on the Park) in Sydney. Having by now put behind him his near-miss with corporate death in late 1990 and early 1991 – when a handful of minor lenders refused to refinance a tiny proportion of the group's huge debt – Murdoch was preparing News for a period of rapid expansion in the US and the Asia Pacific region.

This visit to Australia was a crucial one for him, both commercially and in terms of his relations with Canberra and the new Prime Minister, Paul Keating. With his company's finances steady, Murdoch could afford to focus on where it was going and the commercial and political environment in which it was operating. He was also becoming more reflective about larger issues such as technology, communications, the environment, and the evolution of economies. In his speech at the Park Grand he called on Australia to develop 'knowledge industries' such as education and computer software, and to move on from its reliance on resources. Murdoch told his audience of investment bankers, legal and accounting professionals and diplomats: 'The prosperity of this region is not a question of tapping great new reserves of natural resources. What counts in this region is skills. Prosperity in this hemisphere is going to be a great arch of skills, vaulting Australia to the emerging economies of the north.' Australia should be the nexus between the English-speaking world and East Asia. It had the potential to become 'a great cultural and commercial entrepot'. They were stirring and visionary words.

At the back of the audience sat Mark Burrows, principal of the small merchant bank Baring Brothers Burrows. A tall man with a shock of reddish-brown hair brushed back from his forehead, Burrows had been one of Sydney's most successful merchant bankers through the 1980s, taking pivotal roles in a number of the major takeovers and defences of the decade. Like a number of high-fliers of the time, he frequently wore colourful braces over striped shirts, which gave him a reputation for flashy dressing that took him a good part of the more conservative 1990s to allay. If anyone could be categorised as an Australian version of one of Tom Wolfe's 'masters of the universe', it was Burrows. His reputation not just as a facilitator but a deal-maker was sealed when he advised the bankers to Fairfax during the receivership and sale of the print media group during 1991.

When he was retained for the Fairfax job in December 1990, he and the banks were given little chance of getting anything over $900 million for the publishing group. The banks were owed $1.2 billion. Burrows and his small team of professionals, including Peter Breese and Clay O'Brien, managed to build up an auction process among the three main contenders for the newspaper group. These were: Tourang, formed by Black and Kerry Packer, before the Australian billionaire was forced to make a last-minute withdrawal to head off a lengthy inquiry into his media interests; Irishman Tony O'Reilly's Independent Newspapers Group; and the Melbourne-based Australian Independent Newspapers consortium, backed by the country's largest superannuation funds. When the 'auction' was brought to a head in December 1991, after the fortunes of the bidders had waxed and waned, Burrows was able to squeeze a top bid of $1.45 billion for the Fairfax assets from Tourang. His ability to secure a price well in excess of expectations, sufficient to comfortably repay all of the bank debt, earned him a fee of $16 million. This was considered huge for an Australian success fee at the time.

The morning of Murdoch's speech, Burrows received a phone call from Ken Cowley. 'Rupert's giving a speech at the Asia Pacific conference. Could you come along, because we've something we'd like to talk to you about afterwards,' Cowley said. After Murdoch finished his speech he gathered Cowley and Burrows and they jumped in a waiting News car, a white Holden Statesman, for the short drive down Elizabeth Street to News's offices in the run-down garment district of Surry Hills. The three men walked into Cowley's office on the fourth floor of the building. Murdoch opened the discussion. 'Right, how do we get Seven?'

In the weeks following Keating's October 12 briefing to Caucus in which he fleshed out the pay TV policy he had outlined on the

*Sunday* program on May 31, lobbying of Keating, his Communications Minister Bob Collins, Labor faction leaders Schacht and Langmore and the Democrats became intense. The ABC's David Hill was particularly active, urging the Government to give him two channels and the money to set them up. He wanted $15 million in addition to the $500 million a year the ABC received to fund its traditional television and radio services. Keating and his adviser, Don Russell, were deeply sceptical about Hill's ability to provide the service, given the financial constraints on the ABC. They believed pay TV would divert money and resources from its role as a free-to-air national broadcaster and were aware of the growing opposition among Hill's own staff to any pay TV role for the same reason. Seven Network's Bob Campbell was also accumulating frequent flier points on the 40-minute flight to Canberra to lobby for the networks. Peter Barron was on the phone daily to Russell. The networks wanted to ensure that if other players, including foreigners, wanted to play this game then they had to be included as well. The Keating model would leave the door open to the networks to play if they wanted.

On the morning of Monday, November 2, 1992 Keating called Bob Collins and faction leaders Schacht and Langmore to his office to settle the fine points of the pay TV policy that would go to Cabinet for its rubber stamp later that day. They agreed on the plan floated by Keating that the Government would auction two licences of four channels each, one reserved for new players and the other for all comers, which could include established media proprietors. Anyone who wanted to get into the game could do so, providing they were prepared to pay enough at the auction of the licences. This left only the ABC to be dealt with.

Schacht and Langmore insisted that the ABC should be given at least two channels and the money to be able to start the services. Langmore told Keating that if pay TV was to become an important medium later in the decade, then it was essential that the ABC was part of it. Otherwise it might become marginalised in the industry. Schacht wanted the ABC to be a force in pay TV to guarantee some diversity and ensure subscription broadcasting wouldn't be dominated by the commercial networks. The discussion between Keating, Schacht and Langmore was robust without being antagonistic. Keating needed a structure that he could get quickly through Cabinet and the Parliament. Labor's parliamentary party wanted to clear the decks for the election expected to be called early in the new year.

After an hour of discussion, Keating turned to Don Russell and told him to take down the main points of what had been agreed. They still hadn't settled on what to do with the ABC, but Keating realised he would have to give the government broadcaster something or face a protracted debate in the party room and with the Democrats in the Senate. 'OK, two channels for the ABC,' he said to Russell, who was writing down the points of the package. Although Hill had asked for $15 million, Keating said to his minder, 'Let's give Hill twelve-and-a-half million. Now he'll be able to walk up Sunset Boulevard and tell everyone what a great TV mogul he is.'

That afternoon, Cabinet sealed the Keating plan. With the Government still reeling from figures the previous week showing the unemployment rate at 11.3 per cent, ministers wanted some guarantees that this new industry would create jobs. Cabinet decided that pay TV should carry at least 10 per cent local content. When Collins announced the policy that evening, he said the new industry was capable of generating 4,000 new positions. The Government's legislation would demand digital transmission and Australia would be the first country to use it.

This may have sounded attractive to the waiting media and the public, but the undeniable fact was that no-one anywhere in the world had ever broadcast using a digital signal before. There was no standard, and therefore no equipment to transmit and receive the signal. It would be two to three years at least before the lucky buyers of the licences would be able to actually broadcast their digital pay TV service.

Collins tabled the legislation in the Senate on November 4. With most of the political players at least having agreed to the main points of Part 7, there would be little difficulty getting this section of the Bill through both Houses. The buyers of the satellite licences would be protected until July 1, 1997, the same date that the telecommunications industry was due to be deregulated. Pay TV operators also could not show advertisements until this date – a big victory for the commercial networks. Foreign ownership of licences would be limited to 35 per cent, with individual foreigners restricted to 20 per cent.

At one point in the frantic last-minute jockeying to refine and adjust elements of Part 7, Don Russell called the parliamentary draftsman and suggested he insert a clause which would read, in effect, that an owner of a large circulation newspaper could hold a satellite licence, regardless of nationality. A visitor to Russell's office who was privy to the conversation heard the draftsman's voice coming through the earpiece of the phone. 'Come off it!' the rightly sceptical draftsman spluttered down the line.

One small amendment that backbench Senator Graham Richardson managed to insert just before it went before Cabinet stated that consumer subscribers to non-satellite services need give only 30 days notice to terminate their connection. This meant that only satellite, in effect, could sign up subscribers on longer term contracts, say of 12 months. At a party function in Parliament House later that month, as the legislation was in the process of being passed, Richardson mentioned the amendment he had managed to insert in the legislation to a senior public servant. 'That'll fuck MDS,' Richardson bragged.


On the evening of November 11, while the legislation was still in the Senate, Collins received a visitor, Steve Cosser, who had flown to Canberra to give the Minister a briefing about his plans for a pay TV service. Despite the susceptibility of people like Richardson and even Keating to the lobbying of vested interests like the networks, Collins was quite keen to encourage more than one delivery system in this business and achieve some diversity. He agreed to meet Cosser at the suggestion of his department's senior policy adviser, Chris North.

When North took Cosser into Collins' office, it was late evening and Collins had had a long day in the Senate. He was also in pain from one of his frequent bouts of gout and had just received an injection in the buttocks from a nurse. His office was littered with pieces of Aboriginal artwork and cartoons and photographs of Collins, along with several piles of video cassettes and laser discs. Collins was a member of a group of laser disc buffs in Darwin who had built up a library of imported discs. He told Cosser he was one of the few owners of these machines in the Northern Territory.

Cosser turned on his salesman's charm and spoke with some knowledge about Collins' huge Northern Territory electorate and about Collins himself, before moving on to the subject of pay TV. Once the *Broadcasting Services Act* was passed, making subscription television services to the home legal, his company Broadcom planned to use MDS to broadcast its Newsvision channel. It had just acquired the Italian language channel Teleitalia from the Alessi family. 'We're keen to set up a full pay TV service and we'll want to sign up movies and sports programming as soon as we can,'

Cosser explained to Collins. First, Broadcom would need more licences. It had six in both Melbourne and Sydney, plus the channel it was using to narrowcast the Newsvision service in Sydney. Collins sat and listened while Cosser poured out his plans. The Minister was very conscious that he was talking to a salesman with a rather contrived radio voice. Collins, the rough diamond and straight talker, thought that perhaps Cosser was a little too smooth for his liking.

Collins wished Cosser luck, and warned him that satellite looked to be the superior technology because it had far greater reach. Cosser said he believed MDS would still allow Broadcom to cover most of Australia's metropolitan centres. Collins' final words were, 'It's good to see people like you wanting to get into the industry.'


In a portent of the fierce competition to come, on Friday, November 20, Bob Mansfield called a press conference in the NSW country town of Queanbeyan, on the outskirts of Canberra. He wanted to release details of phone services available on Optus's new fibre optic cable network, which the company had only begun laying in March that year by ploughing a trench in a field at nearby Goulburn. Already, Optus was able to offer long-distance phone connections between Sydney, Melbourne and Canberra.

Three days later, Bob Collins and Telecom's new managing director Frank Blount announced that the government carrier would connect 200 homes in the Wollongong area south of Sydney to a fibre optic cable in a trial of services including pay TV, home shopping and programs supplied by the University of Wollongong. Blount said Telecom would launch a similar trial in the Sydney eastern suburb of Centennial Park sometime in 1993. Blount told Collins, 'Bob this is a trial, just small beginnings.' From small seeds mighty trees grow. Blount and Telecom had just planted the seed.


When the Senate passed Part 7 of the *Broadcasting Services Act* to finally legalise pay television on November 27, 1992, the day's newspapers, radio and television were dominated by Kerry Packer's raid on Westpac Banking Corporation. He had picked up 9.7 per cent of the bank's shares in a buying spree which caught the bank in the middle of its greatest financial crisis in its 175-year history. In May, Westpac had announced a record $1.66 billion loss for the half year to March 31 and a $1.2 billion rights issue priced at $3 a share to its shareholders, to replenish its reduced capital. Most of the losses were due to failed property loans, but included $150 million the bank had written off on its exposure to Northern Star, the Frank Lowy company which gained control of Ten in 1987.

The rights issue closed on September 23, with a shortfall of $883 million. The issue was shunned by the bank's shareholders, who declined to take up 74 per cent of the shares on offer. While the issue was running, the share price plunged from around $3.60 to below the critical $3 level. If investors could buy the shares in the market at less than $3, there was no incentive for them to take up their rights to the issue. This guaranteed a shortfall, but nothing like the amount that eventuated. The underwriter, the Swiss-US investment bank Credit Suisse First Boston, was left with 295 million Westpac shares on its books, for which it needed to find buyers.

Westpac's stock price fell even further after chairman Sir Eric Neal and four other directors resigned on October 1. Then, a month later, Westpac was forced to announce an unexpected additional tax liability in the US of $113 million. The stock hit $2.40 in the wake of this latest disclosure, back to levels at which it was trading in 1985. As one blow followed another, the bank announced its annual results, a loss of $1.56 billion, on November 17.

On Sunday, November 22, Kerry Packer was in Argentina for the polo season. Albert J. Dunlap, the American who Packer hired in 1991 to run the Packer family's private company, Consolidated Press Holdings, was in Argentina with his boss and advised him that now was the time to strike. Packer telephoned his favourite stockbroker, Neville Miles, a partner at stockbroking firm Ord Minnett, to instruct him to start buying Westpac shares in the market.[11] Despite the fact that Packer woke Miles in the middle of the night, the stockbroker was happy to take the call. The next day, Ord Minnett started buying both shares and options over shares. The raid would last four days. On Thursday, two days after Consolidated Press Holdings had passed through the 5 per cent threshold when he would be forced by law to reveal his hand, Packer had put his foot on nearly 10 per cent of the bank. A year earlier, Westpac was Australia's biggest and most powerful financial institution. It was now at the mercy of a raider like Packer. Ironically, Ord Minnett was owned by Westpac. Miles saw no conflict. The buying was good for the share price, so it was good for the bank, Miles reasoned.

Packer had picked the bottom precisely. His buying, combined with the rumours that swirled through the market while he was on his share-buying spree, brought other buyers in as well. Australia's richest man would be assured of a substantial profit which would make him far richer still.

Bob Collins rose early on Sunday December 6 for the drive to Parliament House. He was due to pre-record that evening's *Meet the Press* program at the Ten Network's studio in Parliament House with press gallery veteran Barrie Cassidy. With the final part of the *Broadcasting Services Act* having just passed through both Houses, Cassidy wanted to talk to the Minister about pay TV. By now, Collins felt he was on top of the issue, certainly confident enough to give an 'as live' interview with a searching journalist.

Australians would take to pay TV like 'a duck to water', Collins enthused on the program. While the legislation focused mainly on satellite, the law also allowed microwave technology, and embraced new technology, he told the program's viewers. MDS, in fact, would be the first form of pay TV in Australia, he said. Cosser had lobbied well, but Collins was very much aware that very powerful forces in the media were lining up behind satellite. Collins preferred satellite, too, because he was anxious, as a Northern Territory politician, for the bush to have the same access to high-quality programming as the cities. Collins' view was that MDS would work well in remote areas like his own electorate and Tasmania to re-transmit to small numbers of homes signals brought down by a satellite dish at a base station. This would save these remote households the expense of having to buy large satellite dishes. The MDS receiver dish was about the size of a dinner plate, about one-third the cost of a satellite dish. In Collins' view, MDS would be used by the satellite licence holder as a subsidiary technology, rather than the primary delivery system.

It would take longer for satellite pay TV to be offered, Collins said, but for those who took up MDS 'there can be a very easy transition by the consumer to better technology when it's available'. The legislation would give customers of MDS a chance to opt out of leases once other pay TV services became available. He was referring to the Graham Richardson clause that would 'fuck' MDS.

Despite Collins' belief that MDS was only a transitional phase or a complementary technology to more long-term systems such as satellite, Cosser gave him the unambiguous message at their

November 11 meeting that Broadcom wanted as much good programming as it could get and that it would be a long-term player.
Collins had filtered Cosser's salesmanship through the advice of his
department that Broadcom was setting up his pay TV service with
the primary objective of flicking it on to one of the mainstream
players like Murdoch or Packer. Unfortunately, Collins gave out
conflicting signals in his *Meet the Press* interview. He may have
believed in his own mind that MDS was a subsidiary technology,
but by announcing that his department would call for tenders for
the 200 unallocated MDS licences over the coming days and that
he would announce details of the auctions for the satellite licences
in January, he sent entirely the opposite message to the budding
industry.

Collins unwittingly set these two arms of policy on a collision
course and MDS was being given a head start. Three days after the
interview, the department placed its advertisements in the national
dailies and main regional newspapers. It would invite sealed envelope tenders for the MDS licences, with bids closing on January 29,
1993.

Kerry Packer was more than a little concerned at this
announcement by Collins. Until this time, the policy debate had
been dominated by satellite. Although he had heard of MDS, he
wasn't sure of its potential as a pay TV system. He called Nine's
chief engineer, Bruce Robertson, to ask him about MDS. Robertson told his boss it was limited by the fact that it relied on
line-of-sight, but in most situations worked well. The authority on
MDS was a Los Angeles-based American, Robert Schmidt, he said.
'Well, you'd better get on a plane and go and see him,' Packer told
Robertson.

If potential satellite operators were also confused by Collins'
approach, their minds were suddenly cleared on the issue a fortnight later. The Long March rocket carrying Optus's B2 satellite,
which had been configured by Wayne Nowland especially for pay
television with its seven high-performance transponders, exploded
seconds after its launch on December 20 from Xichang. Just days
before Christmas 1992, the balance of this emerging industry
shifted heavily in favour of MDS, despite its obvious limitations.
Steve Cosser could not believe his luck. He had won the lottery.

# 5

# Betrayal

Gary Weiss was lounging in his 14th floor office at the new No 2 Market Street tower in Sydney in mid-December 1992 when he received a phone call from a stockbroker, Peter Gray. 'Hello Peter, what can I do for you?' Weiss asked as he swung around on his chair to take in the magnificent view over Sydney's Darling Harbour and across the city's inner west to the Blue Mountains. Gray was working with Mark Burrows' brother Peter Burrows at his prosperous retail broking house, Burrows Ltd. Weiss knew Gray from the 1980s when he worked for the high-flying stockbroking firm Potts West Trumbull. PWT had been extraordinarily successful during this frenetic decade because of its ability to buy large lines of stock for entrepreneurial companies such as Industrial Equity Ltd, where Weiss was a strategist in the late 1980s. IEL had been one of the most aggressive stockmarket raiders of the 1980s, and had been a major client of PWT.

'Gary, I'm calling on behalf of Steve Cosser and Richard Wiesener,' Gray said. 'Steve and Richard, as you know, have put together about 13 MDS licences which will give them the basis of a good pay TV business. The Government is auctioning more licences next month, so they'll have enough to allow them to provide a full six-channel service in the capitals. They believe this is the sort of asset that Kerry Packer might like to buy. Gary, can you broker a deal with Packer?'

Weiss didn't know Kerry Packer well at all, but his boss did. Sir Ron Brierley had crossed the Tasman in the early 1970s and started

IEL to buy shares in under-performing companies and either take them over or act as a catalyst for another raider to make the acquisition. The target, typically, would then be broken up and its assets sold off for a profit.

In 1974, as Brierley and IEL were finding their feet in the larger Australian market, the New Zealander got to know Kerry Packer through their mutual love of cricket. Packer was preparing to shake up the establishment with his professional World Series Cricket circus. Both men were also instinctive opportunists in the market. When the troubled UK raider Slater Walker was pulling out of Australia and selling its share portfolio, Packer and Brierley sensed a chance to make some money. Packer lent Brierley $12 million to buy Slater Walker's Australian investment portfolio. The company's chief executive in Australia, a Scotsman named Iain Gray (no relation to Peter Gray), was under instructions from his embattled UK head office to liquidate the UK company's assets as quickly as possible.

Brierley was able to on-sell the shares to other investors for a profit of about $1 million. This was considered a lot of money then. He and Packer split the proceeds and remained friends and occasional business associates afterwards.

Weiss, a lawyer also from New Zealand with a doctorate in Science of Law from Cornell University had joined Brierley at IEL in 1984. He was an unusual looking person, of medium height and with a shock of frizzy hair which betrayed his mis-spent youth in the 1970s as a bit of a hippy. At IEL, his job was to identify suitable corporate targets which might offer profitable opportunities. By this time IEL had become a significant corporate raider. It became even more aggressive in the market when Brierley appointed an up-and-coming executive in the organisation, Rodney Price, as the new chief executive in 1986. Price, from Adelaide, had been running the milk and dairy foods processor Southern Farmers, which IEL had bought a year earlier.

As the stockmarket boom continued IEL took control of struggling retailer Woolworths, and made profitable forays into John Fairfax and Sons and Herald and Weekly Times after Labor's changes to media ownership rules triggered the round of takeovers in the industry through 1987. Weiss picked Bell Resources as a potential 'greenmail' opportunity in early 1988 when Robert Holmes a Court attempted to merge the company with the Holmes a Court group parent company, Bell Group. IEL teamed up with Kerry Packer to announce a joint 'bid' for Bell Resources which was then 38 per cent owned by Bell Group. Although they had no chance of succeeding, IEL and Packer focused the market's mind on the true value of Bell Resources, forcing Holmes a Court to call off the takeover. Bell Resources had become a $1.5 billion cashbox after the Perth entrepreneur had sold off most of its investments, including 30 per cent of BHP, in the wake of the 1987 stockmarket crash.

IEL had lived off the rising stockmarket through the 1980s, but fell victim to the post-crash shakeout of entrepreneurial companies. It was taken over in 1989 by an even larger predator, the Adelaide Steamship Group of John Spalvins.

Weiss then joined Malcolm Turnbull at Turnbull and Partners, but left after his 12-month contract expired. The two fell out in 1993 over the allocation of profits from a deal associated with CanWest's purchase of the Ten Network. He rejoined Ron Brierley, who by this time had acquired a small UK-listed company called GPG Plc, which had been shaken loose by the spectacular collapse in 1988 of New Zealand's Equiticorp group. GPG would become Ron Brierley's main investment vehicle through the 1990s.

Weiss told Peter Gray, 'I'm not sure if I can help you take this deal to Kerry Packer, but Ron might be able to.' He added that if the proposal was good enough, then he and Brierley might like to take an interest through GPG. Weiss said that he was just about to take his family to Amsterdam to spend Christmas there. Gray said he would ask Steve Cosser to fly over from Paris to meet Weiss while he was in The Netherlands to talk about his plans for an MDS pay TV service.

Steve Cosser tracked Gary Weiss down in a hotel in the cosmopolitan Dutch city. It was a day or two before Christmas. Cosser suggested the pair get together for lunch. The two men had only met briefly about six months earlier, at Peter Gray's wedding. Over lunch in a small cafe near Weiss's hotel, Cosser talked enthusiastically about the future of MDS and its advantages over other pay TV technologies; its simplicity, its potential coverage of about 60 per cent of the population, and its relative cheapness. A service covering the main metropolitan markets could be set up for around $200 million. A satellite service would cost $400 million to $500 million, and cable billions. All Australis needed, Cosser told Weiss, was some backing and the right sport and movie programming. Cosser said he had already had approaches from Irish media proprietor Tony O'Reilly and the Los Angeles Times group, with offers to finance Broadcom's bids at the January 29 auction. If he could get the business started before anyone else, it would give Broadcom a substantial head start in putting together a subscriber base. This would make it a very attractive business for investors.

Broadcom, Cosser said, was pursuing two, parallel strategies: to try to sell the business to a single buyer; or to float it, with the foundation shareholders keeping a residual interest. Whatever happened, Broadcom would need to raise some money in the next month or so to help it recover the $8 million Cosser had spent so far in getting the business started. Financially things were getting very tight for Cosser, who had been forced to borrow money against his house in Vaucluse to keep Broadcom going in the meantime. His bank, Westpac, was happy to lend against the house because Cosser, after having left to live in France, leased it at an attractive rate to Banque National de Paris for their managing director.

Weiss was impressed with Cosser's infectious salesmanship. He said GPG would be interested in putting in some seed money with a view to making some money on a float or a sale to a buyer like Kerry Packer. Cosser gave Weiss a verbal commitment to issue GPG some shares in his soon-to-be floated company at a discount, say 25c, compared with the 50c share price at which he was contemplating floating the company. In the meantime, Weiss said, he would urge Ron Brierley to talk to Packer.

After Cosser's experience at Ten, he knew privately that he would not be able to take on Packer or Murdoch for long. They would use their muscle to wear him down or take the business away from him. It was in his best interests to get the business in a strong position strategically to make it valuable to one of these men, and then sell it to the highest bidder, or float it and sell his shares for a profit.

Cosser didn't mention to Weiss that he was also talking to Rupert Murdoch's News Corporation. His discussions with Malcolm Colless were coming along well, and News was showing interest in investing in the business. Cosser was hoping to meet Rupert Murdoch himself in Los Angeles in a few weeks. If he could get some interest from Packer, he might be able to play off the two camps and extract a very good price indeed.

As Cosser shook hands and left Weiss to take a taxi to the airport for the flight back to Paris, he was feeling very pleased with himself. Everything was going so well. All he needed was to get sufficient MDS licences at the auction the next month and he would be able to enter serious negotiations with the Hollywood studios to secure the movie programming which would place Broadcom in a strong position strategically. Prospects were looking extremely bright.

On Monday evening, January 4, Steve Cosser and Richard Wiesener were having dinner at the Four Seasons Hotel in Hollywood after a day of talks with sales executives of some of the Hollywood studios. They had seen, or were due to see Columbia Tri-Star, Paramount, Universal, MGM, Disney, and, of course, Murdoch's Fox. Cosser had been talking to Chase Carey at Fox by phone over previous weeks and now in person as part of the broader talks with News. Wiesener was the most active of Broadcom's shareholders and had put money into Cosser's purchase of the MDS licences. He stayed away from the day-to-day running of Broadcom, but remained close to Cosser as a financial adviser.

With the MDS auctions less than four weeks away, Cosser and Wiesener were anxious to get a dialogue going with the studios so they would be in a position to move quickly and sign movie supply contracts once Broadcom could confirm to them that its delivery system was fully in place. Until Broadcom had the six licences in each city to be able to provide its six-channel service, neither the studios nor any other program supplier would talk to them seriously.

While the two men were having dinner a waiter approached them. 'Mr Cosser?' he asked. Cosser identified himself. 'There's an overseas phone call for you. You can take it at that phone over there,' he said, pointing to a phone on the wall near the entrance to the hotel restaurant. Cosser walked over and picked up the receiver. The switchboard operator asked him to wait on. 'Hello, Steve. It's Malcolm Colless here.' Cosser looked at his watch. It must have been lunchtime in Australia. 'Steve, Ken Cowley is on a plane for Los Angeles. He'll be there by the morning, your time. Rupert wants to see you, too. Ken will contact you at your hotel. Speak to you soon.'

Cosser walked back to Wiesener at their table. 'Looks like we've got our meeting with Murdoch.'

The next morning, Cosser and Wiesener met Ken Cowley in the hotel foyer for a brief discussion on the latest developments with

Broadcom and its pay TV plans. Cowley told them he had a car waiting outside and that Murdoch was expecting them at his house. The three men walked out of the main entrance of the Four Seasons to a white limousine which would take them on the 15 minute drive to Beverly Hills, where Murdoch lived in a Spanish-style house built in the 1950s by the founder of MCA studios, Jules Stein. It was set on about 2.5 hectares of land – large, even for Beverly Hills – with a panoramic view over Los Angeles.

As they drove up the red-gravel driveway, past the fully-grown English oaks that Murdoch's wife Anna had transplanted using a helicopter, to give the garden a mature look,[1] Murdoch came to the front door to meet them. He led them into a large lounge room where another man, a Fox engineer named Peter Smith, was waiting. He asked the visitors to take a seat. 'Nice to meet you both,' he said to Cosser and Wiesener. Cosser then gave Murdoch a draft of the prospectus that he was planning to publish for the proposed float of Broadcom, under the name Australis Media Ltd. Murdoch scanned through the document. He had already been briefed by Colless and Cowley.

Cosser started his spiel. Broadcom already had all the licences it needed for the main markets of Sydney and Melbourne, or more than two million homes. MDS was a proven technology, used in 40 countries, and was far cheaper than the alternative technologies. Its reception dish was small, and unobtrusive. MDS could quickly achieve high penetration rates. Satellite was two years away at least. Cable was prohibitively expensive and five years off at the earliest. He argued that Broadcom was in a position to develop a good head start on any rival and establish MDS as the preferred 'gateway' to the home, not just for pay TV, but also data and interactive services such as home shopping and banking.

Cosser believed he had struck a chord with Murdoch. Although News Corporation's experience had been entirely in satellite, with BSkyB in the UK and soon, probably, with Star TV in Hong Kong, the Australian Government's decision to legally mandate digital transmission combined with the destruction of Optus's B2 satellite a fortnight earlier meant satellite pay TV was years away.

Smith, an Englishman, appreciated that MDS was a line-of-sight technology and wanted to know how it would perform in a hilly city like Sydney. 'What area of Sydney would MDS cover?' he asked Cosser. 'About 60 to 70 per cent,' Cosser replied. 'Well, cable will never get that far,' Murdoch commented.

Murdoch appeared to be quite interested. 'We'd like to do a deal,' he told Cosser and Wiesener. Ken Cowley chipped in at this stage. 'What about Kerry?' he asked. Murdoch fired back, 'We'll give him 5 per cent.' He turned to the Broadcom men, 'We'll come back to you.'

Cosser and Wiesener had one or two more meetings that day in Los Angeles and had planned on flying out that night to London. Earlier, they had bumped into Sam Chisholm and Bruce McWilliam, who were also staying at the Four Seasons, and discovered that the News Corp pair would also be flying to London on the same flight.

As the British Airways jumbo cruised at 10,000 metres above the plains of the American Mid West on its way to the Atlantic coast, Cosser, Wiesener, Chisholm and McWilliam were in high spirits as they drank champagne in the first class cabin. Cosser was encouraged by his meeting that day with Rupert Murdoch. All the pieces were falling into place for him. Chisholm and McWilliam weren't so sure that News would go in, but kept their opinions to themselves at this point. Why spoil a pleasant flight?

Although Wiesener was never one to say much, the other three shared a few jokes and stories about their industry. Their loud conversation was starting to annoy a large American, who had his lounge chair tilted right back almost on to McWilliam's lap. 'Would you be quiet, I'm trying to sleep,' he protested. Chisholm, emboldened by liquor, turned to McWilliam: 'Bruce, you're a lawyer aren't you? Show me your ticket and show this man the no-speaking clause.' McWilliam played along with the joke for a few seconds, attempting to find the clause which said passengers weren't allowed to speak. 'I'm sorry pal, you haven't got a leg to stand on,' Chisholm lectured the humiliated American.

Ron Brierley returned to work on Monday January 11 after a short break over the New Year, and rang Kerry Packer at his house at Palm Beach, where he usually spends the southern summer. After an exchange of pleasantries, Brierley said, 'Kerry, you're probably aware that Steve Cosser has acquired a number of MDS licences and is well placed to have a pay TV service up and running long before satellite. We've been approached to see whether you might be interested in buying into the business, or even buying it. It looks quite attractive, and GPG is considering putting in some seed money.'

Packer told him what he had told numerous others asking him for his opinion on pay TV – that he was sceptical that it could work in Australia. The only circumstances in which it could work, he said, would be through a powerful consortium with access to the best programming. This would minimise competition and the potential losses. But if pay TV was going to happen, then his group would have to be a part of it. Packer asked Brierley to take the proposal, with more detail, to his executive assistant, Lynton Taylor.

Brierley phoned Taylor, a long-serving and long-suffering executive of Packer's who had been instrumental in setting up World Series Cricket in 1977. Taylor had become unpopular among other senior executives in the Packer organisation because he had effectively adopted the role of Packer's informant, sitting in on meetings and reporting directly to the boss. He had extensive knowledge of the media, however, and asked Brierley a number of questions. He wanted to know what Broadcom's assets were, the security of the MDS licences it held, and whether there had been much interest from other parties wanting to buy it.

Brierley told Taylor that he understood Broadcom had received a number of approaches, including one offer worth $60 million, but that he would seek more detailed answers to his questions. Taylor asked Brierley to send him a note fleshing out some of the points raised in their phone conversation. On January 18, Brierley wrote to Taylor:

Lynton,

The only asset of the company is approximately $8 million of capitalised expenses.

There has been considerable interest from (I am informed) a number of parties including Murdoch, O'Reilly, Greater Union, TVNZ and Telecom.

At this stage there are only two firm offers, which are:

a) TCI (including Time Warner and others) offer $US25 million (say, $A37 million) for 100% plus $A80 million working capital. Australis retains a 5% profit participation.

b) An undisclosed but 'substantial' US corporation offers $A8 million for 55% plus $A52 million working capital (this is the '$60 million' I mentioned). This proposal envisages renting instead of owning the boxes hence the lower capital requirement. Australis believes the residual 45% will have a value of in respect of a public float or other sale. The 55% purchaser is also seeking a put and call on these shares.

I am personally completely satisfied regarding the licences but will send you a separate memo on this issue.

Regards,
Ron Brierley

Steve Cosser and his friend Peter Gray, at Burrows Ltd, had certainly got 'a bit of an auction' going. Of these offers, the most serious was from the TCI-Time Warner consortium, although by this late stage it must have been doubtful that it was still both firm and current. Time Warner's Peter Frame was actively lobbying against MDS by mid-January.

Shortly after meeting Graham Richardson in New York, Frame moved to Australia, in May 1992, and had found himself very quickly in discussions with Cosser, as he was preparing to move to France. Cosser suggested Frame have lunch with him and Ross McCreath at Doyles at Watsons Bay, a popular outdoor seafood eatery with stunning views westwards across Sydney Harbour to the city towers.

In was a perfect Sydney winter's day, about 20 degrees C. With no wind and the sun shining on the sparkling blue water of the harbour, Doyles is a delightful and impressive place. Cosser and McCreath were giving Frame the rundown on their plans and the promising future they believed was ahead for MDS. It was still early days, with the main body of the *Broadcasting Services Act* only just passed and the pay TV section tied up before a Senate committee. Frame knew about MDS but wanted to know how it would go in Sydney, with its hills. From their table in the sun at Watson's Bay, it was quite apparent that the hills on either side of the harbour would present a challenge for MDS.

Cosser picked up his mobile phone from the table and rang 303 Castlereagh Street. 'Can I speak to David,' Cosser asked the receptionist. He wanted to talk to David Jupp, a former Telecom engineer and chief engineer at Ten during Broadcom's 12-month stewardship of the network. Jupp and McCreath had done most of the work with MDS, and had set up the Newsvision service which had been running for three months.

'David, Steve here,' Cosser said when Jupp answered the phone. 'Can you come over to Doyles and bring your dish. I'd like you to demonstrate to an important client how it works.'

About half an hour later, Jupp appeared on the walkway in front of the restaurant and beckoned the three to join him in the carpark nearby. Cosser, McCreath and Frame walked across to

Jupp, who had the back of an old station wagon open. He was positioning a small television monitor at the rear of the luggage compartment when they arrived. 'Watch this,' he said to Frame. He picked up a black plastic or porcelain dish, small enough for him to hold in one hand, and turned it towards Centrepoint tower in the distance. Immediately, the Newsvision images appeared on the monitor. Frame watched it for a while. Picture and sound were pretty good, even in these less-than-perfect conditions. It was an impressive demonstration.

Frame was very interested and started to spend a lot of time working out how Time Warner could become involved. MDS appeared to be the system which promised the earliest start into pay TV in Australia. Cable, in which Time Warner had virtually all of its experience in the US, looked to be out of the question in the foreseeable future in Australia, with little or no cable infrastructure in place. Satellite was still in the formative stages worldwide and could be years away. But the legislative picture in Canberra was still far from clear.

The American suggested to Cosser that Time Warner bring in other partners, and mentioned Malone's TeleCommunications Inc (TCI). Between the two groups, they had access to a wide source of movie and sports programming in the US along with their subscription television expertise. This was the genesis of the joint offer by Time Warner and TCI for Broadcom.

Frame needed to make his presence known in Canberra. Within days of starting work in June, he retained one of the capital's most effective lobbyists, Eric Walsh. He asked Walsh to introduce him to the key politicians, including the Minister for Communications. Frame was disappointed to learn that his old chilli dog-eating companion, Graham Richardson, was no longer in the portfolio.

Walsh was Canberra correspondent for *Time* magazine from 1964 to 1972. But long before this, he had been a reporter for the monopoly newspaper in the Australian Capital Territory, the *Canberra Times*. Walsh left the *Times* in 1961 to join a print compositor named Ken Cowley to set up *The Territorial*, a weekly newspaper they hoped would take on the *Times*. The name he and Cowley chose was not a particularly good one for a new newspaper, but the *Canberra Times* proprietor, Arthur Shakespeare, had foreseen such an eventuality as competition and registered almost every conceivable name, a list extending over at least three foolscap pages.

Cowley and Walsh spent many hours trying to come up with an original name not on Shakespeare's list. *The Territorial* became Rupert Murdoch's launch pad three years later for *The Australian*, which he started after enlisting the help of Cowley in 1964. Walsh moved back into journalism with Murdoch's *Daily Mirror* briefly, then *Time*, before joining newly-elected Labor Prime Minister Gough Whitlam as his press secretary in December 1972. He branched into the shadowy world of lobbying after Labor lost the election in 1975.

Walsh's connections in politics and the bureaucracy were second to none. His ability to open doors, in Labor circles in particular, made him a much sought-after intermediary in Canberra during this period. Now he arranged for his latest client, Peter Frame, of the Time Warner organisation, to spend 15 minutes or so with the latest Communications Minister.

When Frame walked into Bob Collins' office, he was left in no doubt that he was being treated *very* seriously by the Australian Government. Collins was almost grovelling in his desire to let Frame know how pleased he was that the world's largest media organisation was interested in being a player in pay TV in Australia. It was another get-to-know-you session, as far as Frame was concerned. He was merely paying the Minister the courtesy of letting him know that Time Warner was keen to invest in this emerging industry.

As June rolled into July and August, Frame appeared to remain a firm believer in MDS. Cosser was very confident he would bring in the giant Time Warner organisation as a shareholder, or even as a buyer, of Broadcom's MDS licences.

But events in Canberra were moving quickly over this period, and the pay TV regime was starting to take shape. Paul Keating was beginning to focus on the issue of digitalisation of the satellite signal and how this could help Labor create opportunities in the new industry for its friends. The growing likelihood that the Government would mandate digital and open up pay TV to more channels than was previously thought possible started to swing Frame's thinking back to satellite. On one of his visits to Canberra, Frame dropped in first to see Walsh and showed him a map of Australia on which his company had superimposed the footprints of the Optus satellite. Although large parts of Australia were outside the footprint, these were remote areas with very low population densities. The number of people affected would be measured in the tens of thousands, out of a population of 18 million. MDS, with its 30-kilometre radius for each channel, would only ever be able to service the larger metropolitan markets. This would exclude 25–30 per cent of the Australian population, including the 40 per cent of Sydney which wouldn't be able to receive an MDS signal.

By December, Frame had decided his group, and therefore TCI as well, should pursue the satellite option as part of a consortium. He suddenly went cold on MDS. More ominous still for Broadcom and Cosser, Frame was starting to come to the view that an early introduction of MDS was a real threat to a potential satellite operator like his company. If Cosser was able to use his first-mover advantage to tie up good movie and sports programming and build up a respectable subscriber base, he would turn the favoured satellite into the 'space junk' Paul Keating had so disparagingly termed it. He had to be stopped.


Cosser and his friend Richard Wiesener were pursuing two strategies: the sale of their MDS licences to a trade buyer, or floating the potential business on the stock exchange. But they had not yet decided which course to follow. Whichever option they settled on, they would need a prominent business figure to be chairman of their company. In the week leading up to Christmas 1992, which fell on a Friday that year, they asked Peter Gray to draw up a list of potential candidates. Gray suggested they meet in the Burrows Ltd boardroom the next day to discuss the names.

As they sat around the obligatory heavy wooden board table in the room lined with large wooden cabinets containing books and model cars – reflecting Peter Burrows' enthusiasm for exotic cars, Ferraris in particular – the three picked over Gray's list. It had the names of Andrew Turnbull, the soon-to-retire chief executive of food ingredients company Burns Philp and Co, Mark Johnson, head of corporate finance at Macquarie Bank, Sir Ron Brierley, and Rodney Price. Gray hadn't sounded out any of these people, but mentioned that Price was rumoured to be ready to leave his job as chief executive of Pioneer International to take up a range of directorships. They spoke to all of the people on Gray's list over the ensuing days, but decided Price would be the most suitable, if they could get him.

Cosser and Wiesener asked Price to meet them at Burrows Ltd. He was lukewarm when they offered him the chairmanship of their company. It wasn't exactly what he had in mind. He asked for some more information. Cosser gave him a draft prospectus and some newspaper clippings. Price said he would think about it over Christmas.

What Cosser did not know at this point was that Murdoch and Packer were also talking and were leaning towards satellite as the best way to get into pay TV. Murdoch's executive-at-large, Malcolm Colless, continued his discussions with Cosser to keep abreast of what he and Broadcom were doing. Bruce Robertson made a second trip to the US for Packer in January to see Schmidt, who had promised to take him around some pay TV operations which used MDS. Neither camp was prepared to rule out MDS at this stage. News and Packer's Nine Network both took the view that they had no choice but to keep open the option of taking a strategic stake in Broadcom, or buying the licences outright, so long as there was a possibility that Cosser could use MDS to make an early entry into pay TV, and undermine satellite.

By early January, however, Broadcom was fast running out of money. Steve Cosser estimated he would need between $2 million and $3 million to be able to bid for additional MDS licences in the forthcoming auction. He had been talking to his friend Peter Gray through the weeks leading up to Collins' December 6 announcement of the auction and Gray had assured him Burrows Ltd could raise the necessary money.

After he returned from the US, Cosser phoned Gray and asked him to raise the $2.5 million Broadcom would need to buy the MDS licences. As a result of his meeting in Amsterdam a few weeks earlier with Gary Weiss, Cosser suggested that GPG was keen. Gray knew Gary Weiss anyway, and put the squeeze on him for GPG to contribute. Gray passed the hat around among clients of Burrows Ltd, mostly wealthy individuals, and was able to come up with the money. Cosser was ready now for the auction, just a fortnight away. The money was raised by Broadcom through a company that Cosser had registered, called Australis Media Ltd.

This was a very busy time, too, for Kerry Packer. On top of his rising concern over developments in pay TV, he and his chief executive, Al Dunlap, were also preparing to take up the board seats that the new Westpac chairman John Uhrig had offered them on December 8, but which they were unable to accept at that stage because Westpac had not completed the sale of the Ten Network.

Packer could not be on the boards of the corporations which owned the Nine Network and Ten at the same time.

Nine days after Uhrig asked Packer and his right hand man onto the board, the bank's directors voted to remove the managing director, Frank Conroy, a long-standing Westpac executive, and find a replacement from overseas. Uhrig wanted someone with no sentimental attachments to the bank to implement a tough round of cost-cutting and the sale of most of its offshore lending book. Westpac also had enormous challenges in managing problem loans totalling nearly $10 billion. Uhrig was already courting an American, Robert Joss, from Wells Fargo Bank, who had been identified by a San Francisco-based search consultant, Dan Metz.

With the sale of Ten having been completed on New Year's Eve, Westpac's board was due to meet on January 14 to welcome their two new directors and discuss a business plan for the bank that Dunlap had been working on.

Soon after 11am on Thursday, January 14, Packer and Dunlap drove into the bank's underground car park off Macquarie Street in Packer's white 7-series BMW and took the lift to the 28th floor of Westpac's headquarters building in Martin Place. They were met at the lift and escorted to the boardroom, where nine directors sat around the long table. At the head, closest to the door they entered, was the chairman, Uhrig. Packer and Dunlap walked down one side of the room and took two seats side by side at the end of the table. Although they were not yet directors, Packer asked the board to hear a proposal that Dunlap would put to them.

Dunlap, a short, greying American with a ferocious reputation for ruthless cost-cutting at corporations he had run in the US, had been introduced to Packer by their mutual friend Sir James Goldsmith in 1989. Goldsmith hired Dunlap to turn around the ailing San Francisco timber company Crown-Zellerbach, which Goldsmith had acquired in 1986. He jokingly referred to Dunlap when he introduced him to Packer as 'Rambo in pinstripes', a name he had coined earlier for a British journalist. Dunlap's more common nickname was 'The Chainsaw', an appellation bestowed on him by another of Packer's friends, John Aspinall, the British naturalist and gambler.[2]

Uhrig and the rest of the board were prepared for something fairly spectacular from Dunlap, and he gave it to them. He started with Conroy's five-point plan to cut costs and sell unwanted assets. With a grim expression he said the bank needed to target at least double the amount of problem loans that Conroy had envisaged needed to be dealt with, and the exercise must be achieved in half the time. Packer and Dunlap were impatient for action. Uhrig and the board winced as Dunlap outlined his proposals, but became restless and sceptical when Packer demanded that Dunlap preside over the recovery plan. First Uhrig, then another director, Sir James Balderstone, said 'no' to this element of the Dunlap plan.

The meeting then deteriorated into a slanging match, with Packer going into one of his much-feared rages, banging the table with one of his fists and swearing profusely. Suddenly, he pushed his chair back and barked at Dunlap, 'Al, we're out of here.' The pair stood and walked out of the room. As they made their way to the glass security door leading to the lift foyer, Dunlap told Packer, 'You were too hasty in there.' Packer then turned on Dunlap and the two shouted at each other, and continued arguing as the lift doors closed. The exchange could still be heard by shocked West-pac staff in the 28th floor lift foyer as the lift descended to the carpark.[3]

Packer and Dunlap never took their board seats. Dunlap resigned a few weeks later and returned to the US to tackle the troubled Scott Paper. In May, Packer sold his Westpac shares for more than $600 million to the property and financial services group Lend Lease, giving him a profit on his six-month investment in Westpac of more than $100 million. After being a long-time West-pac client, Packer put his group's banking business out to tender, and it was won by the National Australia Bank.

If Bob Collins and Paul Keating believed they were comfortably in control of pay TV policy, they were sadly mistaken. By mid-January 1993 powerful undercurrents being generated by the media's major players would catch Keating and Collins completely off guard and throw their carefully structured policy into disarray. The strength and determination of the forces of the media establishment – that is, Rupert Murdoch and Kerry Packer – were increased by the fact that they were starting to panic.

Steve Cosser may have believed he was close to bringing in Rupert Murdoch as an investor in Australis, and Ron Brierley on behalf of Cosser may have been hopeful of attracting interest from Kerry Packer. But by now Murdoch and Packer had decided there was no room for MDS in pay TV in Australia, certainly not as a stand-alone system. Time Warner's Peter Frame had earlier reached the same conclusion and had discouraged TCI, whose chairman and chief executive, John Malone, was a friend of Murdoch's.

Yet the harsh reality was that Australis's plans for an MDS pay TV service and the imminent auction of further licences meant that the two moguls could not ignore MDS. Like the complex attitude of the commercial networks towards pay TV, their first preference was to delay or destroy MDS, but if it would not go away, then they wanted it. Whatever choice the large players would be forced to adopt, their plans did not include Cosser and Australis. In the media industry, it is not possible to have more potent and forceful enemies than Packer and Murdoch. The world's most powerful media interests had decided that for Australia, satellite was the technology of their choice, and that cable would be the long-term delivery system in the future.

Kerry Packer decided at this point that the risk of Cosser getting a head start and muddying the water in pay TV was too great. He told Lynton Taylor to offer Cosser $13 million for his 13 licences. Taylor called Ron Brierley to ask him to relay the offer to Cosser. The answer came back quickly. It was 'no'. Cosser knew by now he would make far more through a float of the company.

The rejection infuriated Packer. He rang John Gerahty, who was chairman of Broadcom, the parent company to Australis, and asked Gerahty to come and see him. 'I've made you a good offer for your licences and you've rejected it. I'm warning you: if you stand in my way, I'll crush you!' Packer bellowed at a nervous and shaking Gerahty, who said later it was the most unpleasant meeting he had ever attended.

Bob Collins exacerbated the rising urgency among the major media players when he accepted his department's advice to announce on January 20 that the Government would auction two four-channel satellite licences; one for new players to the industry – 'licence A' – and a second for established media groups – 'licence B'. Bids would close on March 24, and the winners would be announced the following day. The previous day, Collins asked his department to fax to his Darwin office the documents setting out the terms of the auction for him to sign. He glanced at the document, signed it, and faxed it back to Canberra, where his office released the announcement on the auction. But Collins did not read the documents carefully enough. He missed the fact that his senior officials had omitted the all-important clause that bidders would be vetted before being allowed to bid.

The Attorney General's Department had advised their counterparts in Transport and Communications that vetting bidders would breach the competition provisions of the *Broadcasting Services Act*. It could be interpreted as anti-competitive and leave the department open to legal challenge later. The Communications officials decided they had no choice but to leave this clause out and keep their fingers crossed that the bidders would be people of substance. The only requirement for those wishing to lodge an offer was a deposit of $500.

Collins and Keating at this point appear to have been blithely unaware, too, of the conflicts which this second auction deadline would create. Collins' department was pushing the Government down a policy route to introduce competition in the media by encouraging new players and a diversity of delivery systems in pay TV. It was not looking to 'pick winners', whereas the Government's focus on satellite and the wheeling and dealing over channel numbers inevitably meant the politicians were doing exactly that.

The impending trouble for Keating and Collins lay in the fact that they had picked satellite as the favoured technology. Yet, in nine days, Cosser could be in a position to have a six-channel service in all metropolitan centres using an 'inferior' MDS system and start negotiations with the Hollywood studios. It would be at least 12 to 18 months before the satellite operator would be in the same position.

On January 26, the *Australian Financial Review* reported in a front page article that the Australian television networks, representatives of Kerry Packer and Rupert Murdoch, a number of the Hollywood studios and some of the big US cable groups, including Time Warner and Continental Cablevision, had met in the Los Angeles Beverly Wilshire Hotel the previous day to work out a strategy to halt MDS. The newspaper claimed the meeting followed an earlier get-together by the Australian networks to find a common position to halt the allocation of microwave licences for pay TV.

Most of the people allegedly at these meetings denied subsequently that they were there, or that the meetings happened at all. This isn't surprising, given that any collusive action by parties such as these would represent a breach of the *Trade Practices Act*, certainly if the meeting occurred in Australia. One executive of a US cable TV group, who said he had not attended any meeting in Los Angeles, believed it was more likely that a series of meetings occurred in various locations around Los Angeles at this time, rather than one set-piece meeting.

It appears likely, though, that the large media and studio groups did, in fact, have some discussions on the MDS issue. But whether the interests opposed to the early introduction of MDS had one or a series of meetings, the result is undisputed: a concerted lobbying campaign to pressure the Australian Government to ditch the forthcoming MDS auction intensified immediately. Unfortunately for Steve Cosser and Australis, their arguments were very persuasive and fell on fertile ground in Canberra, in particular in Paul Keating's office. After having designed the satellite licence model only a few weeks earlier, Keating personally didn't like MDS. He believed it would muddy the waters for a national satellite service using the latest digital technology.

On Monday, January 25, Paul Keating's senior private secretary, Don Russell, phoned Roger Beale, the acting secretary in Bob Collins' Department of Transport and Communications. The departmental secretary, Graham Evans, was on leave, and although Beale was more involved in the transport area than communications, he suffered the misfortune of filling in as department head while Evans was away. Russell and his boss, Paul Keating, were becoming concerned about stories in the media about the potential impact of MDS.[4] Cosser was being touted as the next Rupert Murdoch if he succeeded in his plans to get an MDS pay TV service up, and running a year or more ahead of his larger and more inflexible potential competitors committed to satellite and cable. If it was apparent that MDS would start well before satellite, it could also destroy the Government's chances of getting a reasonable price for the sale of the two satellite licences. Collins says he was unaware, amazingly, of the pressure starting to come on his own departmental officers from the Prime Minister's office.

Russell asked Beale to prepare a paper detailing the existing licences in MDS; their rights and entitlements and conditions applying to them; how the use of MDS would fit in with the Government's decision on a digital standard for satellite; and whether the Australian Broadcasting Authority was obliged to issue pay TV licences to MDS holders.[5] Beale told Russell he would provide a paper addressing these issues as soon as he could. After Russell terminated the conversation, Beale rang a lower-ranking official and asked him to start work right away on the paper. Beale thought it odd that he was getting this call from the Prime Minister's office, and not from his Minister.

Two days later, Beale was even more surprised when Keating himself rang, asking that the paper requested earlier by Don Russell be provided urgently. He told Beale that Cabinet had been 'notoriously misled' on the extent to which MDS might be used for pay TV. Beale told Keating that the legislation specifically provided for the possibility of MDS being a transitional medium, and that special provisions in the law would ensure that satellite would ultimately be the primary pay TV provider.

It was becoming very clear at this point that the objectives of the department and the agenda of Cabinet, as represented by Paul Keating, were starkly at odds. There had been an uneasy cooperation between the department's officials and the politicians over the last 12 months of the legislative process. The department's policy advisers, mainly Christine Goode and Chris North, had tried to steer through a technology-neutral regime which would encourage all comers to use satellite, MDS and perhaps even cable. The advantage the bureaucrats enjoyed over the politicians was that they knew a lot more about the subject than their political masters. North had been working on reforms to broadcasting services since 1988 and had travelled the world looking at how pay TV was developing in the US, the UK and France.

Keating and, to a lesser extent, Collins regarded the bureaucrats as clear-eyed idealists with little grasp of the realities of setting up a pay TV service. This was certainly the message Keating and Collins were getting from the established media players through Kerry Packer's energetic lobbyist, Peter Barron, and Eric Walsh for Time Warner. The arguments of these seasoned lobbyists were highly sophisticated and compelling. If MDS was allowed to get a head start, it would steal the best movie and sports programming for a small proportion of the population in the cities, and once again leave the regional areas to the mercy of the regional affiliates of the commercial networks. Barron and Walsh were also highly suspicious of the role of the department. The ABC's David Hill, too, was convinced that the department was deliberately pushing the interests of Cosser. Barron and Walsh raised with Keating a meeting in early January, when Chris North broke a holiday in Sydney to brief some executives of the Los Angeles Times Mirror group on the provisions of the new pay TV legislation. Times Mirror owned the *Los Angeles Times* and had cable interests in the US. It was negotiating with Cosser at this stage to take a direct interest in Australis of anything up to 55 per cent, about the same as CanWest had purchased of the Ten Network, and using a similar structure. Collins was forced to defend North, telling Keating that the official had briefed several other groups interested in pay TV, including Time Warner's Peter Frame.

In the three days from January 25, Keating threw the weight of his office behind Kerry Packer, Rupert Murdoch, Peter Frame and the networks, to demonstrate who was running Canberra. The ABC's David Hill was also a persistent lobbyist for the cause of reining in MDS to give satellite time to get up and running. Hill phoned Collins from the US on January 26 and told the Minister 'we were all wrong' on MDS and that if it could not be stopped then the Government and the ABC should try to 'salvage something from the wreckage'.[6]

Optus Communications chief executive Bob Mansfield was also becoming deeply concerned about the potential impact of MDS on satellite. He had just lost his B2 satellite and was worried about the loss of revenue he was hoping to earn from the satellite licence holders once they got their operations started. Mansfield rang Bob Collins to express his fear that Optus would be left in the cold if MDS got a head start.

Thursday, January 28 was a critical day in the brief life of MDS. Press reports over preceding days suggested there was growing pressure on the Government to call off the MDS auction tenders, due to have been lodged by the next day. ABC Radio's *AM* morning news and current affairs program interviewed Bob Collins, and the Minister declared that he would not be bullied. The auction would proceed.

Almost immediately after the interview ended, soon after 8am, Peter Barron rang Don Russell. Barron, a former journalist with Rupert Murdoch's *Daily Mirror* tabloid newspaper, had worked for NSW Premier Neville Wran as an adviser in the late 1970s and early 1980s before joining former Prime Minister Bob Hawke's office after Labor's Federal Election victory in 1983. Even after leaving Hawke to join Kerry Packer's staff in 1986, he remained a sought-after adviser to the Labor Party during elections. He was a cynical and savvy operator with a keen sense of how Labor should react to, or initiate, key issues. Barron can claim much of the credit for Labor's successful defence of its marginal seats in the 1987 election when the 'Joh for Canberra' campaign of septuagenarian Queensland Premier Joh Bjelke-Petersen was gathering a head of steam.

Barron was a highly regarded strategist in the 1990 election too, and despite his previous status as a member of Hawke's 'Manchu Court', his standing was such in the Labor Party that he had ready access to Hawke's successor and to his staff. The fact that he also spoke for Kerry Packer carried enormous weight in the Labor Government. Kerry was a 'mate' to be looked after. And so was Rupert.

The Labor Government would have to call an election before the end of May 1993, and most of the speculation focused on a March date, either the 13th or the 20th. The opinion polls indicated that the Liberal Party Opposition and its coalition partner the National Party would win comfortably. With an election only weeks away, Keating was pragmatic in the extreme. He may have been a man of vision, but he wasn't about to allow his government to make any moves which might hurt or offend Australia's most powerful media barons at such a sensitive time politically.

Armed with the strategy apparently developed at the meetings in Los Angeles, Peter Barron had been calling Don Russell over the previous days to emphasise to the adviser that the MDS auction simply could not go ahead. It was an inferior technology and would destroy any hope of a commercial satellite pay TV service getting underway. If MDS went ahead it would have to be after the satellite service was in operation, otherwise it would turn the forthcoming satellite auctions into a farce.

By the Thursday, Barron's calls were more persistent and urgent. If the tenders for the remaining MDS licences closed as planned the next day, then the more serious potential pay TV players would have no choice but to buy as many of the MDS licences as possible and compete against Australis using the same technology. This was not their preference, but they may be forced into this action.

Russell didn't need much more convincing. He and Keating also held the view that Collins' department had misled the Cabinet and were promoting the interests of Steve Cosser.

While events were coming rapidly to a head in the ministerial suite of Parliament House in Canberra, Peter Frame was in his Sydney office on the phone to Eric Walsh for most of the day, wanting regular updates. Walsh, who was in Melbourne on other business, was in almost constant contact with Barron, who in turn was calling Russell every half hour or so. Or so it seemed. Barron kept hammering home the same points: that the satellite auction will fail if MDS is allowed to get a head start; the serious players will either boycott the satellite licence auction or be forced to invest in an inferior technology. Barron was under orders from Packer to get the auction cancelled. He was doing a very effective job.

Although the pressure from Keating's office to call off, or delay, the MDS auctions intensified through the day, Collins resisted, wanting the auctions to proceed as announced. As the responsible Minister, Collins would have had to wear the political odium and embarrassment of such a major backdown in the face of lobbying from entrenched media interests. Collins' senior private secretary, Jack Lake, had the previous day canvassed the possibility of cancelling or delaying the auction and was told by the department that it would require a change to the broadcasting law, which had only been passed two months earlier.

Christine Goode suggested three options to Collins: the Government insist that MDS be broadcast using digital technology, thus delaying its introduction; continue to require MDS to be used only for narrowcast services; or delay the introduction of MDS until after the national satellite service was available.[7] She recommended the last option as the best because it dealt with the prime concern of the potential satellite users, that MDS would get a head start and grab programming and customers before satellite got started.

By late that afternoon, however, Keating would not be put off any longer. Russell called Lake into the Prime Minister's office and delivered an ultimatum: tell Collins to call off the auctions, or Keating would do it for him. Lake had no choice but to deliver the bad news to his boss.

Steve Cosser had heard Bob Collins' interview on the morning of January 28 too, and rang the chairman of the Australian Broadcasting Authority, Brian Johns, to seek additional reassurance that the MDS auction was proceeding. Johns told him that, as far as he was concerned, tenders for the licences were due to close the next evening and he had the power to issue new licences.

Cosser was due that afternoon to see his lawyers, Freehill Hollingdale and Page, to complete the final tender documents for delivery the next day. He was preparing to go over to Freehills' offices in the MLC Centre in Martin Place when he took a call from a journalist from the *Australian Financial Review*. The journalist told Cosser there had been a major change in policy, that

Keating had become involved, and it looked like the MDS auctions were off. Cosser was alarmed and surprised by what the reporter told him. 'We've just checked with the ABA and the department and have been told nothing has changed,' he told the reporter.

He called out to Ross McCreath and the Australis pair hailed a cab outside 303 Castlereagh Street to take them to the MLC Centre. Once they reached Freehills, Cosser asked McCreath to ring Collins' office to check. Jack Lake took his call and said emphatically that the auction was still on.

About an hour later, a call came through to the meeting room for Cosser. It was Michael Crawford, media and communications adviser to Bob Collins. 'Steve, we're calling the auction off,' Crawford said. 'The Minister is instructing the ABA not to issue any new MDS licences. It will do too much harm to the prospects for the satellite licence auction.'

Cosser was stunned, but not completely surprised given the rumours which had been swirling for the last day or two. He told Crawford, 'We had been hoping to get our business going by the end of last year and that was delayed by the Senate inquiry. This decision will push it back another year or two because you've mandated digital for the satellite.'

'I'm sorry, but that's the Government's decision,' Crawford said tersely. The conversation was over in two or three minutes.

As soon as he replaced the receiver, Cosser's lawyers, who guessed what he had just been told, urged him to lodge the bids anyway. Collins did not have the power to do this, they argued, and Australis probably had a good legal case against the Minister. Cosser could only think of the time and expense this would take. He had just raised $2.5 million from investors to back his MDS purchases, his house was mortgaged to the hilt to keep his business going, and now his business plan was in tatters.

After a brief discussion with his lawyers on tactics, Cosser and McCreath took a taxi back to Castlereagh Street. Peter Gray had heard the news about the Government's decision and called by the Australis office to offer Cosser a lift to Paddington, where Cosser rented an apartment on his regular visits to Australia. Cosser was quiet on the drive to the apartment, opposite the White City tennis courts, so Gray suggested an early morning run along Bondi beach the next day.

After a night of thinking about Collins' decision, Cosser was in a more talkative mood the next day. As he and Gray ran along the beach, Cosser said it was like Ten again. 'Packer's behind this,' he said to Gray. 'He's got to the politicians. This time I'm going to fight.'

It was a Friday, and when he got to the office Cosser sat down with McCreath to work out what they would do. Cosser would go public. There were already a number of calls from the previous night from journalists wanting to talk to him, including the producers of the ABC's 7.30 Report and Seven's Hinch program. The phone was ringing with other requests. McCreath suggested running some newspaper advertisements to highlight what he regarded as the hypocrisy of Collins' and Keating's decision. Cosser also wanted to make this policy backflip an issue for the election, with the campaigns by the two major parties starting to gather momentum.

Cosser phoned the Liberal Opposition leader John Hewson, and was put through to him in his Melbourne office. Cosser suggested to Hewson that he fly down to brief him on Labor's policy turnaround. He told Hewson he intended to conduct a public campaign against Labor on the pay TV issue. This was music to Hewson's ears. Cosser and McCreath were on a plane by lunchtime. Before he left, he instructed Freehills to lodge the bids for the MDS licences with the Department of Communications on Monday and to make a separate application to the Australian Broadcasting Authority. He also wanted a letter sent to Collins giving him five days notice to revoke his order restraining the ABA, or face legal action.

That night Cosser appeared on both current affairs programs and attacked the Labor Government over the MDS auction reversal. They were feisty, combative performances from a man who had plenty of experience in front of a television camera. In an interview that day with Errol Simper, writing for *The Weekend Australian*, Cosser said, 'This sort of thing is turning Australia into a kind of Luddites' paradise, somewhat akin to living in the old Eastern bloc countries where either the government or the friends of the government had to be the voice of the media and where other voices needed killing off instantly. In this case it has involved severely embarrassing a minister and forcing him into a 180-degree change on a consistently stated position.'[8] Simper didn't know it, but Cosser was talking to him by phone from Hewson's office.

When asked whether he had been pressured by big media players, Collins responded: 'There's only one way I can answer it: to say it's not true and challenge anyone to prove I'm a liar.'[9]

Cosser may have been fighting mad, but Labor politicians rarely forgive those who turn on them publicly. In his advertisements, Cosser was able to highlight in spectacular fashion Collins' and Keating's inconsistencies, exposed by the intense lobbying pressure brought to bear on the Government. From the night of his television interviews, Cosser put Australis on a collision course with Keating and Labor. Paul Keating had yet to call the election, but everyone knew his decision was imminent. Cosser had a lot riding on the outcome.

On Wednesday, February 10, 1993, Rodney Price announced his resignation from Pioneer International. He had grown tired of trying to extract profits from pre-mixed concrete and quarrying. Pioneer was not riding well under Price. It would announce a 21 per cent fall in its half-year profit a few days later and the company was still recovering from the hammering its shares had taken in the stockmarket when it was forced to reveal that it had agreed to act as a sub-underwriter to the disastrous rights issue by Westpac the previous year. Pioneer looked likely to lose about $46 million, although the recovery in the bank's share price after Kerry Packer's November raid assisted Pioneer's position.

At the time of his resignation, Price declared only that he wanted to 'pursue personal interests'. In fact, he had decided to accept Steve Cosser's offer to be chairman of Australis Media.

Four days earlier, Paul Keating ended the mounting election speculation by announcing that the Federal Election would be held on March 13. It was a brave call, given that the Liberal Party had just crushed Labor in the Western Australian State election which returned Premier Richard Court with an increased majority.

That Sunday evening, Cosser inserted the first of his full-page advertisements attacking Bob Collins. In large reverse capitals, the advertisement was headed: 'INFERIOR MINISTER – ELECTION LIABILITY'. It listed the 120 or so places in the US which used MDS for subscription television, plus about another 100 cities in South America, Europe and Asia which also used it. Collins had made the mistake on ABC radio the morning after he suspended the MDS auction of saying, 'MDS is used in Ireland and that is the only country in the world it is used.'

In his second advertisement, run in most metropolitan newspapers four days later, Cosser depicted Collins with a long nose using an enhanced photograph. The ad was headlined

'Inferior minister strreettcches the truth', and accused the Minister of launching a 'desperate smear campaign' against MDS to conceal from the Australian public the 'real reason' for trying to kill MDS pay TV. Cosser was playing the role for all it was worth: the wounded David trying to fight in the public interest against the injustices of an insensitive government acting in the interests of media's Goliaths.

In one of the oil industry's biggest gatherings for years, Pioneer International's outgoing chief executive Rod Price hosted a big farewell dinner on Saturday night, March 6, at Sydney's Marriott Hotel to farewell John Hurlstone, who was about to retire as managing director of Ampol. The oil refining and retailing group was then a Pioneer subsidiary. It was a big evening with over 100 executives from the six oil majors and their partners. A guest was Allan Fels, chairman of the competition regulator, the Trade Practices Commission.

Price was close to the Liberal Party, which was expected to comfortably win the Federal Election the following weekend. He helped Opposition leader John Hewson formulate his 'Fightback' tax reform package, which was the centrepiece policy the Liberals would take to the election. Pioneer supported the Liberals with campaign funds and the former Treasury bureaucrat who did much of the work on Fightback, Jim Hoggett, was a corporate affairs executive with Pioneer and did most of his work on the project on Pioneer's time. Price was a firm believer in the tax reforms contained in Fightback.

Fels was invited purely out of courtesy. A bald-headed man with a pock-marked face, Fels was not popular with large sections of big business, the oil industry in particular. Fels liked people to call him 'professor', although he had left his job as a university academic years earlier to pursue a career as a government regulator. As chairman of the TPC he had launched a string of successful prosecutions alleging anti-competitive behaviour by companies in oligopolistic industries such as oil, transport and building products. He took delight in using his extensive and largely unchecked legal powers to humiliate companies he had caught out on price fixing or predatory market behaviour. As a Labor Government appointee, there had been some talk that an incoming Liberal Government would replace him with someone more attuned to the commercial requirements of big business.

Price spotted Fels during the Hurlstone dinner and walked up to him at his table. 'Mate, after next Saturday, you're fucked,' he told the startled bureaucrat. Unfortunately for Price, Fels had a long memory. When he was chairman of Australis, Price would have reason later to sorely regret this rash prediction.

# 6

# Satellite dawn

Rupert Murdoch spent much of December 1992 in Hong Kong. He was busy negotiating on two fronts: the purchase of a 22 per cent interest in the HK-TVB television group from Sir Run Run Shaw and Robert Kuok; and a controlling interest in the potential rival pay TV broadcaster, Li Ka Shing's Star TV. The satellite footprints of this fledgling pay TV service would cover China and India and would give Murdoch's News Corp the capacity to reach 400 million television homes, or four times the size of the US market. His discussions with the TVB partners did not go very far because the authorities in Beijing intervened to stop News buying a pivotal interest in the terrestrial broadcaster. 'The Chinese made it very clear we were not welcome at TVB,' said Murdoch. 'In their view any foreign company is not welcome. And that's when we pulled back.'[1]

Despite this setback, Murdoch was determined to persist in building a business in China. Among Western businessmen, he was quick to recognise the potential of the world's most populous nation (and to a lesser extent India) and was preparing to commit substantial resources into securing a strong position in broadcast media and also through his *South China Morning Post* newspaper. About 10 days before Christmas he phoned Ken Cowley and asked if he, Mark Burrows and Peter Macourt, the finance director of News's Australian offshoot, News Limited, could join him in the Hong Kong to take up their earlier discussions on how News could win control of the Seven Network. The sale of Ten to the

CanWest consortium was about to be completed, and Murdoch was anxious that Seven should not slip through his fingers.

Cowley and Burrows had already talked over possible strategies, knowing that any move on Seven would receive the closest possible scrutiny from the authorities. The cross-media ownership rule dictated that while News owned daily newspapers in all of Australia's metropolitan markets except Perth, it could never own more than 15 per cent of Seven. Cowley had approached Paul Keating to test the water on News owning Seven, and had been told 'no'. News would have to win control while constrained by both cross-media and foreign ownership limits.

Murdoch had seen Conrad Black stitch up control of John Fairfax while holding just 15 per cent of the newspaper group, and Izzy Asper take Ten with a similar stake in that network's voting stock, and knew the structures did not comply with the spirit of the ownership limits. His preference was also to 'do a CanWest' with Seven. If Black and Asper could get away with it, so could he.

But his ambitions were complicated by the fact that with Seven he would not be dealing with one seller, as was Asper. Seven's banks had been forced to write off about $400 million of the $915 million owed to them by the network's failed parent, Christopher Skase's Qintex group, and they appointed the former head of Nissan Australia, Ivan Deveson, as chairman in August 1991. As the Seven network was the most valuable asset in Qintex, the banks decided to leave most of this written down debt, or about $250 million, in Seven to be taken on by the purchaser.

Because the banks had decided to 'take and hold' and build the value of the network rather than sell it cheaply in a fire sale, they also needed to rearrange the ownership of the network so as not to breach foreign ownership rules. Foreigners were limited to 20 per cent ownership of television networks and individuals to 15 per cent. Most of the Qintex banks, such as HongKong Bank, Chase Manhattan and Bank of America, were foreign. ANZ Bank and State Bank of NSW were the main Australian lenders. As part of this technical rearrangement of the ownership structure, the banks relinquished their control over Seven, and allowed each of the four directors 15 per cent, giving them 60 per cent in total in exchange for a nominal sum of money. This gave Deveson and Seven's managing director, Bob Campbell, 30 per cent between them and effective control over the network.

The banks had to take a back seat as it was almost entirely up to Deveson and Campbell to decide the best course, whether this be achieved through a float, or by trade sale to a single buyer or consortium. So long as the sale proceeds covered the banks' loans and a bit for their trouble, they had to be content to accept Deveson and Campbell's direction on how the sale was achieved. The banks estimated Seven would earn $90 million before interest on its debt and tax for the next financial year ending June 30 1994. Based on accepted valuations of businesses being worth about 8.5 times earnings before interest and tax, the banks reckoned they should get between $750 million and $800 million for the network.

Both Deveson and Campbell from an early stage expressed a preference to float the network rather than sell it to a trade buyer. The latter course would inevitably mean the loss of their jobs. In meetings with potential buyers and investors, Deveson in particular stressed that it was important for the network that he remain chairman. Deveson had presided over the demise of Nissan as a manufacturer in Australia and had taken up a career as a management guru doing the lecture circuit before being picked by the Qintex banks to oversee the Seven sale process. Campbell was installed by Skase in 1987 when Qintex bought Seven from Fairfax. He was a resourceful and wily survivor. They were not about to be railroaded into accepting a corporate conjuring trick of the type used by Canadians Black and Asper.

At Murdoch's office in Hong Kong's South China Morning Post building, he told Burrows, Cowley and Macourt he favoured the CanWest approach, which would give News effective control over Seven but keep the group inside the cross-media limit. Burrows and Cowley had already discussed the matter during their numerous meetings in Cowley's fourth-floor office at Holt Street in Surry Hills. Rarely a day passed that Burrows' black 7-series BMW was not parked in the street outside the News headquarters, defying the ever-eager parking inspectors who took rich pickings from the ceaseless flow of cars and vans in the garment district. Burrows and Cowley had reached the conclusion that it would be best not to go through the back door via a CanWest structure. CanWest had generated enough heat and suspicion, and if News tried the same device it would inevitably raise eyebrows. News would best take Seven by putting together a consortium of like-minded groups with each taking an interest separately. These investors would recognise News as the dominant shareholder among them.

Cowley said he was confident he could bring in West Australian Newspapers and Perth entrepreneur Kerry Stokes to take up, say, 5 per cent each. He had also met the new head of Telecom, an American named Frank Blount, whom he believed might be worth approaching to see if the phone company was interested in taking a piece of Seven. Burrows had sounded out Irishman Tony O'Reilly, who was still smarting after missing out on Fairfax a year earlier. O'Reilly told the merchant banker he would be interested in investing in Seven. On top of the maximum 15 per cent that News could own, a consortium of this make-up could take between 35 per cent and 40 per cent – a shareholding bloc that could not be out-voted.

Murdoch accepted this strategy, but insisted that if the Seven board failed to agree to News and its allies taking what would be a controlling interest, then News would aggressively pursue the Can-West-style alternative.

Ken Cowley had been wearing his hat as executive chairman of Ansett Airlines, which was half-owned by News, when he introduced himself to Blount a few months earlier. Cowley was anxious to keep Telecom's very substantial business with the airline and paid a courtesy call on the carrier's new chief executive in Melbourne several months after he started, in February 1992.

Blount and Cowley hit it off immediately. Both men were in their 50s, were industry veterans at the peak of their power and influence. The chemistry between the two was good. They talked about their organisations, Cowley about News's ambitious global pay TV plans and Blount about the challenges that lay ahead for him in turning a government monopoly into an efficient carrier which would cope with the imminent rush of competition. As part of this transformation, Telecom had adopted an electronic communications information plan, which acknowledged that Telecom lacked experience in the content business. Telecom had long planned to eventually extend its cable network to the home. This network had been built to link Australia's main cities during the late 1970s and early 1980s. It was inevitable that Telecom would need to become involved in multi-media services such as pay television, and home consumer businesses such as shopping and banking, to exploit the capacity of its cable. Cowley listened with great interest. News had been contemplating pay TV even at this early stage. Who knows, at a later date it may need a strong partner in Australia like Telecom.

Soon after Blount returned from his Christmas break in South Carolina, where he lived before moving to Australia, he received a call from Cowley. The two exchanged pleasantries and compared accounts of their festive season activities. Cowley's had been more business than pleasure, as he worked to put together the investors he wanted to take part in the Seven float. 'Frank, News is thinking about taking a substantial interest in the forthcoming float of the Seven Network,' Cowley told Blount. 'Would Telecom be interested in coming in too?'

Blount replied that he thought it was a good idea. He would need to sound out the proposal with the appropriate Telecom divisional head and do due diligence on the network. Any final decision would depend on the board. He said it would be a good opportunity for Telecom to learn about the content business from the inside. Blount also realised this would be the first time Telecom had ever invested in a listed company and that it might present political problems in Canberra. 'Sure, we'd be interested,' he told the News executive.

In the meantime, Deveson and Campbell were also fielding offers from potential trade buyers to generate some pricing tension between a trade sale and the alternative of a sale to the public through a float. They had retained Lloyds Corporate Services partners Tim Burroughs and Vicki McFadden, who had advised the Seven pair to pursue the two parallel strategies and eventually play one off against the other to get the best price or, alternatively, strike an arrangement that Deveson and Campbell might regard as being in the network's best interests.

As part of the float alternative, Deveson and Campbell hired Neville Miles at Ord Minnett, probably Australia's hottest investment banker after having orchestrated Kerry Packer's remarkable raid on Westpac. Ord over this period was also in the process of secretly building a stake in John Fairfax for one of its best clients.

The first trade offer for Seven came in late January 1993, typically from an industry 'bottom feeder', television merchandiser Michael Milne, who offered $575 million. Deveson, Campbell and their advisers were uncertain as to where he would get the money, so the offer was never taken seriously. Another offer of $685 million came soon after from a fiscally more muscular player, Seven regional broadcaster Sunshine Broadcasting Ltd, which was controlled by former Packer lieutenant Trevor Kennedy and Sydney businessman Sam Gazal.

Deveson and Campbell promised the bidders they would consider the offers, but all the body language from the pair suggested they wanted to float. The true test of their resolve to take their favoured course would soon come. In early February, Deveson received a phone call from Cowley. 'Ivan, News would be interested in taking some shares in Seven if you decide to float. Could we have a talk?'

Deveson got straight on the phone to Neville Miles at Ord Minnett. 'Neville, I've just had a call from Ken Cowley. He says News wants to take a position in Seven.'

Miles cautioned, 'Ivan, be very careful.'

Ivan Deveson was wary but trying not to show it when he was escorted into Cowley's fourth-floor Holt Street office. Cowley rose from his chair and walked around his desk to greet the Seven chairman, a short, chunky man with grey hair. In a corner of the room sat Mark Burrows. Deveson had every right to be nervous. He was walking into an ambush.

'As I mentioned to you on the phone the other day,' said Cowley, 'News is interested in taking a core holding in Seven if you decide to go ahead with a float.' Deveson reacted coolly. 'We've had some trade offers and we're weighing them up against the possibility of a float. I'm not so sure we're looking for any major investors to come in at this stage. Bob and I are changing the culture of the network and driving it well.' It quickly occurred to Cowley that Deveson was looking to keep his job. 'It would be good for a float if News came in Ivan,' Cowley asserted, with perceptibly more force in his tone.

Deveson sensed that Cowley wasn't about to be deflected easily. 'News would give the float enormous credibility. We could bring across Fox programming, which would strengthen the network,' Cowley persisted. 'And we understand there are a number of other significant investors who might be interested in taking shares in the float.' He mentioned West Australian Newspapers, Kerry Stokes and Telecom.

The Seven chairman was starting to get nervous, sensing a potential bloc of shareholders who would be friendly towards each other but not seen through the prism of the Corporations Law as being associated. In the case of shareholders considered to be associates because of past close business dealings, the corporate regulator would assume that they would act in concert and thus lump together their share parcels. In that case, their combined shareholdings would exceed the control threshold of 20 per cent, above which the shareholder(s) must make a full takeover bid.

These 'friends but not associates' could control the network, Deveson realised. Stokes he knew to be a close friend of Cowley's. 'This process is entirely in our hands,' he told Cowley. 'The banks have recapitalised and the amount we raise isn't an issue.' Cowley replied, with the hint of a threat, 'If you don't like it, there are other ways for News to approach it.'

Deveson left the meeting in no doubt that News would aggressively pursue its objective of taking a core stake in the network. He mightn't be able to stop Murdoch, but he was damned if he was going to let Kerry Stokes in as well, he thought as he got into a waiting car in the street below.

Kerry Packer had only one person in mind to replace Al Dunlap when 'Chainsaw' finished up at Consolidated Press Holdings in mid-February, taking a performance bonus reportedly worth $25 million.[2] He phoned Brian Powers at Hellman & Friedman's offices in San Francisco to ask the American whether he was interested in the managing director's job at CPH.

Packer knew and liked Powers and had tried to hire him in May 1991 just before Trevor Kennedy quit CPH to be chief executive of the Tourang consortium, which was planning to bid for Fairfax. Powers declined, preferring to stay with Hellman and Friedman, which he had just joined and which at that point was trying to find a way to invest in John Fairfax.

A New Yorker educated in economics at Yale and law at the University of Virginia, Powers was the epitome of the fast-thinking, fast-talking American investment banker. After graduating from Virginia and spending two years on a teaching fellowship at Stanford's law school, he managed a $US400 million portfolio of property and venture capital investments for the Ford Foundation's non-marketable investments, mostly property and venture capital interests. His fortunes rose sharply when an intermediary put him in touch with the New York-based expatriate Australian merchant banker Jim Wolfensohn, who hired him in 1981 as an investment banker at Wolfensohn's boutique advisory firm. As Wolfensohn was Kerry Packer's principal adviser in the US, it wasn't long before Powers met Packer. In 1985 he was head-hunted to run the big Hong Kong property group, Jardine Matheson, one of the territory's most powerful positions, before being lured back to New York by Wolfensohn in 1989. After another two-year stint there, he accepted an offer as a general partner at the San

Francisco-based Hellman & Friedman early in 1991, as the US investment bank was casting its eye over the rich media interests in the Fairfax group. Fairfax was attractive because its underlying newspaper businesses were making more money than at any time in its 160-year history. It had been tripped into receivership because Warwick Fairfax had borrowed too much to finance his buyout, and the group was struggling to service its debt of $1.65 billion.

Powers knew Packer had long hankered after Fairfax and saw him as Hellman & Friedman's best way into the group. He called Packer to ask if he was interested in joining forces with Hellman & Friedman to bid for the print group. Packer suggested to Powers that he fly to London, where the Australian had just taken up residence in his suite of rooms at the Savoy Hotel for the English polo season. By the time Powers called, Packer was already well down the track of setting up a consortium and was in the process of bringing in Conrad Black's Daily Telegraph group and US bondholders owed $450 million by Fairfax. The bondholders had taken legal action against Fairfax after it went into receivership in December 1990 and it looked like they would lose their money. Seizing an opportunity to parlay a place at the table as much for himself as for the bondholders, Malcolm Turnbull persuaded the US investors to join a bidding consortium and exchange the money owed to them for shares in the company after it was acquired.

The bondholders' presence in Tourang gave the consortium the power to end the litigation in the event it won Fairfax. This would be the pivotal factor in persuading the Fairfax banks to accept its offer, which was lower in gross terms that the bid by Irishman Tony O'Reilly's Dublin-based Independent Newspapers. Although Packer was eventually forced to quit Tourang only weeks before it won Fairfax, Hellman & Friedman emerged with a 5 per cent stake in the form of non-voting debentures in the print group. Powers was given a seat on the Fairfax board, which he still held when Packer called him in February 1993.

Powers was more amenable to Packer's second approach. He said he'd think about it. 'What are you doing over the next week or so?' Packer asked him. Powers said he was hoping to spend a few days skiing at Park City, Utah, where he had a lodge. Packer said he was about to fly to the US and asked if he could join him at Park City. 'Sure,' Powers told Packer, 'I'll look forward to seeing you.'

The next day, Packer was on board the DC8 airliner which he had fitted out both for his personal use and to fly his Ellerston polo teams between Argentina, Australia and the UK. As Al Dunlap cleared his desk at Park Street, Packer was heading for Salt Lake City – coincidentally only a 45-minute drive from Park City – for talks with Jon Huntsman, a rich young American with extensive chemical industry interests. Packer was contemplating putting his Australian-based Chemplex polystyrene business into a joint venture with Huntsman, to seek opportunities globally in this unpopular, but profitable, industry.

His discussions with Huntsman over, Packer took a hired limousine through the mountains to Park City, an old silver mining town which had been developed into a trendy ski resort and commuter dormitory town for Salt Lake City. Packer and Powers talked about the challenges that Packer saw for his group in 1993, in particular the imminent arrival of satellite pay TV and the desirability of setting up a consortium which would snare the best programming and dominate the new industry. Packer also told Powers he had started acquiring a pivotal shareholding in John Fairfax through Neville Miles at Ord Minnett. Powers was also a friend of Miles. Conrad Black was pressuring the Labor Government to be allowed to lift his interest from 15 per cent to at least 25 per cent – or higher – to cement his control. But the Canadian had no chance, with Packer's lobbyist Peter Barron having convinced the Government this would not be a good idea. Conrad Black, Barron told Keating and Treasurer John Dawkins, was a conservative Cold War warrior who was no friend to Labor. Besides, there were willing Australian buyers who also wanted to invest in the group.

Packer told Powers his plans depended to some extent on the result of the looming Federal Election three weeks away. If the conservative coalition won, as indicated by the opinion polls, then it had promised to review Labor's cross-media ownership rules which blocked him buying Fairfax while he controlled the Nine Network. Packer's legal advice was that if Black were allowed to go to 25 per cent, then even under Labor's cross-media ownership rule, he could go higher than 15 per cent, so long as he didn't exercise any influence over Fairfax. He was taking an each-way bet. It would be an exciting and eventful year. Packer reiterated his request that Powers join him in Australia.

Powers realised he would not be able to decline this time, and agreed to accept Packer's offer. His long-term tenure would be subject to his wife Paula liking Australia. Packer headed back to Sydney, and Powers followed a few days later. He started at Park

Street on Monday, February 21,[3] although CPH did not publicly announce his appointment until March 16, three weeks later.

It was 8am in mid-February and Mark Burrows was getting ready to drive into the city. He was eating toast while walking around his home, Trahlee – which he had bought from businessman Ian Joye in 1989 for $4 million – as he gathered together papers and documents he would need that day. The city was just coming back to life again after a torpid summer holiday that had taken its movers and shakers to France and Colorado skiing, to Palm Beach 40 km to the north, or to Noosa and other Queensland resorts. Burrows was having his breakfast while he waited for some visitors who had just rung to say they were on their way. When he answered the knock on the door, Kerry Stokes and his adviser, the merchant banker Ross Grant, were on his doorstep. Stokes had started his working life as a television repair man in Melbourne and, through a mixture of good fortune and good judgment, had become wealthy through property development, the media and as Australia's largest caterpillar heavy equipment dealer in the country's main mining State, Western Australia.

Burrows had been told a few weeks earlier by Stokes' close friend Ken Cowley that the Perth-based entrepreneur was a potential starter in the Seven float. Stokes wanted to impress directly on Burrows, who had been doing most of the negotiations with Ivan Deveson and Bob Campbell, that he was very keen to be part of the float. He would take any amount of Seven he could get – 5 per cent, 10 per cent, or 15 per cent. Burrows told him that he had met some resistance from Deveson to the prospect of Stokes' involvement in Seven. He said that Deveson had suggested to him that Stokes was too close to News for his liking. This drew a laugh from Stokes and Grant.

Burrows could only assure Stokes that he would attempt to persuade Deveson to drop his opposition, that he had nothing to fear from Stokes. In reality, Deveson had everything to fear. Deveson had correctly detected that he wouldn't last five minutes if the group being put together by News got the positions they wanted in the float. Stokes would have been chairman.

At their next meeting, Deveson dug in his heels and told Burrows and Cowley there was no room for Stokes. He had made up his mind that Stokes was part of a grab for control of Seven. He was contemptuous of Cowley's suggestion that Stokes would be chairman. Cowley's plans of putting together a consortium took another setback a few days after this meeting when West Australian Newspapers pulled out, declining to take up the 5 per cent that Deveson had agreed to. It was a costly decision and was to cost WAN close to $30 million. Had it proceeded and taken up its ear-marked stake at $2 a share, it would have been in a position to sell later for a price two-and-a-half times its entry cost.

Deveson accepted News and Telecom, however, taking 15 per cent and 10 per cent respectively. He was particularly attracted to the possibility of getting better access to programming from News's Fox studio and television production houses, programs such as *Beverly Hills 90210* and *Melrose Place*, which would attract the 16 to 39-year-old audience that advertisers liked so much.

By early March, the key participants in the Seven float had virtually been put in place, although Frank Blount would need more time to get the thumbs up from Telstra senior management's due diligence assessment of the network, and from his board. Stokes would be pushed out of the picture for the time being, but he would return later to exact his revenge on Deveson.

This would be the first foray by Telecom into the sharemarket. It also marked the formation of a powerful new alliance between Frank Blount and Ken Cowley and between Telecom and News Corporation.


Despite Labor's poor showing in the opinion polls for most of the Federal Election campaign, Cowley was confident Keating could win. His perception on the matter was driven by News's commercial imperatives. Cowley wanted and needed Labor and Keating to win. He had known Keating for many years, but drew closer to him during his six months in the wilderness between leadership challenges. The News Limited chairman regarded Keating as the best political leader in Australia, with a vision for the future role of the country in the region. He and Keating became good friends in the lead-up to the December 1991 leadership coup and, during the tense weeks of the 1993 election campaign, when most pundits had written Labor off, Cowley continued to maintain privately that Keating could, and would, win.


Steve Cosser had flown from France to Australia with his wife Sue and two young children, and the family was staying at the Medina apartments in Rushcutters Bay during March. They had been to the wedding of a former nanny on the afternoon of March 13, and when they got back to the apartment that evening, Cosser turned on the television to see how the election was going.

He was stunned to hear the commentators, including back-bench Senator Graham Richardson, talking excitedly about a swing to Labor and the likelihood of a win by his party. Keating appeared to be about to win an election that had been regarded widely as unwinnable for Labor. Labor had closed a two-party preferred deficit behind the Liberal-National coalition of 6.5 points in the Newspoll taken the weekend Keating had announced the election, to a two-point winning margin in the poll that counted.[4] In the last days of the campaign, Keating hammered home at every opportunity, on radio and television, the perils of the 15 per cent goods and services tax (GST) at the centre of Hewson's tax reform package. By studiously ignoring the personal tax cuts and elimination of oil excise and State payroll taxes that were also part of the coalition's proposed changes, Keating persuaded the electorate to turn a blind eye to his own passionate advocacy of a consumption tax in 1985, and to reject Fightback and Hewson. Cosser's aggressive advertising campaign against Keating and Bob Collins over their MDS auction backflip had little or no impact, except to make him a liability to his corporate interests. Keating was furious with Cosser over the ads, particularly as the former Treasurer had saved his skin just two years earlier.

As Cosser sank deeper into despair as the night wore on, the phone calls started to come in from friends like Peter Gray and Ross Grant, ribbing him over the result and trying to make light of the fact that Keating and Collins would make life for himself and his company very difficult. But his enemies weren't confined to Canberra. His provocative ads also attacked the media barons, Packer and Murdoch. He didn't name them, but it was clear who he was talking about. In one ad published on March 5, dominated by a re-touched photo of flies buzzing around a dead fish with Bob Collins' head, Cosser placed a riddle at the bottom.

> Why does the Keating Government want you to wait three years for fewer channels of Pay TV than you can have today?
> Why do they want you to pay $1800 rather than $250 for the equipment?
> Why do they want you to buy a 3ft to 5ft dish when you can have one which is just 3 inches?
> Answer: Because you are not one of the 'mates'.

In the light of the election result, the advertising campaign clearly had had little effect, but the advertisements offended people in some sections of the industry. Cosser and Australis were becoming a nuisance, despite the fact that they had no business thanks to the Keating/Collins decision of January 28. Cosser knew that he was finished in Australia. His company, Australis Media, would get its pay TV business up and running at some stage, but it was unlikely he would be there to achieve it.

While Paul Keating and the Labor Party faithful gathered at the Bankstown Sports Club to celebrate 'the sweetest victory of all', the party was breaking up for a despondent Liberal Party, which had arranged a black-tie dinner at the Intercontinental Hotel in Sydney's central business district. The country's most powerful businessmen had gathered to celebrate John Hewson's anticipated victory. The chairman of Coca Cola Amatil and director of John Fairfax, Dean Wills, gave his invitation to the taxi driver who drove him home. The following day, while watching television coverage of the disappointed faces at the Intercontinental Hotel, Paul Keating noticed Kerry Packer's son James in the crowd. 'I thought the Packers were with us,' Keating said to himself. 'Heaven knows, we've given them enough.'

Brian Powers hardly had time to get his feet under his new desk when Packer suggested they go for a walk down the street to meet Frank Blount. With Labor returned to office, there would be little chance of a change to the cross-media ownership rules in the foreseeable future, so Packer's ambitions on Fairfax would be stunted for the time being. At least Conrad Black wasn't going to be allowed to go beyond 25 per cent, and Packer was able to go to at least 15 per cent legally, and perhaps a little more. He intended to test the 15 per cent threshold, which his legal advisers said meant very little. The key issue in the Act was influence, not an arbitrary shareholding limit. Black would keep. Today, Packer and his new right-hand man had more exciting matters to discuss with the Telecom chief.

Blount had taken Packer's call only a few minutes earlier. He told Packer, yes, he would like to have a meeting. Packer and Powers walked the city block to Telecom's Sydney headquarters in Elizabeth Street. As they stepped into the foyer they couldn't help but notice that workmen were attaching Telecom's stylish new 'T' logo in stainless steel on the entrance wall of the building as part of the re-badging for its future name, Telstra.

In Blount's 15th-floor corner office overlooking the city and the leafy carpet of Port Jackson figs and oak trees of Hyde Park below, Packer outlined his preferred approach to pay television. He wanted Blount's reaction. Packer was well briefed by his executive assistant, Lynton Taylor, who had discussed the issue with most of the potential players, including Bob Mansfield at Optus, and Martin Hannes at Continental Cablevision. Packer reminded Blount that the satellite licence auctions were coming up, but in the long term, he said, cable would be the best technology because it permitted interactivity and could also be used for telephony.

He wasn't telling Blount anything the American didn't know, but Packer said it would be essential that the most powerful media groups join with Telstra to pool their resources to make pay TV a success. This would enable them to invest in the best programming and have a mix of delivery systems: satellite initially, and then cable later with perhaps some MDS. He also said there was a chance that Optus might wish to roll out its own cable network. Optus was in discussions with Continental Cablevision, which had been trialing new technology in the US which would allow telephony and pay TV to be delivered on the same cable.

Packer insisted to Blount that unless the industry agreed to cooperate with the cable roll-outs, it would be beset by huge costs and heavy losses for years to come. Ideally, Telstra and Optus should divide up the country into regions and each would exclusively cable those areas and have interconnection agreements which would give each company access to the other's system. Blount was cool to this suggestion. Telstra was considering the next step of cabling to the home, but it was likely to be a common carrier, and would charge other content providers to use its cable. Telstra was not planning to go into the content business at that stage. Packer's suggestion seemed also to Blount to have trade practices problems.

Still, Blount was attracted to Packer's idea that the country's main media groups such as his own Nine Network, the other commercial networks and News Corporation, join Telstra in a consortium to explore a pay TV strategy. Blount didn't think it necessary to tell Packer that he had been approached by News to take an investment in the rival Seven Network. The discussions were at a very early stage, anyway.

The Telstra chief agreed to see Packer again in a few days, over at Packer's office this time, to further develop his idea of an unbeatable pay TV consortium. The group would later be dubbed by the industry as the Packer-Murdoch-Telstra syndicate, or PMT for short.

Martin Hannes was a regular visitor to Bob Mansfield's office in the Optus tower in North Sydney over this period. Hannes and Mansfield were old friends who were in the same class at Barker College on Sydney's north shore in the 1960s and played rugby together. Mansfield was aware that Telstra was planning to extend its cable roll-out into the suburbs and was anxious that Optus not be left behind.

Mansfield's first year at the phone company was devoted to establishing its mobile and long-distance phone business, and he had succeeded beyond expectations. Mansfield drove Optus's clever marketing to grab, by March 1993, nearly 30 per cent of the mobile phone market, or more than 50,000 customers, from when it started its analogue service in June the previous year. And it was starting to make inroads into Telstra's dominance of the long-distance call market. By March, with its interstate and overseas service in operation only four months, Optus had reached 7 per cent of the market and 500,000 customers, although many of these were only occasional users of the Optus service.[5]

Mansfield and his board couldn't afford to be complacent or pause to reflect. They had to tackle the young company's most testing and potentially costly challenge yet, and that was to decide the best way to compete for revenue and market share in the biggest of the telephony markets, local calls, worth about $5 billion in annual sales. Developments in telecommunications were occurring so rapidly that if Optus stood still it would be swamped by its competitor. It had to run hard just to stand still, but to move ahead, Mansfield would need to drive the company with breathtaking speed.

The easiest and cheapest strategy would be for Optus to strike an access deal with Telstra to use its copper wire network. But if it took this route it would remain subservient to Telstra and be forced to negotiate access to the Telstra network from a position of weakness at rates dictated by Telstra. Mansfield knew that Optus had little choice but to explore the option of setting up its own network if it was going to compete seriously in this large market. Unless Optus was prepared to bite the bullet, it could never be a gatekeeper to the home offering telephony and services such as data, Internet, and pay TV.

Mansfield was also aware that Optus had a five-year window when it would be Telstra's only competitor. After July 1997, the industry would be deregulated and open to all comers. If it was to lay out a new cable network, the more it could put down before that deadline, the better positioned it would be in a deregulated environment.

He was greatly encouraged by Hannes, who briefed him regularly on progress Continental Cablevision was making with its trial of using telephone and pay TV signals down the same fibre optic cable. It would be an enormous technological breakthrough if Continental Cablevision could make this work. Until then, phone signals interfered with video and audio being carried on the same cable. To overcome this, the UK's second carrier, Mercury, used a 'Siamese' system in which copper wire carrying the phone signal was spiralled around the outside of coaxial or fibre optic cable to enable the carrier to offer both phone and broadband services on the 'same' cable. This was a cumbersome and strictly short-term solution only. Hannes told Mansfield it was only a matter of time before the equipment was developed to allow telephony and audio/video signals to be carried at the same time on the one cable.

Bill Schleyer, in Boston, was urging Hannes to find a partner to open the way for Continental Cablevision to get into the pay TV business in Australia. Hannes had spoken to Steve Cosser, but decided MDS was not the way to go, because its reach was too limited. Continental Cablevision would be a bidder for both satellite licences, but with cable starting to loom large on the industry horizon, this would be the most suitable technology. Bob Mansfield wanted Optus involved in cable to give him local call telephony and broadband services, using pay TV as a carrot to attract subscribers for phone and other on-line services. Cost would be the main hurdle. A full national roll-out might cost $7 billion or more. A more limited roll-out, targeting affluent suburbs in the metropolitan areas, would be less than half that amount. To reduce costs and ensure greater coverage of the population, Optus had been toying with a proposal for regional monopolies, as was the case in the US. Optus would cable one area and Telstra a neighbouring region and the two would negotiate access to each other's systems to achieve near-national coverage. Still, this was a concept for refinement later. In the immediate term, it was clear that the objectives of Optus and Continental Cablevision were complementary. The two groups were ideally matched.

With each day that passed, Optus and Telstra edged closer to the decisions that would ultimately set them on course for a mighty set-piece battle of wills and budgets. It would be fought on the nature strips and footpaths of the suburbs, in Hollywood over movie rights, and in the committee rooms of the sporting codes which would provide the endless hours of sports programming deemed essential for the voracious appetites of multi-channel pay TV services.

Ultimately too, there could only be one winner from this engagement. One would fall by the wayside, financially spent and its programming line-up at threat. As the two phone companies started to shape up for their toe-to-toe struggle, the newly-elected Labor Government prepared to auction its two satellite licences and on the advice of the Department of Communications had set an April 28 deadline for bids.


Albert Hadid made his way across windswept Goulburn Street on a late March autumn evening with his hairdresser, Mark Montgomery, towards the front entrance of the Southern Cross Hotel. It was a nondescript pink building in a part of Sydney where the central business district melts into the seediness of Surry Hills and the noise, shabbiness and decay of the precinct around Central Station.

Hadid was running late and had agreed reluctantly to go to this meeting. He was persuaded by Montgomery, who had good contacts with a number of people looking to get involved in the pay TV industry. Montgomery had only discovered a few months earlier that he had a half-brother, Leo Gray, who was a barrister specialising in media law and a former licensing officer with the old Australian Broadcasting Tribunal.

Hadid was a cautious person by nature, but Montgomery had convinced him through his infectious enthusiasm to talk to these people and perhaps back them financially if they could persuade him that their ideas were sound.

Born in the village of El-Koura in northern Lebanon, Hadid was the son of Yasser Hadid, a gunsmith who migrated to Australia in 1964. His mother, Minor, worked as a process worker at the WD & HO Wills cigarette factory and the family lived in Paddington, before the suburb became gentrified and trendy. Hadid was educated the hard way at Darlinghurst Primary and Cleveland Street High School where, as a young migrant boy, he felt it wise for his survival to do some boxing training. He had to defend himself with his fists more than once.

At Sydney University, where he studied computer science and pure mathematics, Hadid developed a keen interest outside of lecture and tutorial hours in film-making, eventually becoming president of the University Filmmakers Society. He accepted he was not destined for stardom as an actor, but enjoyed the behind-the-camera logistics work as a producer or director of the experimental films the society made. Hadid also accepted that – like Bruce Lee, who disciplined himself to become the world's best kung fu practitioner to get into acting – he would probably have to own the studio to deal himself into film-making.

After graduating, Hadid needed to make money to support his celluloid ambitions and got a job as a salesman for Burroughs, the US mainframe computer maker, then worked for Sperry Univac, before the two companies merged to form Unisys. During his rounds, he did some business with a rag trader, Stanley Falinski, who was impressed with Hadid's salesmanship and offered to set him up in partnership buying personal computers in bulk, then retailing them. Hadid quit Sperry and he and Falinski concentrated on the Osborne computer brand, building their business in a three-storey terrace building in Riley Street, East Sydney, into one of Australia's biggest outlets. When the US parent got into trouble in 1983, Hadid and Falinski took over the brand in Australia, imported the parts from Taiwan and assembled the computers in Sydney. The business thrived until 1987, when Hadid and Falinksi fell out and went their separate ways.

Hadid made his first killing in 1985, when he negotiated with the Boston-based Comdex computer trade fair group to bring the exhibition – normally held each year in Las Vegas – to Australia. He was able to strike a partnership deal with Comdex, but the partnership soured and Comdex bought Hadid out for $250,000, regarded at the time as a substantial amount of money. Using the money he was able to expand his dealership into the Epson, IBM, Compaq and Novell software brands. He moved his shopfront to busy Parramatta Road at inner-western Stanmore and traded under the Microland business name. His office, continually cluttered with paperwork, was on the first floor of the building. It overlooked a small car park and the motley corrugated-iron roofs and old brick chimneys of Stanmore. Although he could afford far better premises in a smart suburb, Hadid preferred the dull ordinariness of the inner west to the distractions of a harbour view. It kept him focused on the reality of life.

Hadid developed a reputation as a litigant, although he maintained he was only standing up for his rights. In 1992, he sued Epson and accepted a $1 million settlement offer after the two become embroiled in a dispute over the ability of dealers to advertise individually. Epson had a policy of not allowing dealers to advertise, preferring to conduct its own national advertising. When it appeared to allow a handful of dealers to do their own advertising, yet insist that Microland continue to adhere to the policy, Hadid sued.

The same year he took the US software company WordStar to court when he believed he had a verbal agreement to be sole distributor of the group's software products and it later began distributing through other outlets, including Jodie Rich's Imagineering. Hadid's barrister told him there was no chance of making a verbal agreement stick in court, but he persuaded the judge that the deal was firm and was awarded $4.5 million in damages. Hadid emerged from his years in the computer business a relatively wealthy person, but a demanding and prickly partner ready to go to court if he felt his rights were being trampled.

Hadid and Montgomery walked through the Southern Cross Hotel's reception area to a private lounge, where he came amongst about 10 people milling around a whiteboard. Montgomery introduced Hadid to the people called together primarily to meet him. Hadid pressed the flesh among the group. His main interest remained making films to help any pay TV licence holder meet local content levels, set by the Government at 10 per cent. While most of the people in the room were interested in manufacturing or importing MDS equipment and had formed a company called Hi Vision to supply MDS pay TV providers such as Australis Media. There was little common interest between Hadid and the Hi Vision group, yet the discussion was very lively. At one point, a Dr Simon Gadir, a slim, curly-haired man in his late 40s, suggested that if the group could marshal the resources, then perhaps it should bid for the satellite licences.

Hadid, who the group clearly regarded as a potential source of funds for whatever venture they embarked upon, said they needed to be sure about the business side of a licence bid. 'Otherwise you'd be kidding yourselves and the rest of the world,' he told them. Gadir wasn't discouraged. He had done a business plan two years earlier for the cinema and film distribution group Village Road-show, which had been keen at one stage to pursue pay TV. His plan was based on the experience of the French Canal+ group, which started with a one-channel MDS service, but later built the service as it became more profitable. Canal+ could afford the luxury of starting modestly because the free-to-air television in France is so appalling. The concept was a good one, however. After the meeting broke up, Gadir approached Hadid and asked him if he was interested. 'I could be, but I'm not sure we could do it . . . I'm definitely interested if I can be convinced.'

Gadir grabbed two others out of the group – Ian Wright, a former Navy telecommunications technician, and Leo Gray – and with Hadid they took the 15-minute drive back to Hadid's shop at Stanmore.

Hadid was beginning to be convinced, but suggested they put some of Gadir's ideas to a partner at Price Waterhouse, Frank Fischl, whom Hadid knew. Fischl introduced the men to another partner, Tony Gall, who agreed to check the credibility of their projections and assumptions.

Hadid also wanted to get some advice from someone who knew the media industry. About a week later, three weeks before the bids were due on April 28, he rang Malcolm Turnbull. By this time, Hadid had decided he could not work with the whole Hi Vision group. Their objectives were too diverse. He decided it best to set up his own group and asked Gadir to join him. Gadir, who knew more about pay TV than anyone in the group, had become disenchanted with Hi Vision because he felt he wasn't being listened to, and agreed to join Hadid. They would pursue his proposal to bid for one of the licences, using a company called United Communications Pty Ltd (UCOM) that Hadid had set up late in 1992 to house any investments in the media, including pay TV.

Hadid agreed with Wright and the Hi Vision board (which included Montgomery), that UCOM would cooperate with Hi Vision on every aspect of their bids, including the crucial business plan and assumptions, but they would not be able to collude on their final tenders. Hi Vision was interested mostly in the less-restricted B licence, which was open to all comers, whereas Hadid focused on the A licence, open only to new players in the media industry in Australia. It would be cheaper, for a start. The two groups would move together towards the auction, but go their separate ways once the tender closed. That was the intention, at least.

When he arrived the following day at Turnbull's offices at 1 Chifley Square, Hadid was impressed that Turnbull was accompanied by Neville Wran, the former NSW State Premier who was his partner in Turnbull & Partners, and his colleague Cass O'Connor, a highly knowledgable media analyst who had spent many years with stockbroking firm Bain & Co before joining Turnbull in 1987.

Based on his initial workings with Gadir, Hadid told Turnbull UCOM was preparing to bid into the high $100 million range for the A licence and that it believed it would cost about $300 million all up to get the service running. Hadid and Gadir assumed 2.2 per cent penetration of Australia's 5.66 million homes by their service after 12 months, rising to 30.7 per cent in year 10. Total costs in the first year, including the licence fee, would be $205 million, and $280 million in the second, when programming ($71 million) and marketing ($25.3 million) would be the major costs. They estimated gross revenue would rise from about $42.2 million in the first year to $793 million in the 10th year. The business would become $197 million cashflow positive in year five. Hadid explained that he and Gadir were still refining their figures to work out what they were prepared to pay for the licence.

The *Broadcasting Services Act* permitted the A and B licence holders to jointly own a company which would operate the back-room functions of their businesses. These included the subscriber management systems for both licences, customer service and the physical transmission of the programming, thus saving them tens of millions of dollars in costs. However, the two licensees would have to market their services and programming packages separately to give at least the outward impression that they were competing.

Hadid proposed that under his plan, subscribers would lease the set-top boxes separately through a finance company, thus relieving the business of the capital cost of buying them and making an additional charge on the rental cost to cover the cost of the set-top box. Hadid said this would be expected to keep the disconnection rate, or 'churn', to just 3 per cent in the first year, rising to 12 per cent after three years. The churn rates were based mainly on the US experience.

Hadid and Gadir also assumed some competition from MDS and slow-down in subscription growth with the arrival of cable five or so years later. On his figuring, Hadid reckoned the licence was worth considerably more than the more established media players, who were more cautious in their estimates and would bid accordingly.

Turnbull pointed out that quite a few major players had also come through his door looking for an opportunity to take part in pay TV. These included the big US cable groups Comcast, Continental Cablevision and Cox Communications. Also, Kerry Packer and Rupert Murdoch were likely contenders. He had not been retained by any of these people, but he knew of their interest. If any of the big players decided individually or in partnership to go for the licences, then a small player like Albert Hadid would be pushed aside in the rush.

He suggested that if UCOM wanted to win the backing of Australian institutional investors to help finance the heavy costs of setting up the business, then it should find an American cable company or bank with knowledge of the industry to support the figures that Hadid and Gadir had cobbled together. This would give their business plan more credibility. Hadid said he would, and also asked Turnbull if his firm could act as an adviser. The two were keen to work together, but agreed that the relationship should remain informal at that stage, and that they should keep talking.

But the UCOM pair needed more information. Gadir had met the president of the US Cable Association, a tough but affable woman named Margaret Combes, in 1990 while doing his pay TV research for Village Roadshow. She possessed encyclopaedic knowledge of subscription television. Gadir had kept in touch with her as he continued to pursue his interest in pay TV after leaving Village Roadshow. The morning after their meeting with Turnbull, Gadir and Hadid rang Combes at her Boston office. Gadir introduced her over the speaker phone to Hadid. After an exchange of pleasantries, Hadid explained that they were intending to bid for one of the satellite licences with a reasonable chance of success. His group needed a US investor or partner to make their venture attractive to investors.

Combes suggested two US cable groups she knew were looking at Australia, Continental Cablevision and Time Warner. Hadid said he already knew of their interest and intended to talk to them. He also asked her some questions about the US experience with rates of subscriber penetration, pricing based on net disposable income and market trends generally. Hadid's contact with Combes would prove critical to the fate of both the A and B licences over the coming months.

Peter Frame was intrigued to receive Albert Hadid's call. Time Warner had also been preparing to take part in the satellite licence auction. Frame was in regular contact with Fred Vierra, international division head with John Malone's TeleCommunications Inc (TCI). With TCI and another large US cable group, Comcast, Frame was contemplating making joint bids for both A and B licences. They had also negotiated with the Australian electronics group, AWA Ltd, to come in as a local partner. As total foreign ownership was limited to 35 per cent, each of the US companies would own 11.66 per cent and AWA ostensibly 65 per cent. The dominant members would clearly be TCI, the world's largest cable (ie, subscription TV) company, and Time Warner, which was perhaps the globe's most powerful programming house, boasting the Warner Bros studios, interests in CNN and the MGM studio library, and extensive magazine titles, including *Time*. The Time Warner Cable division was also second only to TCI in the US in terms of cable subscriber numbers. It would not be possible to put together two more richly endowed media groups.

'To be honest, I've never heard of you,' Frame told Hadid. But despite his misgivings, Frame agreed to meet him. The American took the view that it was best to be informed about his potential rivals in this auction. 'Let's meet tomorrow at the Regent,' he suggested.

Frame was waiting on a leather lounge in the atrium of the Regent Hotel, a few steps up George Street from Sydney's famous Rocks district, when Hadid and Ian Wright walked past the concierge holding open the hotel's heavy glass doors. 'What are you guys up to?' he asked of the UCOM-Hi Vision pair after they introduced themselves. What followed was a game of cat and mouse, with Frame trying to tease out the level of bidding Hadid and Wright may be contemplating and whether they had any backers of substance. Hadid wanted to assess whether Frame was going to go for it in the auction. Frame suggested that it might be possible for the two groups to do business together. As they parted, neither party was any the wiser, but Hadid was fairly confident that Time Warner would not be bidding anywhere near UCOM's estimate of what the A licence was worth. Frame thought Hadid was very committed but, without a substantial backer, would get nowhere. 'Now I've met you, I'll never forget you again,' Frame told Hadid cryptically.

Hadid's next call was to Martin Hannes at Continental Cablevision. As he drove along Chatswood's Eastern Valley Way to

Continental Cablevision's offices in a 1980s semi-industrial commercial block, Hadid was impressed by its modesty. There was no Harbour vista here. An indoor cricket centre and a clutch of tennis courts over the road were the salient features of this locale. It was akin to the suburban ordinariness of the clutter of chimney pots and rusted corrugated iron rooftops that greeted Hadid when he looked out from his Stanmore office.

Hadid asked him whether Continental Cablevision would be interested in joining UCOM if it won the A licence. Hannes said yes, he was interested. It depended on the cost of the licence and how well the numbers stacked up. He wasn't giving much away. Like Frame, he was far more cautious on the value of the licences than the value levels at which Hadid was hinting. As a foreign group without any Australian media interests, Continental Cablevision was in a position to bid for either or both licences.

The two agreed to keep talking. When Hadid went back to Turnbull to report on his meetings and phone calls, he commented that no-one seemed to be prepared to commit. Everyone was being very cautious and giving nothing away. Turnbull replied that they were all talking to other people. Neville Wran chipped in, 'It's like a country dance. Everyone is standing around the walls and no-one's game to go into the middle and start dancing.'

It was 8am on a sunny March morning. Kerry Packer was hosting a meeting on a patio overlooking the lawns of his family compound in Victoria Road in the heart of Australia's wealthiest suburb, Bellevue Hill. He and his guests were sitting around a large table laid out with fruit and cereal while a waiter took orders for hot breakfast. With him were his son James, Brian Powers, Peter Barron and Lynton Taylor, and the chairman of News Limited, Ken Cowley, and his special projects executive, Malcolm Colless.

Packer was pressing on with his objective of establishing an unbeatable consortium to set up and run pay TV in Australia. He had invited Cowley and Colless to his home to formally invite News to join his group. He also wanted to seek Cowley's views on whether it would be sensible to ask Telstra, too. Packer said he had already had some conversations with Frank Blount, and the Telstra chief was receptive to the idea. Cowley agreed it would be a good idea. He couldn't reveal that he, too, had been talking to Blount on another matter – taking an interest with News in the soon-to-float Seven Network. Telstra was still going through its typically lengthy process of making up its corporate mind whether or not to join News in Seven, so it would have been unwise for Cowley to have said anything at this early stage. Packer would not have been pleased to learn that Australia's largest media group and its dominant telecommunications company were about to take pivotal interests in Nine's main rival network. But today the subject was pay TV.

It was agreed then, Telstra would be invited into the consortium. Cowley suggested it might be a good idea to invite Seven, which had the programming rights to the 1996 Olympics and the rights to the popular Australian Football League. Packer added, 'We may as well get Ten in as well.'

The discussion around Packer's breakfast table that early autumn morning didn't dwell on specifics, but ranged across the broad issues of pay TV. Packer was close to marshalling the country's most powerful media and communications groups. Such a consortium would include the three commercial television networks, the country's largest newspaper publisher (which also happened to own Hollywood's 20th Century Fox studio), and the dominant telephone carrier, which was within 12 months of starting to roll out cable through Australia's cities and towns. Packer's group possessed the financial firepower and the movie and sports programming rights that would leave no room for anyone else. All that was required now was to decide how much to bid for the B satellite licence, which Packer expected would be the dominant partner in any cooperative venture with the holder of the weaker A licence. Rather than two four-channel services, the likelihood was that the two licence holders would cooperate to the extent that they would both show the same eight-channel program package.

Grabbing the first-mover advantage that satellite offered was crucial to the new consortium's objective of crushing all potential rivals. But from the day of the breakfast at his house, Kerry Packer made it clear his new consortium would not over-pay for the licence. Packer wasn't going to pour money into a black hole and wait years for a return. The bid would be a sensible one and take account of the fact that it would cost at least another $200 million to $300 million to set up the business. When the consortium was finally announced on April 23, after much anticipation in the marketplace, and just five days before bids were due, it sent a powerful signal to other aspirants: keep away, this business belongs to Kerry Packer, Rupert Murdoch and their powerful new ally, Telstra. Who else would dare bid now?

Albert Hadid was becoming increasingly confident after his discussions with Price Waterhouse's Tony Gall that the A licence he intended to bid for was worth up to $200 million. The night before tenders were due to be lodged with the Department of Communications in Canberra he worked into the early hours calculating his offers. Like most of the satellite bidders, Hadid knew that he could offer more than one bid. The tender terms set by the departmental task force headed by a senior official, Chris Dalton, were remarkably free of conditions and limitations. It was the same group which sold the second carrier's licence and Aussat. For the satellite auction, it deliberately refrained from including any high barriers such as a large deposit or onerous terms which would discourage new players from bidding. The main condition was a deposit of $500 for each bid and, clearly, payment of the full bid amount 30 days after the Australian Broadcasting Authority and Trade Practices Commission had completed their inquiries into the winning tenderers.

Hi Vision and UCOM were to apply the concept of 'more than one bid' very aggressively. Instead of following the normal auction practice of bidding progressively higher to win, Hadid would turn the process upside down. He had been exploring the concept of lodging multiple bids cascading from his highest offer down to relatively low numbers, using different companies. If he was unable to attract support at the highest offer, then as the bids fell lower, he would inevitably find a backer at some stage. His strategy would only work so long as he remained in control of the bidding process. Hadid had made some tentative inquiries with the Department of Communications and the ABA, but did not want to fully reveal his hand. He called Mark Montgomery – who was driving across Sydney Harbour Bridge at the time – to ask him to check with his half-brother Leo Gray whether the idea of lodging multiple, cascading bids was legal and to suggest that Hi Vision should consider the idea. Gray was a specialist media barrister and a consultant to the two-volume Butterworths' reference work, *Communications Law and Policy in Australia*. Before Montgomery had a chance to call Gray, his mobile phone rang again. In a remarkable coincidence, it was Gray on the phone. 'I've been thinking about this and it looks like we can put in more than one bid,' said the lawyer. 'We should get together and discuss it.'

The one uncertainty about the tactic of allowing bids to fall lower was that Gray and Hadid needed to be confident that theirs was the next highest bid.

Brian Powers, also a lawyer by training, warned Kerry Packer in the days leading up to the auction that it was possible some high, speculative bids might be lodged. 'They should all be forced to pay a deposit of $20 million,' Packer told his chief executive. 'That'll sort out who's serious and who's not.'

As he played with some numbers on a notepad in his office, Hadid started with the $200 million top end valuation for the A licence supported by Price Waterhouse's workings. He took off 10 per cent he regarded as a contingency margin, then a bit more to come up with a figure of $175 million. He thought most of the bidding would be in the $30 million to $40 million range for both licences, but there were sure to be others like him who believed the licences were worth more. He added $2 million to his number, then $1,000 to produce his best offer of $177.01 million, just in case someone else bid $175 million, or even $177 million. The extra $1,000 might prove crucial.

Then he came down in $20 million increments for the next four bids – $157.01 million, $137.01 million, $117.01 million, and $97.01 million. He changed the pattern to $10 million increments below this number because he felt sure he would encounter competition below $100 million. In all, Hadid lodged 11 bids down to a low of $37.01 million. Just to cover all scenarios, he also lodged an ambit offer of $1 million above the highest bid, on the off-chance someone topped his highest offer. He would lodge these bids for both licences. He knew Hi Vision was chasing the B licence, and would be making multiple bids a little higher than his range. Although the two groups had worked off the same business plan and cooperated in virtually every aspect of the bidding process, they did not know each other's precise bids. Hadid was hoping to pick up the A licence, but if he picked up the B licence in the process, then so be it.

Later that morning Simon Gadir arrived with UCOM's lawyer, Stephen Blanks, from the law firm Gilbert & Tobin, and the three inserted Hadid's numbers in the gaps in the documentation. They were joined by a former employee of Hadid's, Bert Noah, who had agreed to drive to Canberra to lodge the bids and cheques – totalling $5,500 – with the department. Ian Wright was flying to the capital to lodge Hi Vision's bid documents.

Two days later, Hadid and Simon Gadir were waiting in the office above Hadid's computer storeroom for the phone to ring. At midday, the call they were expecting came through. It was Christine Goode at the Department of Communications. 'We would like to inform you that the offer of $177 million by UCOM Pty Ltd is the successful bidder for licence A. The Minister will notify you in writing that the offer has been accepted. You should have a letter by this afternoon by fax and courier.'

Ian Wright and Mark Montgomery received a similar call from Goode a few minutes later. Hi Vision had bid $212 million for the B licence.

That night the members of the two consortiums got together at the Camperdown Travelodge to work out how to conduct themselves from then on. To what extent could they cooperate without alerting the competition watchdog?

The meeting quickly became a celebration. It was a motley collection. There was Hadid the computer entrepreneur; Wright the technology enthusiast; Gadir the intense academic; Montgomery the hairdresser and his half-brother, barrister Leo Gray; Graeme Harrison, the UCOM chairman and Harvard graduate; Thomas Bassett, a student; Danny Mackay, a former programming executive with the Ten Network in the early 1980s; Lars-Erik Holmberg, a leather clothing merchant; Barry Taylor, a director of an X-rated video company, Climax Video Productions; and Robert Lynch, general manager of Hadid's group of companies.

While the 15 or so planners of this remarkable coup ate, drank and made merry in Camperdown, telephones were ringing all over the city as dozens of journalists from the print, radio and television media tried desperately to get in touch with them to find out who they were.


At his North Sydney office, Peter Frame held the fax letter he had just received from the Department of Communications and stared in disbelief. 'We are sorry to inform you that your bid has been disqualified. It did not meet the conditions of the tender.' Frame was in deep shock. The solicitors to the TCI-Time Warner consortium, Mallesons Stephen Jaques, had neglected to write the bidding syndicate's name, Capricorn Entertainment, on the front of the envelope. The bid was for $71 million for the A licence. The world's two largest pay TV groups were knocked out of contention for an Australian satellite licence on a technicality.

Ross McCreath received a similar letter the same day from the department. He had written Australis's name on the back of the envelope, instead of the front, for its two bids of $20 million and $10 million for the B licence. McCreath had lodged the speculative offers believing Australis had little hope, but thought that it might be worth pitching in a couple of low bids on the very slim chance that the auction attracted little interest.

Frame's and McCreath's concerns at having been ruled out of contention for a licence subsided when they heard the radio reports that afternoon of the winning bids by Hi Vision and UCOM. Neither could believe the prices offered. Frame's threats over the phone that morning to sue Mallesons also dissipated. How could anyone make the business work by paying so much, he thought. Time Warner and TCI were never in the race at these levels.

Sydney's late afternoon *Telegraph Mirror* and the following day's morning papers went into a frenzy. 'Shock Win in Pay TV' screamed the *Telegraph Mirror*'s 96-point headline in the morning edition on May 1. 'Unknown firms triumph' and 'A complete and utter farce', the second deck headlines shouted. 'TV Minnows Pip Packer, Murdoch', was the *Sydney Morning Herald*'s headline.

Everyone had been expecting Kerry Packer's PMT consortium to win. Who were these other people? The size of the headlines were in inverse proportion to the ability of anyone from the media to talk to the Hi Vision and UCOM principals – Ian Wright, Leo Gray and Albert Hadid.

Brian Powers was sitting in the conference room at 54 Park Street with some News executives the evening the news broke about the auction result. 'Let's look forward to a bright cable future,' was his comment.

PMT had lodged two bids, one structured to account for payment over time in the $50 million range. The second bid of $36 million was essentially the same offer but expressed in net present value terms.

Martin Hannes had been more adventurous. He bid $60 million for Continental Cablevision. The favourites were beaten, but they were highly sceptical that Hi Vision and UCOM would attract sufficient backers at the high prices offered to pay for the licences. Hadid wasn't very confident about Hi Vision's chances of attracting the finance, but UCOM was well down the road, he thought.

Wayne Burt returned to work at Macquarie Bank after his Christmas break to discover that Steve Cosser and Richard Wiesener were well into discussions with Peter Gray at Burrows Ltd and

Trevor Jones at County NatWest to float Australis. Burt had kept in contact with his friend Cosser before he left the previous August for a four-month post-graduate course in advanced management at the Harvard Business School, paid for by Macquarie Bank. He had a reasonable idea of what Cosser was doing. Still, he would have liked to have been part of the proposed float.

Cosser and Wiesener still hadn't given up on a straight sale of Australis's MDS licences, and had just returned from meeting Rupert Murdoch in Los Angeles. Despite his initial enthusiasm, the News Corp chairman appeared to cool towards the technology soon after the meeting. Two days after his meeting with Murdoch, Cosser received a phone call at his London hotel from Sam Chisholm. The BSkyB boss told Cosser that Murdoch had been holding talks with John Malone of TCI on the subject of Australian pay TV and had decided not to pursue the Australis option as a result. Chisholm didn't elaborate any further. Cosser could only guess that TCI may have decided to team up with Time Warner in a joint bid for the satellite licence.

Ron Brierley continued his discussions with Lynton Taylor at Consolidated Press Holdings, but Cosser couldn't count on any big offers from Packer, who was renowned for his tight-fistedness. The Los Angeles Times Mirror group was probably his best prospect at this stage. A delegation from the company had been impressed by the presentation given by the senior Department of Communications official, Chris North, and were ready to back Australis and MDS. But after the auction was cancelled on January 28, the group packed its tent and returned to the US. The senior vice-president of Times Mirror Cable, Jim Guthrie, said later that North had given Times Mirror 'a lot of comfort'[6] in stressing the Government's intention of introducing technology-neutral pay TV. Asked whether North had given the briefing as an adviser to Cosser, Guthrie said, 'He did not hold himself out as that. He was there as an expert on the Act, and obviously knew Cosser well.'[7]

Burt could sense through his friendship with Cosser and the behind-the-scenes activity by the media industry's heavyweights that Australis was well positioned and that the float could go well. He had to bide his time, though, while Burrows and County NatWest readied Australis for its float and earned the normally generous fees attached to such an exercise.

Over dinner one evening in April at the fashionable Tre Scalini restaurant in East Sydney, Cosser gave Burt the opportunity he wanted. Cosser said that he and Richard Wiesener had invested millions of dollars getting Australis to the point where it was, and the two wanted to sell down their interest in the company and recoup some of their money before the float. The two men owned 90 per cent of the company at that stage. Ron Brierley and Gary Weiss had put in $2.5 million in January to buy 10 per cent for GPG Plc. Could Burt put together a group of institutional investors to buy, say, another 20 per cent of the Cosser-Wiesener stake in Australis? Burt said he was sure he could.

The next morning, Burt went to see Warwick Evans, the head of Macquarie Bank's equities division, to tell him about this opportunity to earn a good fee by raising between $8 million and $10 million for Cosser and Wiesener. Evans said, 'That's funny, I had a call yesterday from Andrew Cormie at J.P. Morgan in Melbourne and he asked me if there were any good investment opportunities in pay TV.'

Burt was on the phone to Cormie straightaway. He then flew to Melbourne and joined Cosser, who was already in the city, and the pair went to see Cormie. After Cosser gave one of his impressive sales pitches lasting a good one-and-a-half hours, through which Cormie sat impassively, the J.P. Morgan man said, 'How much do you want?' Burt said, 'About $3 million.' Cormie then said, 'I'll take the lot.'

Burt urged Cosser to sell down more. He would talk to the bank's analysts and dealers and come up with more names. A dealer, Stephen Aboud, suggested to Burt he contact a Swiss bank, Union Bancaire Privee, through its London-based funds manager, Connor Maloney, as a likely investor. Another large client of Macquarie's was the large Los Angeles-based Capital group, which was the biggest shareholder outside the Murdoch family in News Corp and an active buyer of Australian stocks. Burt arranged conference calls between himself, Cosser and these groups over the next few days. Union Bancaire came in for $2 million and Capital $3 million.

In a period of three days in mid-May, Burt raised more than $8 million for Cosser and Wiesener, who held their Australis shares in a company called Regent Communications. On top of the money GPG and the Burrows Ltd clients had pitched in back in January, the two European-based men had recouped several times their investment. The float was yet to come.

Burt's ability to raise money quickly caught the notice of Ken Borda, head of corporate finance at Bain & Co, one of Australia's largest stockbrokers. Burt and Borda had worked together twice before when they pitched for underwriting work on the 1992 GIO float, and the aborted initial attempt to float retailer Woolworths. Borda liked Burt and regarded him as an effective deal maker. Burt said he had at least two large floats in the pipeline that he could take to Bain.

Within a week or so of Burt moving across to Bains in June, he introduced his new firm to the $100 million float of the Sunbeam Victa group, which the Byvest group, run by his friend Ross Grant, was looking to sell after having bought it from Bob Mansfield and Phil Cave's Reil Corp five years earlier. This underwriting earned $1.5 million in fees for Bain. Borda didn't have to wait long for a quick return on his decision to hire Burt.

On April 29, the day before the satellite licence winners were to be announced, Rodney Price called a press conference to announce that Australis would be floated by the end of September and that he would be the company's new chairman. The company's 25 shareholders would sell half of their shares to the public to raise about $30 million.

Cosser and Wiesener had accepted Peter Gray's advice that it would be best to start preparations for a float and, in view of the bad blood between the newly-elected Labor Government and Cosser, that it would also be best for Cosser to distance himself from the company. The single biggest winners from the float would be Cosser and Wiesener, who would be paid $15.2 million in cash from the float proceeds. Australis would also issue them with 57.3 million non-voting debentures with a face value of $28.65 million. Cosser and Wiesener would be able to convert these securities into ordinary shares after 12 months and sell them through the stockmarket. This would be on top of the $8 million that Burt was just about to raise for them. In all, the two men would be expected to be paid in cash and shares more than $51 million for licences which cost them less than $300,000.

Australis didn't have much to sell at that stage. It had only its single-channel Newsvision service and was trialing an Italian language channel, Teleitalia, which it had bought along with four MDS licences from the Allesi family in Melbourne in exchange for 8.2 million 20 cent shares in Australis.

The success of the float would depend on the Government softening its stand against MDS. So long as Australis was permitted only to narrowcast a limited range of programs to restricted audiences, it could never be a significant player in pay TV. Price could not say with any certainty when Australis would make a profit. Its only strategy at this stage was to expand its narrowcast service to other foreign language groups, the Greek and Chinese communities, and build up a subscription base in expectation that the Government could be persuaded at some stage in the future to allow Australis to use its licences to broadcast a multi-channel pay TV service. By the time it floated, Australis expected to own, or have access to, 24 licences.

Although Australis was confident of winning its legal action against Collins over his cancellation of the MDS licence auction, the Government had foreshadowed an amendment to the new Act to support the January 28 decision to delay the introduction of MDS-based pay TV broadcasting. Justice Whitlam had reserved his decision in Cosser's case and it could be weeks or even months before the outcome was known. Cosser and his new chairman knew they would have to reach a compromise with Collins, or face the prospect of the Government blocking them indefinitely. Collins needed a deal, too. If Cosser won his case, then he would lose his bargaining power and face a damages claim as well.

To get new legislation through the Parliament, Collins would rely on the votes of the seven Democrats who held the balance of power in the Upper House. Cosser and Price knew the Democrats were pivotal to any legislation and paid them a visit in May to suggest a compromise. They suggested that the Democrats push for the compromise of confirming MDS as a broadcasting technology, but prevent its use until the satellite licence holders had their services going, or until December 31, 1994, whichever was the earlier. This would give satellite licence holders, including the ABC, a clear run for 20 months to get their services up and running. It would also give certainty to MDS and Australis.

Collins was still reeling from the working-over he had sustained during his one-day appearance in the witness box for the Australis legal action against him, when he heard that Hi Vision and UCOM had won the A and B satellite licences. Who were these people, he thought, as he read the provocative newspaper headlines. Wasn't the department supposed to vet all contenders before the close of the bidding?

With the MDS debacle still ringing in his ears, he realised he had another crisis on his hands. He called in his department head, Graham Evans, and Chris North and Christine Goode. 'How in the fuck can a bunch of shonks get through when the department was supposed to check them?' he bellowed at the public servants.

'Minister, we didn't do that,' Goode confessed to a quivering Collins. She handed Collins a 14-page briefing paper from the Attorney-General's Department, stating that credibility checks could be seen as anti-competitive and therefore inconsistent with the competition requirements of the *Broadcasting Services Act*. So the auction was run without the checks and without telling the Minister about this problem. Collins was dumbfounded. He asked Goode and North to leave the room.

'How in the hell could the A-Gs have given this advice without the department telling me?' Collins ranted at his department head. Evans confessed he also had not known about the advice, or the decision by the senior bureaucrats not to vet the bidders. He offered to resign. Collins replied, 'If I thought you were personally responsible for this, I would accept. But I don't believe you were.'

Evans survived, Goode stepped aside from her position by 'mutual consent' and Collins ordered an inquiry by a former Commonwealth ombudsman, Dennis Pearce, whom Evans suggested for the job.

Still dazed and demoralised from their March election loss, the Opposition parties seized on this heaven-sent opportunity to boost their stocks by going for Collins' jugular. When he admitted in the House of Representatives that he had signed on January 19 the departmental document setting the auction rules, including the need for a deposit of just $500, Parliament went into uproar. Collins attempted to deflect the blame by saying his department had not informed him that it had changed the auction rules. 'It is, if you like, a standing order which says that when any variation is made, or even a relatively minor one, the obligation is on the department to flag it specifically with the minister.'[8] Collins was looking increasingly shaky in his job as he searched desperately for scapegoats.

While the political storm raged in Canberra and the media continued to exert pressure on his consortium and the Hi Vision group, Albert Hadid remained out of sight while seeking the financial backing to enable him to pay for the licence. He estimated he had about 75 days to find the money. That was how long he thought it would take the ABA and the TPC to make their inquiries before he was given 30 days notice to pay the $177 million he had offered for the A licence. If he couldn't find a backer, or a group of supporters, then the licence would fall to the next highest bid, which he believed was probably his, although he couldn't be sure. Sooner or later he would find a partner at one bid level or another, but he could not waste too many opportunities. At some point, the bidding would cascade down to someone else.

Hi Vision would do the same. Both groups regarded this tactic of allowing the bids to cascade downwards if they failed to find backing at one price as being quite reasonable and, according to Leo Gray's interpretation of the rules, quite legal.

Hadid's first call was to Margaret Combes, the president of the US Cable Association. Because its cable industry was so large and there was so much financial expertise in the US, it was the obvious place to look for bank funding or investors who would understand the subscription TV business.

Hadid wanted to know which US banks or investment banks would be most likely to lend money or underwrite a share issue to raise funds for a pay TV business in Australia. Combes suggested an investment banker, Kirsten Beck, who specialised in media and cable TV financing. Beck would have good contacts among the investment banks and fund managers. Combes also said a cable industry trade fair was scheduled in San Francisco in the first week of June and that Hadid should fly over for it. He would make some good contacts in the cable industry and she would introduce him to Beck.

UCOM and Hi Vision were starting to crack under the intense media scrutiny in the days after they won the licences. Barry Taylor resigned on May 5 as a director.

On the same day Graeme Harrison, listed as chairman of UCOM on the licence bidding documents, denied through his solicitors, Allen Allen & Hemsley, that he had been, or consented to be, a director of UCOM.

The newspapers were portraying the licence winners as being in a state of chaos, with no funding and little chance of keeping control of the licences. Hadid and Gadir refused to speak to the press, choosing instead to focus on finding financial backing. Wright gave an interview to the *Sydney Morning Herald* on May 6, hoping that it would satisfy media demands for information on his group and that the press would then go away. He complained in the interview that his group was finding it difficult to talk to potential partners. 'We're being hounded and monitored and no-one can come near our office without being splattered all over the daily press . . . we know there's a campaign of ridicule out there. There are powerful people who are upset that we won, fair and square. I find that strangely satisfying; they're taking us seriously.'

Hadid and Gadir spent the rest of May on the phone and facsimile to US investment banks, Salomon Brothers, Donaldson Lufkin Jenrette, and Nomura in New York, trying to persuade them to endorse the UCOM business plan on which Tony Gall at Price Waterhouse had worked. They also spoke to potential program suppliers, Viacom, Time Warner, ESPN (Time Warner's sports channel), Turner International (which owned CNN and had rights to the MGM film library), Paramount and Universal. They quickly realised that until they had their licence paid for and in place, the program suppliers were not ready to talk to them. Their most urgent priority was to find $177 million.

Another catalyst in this highly volatile situation was the legal action against the Government mounted in January by another bidder for MDS licences, Kerry Stokes. His Australian Capital Equity group wanted to use MDS to operate a business data service in the State capitals. He sued even more quickly than Steve Cosser and persuaded a judge in the Federal Court in Perth to order the tenders to be reopened. When the Government attempted to cancel the auction once again in mid-May, claiming technical deficiencies in the bid documents, Stokes sued again and the court ordered the Government to continue the process. With the new bids due to close on May 28, the Government and Stokes settled their action, allowing the Government once again to pull the auction. The combined blundering of Collins, his junior minister David Beddall, and the Communications Department had reduced the MDS auction process to new depths of absurdity.

The MDS bungles acted as a backdrop to the continuing media and political scrutiny of the satellite licence auction process. Collins was by now coming under intense pressure daily to end the potentially lengthy delays between the acceptance of the bid and the 75 days or so before the department knew whether or not the balance of the money would be paid. If the Hi Vision and UCOM bids lapsed, there seemed every chance that these two groups, or similar bidders, might be positioned to win the next highest bids and the process would start again. It might take six months to find a buyer.

Bob Collins issued a fresh regulation, forcing successful bidders for the licences to lodge a non-refundable 5 per cent deposit within three working days of a bid being accepted. This was expected to dramatically increase the likelihood of successful bidders completing their purchase of the licence. They would have real money on the line now. The new regime would come into effect if the current bids cascaded down.

As each day passed, Hadid and Gadir could sense that time was running out for them. The past month had produced very little except for some huge phone bills. They had about eight weeks to come up with the money. They would have to get on a plane to the US and start seeing people.

The cable show in San Francisco would be a good place to start. After the flight across the Pacific, Hadid and Gadir checked into the San Francisco Hilton before their expected round of meetings at the trade fair the next day. After meeting Combes there, she arranged for them to meet Mike Fries, the chief executive of United International Holdings (UIH), a US cable group which had sold its US interests to TCI and, under a non-compete clause in the sale documents, could only invest offshore. The Australian situation would be ideal. Fries told Hadid and Gadir he was certainly interested, not so much in one of the main licences, but a smaller role as a franchisee or a regional MDS operator.

Combes then brought Kirsten Beck to meet Hadid and Gadir in the Hilton hotel lobby. Hadid's initial impression was that she lacked substance, but after questioning her, he changed his mind to the extent that he believed she would be ideal to help him. Hadid nominated some banks, and she agreed that Salomons, Donaldson Lufkin Jenrette, and Nomura would be the most suitable.

That evening at a drinks party hosted by the fair organisers, Combes introduced Hadid and Gadir to two senior TCI executives. After some introductory small talk, one of them said, half jokingly, 'You know we'll do everything in our power to stop you.'

The Falcon jet circled over Hamilton Island before coming in to land on the resort's huge concrete airstrip which cuts the island in half. As the side door opened and the aircraft's steps folded outwards on to the ground, Paul Keating stepped on to the tarmac. The Prime Minister had been on holiday on the Barrier Reef and was returning to Canberra via the Whitsunday island group, which was serviced through Hamilton. Despite the airstrip's desecration of this once unspoiled paradise, Hamilton became the entry point for the numerous resort islands nearby. It was June, and for Keating, this was his first break since Labor's remarkable election victory in March. By winning the 'unwinnable' election, Keating had secured the electorate's endorsement of his politically bloody leadership coup over Bob Hawke in December 1991.

The Hamilton stop-off marked the end of Keating's brief Queensland holiday, because he wasn't there for further relaxation. Now he was on business. As he stepped off the executive jet, he was met by News Corporation's Australian head, Ken Cowley, who would accompany Keating on the 20-minute trip across the aqua blue waters of the Whitsunday Passage by large cruiser to Hayman Island, which was owned by News's 50 per cent affiliate, Ansett Airlines. Keating was due to speak at one of News Corp's irregular executive conferences on Hayman, outlining his vision for Australia to 200 or so senior News executives.

The previous News get-together was at US ski resort Aspen a year earlier and, before that, also at Aspen in 1989.[9] Murdoch was a global player and went to considerable lengths and expense at times to educate his senior executives in world developments. In 1992, the guest speakers were the US Secretary of Defense, Dick Cheney, and Margaret Thatcher's former foreign affairs adviser, Charles Powell. Another speaker in 1993 on Hamilton was the recently-elected leader of Britain's Labour Party, Tony Blair. Labour and its former leader, Neil Kinnock, had been humiliated by the Murdoch press in the last UK election 16 months earlier. The opinion polls had pointed to a Labour win over the tired Conservative Party Government of John Major, but Kinnock could not combat the barrage of anti-Labour stories, coming mostly from Murdoch's mass circulation newspapers, *The Sun* and *News of the World*. Murdoch liked to pick and back winners. He expected Kinnock would lose, so had little hesitation putting in the boot. But he liked his successor, Blair, whom he saw as a winner. Blair accepted the invitation to speak at the News gabfest on the other side of the world and meet the men and women of the News empire which made and broke governments and oppositions. But at this conference Blair had to take a back seat to Paul Keating, who was elevated to centre stage. In the wake of Labor's election win, Keating and Cowley had become very close. Cowley used to boast to friends that if he was any closer to the Lodge, he would have to move in.

Over dinner on a cloudless night with hundreds of candles lighting up the expensively decorated resort's dining area, Keating gave a stirring speech to the News executives and their wives, outlining his vision for Australia as a pivotal player in the region. It was another enunciation of his initiative to form the Asia-Pacific Economic Conference (APEC) forum which would bring together the nations of the Pacific rim.

Keating's acceptance of Cowley's invitation to speak at this very private gathering marked the start of what would prove to be a turning point in Keating's relations with Australia's media moguls. Until that time, Kerry Packer and Peter Barron could ask and get from Keating and Labor virtually anything that was deliverable politically. But Keating was starting to tire of Packer's constant requests. He was impressed by Murdoch as a man of vision, like himself. From June 1993 onwards, Packer would find it more difficult to get his way. The decisions would soon start to go the way of Rupert Murdoch and News.

After dinner, Murdoch invited Keating and Cowley back to his room for a nightcap. As they stood around talking about the forthcoming float of Seven, in which News and Telstra were taking pivotal interests, Murdoch asked Keating to consider another proposal: 'We'd like to buy Fairfax, but realise we can't so long as we own our newspapers. I'd like to float the papers and put Ken in charge as chairman. He would be entirely independent to run his own show. I think News would then be in a position to move on Fairfax.' Keating had been impressed with the evening and the vision Murdoch had been painting, but he knew this idea was fraught with political dangers. Keating said he would think about it. In his mind, however, he doubted it would be possible. The subject was not raised again.

Holidaying on Hayman Island at the time of the News Corp conference was the chairman of the Australian and NSW Rugby League, Ken Arthurson. A grizzled veteran former half-back with the Manly Warringah rugby league team and now a football administrator, Arthurson ran into Ken Cowley in the small resort area. The two men had known each other for several years, Cowley's involvement in the sport being confined mostly to News's indirect interest in the Brisbane Broncos football team. Cowley invited Arthurson onto the cruiser which News had hired for the time of the conference and introduced him to Rupert Murdoch. Constantly looking for opportunities, Murdoch told Arthurson he wanted to show rugby league on his new Star TV satellite network in Asia. The deal was done later, but Arthurson complained later that Star paid the league nothing for the rights.[10]

Arthurson wrote later about the meeting: 'I was impressed with Murdoch that evening. I must say that I thought he came across as a very humble sort of bloke, relaxed and friendly on what turned out to be a most enjoyable occasion. I have always admired him as a businessman.'[11]

This friendly encounter would be forgotten two years later when News's pay TV ambitions in Australia included building a new rugby league competition.

Within days of the Hayman Island conference, the Telstra board, after months of deliberation and discussion, decided to join News in the imminent float of the Seven Network. It would buy a 10 per cent interest and News 15 per cent. When the network floated a short time later, raising $725 million for the bankers to the collapsed Qintex group, News and Telstra received sub-underwriting fees of more than $2 million for their role in the float. This was icing on the cake for the two partners, who would have the last laugh at the expense of the reluctant Seven chairman, Ivan Deveson.

This investment was a big step for Telstra because it was the government monopoly carrier's first stockmarket exposure. It marked the start of the significant cultural changes that Frank Blount was making in this huge organisation. As its only shareholder, the government also needed to approve this first tentative step into the sharper end of the marketplace. But Keating's Labor Government believed the partnership with News would help speed the evolution of Telstra into a telecommunications group of world standing. At a meeting with Murdoch the previous October, Keating had been impressed with the News chairman's grasp of global telecommunications developments. Murdoch emphasised to Keating the need for Australia to keep pace with developments in the US, where phone and cable companies were linking to form a national data highway over their cable systems, the Internet being the most apparent manifestation. The success and potential impact of this development would depend on cable going to the home.

Murdoch was making equally visionary statements publicly. In an interview with Kerry Packer's *Australian Business Monthly*,

Murdoch said, 'You can have anything you want if you press the right button. A fibre-optic cable will take you anywhere, from your home to any other person's home, office, newspaper library. It's in this country. People dream about a world highway.'[12]

# 7

# Midsummer manoeuvres

As he stood in the Nomura conference room high in the World Financial Centre building at the Wall Street end of Manhattan, Albert Hadid could see the 110-storey twin towers of the World Trade Centre dominating the view from one window and, turning his head to look out of the opposite window, he could see across town to the Empire State building with the sprawling thicket of high-rise buildings in between that housed the world's most powerful financial institutions and corporations.

He was in the process of completing an agreement with Robert Long, chief executive of the US subsidiary of the giant Japanese financial group, Nomura, and a senior executive, John Casale. Nomura would act as adviser to UCOM with an option of also underwriting any capital raising by UCOM to fund its licence and its start-up costs. If it couldn't find investors to finance the licence development, Nomura would lend its own money. Nomura would send a team of three or four senior executives to work with UCOM from the bank's small Sydney representative office.

'Thank god I'm dealing with a large reputable bank,' Hadid thought to himself. 'We're covered.'

That evening he sat in the foyer of the Hyatt Hotel with Kirsten Beck as faxes from Nomura came through with the appropriate signatures on the agreement between the bank and UCOM. Gadir had to fly back to Australia a week earlier, leaving Hadid to continue the negotiations with the bank. Beck had been pivotal in introducing Hadid and Gadir to Nomura, which had been so enthusiastic about the satellite pay TV venture in Australia. Hadid had felt it unnecessary to have any discussions of substance with other banks. He had spent a crucial three weeks in New York talking to Nomura, painstakingly sifting through UCOM's projections and assumptions to satisfy the bank that the proposal would work.

Nomura was happy with the price bid for the licence and the expectations of costs, subscription growth, and revenues. UCOM had counted in a 'free carry' of between 25 per cent and 30 per cent, which meant that any partners or investors which came in to develop the business would pay 100 per cent of the future costs, and still leave UCOM with 25–30 per cent of the business.

Hadid had spent about $800,000 to that point on consultants' fees, staff costs, legal fees, air fares and phone bills and believed he had done much of the groundwork. He looked forward to reaping some reward for his efforts.

Now he had the support and endorsement of a major global institution, Hadid was confident his pay TV plans would come to fruition. He could thumb his nose at the media establishment in Australia, which had been so sceptical about his strategy and which he believed had tried to sabotage his plans with its intrusive and highly critical coverage. Hadid was a little uneasy that he was investing so much time and effort with Nomura with the deadline for payment less than four weeks away, but now he had a signed agreement, the risk had paid off.

The next day, Hadid was on a flight back to Australia. After the 20-hour trip, including a stop-over in Los Angeles to change aircraft, he arrived at 6am the same day he left, and took a taxi to his Stanmore store. Walking into his office with the day just breaking, Hadid noticed a letter on his fax machine. It was from Nomura's Robert Long in New York. The deal was off. There appeared to be a conflict of interest because the Sydney office had done some work with Hi Vision.

Hadid was dumbstruck. He didn't believe a word of this excuse. The potential for conflict had already been discussed. That was why Nomura was to send over some fresh people and put a 'Chinese wall' between them and the people in the Sydney office. The previous day he had shaken hands with some of Nomura's most senior people and the deal was on.

Immediately, he called Long and Casale. They said they were really sorry, but someone even more senior had stepped on their toes, instructing them to withdraw their support for UCOM. Hadid reminded them he had a signed agreement and intended to keep them to it. He did not have time now to find another backer. He had spent too much time getting Nomura on side. Even if he did sue, it would take months to get anywhere. Hadid had less than four weeks. In a last-ditch effort to save his licence, he went to see Cass O'Connor at Turnbull and Partners, who offered to see Salomon Brothers in Sydney to try to get their support. Salomons wanted more time to assess the business plan and test the market's willingness to invest in the venture.

On the evening of July 30, Hadid arrived at his home in Sydney's Greenacre at 5pm, for the first time in perhaps six months. At midnight his bid would collapse and the auction process would go down to the next highest offer.

The next day, a Saturday, at 11am, Hi Vision was informed that its offer of $211 million for licence B had been accepted, as was UCOM's $157 million bid for the A licence. The difference this time was that Hi Vision had until 5pm the following Wednesday to produce $9.3 million, and UCOM $7.85 million. If they failed to produce this money, then the bids cascaded again.

This added considerable new urgency to the attempts by Hadid and the Hi Vision people to raise not only the deposit, but also the full licence amount. They would lose the deposit money if they failed to raise the balance.

Both syndicates failed to get the deposit money by the following Wednesday, so the auction cascaded once again, this time to $195 million for Hi Vision and $137 million for UCOM. These bids lapsed on Tuesday August 10, and the following morning, Hi Vision and UCOM came in again with their next bids, $186 million for Hi Vision and $117 million for UCOM.

Peter Frame was getting anxious again. What if the bidding fell to the price that Time Warner-TCI-Comcast-AWA had offered, but which had been ruled ineligible? He and Eric Walsh went to see Bob Collins to see if there was any way the Time Warner bid could be reinstated. Collins assured them he would try to do so, but unfortunately he couldn't.

On Friday evening, the 13th, the latest Hi Vision and UCOM bids expired, and cascaded again. They cascaded again on the evening of the 18th, the 23rd and the 26th. This was Hi Vision's lowest bid, of $130 million. It was out of the race now. On the morning of August 27, the department informed UCOM that it had won both licences, an offer of $97 million for the A licence and $117 million for the B. It had until 5pm the following Monday to pay a total of $10.7 million in deposits. UCOM had made these bids through an entity called New World Telecommunications Pty Ltd, for the B licence, and United Airways Pty Ltd, for the A.

The moment of truth had arrived for Hadid. He now had both licences, but only briefly. If he did not come up with the deposit money by this latest deadline, he would be out of the race too, at least for the B licence. A consortium headed by former Fraser Government Communications Minister Neil Brown had the next highest offer, of $103 million. But it is unlikely he, either, would have been able to hold it for more than three days. There appeared to be every chance that the B licence would cascade all the way down to the PMT consortium's offer.

Hadid and Gadir walked around the corner from the temporary offices they were renting in Sydney's Bligh Street to Turnbull and Partners in Chifley Square for an appointment with Cass O'Connor. Every minute now was precious. The UCOM pair had kept in contact with O'Connor through the auction process, and O'Connor had told them she was confident there were one or two serious players who were keen to do a deal on the licences.

She asked Hadid if UCOM was now prepared to sign up her firm formally as an adviser, which he agreed to do. Hadid had with him the Nomura agreement, with the detailed financial projections he and Simon Gadir had provided to Nomura in New York. Now Nomura had pulled out, O'Connor said UCOM should look at the option of raising money through a float, and they would need an underwriter. She phoned Rowan Johnston, head of corporate finance at her old firm, Bain and Co, and Andrew Price, head of Nomura Australia, which had been working with Hi Vision. Hadid and Gadir had to leave for a short time, but said they would be back.

When he received O'Connor's call, Price said he would come straight over. As Johnston was leaving Bains' office on the 21st floor of the Grosvenor Place tower, he called by Wayne Burt's desk to suggest he join him to meet O'Connor and a client of hers about whom they had read so much, Albert Hadid. Burt eagerly agreed.

When Price, Johnston and Burt arrived at Turnbulls, they were shown into a meeting room where O'Connor joined them. She told the three merchant bankers that Turnbulls had been retained as the sole adviser for UCOM to seek ways to raise money to fund the two licences.

They were talking about the prospects of raising money in a float when, in the middle of the conversation, Hadid walked in. O'Connor introduced him and he explained how UCOM had allowed earlier bids to lapse but was on a tight schedule with the two current bids. UCOM needed someone to pay the deposits.

He turned to Burt and asked him his views about an underwriting. Burt was very persuasive when he told Hadid that he had recently raised $8 million for Australis from institutional investors and believed it was the first money raised for pay TV in Australia. He thought there would be a lot of corporate and institutional money available. Burt said UCOM needed a larger partner or foundation investor and that would make the underwriting more achievable. Hadid thanked him, then made his apologies. He had other meetings to go to and calls to make. This was a very busy day.

When Hadid got back to his office, there was a pile of messages to return calls. But before he could start ringing, one of the half dozen people working the phones for him called out, 'Martin Dougherty's on the phone.' Hadid knew Dougherty, a knock-about former public relations operative and adviser to Warwick Fairfax in his ill-fated privatisation of the John Fairfax group. He had bought Lars-Erik Holmberg and Barry Taylor's interests in Hi Vision in July after the two men quit the consortium. With Hi Vision out of contention now, Dougherty was keen to do a deal with Hadid.

Dougherty had put together a fresh consortium and had secured the backing of stockbroker Burdett Buckeridge and Young, which was prepared to help raise the necessary funds. He wanted to pay the deposit, buy the B licence for $10 million, but leave UCOM with a 5 per cent interest free of cost.

Hadid replied, 'The offer is not good enough. I want $30 million plus 6 per cent, plus a commissioning agency for all the local drama productions. Then we'll talk.'

Dougherty was not put off. 'I think it is a good offer. In effect we're giving you a $25 million payment and you should also do well in the float. The alternative if you delay is that you could lose everything, like Hi Vision.' To this Hadid replied, 'I think we've got enough interest to get our bids up by Monday.'

Hadid was bluffing to some extent. He was relying on Cass O'Connor's assurance that Turnbulls was talking to two US groups wanting to play, although she did not tell Hadid who they were. The other card he had up his sleeve was Margaret Combes.

At 1am on Saturday, Hadid called Margaret Combes. She had just taken a job as head of a new cable network called Americana, but was pleased to take his call. It was 10am in Boston. Hadid explained to Combes that he had won both A and B licences in the auction but had three days to pay the deposits of nearly $11 million. Was there any interest she could raise in the US?

Remarkably, she had just spoken to Don Heller, a vice president of a large cable group based in Philadelphia called Lenfest Communications. Lenfest operated a business called NuStar, which used satellite to deliver to 11 cable networks throughout the US, promotional spots to be inserted between programs. Heller had a spare transponder and had called Combes to ask whether Americana, which had national ambitions, would be interested in leasing it. Combes told him she would think about it, but after Hadid's call she immediately rang Heller back with another proposal.

Would Lenfest be interested in a satellite pay TV business in Australia? she asked Heller. Heller said he would have to talk to the company's president and chief executive, Harold Fitzgerald ('Gerry') Lenfest.

Lenfest Communications was the 14th largest cable group in the US with one million subscribers and interests in the smaller Susquehanna Cable and Raystay Co regional networks, with another 220,000 subscribers. Gerry Lenfest started the company in 1974 and aggressively pursued the strategy of 'clustering', or buying up adjacent regional cable systems to create a large aggregation stretching 330 km from Atlantic City on the east coast to Harrisburg in Pennsylvania. The industry in the US was highly regulated at federal, state and local levels, but operated essentially by permit from municipal authorities. Although Lenfest had been relatively successful in acquiring neighbouring cable groups, expansion opportunities were limited. To grow strongly, the US cable groups had to look overseas. Combes suspected Lenfest might be prepared to invest in Australia because it had shown its appetite for foreign acquisitions with the purchase of 29 per cent of the French cable operator, Videopole.

Like most US cable groups, Lenfest was losing money ($US16.97 million in the year to December 31, 1992), but its corporate strength lay in the fact that it was 50 per cent owned by a subsidiary of John Malone's TCI, an investment dating back to the early 1980s. When Don Heller called Gerry Lenfest to tell him there was an opportunity in Australia, and that Margaret Combes was about to ring him, Lenfest was very interested.

Combes called Hadid and told him Lenfest wanted to do a deal. Fax him your business plan, then give him a call, she said, giving Hadid Lenfest's fax and phone numbers at his office in Pottstown, a light industrial suburb about 70 km north-west of Philadelphia. 'This guy is hot. Go for it,' Combes urged Hadid.

Hadid had the Nomura proposal with the business plan on his desk and faxed it to Lenfest. Half an hour later he called. By now, it was about 2am Sydney time. Hadid was extremely nervous. He had never spoken to Gerry Lenfest before and he was about to ask him, over the phone, for nearly $11 million, just to pay the deposits. 'Gerry, it's Albert Hadid. You spoke to Margaret Combes a short time ago, can we have a talk?' Hadid asked the American.

'Sure, I hear you have a couple of satellite licences. I think we might be interested in doing something with you,' Lenfest replied. Hadid was amazed that Lenfest had no quibble with the $117 million and $97 million UCOM was due to pay for the licences. Lenfest was more concerned that no-one else should muscle in on the situation. He urged Hadid to 'move on those two licences because we don't want to take any risks [of losing them]'.

The two spent the next 20 minutes or so negotiating over ownership percentages and control in view of the 20 per cent limit on individual foreign investors and the level of investment the business would need. As they talked, Hadid wrote down the agreed points, then penned a rough agreement which he faxed to Lenfest to sign. Lenfest agreed to finance the two deposits and would take 50 per cent of whichever licence he wanted, with Hadid owning the other half. Hadid would keep 100 per cent of the licence Lenfest didn't want. Lenfest expressed a preference at that initial stage for the cheaper A licence. Hadid said he probably had a buyer for the B. Hadid didn't want to press him at this point on how the deposits would be paid in time. Lenfest ended the conversation by asking, 'Albert, this will be a good business, won't it?' Hadid assured him it would be.

As soon as Lenfest hung up, Hadid tried to call Cass O'Connor at home. Her number was engaged. Hadid figured the phone was off the hook. He sent her a fax, 'Cass, wake up – Albert.'

She didn't get the message until she woke up late that morning. She called Hadid. 'Cass, I've spoken to Gerry Lenfest, head of

Lenfest Communications, and he's agreed to finance the two deposits. I've no idea how we're going to get the money from him in time to pay the Department of Communications on Monday. He's probably not aware, either, that we're 15 hours ahead.'

He asked O'Connor to call Lenfest. It was late evening by then in the US. Lenfest had told Hadid earlier he was going to spend the weekend at his beach house at Ocean City, about an hour's drive away, 20 km south of Atlantic City.

O'Connor agreed to ring Lenfest and try to work out a way to have the money transferred in time. She phoned the number given to her by Hadid straight away. When Lenfest answered, O'Connor said she was acting for Hadid, and then emphasised the need for Lenfest to have the deposit money transferred to Australia by Monday morning, eastern Australian time, which was Sunday night his time.

Could the two of them arrange a bridging loan provided by Turnbulls until Lenfest could pay the money? Lenfest started to get edgy. It was late and he didn't appreciate this sort of pressure. The conversation became heated. He demanded to know who O'Connor was. She backed off, then asked him who Lenfest's bankers were, hoping at least one of them was represented in Australia. He started naming American banks, none of whom had any presence in Australia, then dropped the name Toronto Dominion. The Canadian bank was a specialist lender to the media and had offices in Melbourne. O'Connor asked Lenfest if she could call the bank on his behalf to see whether it was prepared to extend a short-term facility.

He agreed. O'Connor said she would call back if she had any luck. 'Not until the morning please,' Lenfest pleaded. She only knew one executive from the bank, a man named Mike Wozniak, who was not hard to find in directory assistance. Wozniak was receptive, but said he would need to discuss the matter with the bank's main account executive in New York. He would call O'Connor back.

He didn't ring back until the next morning. The New York executive was encouraging. Wozniak then called Lenfest to offer him the bridging facility, totalling $10.7 million.

Hadid and O'Connor were on the 11.30am shuttle flight to Canberra the next day. They had an appointment with Pauline Selmes, a senior official with the asset sales task force in the Department of Communications. Hadid handed her two Westpac cheques, one for $4.85 million for the A licence and the other for $5.85 million for the B.

Albert Hadid had finally hooked a big fish for a partner, and got not one, but two, pay television licences. He stayed on at the department to settle the documentation for the licences. O'Connor got into a taxi for the five-minute drive to Parliament House. She had been called just before she and Hadid left Sydney by a friend of hers, Sam Mostyn, a senior adviser to Bob Collins. Mostyn invited O'Connor to brief the Minister on the new licence holder's plans.

O'Connor rejoined Hadid in the lounge bar of Canberra airport in plenty of time for the 6pm flight back to Sydney. Hadid ordered two glasses of sparkling white wine. He asked O'Connor where she had been. She replied that she had been to see her friend Mostyn at Parliament House and spoken to Bob Collins. Hadid noticeably cooled. He didn't say anything, but O'Connor realised he was offended he hadn't been asked to see the Minister too. Relations between Hadid and Turnbull and Partners also chilled from that day.

Two days later, in a statement bursting with enthusiasm, Lenfest issued out of its Pottstown, Pennsylvania headquarters a one-and-a-half-page press release headed, 'Lenfest Group to join in operation of Australia's first satellite pay TV service: New service will reach millions'. It went on, 'A number of prominent Australian businessmen and communications experts have worked with Lenfest and its associates on the venture. They include Albert Hadid and Dr Simon Gadir. They were assisted in their search for a US cable television operator by Margaret Durborow Combes . . .'[1]


When Don Heller flew into Sydney the following Saturday he checked into the Ritz Carlton in Macquarie Street, taking a 10th floor room overlooking the Harbour Bridge and the Opera House. It was his first visit to Australia and he was impressed. Heller had only recently joined Gerry Lenfest, who was throwing him in at the deep end on this assignment. An accountant, Heller had worked through the 1970s with a number of manufacturing companies in Philadelphia before joining Spectrum Arena, an entertainment company which owned or managed sports teams and a circus as well as having cable TV interests through its PRISM subsidiary. PRISM packaged home and away games for cable TV stations in a particular team's orbit of influence and one of its largest customers was Lenfest Communications. Heller moved across to Lenfest early in 1993 and, in his role as vice president in charge of business development, launched a news channel. Lenfest's bold move into Australia was very much his responsibility, but creating a national pay TV service using satellite was entirely beyond Heller's experience.

Heller brought with him to Sydney a former banker with Pittsburgh National Corporation, Stephen Plant, who had been hired as a consultant to keep an eye on the numbers for the difficult negotiations ahead. They would need to devise the best way to raise the money to pay for one, or if necessary, both of the licences, define and refine their working arrangement with Hadid, and ensure that the two licences cooperated on key issues such as a common digital standard.

Their primary job, however, was to protect the $10.7 million in deposit money, which had been guaranteed personally by Gerry Lenfest. Before he left Philadelphia, Heller was told by good friend Allan Sonnenberg, who controlled the main microwave pay TV service in the city with 50,000 subscribers, to be sure when he was in Australia to introduce himself to an impressive young Australian he had met, named Steve Cosser.

After spending Sunday recovering from jet lag, Heller and Plant embarked on a whirl of meetings the next day. They visited a number of merchant banks to find an adviser to look after their interests in Australia and keep them informed while they travelled to and from the US over the coming weeks.

Most of their meetings and discussions on their Australian visits would be held in a large, third-floor meeting area of their hotel which, like all Ritz Carltons, is a contrived mixture of 18th century American regency style with elements of French rococo. They have formal, discreet meeting rooms, and a cosy cocktail bar with an open fire. They are designed more for the cooler climes of New York, London or Boston, where the hotel group is based. They look gauche and slightly out of place in the light and heat of Australia. Still, once inside the darkened, air-conditioned foyers and meeting rooms where the lights need to be kept on in daylight hours, the guest or visitor could be in a Ritz Carlton anywhere in the world.

That afternoon in the third-floor meeting room, Hadid introduced Martin Dougherty to the Lenfest men. Dougherty wanted to buy the licence that Lenfest didn't want. Heller was more interested in knowing how Dougherty would finance the acquisition. He wanted a letter from Dougherty's proposed underwriter, BBY, on their experience in similar underwritings and also his offer for the licence in writing.

A short time later, Heller and Plant, along with Hadid and Gadir, were hosts to another delegation, this time Ken Borda, Rowan Johnston and Wayne Burt from Bains. The Bains trio gave Heller and Plant a rundown of their past experience at underwriting large capital raisings of the type anticipated by Lenfest in Australia. Burt said it was difficult to be precise about such an exercise without some detailed information about the business and without knowing whether any other large overseas groups might be joining the partnership as a cornerstone investor.

After they left the meeting, Borda and the Bains men agreed it would be best to approach Lenfest directly to try to win the underwriting business. They wrote to Heller and Plant on September 8 asking to be considered for the role of underwriter, but did not tell Hadid.

Two days later Johnston and Burt met Hadid again to discuss UCOM's business plan in more detail. Hadid and Burt disagree about what happened next. Hadid says Burt asked for a copy of the document and Burt says Hadid was keen to show it to Bains. Whatever the case, Hadid gave Burt a copy of the detailed assumptions and projections, after asking him to sign a confidentiality agreement.

Heller and Hadid flew to the US on September 12 for meetings with Gerry Lenfest, leaving Plant to continue the dialogue with the UCOM people and Bains. Cass O'Connor flew to the US for the same meetings. She and Hadid had agreed that Turnbull not continue as adviser to UCOM, and at Malcolm Turnbull's urging, O'Connor would try to get Lenfest to retain their firm. Turnbulls could sense that events would soon move quickly, and they wanted to attach themselves to a party with more money than UCOM.

In Sydney over the next four days, while Hadid was away, the meetings between Plant, Gadir and Bain continued. Once again time was becoming an issue. The balance on the A licence was due on November 17, and the Australian Broadcasting Authority had frozen the B licence until the A was dealt with. But until Lenfest had decided which of the licences it would develop, this date effectively was the deadline for both. Even before he left for his meeting with Gerry Lenfest in the US, Hadid was becoming frustrated with the apparent lack of progress. He complained to Plant and Heller that he wasn't being briefed on developments. Hadid had agreed to give Lenfest the responsibility of financing the licences and looking for partners, because the Americans had paid the deposits and had money on the line. Hadid held the power of veto over any decision Lenfest made because of the joint venture arrangement he had struck with Gerry Lenfest in the early hours of August 30.

As the days rolled by in September, Hadid noticed a distinct change, a cooling, in the attitude of Heller and Plant towards him. The Lenfest men in turn claimed they were finding it difficult to deal with Hadid and expressed the view privately that it would be hard to attract another large US cable company into the consortium so long as Hadid insisted that he take an interest without cost, or free carry, of up to 30 per cent.

Hadid suspected that Heller and Plant might be considering another deal behind his back. Soon after UCOM won the licences, Gadir had urged Hadid to talk to Steve Cosser and Rodney Price. He argued that it would be a good idea for at least one of the satellite licence holders to join Australis with its 24 MDS licences. Hadid brushed him off initially. Cass O'Connor had advised against it. She saw them as competitors, but warned Hadid she suspected Lenfest and Australis were having discussions behind his back. Soon after he returned from the US in mid-September, with discussions with Lenfest in hiatus, Hadid agreed to a meeting. Gadir said he would arrange it.

At 3pm on October 1, Cosser, Price and Wiesener walked into the Ritz Carlton and made their way to the third-floor meeting room. They had just come from Burrows Ltd, around the corner in Spring Street, where they had been interviewing a promising applicant for the chief executive's position at Australis. His name was Neil Gamble.

Cosser told his colleagues as they left the building, 'I've agreed to meet the Lenfest people around at the Ritz Carlton. Would you like to come along?' When they walked out of the lift on the third floor, Heller and Plant were waiting in the meeting area, known as the concierge's room. Heller had already met Cosser. The American contacted him on the recommendation of Sonnenberg soon after he arrived in Australia and the two had talked about their plans. This time, the five men chatted between themselves for about 20 minutes before Cass O'Connor arrived, late, in her new role as Lenfest's adviser. A few minutes later, Hadid, Gadir and Anne Keating, the sister of the Prime Minister, walked in.

Gadir broke the noticeable tension in the air. 'Steve, would Australis consider coming in on one of the satellite licences?' Cosser was non-committal, saying only that he would think about it. Price sat in a corner of the room and Wiesener to the side. Neither said a word.

The UCOM party had only been in the room a few minutes when Cosser said he and his colleagues had to go. Although Hadid wasn't particularly keen on doing a deal with Australis either, he was amazed that the Australis people appeared to be giving this serious proposal so little consideration. As Cosser, Price and Wiesener walked out, followed closely by the Lenfest pair, O'Connor turned to Hadid, 'They were eyeballing each other.'

Australis's debut on the Australian Stock Exchange on September 30 was almost guaranteed to be a success. Peter Gray and Steve Cosser had planned to restrict the sale of the 70 million 50 cent shares substantially to a few dozen associates, friends, and clients of Burrows Ltd and to those of the other underwriter, County NatWest. In concert with the snowstorm of hype that Cosser and Price were able to generate in a compliant media, the scramble for the shares by outsiders wanting to invest in this new industry went largely unsatisfied. The shares started trading at 60 cents, 10 cents above the issue price, but over ensuing days dipped as some of those who bought the stock ahead of the float made a quick profit. Cosser and Richard Wiesener had raised a total of $15.17 million in the months leading up to the float by selling shares through Wayne Burt at between 20 and 38 cents to selected institutional investors, such as Union Bancaire Privee and the Capital group. The company also issued to Cosser and Wiesener's Regent Communications another 57.3 million debentures which could be later converted into ordinary shares and sold on the market. Of the 122.7 million shares which would be circulating in the market after the float, 52.6 million were sold to friends and associates of Cosser and Wiesener.

Gary Weiss's GPG Plc already had 10.8 million shares, which it had bought earlier in the year for 20 cents. Rod Price was issued with 2.142 million shares and nine million options in the float, George Bennett 798,000 shares and 250,000 options, Mark Johnson 666,000 shares and 500,000 options and Phil Scanlan 666,000 shares and 250,000 options. The directors paid 38 cents for their shares, compared with the 50 cents at which they were offered to the public. Their options were exercisable at 50 cents, so the directors could convert the options at this price and sell them for a profit once the share price traded above this level.

Although the legally required information was contained in the August prospectus, the document required careful reading by an experienced eye to gain the full picture. Rodney Price mentioned in his opening letter in the prospectus that broadcast licences would not be available until after December 31, 1994, or 16 months later. 'The Directors expect that Australis will qualify for and be granted broadcast licences and intend to apply for them as soon as possible,' Price wrote to prospective investors. This did not disclose the full position. The broadcast licences were easily enough obtained over the counter from the department. What Price did not explain was that Australis would first need to bid for additional MDS licences in open auction against potential rivals before qualifying for broadcast licences.

The prospectus touched on this in passing only. Under the heading 'risk factors', the prospectus mentioned that '. . . the effect of any future tenders for as-yet unissued MDS licences . . .' may have a potential impact on the profitability of Australis.[2] What was not spelled out was the fact that it was absolutely necessary for Australis to successfully tender for the overwhelming majority of the 200 licences that were to be auctioned, or face the prospect of having a commercial rival buying the licences and leaving Australis with the limited number of licences it had already acquired. There was no mention either that the MDS auction process was subject to political interference, as had been the case in January when Bob Collins suspended the auction.

Australis had very limited programming, and could not even begin to negotiate program supply arrangements with the Hollywood studios until it had broadcasting licences. Price, in his open letter to investors, also stated that Australis 'rejected satellite' and had 'selected proven technology' – that is, MDS.

Australis and MDS was promoted as 'the first subscription broadcast delivery system' which would become 'the gateway through which all other programmers operate'.[3] In a report issued to coincide with the float and listing, Macquarie Bank analyst Alex Pollak valued the shares at $1.12 a share 'as it stands today'. Pollak warned in his report that the only serious risk to Australis was that the unallocated MDS licences yet to be auctioned in the key markets of Sydney and Melbourne might be bought by 'an existing major media player', that is, Kerry Packer or Rupert Murdoch. This very real possibility was not mentioned in the prospectus.

There can be no doubting Pollak's independence, but it did not escape the market's notice that Australis's deputy chairman was Mark Johnson, an executive director of the bank which employed Pollak. Johnson was the same person who advised John Fairfax in its purchase of Melbourne's HSV 7 television station from Rupert Murdoch in 1987 for $320 million in defiance of the cross media ownership rules which had just been introduced by the Hawke Labor Government.

Neil Gamble was working in Brussels for Tyco International running the fire protection business that the US group had acquired from Wormald in 1990 when he received a phone call out of the blue from his old boss, Bob Mansfield, now running Optus. 'Neil, I've just been speaking to Steve Cosser,' Mansfield told Gamble. 'He's looking for a chief executive for Australis and I suggested your name. You'll probably get a call from him in the next day or two.'

The next day, Cosser called from Australia and told him about Australis's plans to eventually expand its number of MDS licences to run a full pay TV service, but in the short term was moving ahead by adding to its ethnic narrowcasting operations. 'Would you be interested in the chief executive's job?' he asked Gamble, who wasn't at all sure whether he wanted it or not. His initial reaction was probably negative. Cosser asked Gamble if he could fly to London to meet Rodney Price, who had just moved to the UK and who had accepted the chairman's role at Australis. As the chief executive would be working closely with Price, it was essential that the two should get on well. Gamble agreed to go to London, and met Price at one of the Thistle chain of hotels owned by Brierley Investments, of which Price was also a director. The two talked for some time, Gamble telling him about his experiences at Wormald. At the end of the talk, Price said to him, 'We really are looking for someone with pay TV experience. We've got two Americans lined up to interview, but I've been impressed with what I think you can offer.'

Two days later, Price phoned Gamble in Brussels. 'I've thought about it, and I'd like you to go to Australia for an interview with the board.' Gamble agreed to do it, although he still had nagging doubts about the job. He put the phone down in his apartment and turned to his wife Jean. 'There's no way I'm spending 24 hours in a plane only to have a one-in-three chance of getting the job.' At that moment, an announcer on the television said the network would soon cross live to Monaco to bring the decision on which city would host the 2000 Olympic Games. Gamble joked to his wife that if Sydney won, then maybe it might be worth considering the Australis job more seriously. At 7.30pm, when the live cross to Monaco showed International Olympics Committee boss Juan Antonio Samaranch declare Sydney as the 2000 Olympics host, Gamble decided that he'd better make the flight.

His interview with the Australis board in the Burrows Ltd boardroom was scheduled for 2pm on October 1. The talk went well, and Gamble was confident he would get the job, particularly as he had been so glowingly recommended by Bob Mansfield. Just as the interview was finishing, Steve Cosser said he had a meeting to go to and left, taking Richard Wiesener with him. He asked Price, who was also there, to come with them. They were on their way to see Albert Hadid, and Don Heller and Steve Plant from Lenfest Communications, to hear a proposition they wanted to put. Cosser had a pretty good idea what it was going to be.


As October rapidly came to a close, Albert Hadid was becoming increasingly agitated that another month had nearly gone and nothing was happening. Hadid was completely in the hands of Heller and Plant. Yet, he was hardly on speaking terms with them, and his previously good relations with Cass O'Connor and Malcolm Turnbull had also soured. He was getting most of his information about what was happening from Wayne Burt.

On October 22, Steve Plant and Cass O'Connor visited Burt at the Bain offices on the 20th floor of the Grosvenor Place building in George Street. Plant complained to Burt that Lenfest was getting nowhere trying to find another US cable company to join their venture to shoulder the costs. He said both Time Warner and TCI had refused to take any part so long as Albert Hadid had a prominent role in the venture. Lenfest was also trying to persuade Continental Cablevision and Cox Communications to come in to split the funding of the A licence, but the other groups were baulking at the level of free equity Hadid wanted. Plant said the only way Lenfest would find backing and/or other partners would be to reduce Hadid's role in the process. The adverse publicity which accompanied the awarding of the licences to Hi Vision and UCOM appeared to have scared potential investors away. Hadid still had a joint venture agreement with Lenfest, so this would not be easy. Plant said Lenfest had sufficient credit facilities available to develop one of the licences, but it wanted another partner with cash to help develop the business.

After Plant and O'Connor left, Burt phoned Hadid. 'Wayne, how did the meeting go?' Hadid asked. 'It went well,' Burt replied. 'I was surprised that Cass O'Connor came because I thought I was going to see Steve Plant alone, but anyway . . .'[4]

Hadid broke in, 'Well, at least you're having communication with them. We have no communication at the moment. Things have broken down, and I'm inclined to go my own way on this.'

Burt replied, 'Albert, that seems a little bit extreme because Lenfest said in the meeting, and I'm sure you're aware, that they had facilities available, cash and credit, sufficient to fund one of the licences and that they appeared to have an inclination to do so. If that's the case then clearly you should be talking to them.'

Hadid said, 'Well, that just doesn't seem possible at the moment, we've reached a stalemate. I am totally frustrated with them. I'm definitely inclined to go off on my own.'

That evening, Burt met Steve Cosser for dinner at the Bayswater Brasserie in Kings Cross. The two had been close friends and occasional business associates for over eight years. They had similar interests, similar personalities and there was little in their lives that they did not tell each other. Burt told Cosser about the tensions between the Lenfest and Hadid camps and that this opened an opportunity for Australis to take a role in one of the satellite licences, preferably the B licence. Because this was the only licence that Australian media interests could acquire (as well as foreigners, if they wanted it), it was intrinsically more valuable. Taking control of the B licence would freeze the established Australian media players out of the game because this was the only licence in which they could take an interest.

Burt believed he had some ideas on how Australis could effectively acquire the licence from Lenfest, while keeping the Americans in as a partner. Cosser was concerned about the delays in getting his MDS service in operation and he was interested in trying to do something with Lenfest, although he was sceptical about the price being proposed for the satellite licences. Burt said he was driving the next day to Palm Beach, where he was spending the weekend at a house owned by an old Macquarie Bank colleague, David Fitzsimons, only a few doors along from Kerry

Packer's large holiday home at the southern end of the ocean beach. His girlfriend Skye was preparing for an art exhibition and their flat in the inner eastern suburbs was crowded with paintings. 'I'll put the ideas on paper and we can talk early next week,' he told Cosser.

Burt thought further about his plan for Australis on the 40-minute drive to the beachside suburb of Palm Beach, with its ocean surf beach on one side of the narrow isthmus at the end of Barrenjoey peninsula and the stiller waters of Pittwater on the other.

After unlocking the front door of the house, Burt went into the bedroom and threw his bag on the bed. He took out a tape of Tibetan music and sat on the floor to meditate for an hour or so. Burt was a practising Buddhist, but commercial matters were never far from his mind. After relaxing with some meditation, he picked up a pen and notepad and sat at a small table while the ocean pounded the beach just below. He wrote in large letters at the top of the page the words, Project Midsummer.

Burt was on the road early on Monday morning for the drive back to the city. He had struggled to wake after a late night playing poker with Kerry Packer's son-in-law, Nick Barham, at Packer's huge Ocean Road house. The cold light of day brought with it the reality that he had yet another meeting, at 9.30am, in his office with Steve Plant and Cass O'Connor.

Plant reiterated Lenfest's desire for Hadid not to have any control over the operation of whichever licence Lenfest decided to capitalise because of the problems he claimed he had met in the United States with both investors and potential programmers. He said Lenfest needed to reach a deal by mid week with UCOM because time was short. The A licence bid lapsed on November 17, less than three-and-a-half weeks away. He said that Lenfest could put $US45 million into one of the licences, probably the A licence, and perhaps another US cable company like Continental Cablevision another $US30 million to fund the $97 million for the A licence. Plant brought up the CanWest structure as a way for the US companies to get around the foreign ownership limits of 20 per cent on individual investors, or 35 per cent in total.

Plant said the problem for Lenfest was that it needed to get Gerry Lenfest comfortable with spending $100 million, 'and he's not there at the moment'. Lenfest was worried about losing his $10.7 million in deposits. The meeting traversed a lot of territory, but it was all talk. Burt was waiting for a chance to talk to Plant privately. As they filed out of the meeting room, Burt whispered to Plant, 'Can I call you. I have something I need to discuss with you.' Plant replied, 'Sure, call me at the hotel.'

An hour later, Burt called Plant at the Ritz Carlton. 'I'm sorry I couldn't raise this at the meeting with you, but I wanted to have a private discussion with you about an idea that you may or may not have considered. It relates to your licence strategy and how you might fund it. Can we meet to talk about it?' Plant said, 'Yes. Meet me at the hotel tomorrow at 3.30pm.'

The American was waiting for Burt in the hotel's concierge room. Burt produced the page of notes that he had written at Palm Beach. Under the heading, Project Midsummer, Burt outlined, using code names, a strategy by which Lent (Lenfest) would acquire full control of the B licence, and sell it into Autumn (Australis), in exchange for shares in Australis.

'It's embryonic, we haven't fleshed it out and developed it in terms of a formal proposal, but I'm able to articulate the key aspects to you,' Burt told Plant. 'Before I do, I'd like to establish two parameters, if I may be so bold. One is that we would expect to be retained as the exclusive adviser on any transaction that results from this idea, assuming that it's something that you see merit in.

'Secondly, of course, we would expect you to pay the success fee and we think there are significant benefits accruing here and we would want to make the normal investment banking success fee on it which you, Steve, better than most know the sort of order we are talking about.'

Plant replied, 'Yes, I understand. Obviously I'd have to check with Gerry, but on that basis, assuming we like the idea and want to use it, then both of those aspects, the fee and the advisory role, would not be a problem.'

Said Burt, 'I want to stress this is entirely confidential.' Plant said, 'Absolutely, this has to be kept completely confidential between us at the moment until we see which way it's going to go.'

'The simple point is that we think you should consider forming an association or joining with Australis in some manner to be precisely worked out, but that would generate a significant number of benefits to you both,' Burt said. 'It's not earth shattering, as I say as an idea, but if I read through some of the benefits, present to you some of the benefits, then you will see it has some real impact.'

Burt had listed a number of benefits to both Lenfest and Australis individually, and also for the combined business. These included, most importantly, that if they invested in the B licence, it would remove the threat of competition from the Packer-Murdoch-Telstra syndicate, which could only buy into this licence.

Other benefits were faster and simpler fund raising, because Lenfest and Australis wouldn't be competing in the marketplace for funds; satellite and MDS could be used in conjunction with each other rather than in competition; and, because of this, MDS could be used almost immediately. If licence A was then bought by third parties it clearly would be a less effective competitor.

It would allow Australis to develop from being a small player in a fragmented industry to being part of a major group which was dominant. They would gain immediate access to broadcast television. Under the current moratorium on MDS, Australis could not broadcast, but only narrowcast. It would also lower programming costs because the two groups would not be competing against each other in Hollywood.

'Of course, as in all deals like this, the whole is hopefully greater than the sum of the parts,' Burt told an interested Plant. 'Australis is already listed. The combined capital to be raised would be less because you are raising it for one operating system. The technologies, to a certain extent, are compatible and overlap and could use similar uplinks. And the pool of institutional money that's on the sidelines – and this is where Bain's experience comes in – would be able to be committed to support the venture because the analysts would be able to sleep at night knowing there's not an active and already existing competitor.'

Plant told Burt, 'I see what you're saying. I appreciate that. I like it, it sounds very interesting and you have given me a lot of material.' He would speak to Gerry Lenfest and the other executives in the US overnight, and see what they thought about it. 'I'll get the feedback and call you tomorrow morning. Is that satisfactory?' Plant said. 'I look forward to your call,' replied Burt.

Plant appreciated Burt's insistence on confidentiality for a number of reasons, but from the point of view of both men, it was essential that Albert Hadid not find out about these talks.

When he returned to the Bain offices, Burt had a message to ring Hadid. He wanted a meeting, now. 'Come around,' Burt said to him.

Hadid walked into Burt's office and repeated his earlier claim that he was having trouble with Lenfest and Turnbull and Partners, that they were no longer on speaking terms, and that he would have to let the licences cascade again. The main point of conflict between Hadid and Lenfest was Hadid's insistence on UCOM having 30 per cent of the satellite business without having to invest any more money.

Both Burt and O'Connor had told him this was unrealistically high and that no outside investor or potential partners would come in on those terms. Burt told him, 'Listen, Albert, let's be frank about this, rather than cascading or whatever, talk to Lenfest and Turnbull, they're the people who have funded you. We've consistently said that. Just open the dialogue even if it's strained or frustrating at the moment. These things are always capable of being reopened and I recommend that you go and have conversations with them.'

Hadid agreed to try. But by this point a new agenda was taking shape and there would be no room in it for him. Events were spinning out of his control. The only hard bargaining chip he possessed was his ability to force the licences to cascade down to the next price levels, an event which would cost Lenfest the $10.7 million it had paid for the two deposits.

Soon after Hadid left, Burt walked quickly over to the Wentworth Hotel, where he had arranged to have a drink at the lobby bar with Steve Cosser. Burt was running late and Cosser was about to give a presentation on Australis and to introduce to analysts and fund managers the company's new chief executive, Neil Gamble, at a nearby stockbroker's office.

In their brief discussion, Burt asked Cosser to make some time for a meeting the following day to talk about the rapidly unfolding developments. Steve Plant was due to make calls overnight to the US and Burt would be in a better position to brief Cosser the next day on what was happening.

The next morning, Burt received an early call from Plant, who had spoken to Lenfest and Heller overnight. They were 'receptive' and willing to take the proposal a step further. But Plant warned, 'He is far from committed, because he still has to write a very large cheque.'

Burt suggested it was time to have a direct discussion with Steve Cosser. Plant said he would have to do it that day because he was flying back to the US the next day. Burt said he would arrange it. Before hanging up, Burt needed to know that he and Bains were going to make some money out of his ambitious plan. 'Did you put to Mr Lenfest the question of the Bains success fee?' he asked.

Plant said, 'Yes in general terms, I did.' Burt persisted: 'Will Bain be appointed to carry through the transaction?' Plant replied, 'Yes, in principle, that's been agreed by Mr Lenfest.'

Burt was straight on the phone to Steve Cosser, who was staying at the Ritz Carlton in Double Bay. 'The Lenfest people have agreed to meet you. You should do it,' he told Cosser. 'There's a possibility that they will fund one or other of these licences. I think they have the capacity to do that, and if they do it then you're going to have a pretty strong competitor if you don't join them.'

Cosser expressed scepticism that Lenfest would pay $97 million or $117 million for either the A or B licence. He added, 'Look, I'm prepared to meet, but I have to be absolutely categoric in stating that we don't have any funds, we're not interested in raising any funds and we're not interested in putting a dollar into the satellite game. Also, this has to be extremely confidential. This is a small market. We're a listed company and we believe in MDS. To have discussion with a potential satellite operator cuts across our business philosophy, our aspirations in our prospectus. If it comes to nothing, then it would be very damaging, potentially, if it came out.' Burt agreed. He suggested they hold the meeting in his room at the Regent Hotel, where he had been staying after returning from Palm Beach.

In his hotel room, Burt introduced Plant and Cosser and urged them to have a free discussion to see if there was any prospect of reaching some sort of association. Cosser very quickly took a negotiating position by stating that Australis believed in the technology of MDS and eventually it would be a broadcast television operator. The meeting shouldn't be taken as any sort of admission or concession that they were concerned by the presence of satellite television, he emphasised. Plant sensed that the opposite was the case. Australis was vulnerable so long as government legislation stopped it using its MDS licences for broadcasting, at least until December 31 the following year.

Plant said Lenfest was inclined to pay the $113 million balance of the B licence, indicating clearly that his group would be a force in this industry. Cosser said, 'Look, as you probably know, I'm standing down as chief executive. I'll tell Rodney Price the chairman and some of the executives of Australis and see what their reaction is. I wouldn't have your hopes too high at this because I think they'll be sceptical given our stated business strategy.'

The two were clearly wary of each other, neither wanting to give much away, but also wanting to give the impression each was confident of his position. Burt wanted to cut through all this, and suggested that the two principals, Price and Gerry Lenfest, meet as soon as possible. The three talked about the best location for such a meeting. Burt recommended Los Angeles. Given that Australia was separated from the US by the Pacific Ocean, LA was as close as possible to being half way between Sydney and Philadelphia. Plant and Cosser left Burt's room and took separate lifts down to the lobby. Cosser was acutely aware of the need to keep these discussions secret. The Regent is a popular watering and dining hole for Sydney's merchant bankers and lawyers. To have been seen with Plant would have set the rumour mill running.

For Burt and Bain, the situation was developing nicely. With his Project Midsummer concept finding some interest with Lenfest and Australis, he had managed to snatch from under the noses of Malcolm Turnbull and Cass O'Connor the potentially lucrative underwriting and advisory roles which would surely follow.


Burt and Cosser arrived in Los Angeles at about the same time, Burt having flown directly from Sydney and Cosser travelling via New Zealand. Cosser was paranoid about being found out or spotted dealing with Lenfest and wanted to cover his trail. The two had arranged their flights so they could meet up in LA, then fly on together to St Louis, where the meeting would now take place. As it was, their timing was good. They met at the luggage carousel at LA airport. Burt had negotiated with Steve Plant for Lenfest to pay his air fare. Rodney Price was as paranoid as Cosser and insisted that the meeting not take place in Los Angeles because he feared that they all might be spotted in a hotel foyer. LA was full of Australians. Instead, he agreed with Gerry Lenfest, with Burt and Plant acting as intermediaries, to meet in St Louis, Missouri. It was only an hour's flight from Philadelphia and Price was in St Louis anyway, ostensibly visiting the wheelchair manufacturer Everest and Jennings, owned by the Graham Field health care company of which Brierley Investments was a shareholder.

After arriving in St Louis, the port city at the junction of the mighty Mississippi and Missouri rivers, on the evening of November 1, Burt and Cosser took a taxi to the Ritz Carlton Hotel, where they were staying and where they were due to meet the Lenfest people the next day. Price was waiting for them at the hotel. Cosser introduced Burt to the Australis chairman. Price, a suspicious and cynical business veteran, wanted to know what Burt's relationship was with Lenfest. Burt told him he was advising Lenfest on its fund raising, but also that Bain and Co stood to earn a success fee if Australis and Lenfest got together to buy the B licence. Price was sceptical about the whole proposal that he knew would be put to him, but in particular he didn't believe anyone would be foolish enough to pay the high prices being suggested for the licences. Burt made the point that there was considerable tension between Lenfest and UCOM, that their arrangement could break down and Lenfest would not only lose control of the licences but also its deposit money.

The next morning in a conference room at the hotel, Burt gave Gerry Lenfest, Heller and Plant a brief outline on a white-board of his Project Midsummer plan. Before going into detail, Burt sought an assurance from the Lenfest executives that he would be retained as the exclusive adviser to Lenfest and that he wanted a 'healthy' success fee if the deal was consummated. Gerry Lenfest said he liked the idea of success fees, but when he heard what sort of percentage Burt wanted – 3 per cent of funds raised – said it was too much. Burt backed away. 'Let's sort it out later,' he told Lenfest. He didn't want to put the deal at risk at this early stage. He turned back around to the whiteboard and continued his briefing.

That afternoon in the same room, Cosser and Price joined the Lenfest people and Burt, who gave yet another rundown of the objectives and benefits. One of the most crucial elements of the plan was for Lenfest to secure control of the B licence from Hadid to enable it to deal with Australis. Price reiterated his view that Australis would not do the deal if Hadid was there. Gerry Lenfest said Heller would continue to try to reach an accommodation with Hadid, and that if this failed he would fly Hadid to the US and deal directly with him.

The discussion then moved to ways to consummate the deal. Price said Australis was in no position to provide any money for the licence. Lenfest would have to do it. Perhaps Lenfest could take a substantial issue of shares in Australis in return. The meeting went on for most of the day. That night in his room, Don Heller drafted an agreement between Lenfest Communications and Australis. It was in the form of a letter to Gerry Lenfest to be signed by Price and Cosser.

November 3, 1993
Mr H.F. Gerry Lenfest
The Lenfest Group,
202 Shoemaker Road,
Pottstown, Pa, 19464

Dear Gerry,

This letter is to confirm the agreement reached between Australis Media Limited (Australis) and the Lenfest Group (Lenfest). Lenfest agrees to sell its interest in New World Telecommunications Pty Ltd (New World) to Australis under the following terms and conditions:

1. Lenfest will obtain ownership and/or control of at least 90% of the shares held by at least 75% of the shareholders of New World.

2. New World must acquire the Australian pay television satellite licence B which it has bid on and was awarded.

3. Lenfest and New World must terminate and be released from its current business relationship and agreements with Turnbull & Partners.

4. Australis will issue new shares of Australis stock to Lenfest. The shares will be valued at $A.80c. Lenfest will surrender its shares of New World which will be valued at $A130 million. The number of shares to be issued will be 162,500,000 and the number of Australis shares/share equivalent issued prior to this transaction will be 180,000,000.

5. Australis will enter into a ten year technical services agreement with Lenfest. Lenfest will provide services as will be detailed in the formal agreement including but not limited to developing an operating structure, subscriber management system, marketing and pricing policy and management team. All personnel will be trained by Lenfest. Lenfest will also be responsible for the selection, acquisition and packaging of program offerings and have responsibility and authority to negotiate appropriate programming contracts. Lenfest will be reimbursed its out of pocket expenses incurred during the first two years of the agreement. These expenses will be budgeted and/or approved by the Australis board of directors. Lenfest will also be paid a fee calculated as a percentage of all revenue as scheduled below. The fee regardless of the calculations will not be greater than $A5 million in any one year.

*Technical service fee:*

| Year | Percent of revenue |
|------|--------------------|
| 1    | 5                  |
| 2    | 4                  |
| 3    | 3                  |
| 4    | 2                  |
| 5    | 1                  |
| 6    | 1                  |
| 7    | 1                  |
| 8    | 1                  |
| 9    | 1                  |
| 10   | 1                  |

6. Lenfest will be represented on the Australis board of directors with a minimum representation equal to its percentage share holdings.

7. A public offering of Australis stock will be undertaken to raise additional capital for the operation of the company. The principals of the company (Rodney Price and Stephen Cosser) will not make available any of their holdings as part of the offering.

8. Lenfest will have the rights to participate in any future public offerings to prevent its percentage ownership from being diluted.

9. All appropriate Australian laws and regulations with respect to ownership and structure will be strictly adhered to in the completion of this transaction. The agreement and negotiations on which it is based will be subject to the laws of New South Wales and exclusive jurisdiction of the courts of New South Wales.

10. The parties agree Bain & Company will be engaged under the terms detailed on the attached Exhibit A.

11. A formal agreement will be prepared incorporating the points agreed in this letter along with other appropriate provisions.

12. No communication or announcement of this agreement is to be made without the prior written consent and agreement of both parties except to those needed to complete the transaction. Those persons will also be bound by this restriction.

If the above has your approval, kindly acknowledge your acceptance by signing and returning the enclosed copy of this letter.

Sincerely,

Rodney Price    Stephen Cosser

Agreed to this 3rd day of November 1993
The Lenfest Group
By Gerry Lenfest

Heller worked on the agreement until well after midnight. Later that morning, the Australis and Lenfest people reconvened and asked Burt to remain outside the room. They had to agree on a fee to pay Burt in the event the plan proceeded to fruition. After a few minutes discussion, and in recognition of the benefits that would flow to both companies, they agreed to a total fee of $1.5 million to be paid half each by Australis and Lenfest. Price signed the agreement for Australis. Cosser declined, insisting that the signature of the chairman was more than sufficient to bind the company.

It wasn't entirely what Burt was seeking, but it was a reasonably good fee. From St Louis, Cosser flew on to France, Price remained on business in the US and Burt flew back to Los Angeles the following day. The following morning he ran along Santa Monica beach and pondered to himself just how well things seemed to be going. The only potential hurdle would be removing Albert Hadid if not entirely from the equation, certainly enough to reduce his influence to virtually nothing. That evening he had dinner with an old girlfriend living in LA, Susie Thurlow, and the next morning took the 10.30am flight back to Sydney.


Burt had hardly sat down at his desk on the morning of November 8, when Albert Hadid called. Hadid had no idea where Burt had been and, fortunately, didn't ask. The merchant banker had other transactions going at that time, and Albert had become used to him disappearing for a day or two at a time.

'Wayne, the situation is getting impossible. We're in danger of losing everything and I really need some clear thinking on all of this. Could I come and have a meeting with you?' he asked Burt. Burt was very cautious, and said no. 'We've been retained by Lenfest on some aspects of capitalising the bid and I don't want to get into a situation where I'm caught between the two of you involved in your discussions,' he said.

Hadid said, 'I understand that, but there's one particular idea that I really would like to run past you. Is it at all possible that we could just have a brief chat on an off-the-record basis about this idea?' Burt agreed.

'Wayne, I have this new avenue, new initiative which is fantastic and will enable us to fund the licence and I would like to get your view on it,' an excited Hadid told the merchant banker. 'It involves an insurance company called Financial Surety International, which is part of or associated with the Metropolitan

Reinsurance company. There's a proposal whereby they would put up the money for the licence – either licence but one of the licences – against a bond or an insurance policy or a life insurance policy that was going to be underwritten in London. I have had discussions with the underwriters and I am confident that it could be underwritten and they are going to advance me the money.'

Burt had never heard of this sort of proposal before. 'What do you mean, as a loan?' Hadid said, 'No it's an investment against a life policy that can be underwritten.'

This left-of-field development worried Burt. 'I think at this stage in the piece that sounds like a crazy idea to me and I'm not sure why you're wasting time on it. It sounds totally implausible. Lenfest are the people who have put up the deposit and I think you should be talking to them at the moment.'

Hadid said he intended doing that. 'I've been speaking to my group and I think I'll end up speaking for my group and we'll be asking Lenfest for some sort of a way to recoup our costs, repayment of our expenses. Then we will try to get some equity in the business.'

The insurance idea seemed to have gone away for the moment. Burt was relieved.


Rod Price flew back into Sydney the following day and called a meeting of the Australis board at the company's offices in the deteriorating 303 Castlereagh St building. Price said he had been to the US where he and Steve Cosser had agreed with Lenfest to acquire the B satellite licence in exchange for shares. This news came right out of the blue to the other directors, Mark Johnson from Macquarie Bank, George Bennett, a retired accountant, Gary Weiss and Phillip Scanlan, a former managing director of Australian-based Coca Cola bottler, CCA Beverages. The deal still faced some significant hurdles, but Price was confident it could be pulled off before the A licence expired in eight days' time.

He urged his fellow directors to keep the information totally confidential. Despite all of the behind-the-scenes activity involving Australis, the market got no hint of its deal with Lenfest. Australis shares, in fact, had slipped to 50 cents after its strong debut on the stock exchange. For anyone in the know, it was a superb time to buy the stock.

Over the next three or four days Hadid and Heller continued to haggle over the issue of how much free carried interest UCOM would have in the licence they developed. Hadid stuck with the 30 per cent, of which he said UCOM would have half and Lenfest the other half. Heller insisted that the maximum that would be accepted by US investors would be 10 per cent, or 5 per cent free equity interest each. The gap was so great it would never be resolved. Heller was hoping that Hadid would give up and ask to be bought out. In the meantime, he decided to continue the pretence of negotiating over free carry, when his primary goal now was to have Hadid removed.

Both started to consult their lawyers. Hadid sought the advice of media and entertainment solicitor Martin Cooper, and Heller a partner at the firm Clayton Utz, John Elliott. The two sides were each threatening to sue the other for preventing the completion of the licence purchase.

Hadid was pushing his case very hard. He was determined to reap some rewards for the work he had put into winning the licences and put himself in a position where his desire to produce local content material for the multi-channel service could not be refused by his partner. He was prepared to take the risk of the deal collapsing and the licences expiring because he would pick up at least the A licence at the next price levels below. He stood to lose the B licence because he believed that the next highest bidder for this licence was the Meridian consortium of the former Communications Minister in the old Fraser Coalition Government, Neil Brown. The specialist monthly newspaper, *Pay TV News*, reported in May that Meridian had offered $103 million for the B. Hadid was sure his next bid of $87 million for the A licence was the next in line. At the very worst, he would end up with one licence and be free to negotiate with a fresh partner.

Lenfest, however, stood to lose its deposits if it failed to buy out Hadid in time. It might be forced to agree to Hadid's 30 per cent free carry proposal, if it could not manoeuvre Hadid into a position where he would agree to sell. With full payment due on the A licence on November 17, Gerry Lenfest, back in Philadelphia, was forced to consider the harsh prospect of having the $11 million in borrowed money which he personally guaranteed evaporate before his eyes.

What was also becoming clear was that if Lenfest were to purchase the B licence, it would have to let go of the A licence and lose its $4.3 million deposit. It couldn't own both licences.

Wayne Burt knew too that Neil Brown was next in line for the B licence because Albert Hadid had told him at one of their meetings in the tense days following Burt's return from St Louis. On the night of November 12, however, Burt had dinner with Rodney Price at Darcy's, an upmarket Italian eatery in Paddington. The two talked generally about the proposed deal and the difficulty Don Heller was experiencing in trying to buy out Albert Hadid. Price was adamant that if Australis was to get involved, Hadid should have no continuing role. The adverse publicity associated with the licence bidding process and Hadid's efforts to find partners and raise money over the previous six months had been a turn-off for Price. The Australis chairman was concerned that if Lenfest was unable to deal with Hadid, that it would lose control of the B licence and the planned merger would fizzle. Price asked Burt whether he knew who stood at the next price level if the B licence cascaded. Burt said he believed it was Neil Brown's Meridian consortium. Price was very interested. Perhaps we should have a talk to Mr Brown, he suggested to Burt.

The next morning, a Saturday, Don Heller phoned Burt and asked him to meet him at the Ritz Carlton in the city. Heller was getting increasingly anxious about his inability to persuade Hadid to cede control of the B licence to Lenfest as part of his commitment under the St Louis agreement. Heller had made his latest offer, of $3 million, to Hadid over lunch the previous day. Hadid laughed and declined the offer. The American now called in Rod Halstead, another partner at Bain and Co's lawyers, Clayton Utz, and the two were going over some documents when Burt arrived at Heller's room just off the third floor meeting area of the hotel. One of the documents was the August 29 agreement between UCOM and Lenfest.

Heller told Burt he believed Lenfest's deposit money was in jeopardy because of the 'recklessness' of Hadid in not accepting a reasonable commercial offer. He had been discussing with Halstead the legal options open to Lenfest, in particular going to court to seek to enforce a solution on Hadid. Soon after Burt arrived, Halstead took the papers and left to do further work on these options.

Burt told Heller about his discussion with Price the night before, and said he would try to contact Neil Brown. Price wanted to explore his willingness to do a deal with Australis on Meridian's bid for the B licence. If Australis could buy or gain an option over the next lowest bid, then it would be insurance against the possibility of Hadid forcing the current bids to cascade. It would also strengthen Heller's hand in talks with Hadid. Although Lenfest stood to lose its deposits if Hadid forced the bids to cascade to the next level down, at least Australis and Lenfest would be able to pick up the B licence for $14 million less than the price being contemplated.

After leaving Heller, Burt phoned Brown's Melbourne home on the morning of Saturday, November 12. He had done a company search of Meridian and established Brown's home address and his phone number. He was told that Brown was staying at the Australian Club in Sydney. The merchant banker phoned the club and he was put through to Brown's room. When Brown answered, he introduced himself, and told Brown he was making an approach on behalf of Steve Cosser and Australis and had a proposition to put to him regarding the B licence. Brown suggested Burt meet him at the club. Burt had expanded his advisory roles yet again.

The two walked to the nearby Wentworth Hotel, where Brown said he believed his group was, in fact, the next bidder down. Burt asked him what his aspirations were for the licence if Lenfest and UCOM forfeited. He offered any assistance in the form of underwriting if required. Burt then suggested that Brown meet Rod Price and explore the possibility of cooperating with Australis over the licence.

Brown and Burt walked the 10 minutes to the Quay West apartments in the Rocks where Price was staying. When they entered the apartment, Price greeted them and introduced Brown to John Crase, an Adelaide accountant who looked after Price's complex financial affairs. Crase was a short man, almost bald, but clearly very close to Price. The Australis chairman explained there was a possibility of the B licence expiring because of the tensions between Lenfest and UCOM. He pointed out to Brown that his Meridian consortium would need partners if it won the licence and suggested that Australis with its MDS licences would be ideal. Brown agreed and was attracted to the idea. Price said that the Meridian bid would provide an avenue for Australis to enter satellite pay TV. He offered Brown the prospect of becoming a director of Australis. After an hour or so of talks, Brown asked to be excused. He had a dinner appointment, but would return later.

His appointment was with Albert Hadid, who wanted to see whether Brown was interested in selling the bid to UCOM. Hadid could then tell Lenfest to go to blazes and take up the licence at the next level. Brown didn't tell him he had been talking to Australis. After their meal, Brown agreed to think about Hadid's proposition. About 10.30pm, he walked back to Price's apartment.

Brown and Price negotiated for several more hours, during which time Price persuaded Brown that it was probably best for him to sell his interests to Australis rather than go through the trouble of capitalising the licence. Brown agreed to sell Australis an option over his bid for an immediate payment of $50,000 and, if the bid did in fact cascade, that Australis would buy the licence from him for $5 million. Price asked Crase to pass him his cheque book and he wrote a $50,000 cheque and gave it to Brown. By the time the arrangement was documented, it was after 4am.

Brown returned to the Australian Club with a big cheque in his pocket and the prospect of a lot more money. He expected to be pay TV's first millionaire. Burt went back to his apartment in Elizabeth Bay to get some sleep. He had a lot of work ahead of him over the coming days. That night, he was due to have dinner with Don Heller at the Ritz Carlton. With the next bid secured, Burt suggested that Heller could now afford to take the risk of allowing the bid to cascade. Sure, it would lose Lenfest its deposits, but they would be able to save more on picking up the licence at the next bid. Heller said they should fly to Canberra the next morning to tell the Department of Communications that the bid might, in fact, cascade again, but that it had been secured at the next level down. He feared that without assuring the department that things were in hand, further bad publicity over the bidding process might force the department and the Australian Broadcasting Authority to intervene.

The first preference was for Lenfest to reach agreement with Hadid. Burt offered to act as an intermediary. He would sit Heller and Hadid down together and thrash out a compromise. The next morning, before driving to the airport for the flight, Burt phoned Hadid, who was still fuming after Neil Brown had sold the option over Meridian's bid to someone else.

'Albert, things seem to be worsening in your discussions with Lenfest. I've met Don Heller over the weekend and he tells me that you're miles apart and not close to coming to any commercial resolution or agreement.'

Hadid said, 'That seems to be the case.' Burt then raised the temperature by informing Hadid that Lenfest was taking legal advice. 'Well, they can start taking legal advice. I've already taken my own and I'm well advanced with my own case and no-one takes me on. I'll strike first and I'll bring them all down.' Hadid was angry.

Burt tried to settle him. 'Hang on, Albert, calm down, I wasn't meaning to provoke you. I was just meaning to point out that they are taking legal advice and there's a very short time frame before at least one of these licences lapses. Things could get out of hand. Look, let's see if there's a commercial resolution first. Is that what you want?'

Hadid had just lost his fall-back position, so he had no choice now but to strike an acceptable arrangement with Lenfest. Burt then offered to bring the two men together to focus on the outstanding issues and try to bring some clarity to the situation.

'There would be a couple of conditions upon me getting involved in this because, as we've just discussed, there's all sorts of legal threats,' Burt told Hadid. 'I would propose having some sort of indemnity drawn up and signed by both parties which removed Bain and myself from any potential action that you may take against each other or against even third parties. I don't want to get drawn into all that stuff and I wouldn't sit down with either of you if that was going to be the case.'

Hadid was reluctant to agree. 'I've never signed anything like that and I wouldn't do it lightly.'

Burt went on, 'I suggest we meet at the Regent Hotel which is where I have a room. Would that be acceptable?' Hadid agreed to meet Burt and Don Heller at the Regent at 6.30 that evening.

After landing at Mascot, Burt and Heller took a taxi straight to the Regent and arrived just on 6.30. Hadid was late. While they were waiting in the hotel foyer, Heller said, 'I think the emotional level between Albert and me is too high. I don't think it is particularly conducive for me to be in the room for the initial meeting. You should meet him alone initially.'[5] Burt said the point of the meeting was to have the two sit together, but if Heller was uncomfortable, then he should take his own room, Hadid would have another, and Burt would shuttle between the two.

Hadid arrived about 7pm and after phoning Burt's room from reception, took the lift to the 19th floor. Burt told Hadid that Heller preferred not have direct contact at this stage. Could he take his own room? Burt would relay messages between the two men. The situation was becoming bizarre.

First, Burt wanted to make sure Hadid was prepared to do a deal. 'Are you here with serious intent?' he asked Hadid. 'Yes, I'm here to try and reach a deal and I want to do that because Gerry is our only option left,' Hadid replied. Second, Burt wanted Hadid's signature on an indemnity agreement. With legal threats flying around already, he didn't want to end up in court if his efforts to broker an agreement turned nasty afterwards. Hadid replied, 'Well Wayne, that would be extraordinary, an extraordinary thing for me to do because I've never signed a document like that. I'm not in the habit of limiting my legal remedies or legal options.'

Burt dug in his heels, 'I should imagine you would say that, Albert. But in this situation I'm not prepared to go much further – in fact, any further – unless this is signed. I've had Don sign it – you can see his signature on it – so he's in the same position as you.'

Hadid recounted the cases and the money he had won in the courts, then said, 'I'll sign it, I want to do a deal.' He corrected a mistake in the document, inserting the correct name of the company which held the B licence, New World Telecommunications, rather than UCOM, then signed it.

Burt asked Hadid to go and check into his room while he took the document to Heller to initial the change. Before Hadid left, Burt said, 'Well, at least I'd better fill in some fee for this so that there's some consideration on the document.' Burt filled in $1. He and Hadid joked about it. Hadid handed over a $1 coin. Burt said, 'Albert, I've got success fees on capitalisation of this licence and, hopefully, I'll get the underwriting. But if we don't reach an agreement here, this dollar will be the only dollar I make out of pay TV, so I'm going to keep it.'

Hadid returned to Burt's room about an hour later. Burt asked him what he wanted. Hadid said he had conferred with the other shareholders in his group and they had given him the power to conclude a deal. He gave Burt a one-page letter setting out six requirements, or alternatively a cash payment of $US25 million to walk away. The six points were a 5 per cent free interest in the B licence, or about $12.5 million worth of shares assuming a value of $250 million for the licence, $2 million payment up front, plus a further $5.5 million to cover UCOM's expenses. The third point was to make Hadid a commissioning agent for local content for the licence. Fourth, he wanted to appoint a director to the board of the licence holder. Fifth and sixth related to a request to Lenfest to pay the deposit on his next highest bid on the A licence, which would invariably cascade down later that week.

Burt took the list to Heller. He ruled out the board seat, the drama commissioning agency, and the payment of the deposit on the next A licence bid immediately. He described the expenses claim as 'outrageous'. His only concession was on the 5 per cent free carry, but on the much lower figure of the cost of the licence rather than value of the business after a subsequent capital raising.

The two men, as had been the case over the last three months, were miles apart. While Burt was in Heller's room on the 18th floor, Hadid was standing at the window of his 20th floor room looking directly into Bain and Co's offices in Grosvenor Place, next door, where people were still working.

As the night wore on, and Burt shuttled between Hadid and Heller's room, their positions gradually came closer together. The threats and posturing subsided. At around 4am the next morning, Hadid finally agreed to a payment of $13 million to sell his interest in the licence to Lenfest. Heller also conceded to his request to be appointed as the drama commissioning agent responsible for the 10 per cent local content for the new service. After the St Louis meeting, Heller had expected this would be one of Hadid's demands to be bought out of the licence and in a fax to Gerry Lenfest on November 4 had recommended that Lenfest 'give him a bone, but only verbal' on the agency request.[6] Lenfest later admitted that a verbal undertaking meant there was no commitment to the offer.[7] That was to prove to be the case.

When Burt delivered the news to Hadid that Heller had agreed to the $13 million plus the commissioning agency, he replied, 'It's not a bad night's work, is it?'[8] Burt called Heller in his room and asked him to come up to Hadid's room. The two shook hands.

At 2.30pm that day, Hadid, his lawyer Martin Cooper, Don Heller, Clayton Utz's John Elliott and Burt met in Burt's room in the Regent to sign the formal agreement drawn up by Elliott on the deal agreed early that morning. Cooper took the document and those present agreed to meet back at the room at 6.30. At the appointed time, Cooper and Hadid came to Burt's room. Hadid was agitated and angry. 'This is a disgrace. This document doesn't represent what we agreed. Everything's off. There's no deal.' Burt urged Hadid to calm down. 'What's going on?' Hadid continued. 'I'm not agreeing to this deal. It's a joke.' He then stormed out of the room.

Burt turned to Cooper. 'What was all that about?' he asked. Cooper said, 'Look, there's not really a problem. Albert's so emotional about all of this. He's giving up something that's been in his life for months and he can't bring himself round to let it go. He'll cool down eventually.' Before he left, Cooper asked for an assurance that Lenfest wouldn't onsell the licence to the Packer-Murdoch-Telstra consortium, as Hadid now suspected. Burt said, 'As far I know, there's no PMT involvement. You have my assurance.'

Cooper brought Hadid back a short time later. He was much calmer. Hadid told Burt he wanted Lenfest to pay the deposit on the next bid on the A licence when it cascaded down to $87 million two days later. 'That was not agreed last night,' Burt said. 'I don't care, I want Lenfest to do it,' Hadid said.

Burt went down to see Heller, who was still in his room. Heller wouldn't hear of it. 'We'll let it cascade and exercise the option over the Meridian bid.' Burt went back and told Hadid that Heller would not budge. 'Lenfest has its options, too.' Hadid suddenly realised that it may have been Lenfest that bought the Meridian option. 'OK, I'll agree to the original deal.' It was about 1am. Burt escorted him down the lift to the hotel lobby. Hadid had forgotten that his shareholders had been waiting downstairs expecting to sign the document while Hadid argued upstairs with Burt and Heller over the previous four hours. They were asleep on the couches in the foyer as the cleaners vacuumed around them. Hadid woke them up and they walked out of the hotel.

Early that afternoon, the same players reconvened at Clayton Utz's offices at 1 O'Connell Street in the city. This time, they would sign the agreement. Immediately after Hadid and his shareholders left, John Elliott told Don Heller that Lenfest could not own 100 per cent of the licence. It was illegal. It would need Australian shareholders technically to own at least 85 per cent. He asked Burt if he could be the nominal owner of 85 per cent of the licence until the Australis deal was announced, probably the next day. Burt agreed and Elliott drew up the documentation. Burt's colleague, Rowan Johnston, then pointed out to Elliott that Burt was a New Zealander. Heller – who appeared to be getting increasingly agitated as the technical ownership of the licence his company was about to pay $117 million for was being tossed around the room – suddenly exploded with anger at Elliott. 'How could you not see that,' he screamed at the lawyer. Elliott tore up the sale document and re-wrote it attributing the 85 per cent to Johnston, who declared himself to be a true blue Aussie.

Burt called Hadid back and asked him, in light of the mistake, to re-sign the sale documents, acknowledging Johnston as the major shareholder, which he agreed to do. Early the next morning, Burt was woken by a phone call from Rod Price. Time zones were becoming meaningless now that the discussions and dealings were being conducted across the international dateline between Australia and the US. Price was in Philadelphia and was close to reaching final agreement with Gerry Lenfest on the Australis purchase of the B licence. They had settled on the final price of $138 million, but were still negotiating the price at which Lenfest would be issued its 162.5 million shares. Price wanted 80 cents, Gerry Lenfest was offering 75 cents. The $138 million was composed of the $117 million Lenfest would pay for the licence, the $13 million it paid Hadid, the $4 million it would forfeit on the A licence and $4 million in expenses incurred by Lenfest. Price asked Burt to get the Australis directors together at Clayton Utz, where Heller would be waiting to sign the formal agreement – as soon as he and Gerry Lenfest agreed on the share value to be used to buy Lenfest's licence.

By mid-morning the Australis board, along with managing director Neil Gamble and company secretary Ross McCreath, Rod Halstead, Burt, Heller and Price's accountant John Crase were assembled in the Clayton Utz conference room awaiting the final word from Pottstown. Halstead and Heller were on a speaker phone to Price and Lenfest as the two reached final agreement on the share issue price of 75 cents to Lenfest. Gary Weiss and Neil Gamble started drafting a rough press release, which Crase recognised as being not very informative. Crase phoned a public relations operative who Price had known from the IEL days, Murray Williams, and asked him to come around to craft a more readable document. McCreath rang the stock exchange to inquire about the correct procedure for suspending trading in a stock pending an announcement.

About midday Sydney time, Price and Lenfest told Heller and Halstead over the speaker phone they had agreed on the 75 cent issue price to Lenfest Group. Halstead and Australis's new lawyer, Robert Mangioni, would begin drafting the final documentation. At 2pm, Williams took Weiss's rough press release draft and walked back to his office in Clarence Street to put it into a more readable form and prepare it for distribution. There had been some discussion in the Clayton Utz meeting room about a letter being sent to the stock exchange. Before he left, Williams asked the Australis lawyer, Robert Mangioni, whether the letter had been sent. Mangioni said it had.

But the two men were talking about entirely different letters. When he got to his office, Williams rang his stockbroker and put in an order for 125,000 Australis shares. The stock was trading at 49 cents.

It wasn't until 2.40pm, when he was reminded by Gary Weiss, that Neil Gamble told McCreath to ring the stock exchange and ask for a trading halt pending an announcement. The market had no idea what it could be. Apart from one significant line of shares which went through about 2.30pm, there had been little interest in Australis stock over previous days.

At 4.10pm, just after the close of trading, Murray Williams sent out the press release under Australis Media Ltd letterhead announcing that the company had bought the B licence from Lenfest for $138 million through an issue of shares. The acquisition of the satellite licence would permit Australis to develop at the same time its MDS narrowcast services to full broadcast television as well. Despite Cosser and Price's initial resistance to the deal, it was an ideal fit for Australis. The last paragraph of the release written by Williams stated, 'Lenfest was advised in this transaction by Dr Wayne Burt, a director of Bain and Company, who are retained to underwrite the public equity issue proposed for early 1994.'

The announcement caught the market completely by surprise. The heavy manoeuvrings behind the scenes by Cosser, Price, Burt, Hadid and the Lenfest people had gone undetected by the normally alert eyes and ears of the investment community. When the share-market opened the next morning, Australis shares jumped straight to 90 cents. The initial reaction of investors was that this was a brilliant move.

Murray Williams had made $51,000 overnight. But he was a little concerned that the letter Mangioni said he had sent to the stock exchange may not have gone, or had related to something else entirely. He should have made absolutely sure before he bought the shares. Foolishly, Williams said nothing.

Albert Hadid was mulling over his next move in his temporary offices in Bligh Street on the evening of November 18 when the fax came through from Andrew Price at Nomura. It was the two-page Australis announcement. Hadid picked it up and read it. He had been through an extraordinary corporate voyage over the previous six or seven months, but this document shocked him more than anything he had heard or read over that time.

He couldn't speak or comprehend what had happened. A little over 24 hours earlier he had been shaking hands with the Lenfest people and wishing them good fortune. Now they had sold out to Australis. Memories of the early October meeting at the Ritz Carlton with Steve Cosser and Rod Price, and Cass O'Connor's comment about the eyeballing across the room came flooding back. Where was Wayne Burt when he disappeared for nearly a week earlier that month? Here he is, credited with advising Lenfest on this transaction.

Hadid had been worried Lenfest would flick the licence across to PMT. Australis? That was far more hurtful. Hadid picked up a pen and started writing on a lined notepad.

Wayne Burt     258 1124
November 19, 1993

CONFIDENTIAL

Wayne,

You have betrayed my trust. As a director of Bain this is most concerning.

The shareholders are incensed. They want their money NOW. Wayne, we mean NOW. There is only undesirable alternatives for you (all of you).

Now it makes sense why you suddenly shifted from 30 per cent free carry to 10 per cent free carry. Why $117 million licence will be valued for $490 million after its payed for. Why you didn't care for Turnbulls dismissal and advised me not to be depressed about it, that Lenfest and you didn't care for them.

All the promises you made and that being in your hands and trusting you payed off. I trusted you, you virtually single mindedly plotted and directed me into believing you and accepting everything you proposed. Even the price twist of $13 million instead of $12.5 million was a wonderful performance. I can write a book. You as my professed adviser, friend and underwriter have a lot to answer for. We demand a meeting with you immediately. Before we lose licence A then you, Bain and Lenfest will be held totally responsible. You have already caused great damage to our business, including licence A.

Albert, on behalf of UCOM

Hadid sent copies of his letter to John Barnes, the chief executive of Bain and Co, and to the firm's chairman, Maurice Newman.

Burt phoned Hadid later that day. 'Albert, you're out of order sending such an abusive letter to me and my superiors . . .' Burt had hardly started talking when Hadid broke in. 'I want my $13 million immediately and you'd better get it for me.' Burt tried to explain that the $138 million included all costs, including the $117 million for the licence, and that Lenfest hadn't made a profit on the sale to Australis. Hadid said, 'I don't care about that. I want my money and you'd better get it for me.' He then hung up.

Burt was worried now. He had an indemnity against legal action signed by Hadid, but the situation had clearly enraged Hadid and there was no telling what he would do now. The next day, Clayton Utz, on behalf of Lenfest and Bain, wrote to Hadid denying the allegations made by him in his letter.

Bain and Lenfest could wait, Hadid thought. His first and most pressing priority now was to get control of the other licence. His $97 million bid for the A licence expired on November 18 and Lenfest lost its $4 million deposit. Its money wasn't completely lost because it was refunded in the form of Australis shares as part of the merger arrangement announced that day. The next day, November 19, the A licence cascaded down to Hadid's next bid of $87 million.

Rather than invest valuable time trying to raise the money for this deposit, Hadid approached the next bidder, John Bulbeck, whose Acocia Press group, which published *Pay TV News*, had bid $85 million. Hadid struck an option deal with Bulbeck similar to the one that Australis had done with Neil Brown: a small payment up front, a second payment if Hadid could raise the deposit, and further cash if the purchase of the licence was completed. In all, Hadid would pay Bulbeck $1 million. Bulbeck had little prospect of finding a backer if the process cascaded down to his bid, so he reasoned that he may as well try to make some money out of it. Hadid had been dealing with Bulbeck on and off over the drawn-out auction period because the publisher was negotiating to buy a maker of satellite dishes and MDS antennas in Newcastle.

Once he had secured the Bulbeck bid, Hadid locked up the next three bids with another two of his bids sitting at $82 million and $77 million. Instead of having just three days to raise close to $4 million, he now had 12 as each bid cascaded every three days towards what he believed would be his last chance offer. He was concerned that the bidding was getting close to the levels of Continental Cablevision's offer. Three days later, the $87 million cascaded, followed by the Bulbeck bid of $85 million. Hadid could see the A licence also beginning to slip through his fingers. On

November 24, the day before the $85 million bid expired and the process would cascade down yet again, Hadid received a phone call from Burt, who had been trying to get hold of him after receiving Hadid's anguished letter on November 19.

Hadid had refused to take his calls to this point, but both men now had reason to speak. Burt, along with Cosser and Price, were concerned that if the A licence fell into hands hostile to Australis, then competition between the licence holders would make it very hard for Australis to make money. The Government had always envisaged that the two licences would compete, but that there could be limited cooperation. Cosser and Price would push this interpretation of cooperation to the limit.

Hadid decided to talk to Burt this time because he was becoming increasingly concerned that he would lose the A licence. He had been talking on and off to Peter Frame from Time Warner, and an accountant that Frame had hired to help him, Anthony Hollis. So far, the offers Frame had been making were unacceptably low to Hadid and the American appeared to be in no hurry to do a deal. Hadid needed a deep-pocketed backer. Burt had promised to find him one during their long night of negotiations at the Regent Hotel.

The discussion wasn't a pleasant one. Hadid wanted to know the extent of his involvement in Lenfest's on-sale of the B licence to Australis. Burt chastised Hadid for sending copies of his letter to Burt's employers at Bain. After the unpleasantness, Burt offered to try to find a backer for the A licence, which could then be floated with Bain as the underwriter. He never missed an opportunity to earn a fee.

Burt's offer to help Hadid was driven largely by Cosser and Price's very real concerns that the A licence find a friendly home. Hadid accepted his offer and threatened to sue him if he failed. He also asked Burt if he could approach Gerry Lenfest and ask if he could pay the A licence deposit, or at least speed up payment of the $13 million Lenfest owed Hadid.

Burt called back on December 1. He thought he had a potential investor. Burt knew that one of the numerous cable operators Lenfest had approached in October and November had been an east coast cable group called Century Communications, run by a veteran of the industry, Leonard Tow. It was the 10th largest cable group in the US, bigger than Lenfest, with about 1.4 million subscribers. Century appeared to have been quite keen in its talks with Lenfest, so Burt called Steve Plant in Philadelphia to ask him if

Century might be interested in backing Hadid on the A licence. Plant, who was as concerned as Australis to have someone they knew own the A licence, gave him the number of the group's chief executive, a volatile Irish-American called Bernard Gallagher, or 'Bern' to his friends.

When Hadid asked Burt if he was calling from overseas, Burt said he was in London on another matter. In fact he was ringing from Steve Cosser's office in Paris. Hadid was still unaware that Cosser and Burt were close friends.

In his first phone conversation with Bern Gallagher, Burt briefed him on the bidding situation with the A licence and asked him whether Century might be interested in investing. After giving Gallagher a rundown, Burt pointed out that his firm Bain would require a success fee for introducing Century to the deal. After some haggling, Gallagher agreed to pay a fee, but it would be subject to later negotiation providing Burt was able to satisfactorily negotiate a partnership arrangement. Over the next three nights, Burt worked the phones in Cosser's offices in the Avenue Montaigne, trying to negotiate with Gallagher in Century's offices in the picture postcard Connecticut village of New Canaan, and Hadid in Sydney. A critical part of the negotiations between Gallagher and Burt was to strike an arrangement to share the estimated $500 million establishment costs of the satellite licences.[9]

Hadid was also negotiating with Burt and Gallagher on his request for 30 per cent of the interest in the licence without cost, or free carry. After the $82 million bid cascaded down to Hadid's last chance bid of $77 million, Hadid agreed to take 8.5 per cent free carry on condition he would have the commissioning agency for Australian content for the licence. Hadid was oblivious to the discussions between Burt and Gallagher on an infrastructure sharing agreement to share the costs of subscriber management, marketing, equipment costs, and perhaps even programming.

Although Burt was in line to be paid a success fee by Century, he was also acting for Cosser, Price and Australis in negotiating this highly sensitive agreement, which Cosser and Price believed was critical to the commercial success of their pay TV business.

With time running out rapidly, Gallagher on Thursday morning Sydney time (late evening on Wednesday in Connecticut) agreed that Century would pay the $3.85 million deposit required for this latest bid. If he didn't, the licence would go to someone else. At these levels, the cost of the licence was looking to be a far better commercial proposition than the $100 million-plus figures the various players had been dealing with until then. Gallagher explained that he did not have the ability to lodge the money in Canberra by the deadline of 5pm the next day, which was Friday December 3. After more frantic calls between Burt, Gallagher and Steve Plant, Lenfest Communications offered to arrange another facility through Toronto Dominion in Melbourne, as it had done when it paid the A and B licence deposits back in August, and lend the money to Century.

Century, of course, could only own 20 per cent of the licence under pay TV's foreign investment rules. Hadid had agreed to 8.5 per cent, but Century would need to find Australian investors for the residual 71.5 per cent. In the flurry of calls during Thursday, Rod Price told Bains, who were acting as the conduit for the negotiations between the various parties, that he knew a venture capital group which might be willing to take the 71.5 per cent Australian interest. At 7pm that evening, Burt's colleague Rowan Johnston hosted a meeting at Bains attended by Albert Hadid and his lawyer Martin Cooper, along with John Lever, chairman of Continental Venture Capital (CVC), the group Price had brought in, and Price's accountant, John Crase. Hadid was a little bewildered to meet these people he had never seen before. Crase introduced himself as a partner from KPMG Peat Marwick, and Lever as a principal of CVC. Lever said to Hadid when they were introduced, 'I got involved today . . . I know nothing about pay TV.'

As he was leaving his Stanmore office to get a lift over to the city, Hadid's mobile phone rang. It was Peter Frame's offsider, Anthony Hollis, from Time Warner. 'Albert, we want to do the deal,' he said. In the wake of the settlement of the B licence, Time Warner had come back with a number of offers for the A, with the last being a $25 million cash payment plus the commissioning agency for the 10 per cent Australian content. Hollis made the offer the afternoon Hadid was due to sign the partnership agreement with Century and CVC. Hadid rejected it, saying that even with an 8.5 per cent stake, his interest would be worth over $40 million once the A licence company floated. It was now 6.30pm, and Hadid was on his way to sign the deal. 'We'll equal or better that,' Hollis said. 'I'm sorry, Anthony, but the deal is done,' Hadid replied. That was the end of Time Warner's ambitions on pay TV in Australia.

John Lever was more than happy for CVC to take a technically controlling interest in the A licence without putting up any money. This CanWest-type ownership structure would lead to fierce arguments between the partners later, but with the deposit money due the next day and the ownership structure to be settled in the meantime, the parties had no time to argue fine details. The ownership documentation was signed that night and the next day Toronto Dominion agreed to lend the money to Century with a Lenfest guarantee. Johnston was on a plane early that afternoon with a Bains cheque to pay the deposit to the Department of Communications.

Although he had 8.5 per cent of the new licence, Albert Hadid was unaware of the negotiations going on between Century and Australis over the sharing of infrastructure costs. He also had no idea that Lenfest had loaned Century the money to pay the deposit. He was quoted in the press over the ensuing days (the CVC people had gone to the US to further negotiate the cooperation deal with Century and were uncontactable) as saying he expected the A licence to be floated and listed on the stock exchange and that it would be a vigorous competitor to Australis and Lenfest for subscribers and programming, in particular movies from the Hollywood studios.

The agreement which CVC and Century were trying to reach with Lenfest and Australis would ensure the exact opposite was the case.

*Lionheart*, Ron Brierley's 55-foot motor cruiser, pulled away from the Man O' War Steps near the Sydney Opera House at noon on February 14 for a lunchtime cruise on the harbour. Aboard were Bern Gallagher and the chief financial officer of Century Communications, a man named Scott. The two had flown from the US to sign the infrastructure sharing agreement with Australis and, once this was done, pay the $73.15 million owing on the A licence. Essentially the agreement provided for Century to pay 30 per cent of Australis's total establishment costs, estimated to be about $580 million, and in return receive an increased return from the business. Both of the four-channel licences would be run through the same marketing and subscriber management systems and revenues would go to a common management company.

As *Lionheart* motored slowly across Port Jackson to the other side of the harbour, where it would drop anchor off Bradleys Head in the lee of the gentle north-easterly breeze, a waiter started serving white wine, beer and mineral water to the 20 or so guests on board. The Australis party included Rodney Price, Neil Gamble and Ross McCreath. Also aboard were Price's friend John Lever and the managing director of CVC, a man called Vanda Gould, along with Wayne Burt, the facilitator working at times for Lenfest, Australis and Century. A notable absentee was Albert Hadid.

It was a brilliantly sunny day and Gallagher was able to put behind him the tough negotiations over the licence and the all-important infrastructure sharing arrangement. This included fee negotiations with a persistent Burt, with the two settling on a figure of $1.1 million. Gallagher also had to endure an interruption to a week of instruction at the David Ledbetter School of Golf in Houston, Texas, when he was visited there by Wayne Burt, Rod Price, and Steve Plant from Lenfest for further negotiations on the cooperation agreement.

All that needed to be done now was for Gallagher and Price to sign the cooperation agreement and they could relax and enjoy lunch. The signing done, Gallagher instructed his finance director Scott to arrange for the residual $73.15 million to be telegraphically transferred to the Department of Communications in Canberra.

As the afternoon wore on and most of those aboard had plenty to drink, Lever, Gould and Gallagher found themselves upstairs in the wheelhouse. Their discussion moved on to the issues of ownership and control of the A licence, which would trade under the name of XYZ Entertainment. As his company was putting up virtually all of the money, Gallagher understandably believed that Century would be running the business. Gould disagreed. CVC had 71.5 per cent of the voting shares of the company and he expected his company to have a large say in what would happen. The combination of drink, several hours in the hot sun and a clearly unresolved issue among the parties triggered a loud argument. Neither Gallagher nor Gould would back away, and Lever attempted to calm the two down.

As the shouting continued, Neil Gamble and Rod Price moved to the foot of the stairs to find out what was happening. Gallagher finished off another bout of shouting by grabbing a copy of the cooperation agreement off a table in the wheelhouse, tore it up and threw it overboard. 'That's it, we're out of here,' he yelled at Gould. He shouted to his colleague Scott, who was among the bewildered group downstairs, 'Get that money back, we're going home.'

As the torn contract drifted in the water, Ross McCreath called to someone with a mobile phone to call a water taxi. Gamble asked

Price, 'What's going on?' As he opened his coat to reveal another copy of the document in an inside pocket, Price said, 'I don't know what's happening. I'm just a simple farmer.'

The boat captain rightly adjudged that the lunch was over, upped anchor and motored quickly back to the Man O' War Steps. Gallagher and Scott jumped off and walked one way, Gould and Lever another, without a saying a word. Everyone else on the boat was still trying to work out what had happened.

It did not augur well for this partnership, nor for Australia's satellite pay TV industry.

# 8

# The coming of cable

On the morning of October 13, 1993, John Malone of Time Cable International (TCI) and Raymond Smith, the chairman of Bell Atlantic, called a press conference at Bell's Manhattan headquarters to announce the world's largest merger, an exchange of shares valued at $US33 billion which would bring together the combined $US60 billion in assets of the two companies. Coming in the midst of the toe-to-toe stoush for Paramount studios between Viacom and Barry Diller's QVC home shopping company for Paramount, which ended with Paramount falling to Viacom for $US10 billion, this deal rocked the communications and entertainment industries. It appeared to achieve in one, very expensive, move what most of the players in these businesses were aiming to do: use the powerful cash flows of a telephone company to energise a rich program storehouse like TCI, which also happened to own one in every four set-top boxes in the US. TCI, through its programming arm Liberty Media, held interests in CNN, TNT, QVC, Court TV, Black Entertainment Television, American Movie Classics, Discovery Channel and half of Lenfest Communications.

No combination of companies globally would be better placed to exploit the opportunities on offer down the information superhighway and through the gateway to the home – the set-top box – than this. Two days after the merger was announced, Rupert Murdoch described Malone as 'a genius'. Said Murdoch, 'He throws up new ideas every five minutes. He surprised all his closest

associates, I'm told. He sprung it on them at the weekend.'[1] Malone
and Murdoch were arguably the two most powerful figures in the
US communications industry. In his book, *The Highwaymen, War-
riors of the Information Superhighway*,[2] Ken Auletta, writes of
Malone:

> Malone transacts his business from an eleventh-floor corner office in
> a corporate park in suburban Denver. A block of gray granite serves
> as his desk . . . the two exterior walls are windows and from them one
> sees nothing but the snow-capped Rockies. There are no mementos or
> plaques. The only touch of whimsy is a large fake-fur gorilla dressed
> in a white T-shirt and a red CNN tie, which sits on a chair facing the
> door. Malone instructs entering visitors, 'Say hello to Ray Smith . . .'
>
> Malone is a private person – so private that he rarely asks even
> close business associates personal questions and expects none in
> return. Not a single photograph is visible in his office – not even of
> his wife of 30 years Leslie, nor of his daughter, Tracy and her one-
> year-old daughter, nor of his son, Evan, a senior at the University of
> Pennsylvania . . .
>
> When Malone appears on industry panels or testifies before con-
> gressional committees, he seems a frosty figure dressed in boxy suits
> and wearing the strained expression of a scientist or an investment
> banker. In Colorado, he seems much more relaxed. He is 52 years old,
> about six feet tall and square-shouldered. He speaks in a monotone,
> but there is about him an unmistakable intensity. His eyes are hazel
> and they fasten on visitors . . .
>
> He is a man of science; he has a PhD from John Hopkins Uni-
> versity in operations research, which centers on the construction of
> mathematical models. In business life he strives for pure logic, unal-
> loyed by emotion, unswayed by friendship or sentiment.

Malone would later play a key role at a turning point in the pay TV
industry of Australia where his furthest flung investment, through
Liberty and Lenfest, was Australis Media. Australia and Australis
barely registered on the scale of priorities for Malone and TCI
as 1993 drew to a close and the new year produced more of the
dramatic manoeuvrings which were reshaping the communications
and entertainment industries in the US.

Not long after its merger announcement with TCI, Bell
Atlantic announced a joint venture with two other regional phone
companies, Nynex and Pacific Telesis, and with Hollywood agent
Michael Ovitz's Creative Artists Agency, to explore interactive
multimedia services across the phone companies' networks. The
phone companies would provide $US300 million in seed capital for
the venture.[3] Deal followed deal. The temperature was rising to

furnace heat and the risks to alarming levels as players jostled to position themselves for the anticipated boom in services transacted via cable or phone line to computers or television sets in the home. Huge deals at unsustainable multiples were being announced almost daily in the race to tie up programming, develop consumer services, and the means to deliver them. No-one really knew where it would end or whether the information superhighway would take them to the pot of gold at the end of the rainbow . . . or towards a high-speed corporate collision. But few dared not join in the frenzy for fear of being left behind.

The massive release of money from the US phone companies, which until this time had been bottled up by regulation, also provided enormous incentives for the equipment providers such as General Instruments and Scientific Atlanta to accelerate their development programs. Digital compression – the asymmetric digital subscriber loop (ADSL) technology allowing video to be transmitted down phone wires – and the research backed by Continental Cablevision into sending voice and video traffic down the same fibre optic cable were coming rapidly to fruition. The potential rewards were huge for companies able to translate these technologies into commercial use.

The Bell Atlantic-TCI merger fell over in February 1994 after the US Federal Communications Commission, in a left-of-field decision, ordered all US cable companies to freeze their rates. By preventing further increases, the decision would reduce TCI's cash flow by about $US300 million a year.[4] Bell wanted to reduce the purchase price, and the deal died.

But by now the momentum was so powerful that it was not diverted or even diluted by the demise of the world's largest merger. The waves from these tectonic movements in America's corporate geology rippled quickly across the Pacific, splashing over Australia. Bob Mansfield at Optus and Frank Blount at Telstra could both see that the rush in the US to bring together content (movies, sport, home shopping, Internet, telephony) and new and more powerful delivery systems to the home would set the cast for their own businesses.

The question confronting them both was how they should react, not whether they should. The rewards would go to the company which moved first and secured the best content package. More particularly, the penalty for allowing the rival to take the initiative would be fatal for the emergent Optus or, for Telstra, come at heavy cost in terms of its market share in its main business of telephony. Blount was also aware that if the Keating Labor Government did not privatise Telstra, then an incoming Coalition government certainly would. If he presided over a massive erosion in the value of Telstra by allowing Optus to take half of his phone customers using an attractive pay TV and content package, he would be lose his job.

To assess the impact on its revenues and value of doing nothing, the Telstra board retained Chris Beare, a former Telstra executive who had joined the merchant bank Hambros as a telecommunications specialist. Beare built a computer model which he called his 'black box'. When he fed in assumptions about a cable roll-out by Optus and potential rates of take-up of its pay TV and phone services by households, Beare estimated it could reduce Telstra's value by between $6 billion and $8 billion. These were large sums, especially when Telstra was being valued by market analysts at between $15 billion and $20 billion in anticipation of a float of the carrier in the near future.

As he stared over leafy suburbia and the public tennis courts from Continental Cablevision's modest offices, Martin Hannes knew more than anyone that the dramatic developments in the US would have immediate implications for Australia. He was a persistent caller and visitor to his old school friend Bob Mansfield at Optus in North Sydney. It was now or never, he told Mansfield. The trials Continental Cablevision had been conducting had reached the point where his group was confident the technology would work. Optus needed to decide whether to build its own network using new technology, or continue to ride on the back of the Telstra networks and risk being marginalised by the rush of new competitors which would come into the market after deregulation in July 1997. It was now early 1994. Optus had a three-year window of opportunity in which to establish a serious rival service to Telstra's. If it delayed, it would open the door to a large overseas carrier such as British Telecom or AT&T to come in after deregulation and build a second national network.

If Optus agreed to go ahead, it could offer its own phone service along with pay TV and other applications, such as home shopping, banking and gambling, down the same cable and strike deep into Telstra's phone revenues running at $13 billion a year. Mansfield was receptive, but as much as it was a risk to do nothing, it was also a huge gamble to proceed. To build a cable network would cost anything between $3 billion and $10 billion, depending on how far Optus wanted to go. Optus's total revenue that year was expected to be a little over $800 million and it would be lucky to break even after accounting for its costs. After paying debt interest, it would lose close to $100 million for the year.[5] Mansfield reflected later:

> I spent three years at Optus on the edge of my seat on a lot of approvals and time lines and executions that were right at the leading edge of world technology. We took different components from companies that had not worked together and set an unbelievable time line that presumed that we'd make them work together. Having been on the edge of this technology juggernaut there was full recognition at Optus that we were right at the leading edge. We would have been the first in the world to apply this, but having won the challenge with so many previous steps we weren't overconfident, but had some expectation that it would happen.[6]

Until this time, Telstra had moved in slow, deliberate steps towards the long-term objective it identified in the early 1980s, of eventually cabling up households and offering its nine million accounts other services beyond a generic phone line. In the late 1970s it built fibre optic cable links between the main metropolitan centres of Australia to cope with the increasingly heavy voice and data traffic between the cities. As communications developed in the 1980s with the introduction of video conferencing, facsimile, and high-speed data transmission by corporations and information services such as AAP, fibre optic cable was extended into the cities, where it formed a core loop.

Fibre optic cable consists of a number fine fibres – usually eight, 12, or 16, depending on the requirements – which transmit laser light pulses carrying the voice or data. Each fibre is capable of carrying about 150 megabits per second of information, or about 2,500 times the capacity of a phone line. As the intensity of the signals diminished away from the city centres, so did the need for high-capacity fibre optic transmission. Until the development of the Internet for popular use in the 1990s, the two twisted copper wires which made up the great bulk of Telstra's phone network were more than adequate for domestic use. The arrival of the Internet, combined with the dramatic growth of data transmission by corporations in the 1990s, forced phone companies worldwide to the realisation that their old systems could not cope much longer. As the voice and data traffic loads moved out into the suburbs, the phone companies were forced to take cable nearer and nearer the home.

By 1994, Telstra had renovated its old copper wire network to the extent that its fibre loop reached to within 600 metres of 50 per cent of Australian homes. With the copper network starting to reach the end of its shelf life, it was only a matter of time before Telstra would be forced to take the biggest and most expensive step yet – to extend the cable the 'final mile', in industry jargon, from the main metropolitan loops to the country's six million homes. This would be an enormous task, and rank in terms of scale and cost with the largest infrastructure projects ever undertaken in Australia.

For this final stage, Telstra would use the slightly cheaper but more suitable coaxial cable. This consisted of a central copper core, surrounded by plastic insulation which in turn is wrapped in a sheaf of woven metal, usually aluminium, over which is the outside protective covering of grey or black plastic. Whereas fibre optic cable transmits pulses of laser light, coaxial transmits an electronic signal. The mixture of fibre optic and coaxial was colloquially known as a hybrid fibre-coaxial cable, or HFC.

It was possible to take fibre optic all the way to the home, a long-held dream of phone companies. But in reality, this would be impractical. Martin Hannes used the analogy of the water main into a home. If a copper wire telephone line was like the traditional half-inch water pipe, coaxial cable would have the capacity of a one-foot wide pipe and fibre optic would be like a one metre conduit. 'How much water can you use?' he asked.[7]

In September 1993, the Telstra board agreed to a senior management plan to run a very limited trial in which it would connect 100 homes in the Sydney suburb of Centennial Park. This was primarily to test the set-top boxes made by General Instruments, News Corporation's Datacom, and Scientific Atlanta which were on offer at the time. It would also allow Telstra to develop the interface between the fibre optic cable and the coaxial cable. The following month, just a few days after Bell Atlantic and TCI announced their merger, Telstra asked for expressions of interest from technology groups globally to supply the infrastructure for a cable network. Potential tenderers such as Japan's NEC, America's AT&T, Germany's Siemens and Holland's Philips would be asked for proposals to build and operate the network; from laying the cable, supplying set-top boxes, to providing subscriber management and billing systems. Interested parties had five days to convince Telstra they were serious before formal tenders were called on October 22, with bids closing on December 17, a period of just nine weeks.

Telstra's head of network products, Gerry Moriarty, a bearded, bespectacled New Zealander hired from Television New Zealand earlier that year, gave the first hint that accelerating events may force Telstra to pick up its pace. The short tender period was 'tight but realistic', he said. 'Time and speed factors will be part of the costing factors for this.'[8] Moriarty stressed that the cable would be a common carrier offering 64 channels to be used by information suppliers or program packagers.

By early 1994, Telstra was aware that Optus was close to striking a deal with Continental Cablevision. Telstra had also been talking to Martin Hannes, but Hannes had left his meetings with Telstra executives unsure of what the carrier wanted to achieve with its cable roll-out, and whether it was more a defensive move than a strategic advance. One point on which the Telstra people were firm was that pay TV revenues would have to finance the construction of the cable, and that the telephone business would be kept entirely separate.

Hannes felt he was making more progress with Optus's Bob Mansfield, who appreciated that he had to proceed to build a new network, or face being sidelined after deregulation. Apart from a long friendship since their school days, Mansfield was enormously comforted by Hannes's offer to back Optus if it decided to build a network and use the phone-and-video technology Continental Cablevision was offering.

Despite its lack of a clear vision, Telstra knew that time was ticking away and it had to make some big decisions on the future of its network. The strategic issue for Telstra was entirely different to Optus's. As the former monopoly carrier, its market share could only go one way with the introduction of competition, and that was downwards. As desperate as Optus was to attack Telstra's soft underbelly, so was the awakening Telstra anxious to defend its exposed position.

Kerry Packer was also watching the corporate upheavals in the US and the unfolding developments in Australia with great interest. As usual in matters which might affect the commercial interests of his Nine television network, or from which he might make some money, Packer and his American lieutenant Brian Powers were in the thick of the negotiations.

Although his PMT consortium had gone into hibernation after its failure to secure a satellite licence, Packer was still very much aware of the advantages of being involved in a powerful consortium which would dominate pay TV and home gambling. After he and Brian Powers spoke to Martin Hannes, the pair were very attracted to Hannes's idea of including potential revenues from telephony to rapidly shorten the pay-back period for such a large investment.

Packer's initial preference was to deal with Telstra to negotiate cable delivery of the service he envisaged. Packer and Blount were still partners in the consortium and Telstra would always be a tough player to beat in the Australian market because of its dominance of the communications industry. The long delays with the satellite bidding process and setting an international digital standard, which in turn delayed development of the appropriate digital set-top boxes, convinced Packer by early 1994 that satellite should be by-passed. He had always regarded satellite as a transitional technology that would be a useful way of building a large subscriber base with a pay TV package before migrating that customer base across to cable. This would be the ultimate delivery vehicle because it was interactive with the household subscriber and could carry many more channels, once digital technology was developed for an almost unlimited range of interactive services.

In their early meetings through January and February 1994 as the various parties pushed and prodded each other to test their commitment to cable, Blount agreed with Packer and Powers that telephony would make the package a better commercial proposition. But the Telstra boss met stiff resistance among his senior executives to the proposal. After weeks of discussions and negotiations, he was unable to meet Packer's insistence that Telstra would include a proportion of its telephone revenues in the income derived from the services to be offered on cable. The Telstra culture dictated that it would share its phone business with no-one, particularly if it was footing the cost of rolling out the cable. Also, to maximise its revenues, Telstra wanted its cable to be open to all comers who wanted to use it. Blount could only provide about 20 channels for a PMT pay TV service. The set-top box in the home would have another 40 or so channels provided by other program or service suppliers.

Packer and Powers were drifting across to Optus, despite the fact that the second carrier would be coming from a long way behind to catch Telstra's fairly advanced cable roll-out. Packer believed the economics stood up far better when telephone revenues were included in the mix. He also agreed with Optus's desire to keep the cable exclusively for the services provided by its own consortium members. Mansfield's marketing instincts told him that if he was to use the Optus brand name to attract customers, he didn't want a hotch-potch of other, potentially competitive, services cluttering up the programs coming through the receiver box.

During their discussions, Mansfield asked Packer to take an investment in Optus. This would be a very public demonstration of faith by Packer in Optus and its strategy. It would also help Optus attract more partners and smooth its efforts to raise funds for its cable roll-out. After some haggling over price, Packer agreed to buy 15 per cent for $318 million, representing a notional price of $1.20 a share. Packer and his senior people, Powers and Nick Falloon, were comforted that Optus would make its phone and pay TV technology work because it would be backed by Continental Cablevision. Although Optus wasn't listed, Mansfield anticipated that it would be floated perhaps as early as the end of the year. The foundation shareholders wanted to sell down or quit completely once the business was running strongly and they could only do this effectively through a listing which would put a market price on the shares.

The float price being contemplated at the time of Optus's negotiations with Packer was about $2.10 a share, which would have valued the Packer parcel at $556 million. Mansfield and the Optus board recognised they were selling the shares cheaply to Packer, but it would be worth it to have him and his reputation for possessing a 'Midas touch' being closely associated with the company.

The announcement on April 11 caught the communications industry and the investment community by surprise. Mansfield was hailed as a hero for pulling off such a major coup in bringing Packer in like this. But Packer's decision to back Optus rather than his PMT partner Telstra raised a few eyebrows. Would Optus be brought into the consortium too? How would it get on with Telstra? Or, more to the point, was this the beginning of the end for PMT?

At its April meeting the Telstra board, chaired by David Hoare, voted to accept Frank Blount's recommendation that the carrier proceed with a limited cable roll-out from the fibre-optic loop to 1.1 million homes in the Sydney and Melbourne metropolitan areas. The project would take three years and cost $730 million. Although it took no-one by surprise given the build-up towards the decision, it was as significant as Japan's raid on Pearl Harbour as a declaration of hostilities against its opponent.

Optus was arming for its response. Three weeks later it culminated months of negotiations and signed a formal joint venture agreement with Continental Cablevision to work towards construction of a multi-billion-dollar cable network to offer phone and pay TV services. Telstra had been half expecting this announcement too, because it had assumed Martin Hannes would also have been talking to Optus about his plans to put phone and multimedia services down the same cable. It was dawning on Telstra that the days of its comfortable monopoly in the local call market were numbered. Bob Mansfield had come cap in hand trying to negotiate from a position of great weakness with Telstra to obtain access to its network at reasonable commercial terms, but had failed. Why would Telstra give cheap access to its core network to a rival intent on stealing its business? Telstra reacted predictably and sent Mansfield on his way. Now, it was suddenly confronted with serious competition from a reinvigorated Optus backed by one of America's biggest cable companies. Unless Telstra fought back with even more firepower, it would realise the worst scenarios foreseen by Chris Beare's 'black box'.

Michael Lee had only been in his new job as Communications Minister a few days when he paid a courtesy call on Frank Blount in his Sydney office. Blount wanted to see the new minister to discuss the main issues confronting the government-owned carrier. And Lee was keen to see Blount. After all, Telstra was the Government's single most valuable asset and it was being drawn increasingly into the corporate storm starting to engulf the telecommunications industry. When Lee walked into Blount's 15th-floor office, the American introduced him to David Hoare, the silver-haired Telstra chairman. Lee knew straight away this would be no ordinary briefing.

Lee was given the Communications job in January after the resignation before Christmas of Labor Treasurer John Dawkins, which gave Paul Keating the opportunity to reshuffle his Cabinet and split Transport and Communications into separate ministries. Dawkins had had a gutful of politics, dealing with an obstructive

Senate, and the endless hours of flying between Canberra and his Fremantle electorate in Western Australia.

Keating liked Lee and respected his strong Labor background. A boyish 38-year-old, Lee had joined the party in 1972 while in year 11 at De la Salle College with other boys who would also become party and union luminaries. These included Seamus Dawes, John Della Bosca and Stephen Hutchins. After moving to the NSW central coast, Lee continued his interest in politics and won a tough pre-selection contest for the seat of Dobell ahead of the 1984 election. He may have looked like an upwardly mobile 'chardonnay socialist' ready to compromise long-held party traditions in the interests of 1990s pragmatism, but Lee was old-school Labor in his thinking. He wasn't about to roll over in the face of pressure from vested commercial interests, but was keenly aware that his party's support came heavily from working-class and low-income groups.

Lee resisted the Communications job initially because he regarded it as a poisoned chalice after Bob Collins' prolonged traumatic experience through 1993 with the MDS and satellite auctions. But Keating could be very persuasive.

Now Lee was in the Government's ministerial hot seat. Blount and Hoare wanted him to resolve a long-running issue between the company and its shareholder. Telstra planned to commit to a number of strategic partnership agreements, or SPARS, with its major corporate clients, such as Westpac. The effect would be to lock these customers in with attractive pricing arrangements. Telstra wanted to use its market power to dominate the large corporate market. There were legal and trade practices ramifications and Lee was cool to the idea. Optus was suing Telstra and the issue had been the subject of lengthy discussions between the Communications Department, Telstra and Optus. Telstra saw the Government's reluctance to allow these SPARS as a restriction on its ability to compete. Blount and Hoare showed every indication of wanting to press this matter further. Later Blount threatened to drop all phone charges to discount levels, if the Government persisted with the view that these agreements might be discriminatory and therefore illegal. The meeting was outwardly friendly, but strained under the surface. It augured badly for future relations between Telstra and its new Minister.

The cable roll-out was hardly discussed. Telstra had telegraphed its plans publicly back in November and in January had formed a company called Visionstream to act as the main contractor for the cable project.


Within days of Bern Gallagher's drunken, document-tearing display aboard Ron Brierley's boat on Sydney Harbour that sunny Monday afternoon in mid-February, the delicate arrangements between the A and B satellite licence holders came under far more serious threat. The PMT consortium launched two legal actions late on the evening of Friday, February 25, aimed at exposing the close links between the two licences. A company associated with PMT, Claybon Pty Ltd, also sued the Australian Broadcasting Authority, seeking a review of the decision to award the licences, alleging that the ABA was in error because it had not been fully informed at the time.

News Limited's lawyers, Blake Dawson Waldron, alleged in the PMT action that the B licence owner, Lenfest Communications/Australis, was in a position to control the A licence because it paid the $3.85 million deposit on behalf of Century Communications, and that it failed to disclose this to the ABA. Blake Dawson Waldron was taking the action on behalf of the main PMT company, Australian Pay Television Pty Ltd, which was seeking compensation for loss and damage at having missed out on the B licence.

In the second action, Claybon sought a review of the licence allocation because Lenfest effectively controlled the A licence as well. Claybon also attacked the CanWest-style ownership structure of the A licence, in which Century appeared to have all the economic ownership, but only 15 per cent of the voting rights. It was this arrangement which had led to the argument between Gallagher and Vanda Gould aboard *Lionheart*.

Interestingly, Claybon declared itself in its statement of claim to have been a bidder for the A licence, despite the fact that PMT was legally prevented from holding the licence. Its court action was prepared by Melbourne solicitors Holding Redlich and Claybon's directors were partners of the firm. Claybon was a classic $2 shelf company, which was de-registered in 1998. Unfortunately, no-one associated with PMT can remember what Claybon was doing bidding for the A licence. Memories conveniently have faded on this matter. The only rational explanation is that while it was not eligible to buy the licence, it could at least lodge a bid to gain standing in the event of any future legal action, like this. None of the PMT partners could hold more than the maximum permissible cross-ownership level of 2 per cent of the A licence in the event they had won the B.

There appears to have been a more solid connection, however, between PMT and the A licence than anyone cares to recall. In a letter dated November 30, 1993, Time Warner's Peter Frame reports to his superiors in New York on negotiations with Albert Hadid to buy the A licence. Time Warner was legally able to buy the licence because it was not an established media player in Australia, apart from its *Time* magazine interests. Frame canvasses the prospect of suing the Government for disqualifying its $71 million bid in April 1993 on a technicality, and asks his superiors for help in deciding whether or not to challenge the decision. Frame writes that he believes a Hadid company is the next bidder in the cascading auction process for the A licence at $77 million. Time Warner's disqualified bid is the next down.[9]

The critical issue for Time Warner was to decide whether to pay the $US8.58 million Hadid was demanding to buy the licence from him at his next bid level, or take a risk that he would not find a backer, in which case the process would cascade down to the disqualified Time Warner offer price.

The US group was clearly very keen to buy the A licence. Frame sets out a series of scenarios if Time Warner sued and won, or if it lost. There were pros and cons of challenging and losing, and challenging then winning. If Time Warner lost an action against the Government, one of the 'pro' factors was to sue Mallesons for neglecting to write the bidding company's name, Capricorn Entertainment, on the front of the envelope as required – the technicality which disqualified the bid. If Time Warner were to win, then the options were quite intriguing. Frame lists them as:

First, Time Warner secures the A licence; two, 'we gain leverage on PMT prior to entry'; three, 'we pay no premium' (ie, Time Warner doesn't have to pay a high price to buy the licence from a bidder such as Hadid); and, four, 'PF (ie, Peter Frame) to secure from Packer . . . PMT desires Time Warner to do this, and support us, publicly and privately.'

According to Frame's letter, PMT encouraged Time Warner to sue the Government to wrest back control of the A licence, before putting it into PMT. Frame points out that, 'Any action taken by TW must begin therefore before the next envelope after Hadid is opened. That means we must begin the legal challenge before the end of business on Thursday December 2 (8 am Thursday December 2, NY).'

He continues, 'Meantime I've begun an intense lobbying effort in Canberra through our new lobbyist (ex head of Hill and Knowlton Asia Pacific – excellent, highest level contacts). His mission: put TW back; we're the only credible company left in 'A' to pay the deposit and back the end payment; neutralise the perceived Packer-Murdoch dominance; start the new industry and proceed to discussions with the B licensee.'

Frame goes further: 'I will also attempt to get Kerry Packer's support to go for it legally with our pledge to put it in PMT (after we negotiate terms) if the political efforts don't materialise.'[10]

Frame was clearly trying to use either the threat of legal action or the purchase of the A licence from Albert Hadid to then place it with the PMT syndicate, which by law wasn't able to own it. The Labor Government was in a position at this time where it was unable to say 'no' to Kerry Packer on most things, but this would surely have been too much to ask. The B licence holder and any number of unsuccessful A licence bidders would certainly have sued the Government, and won. What was Frame doing, trying to procure the A licence for PMT? We'll probably never know.

The PMT legal actions in February 1994 caught Australis and Lenfest by surprise at a most vulnerable time. Australis was about to approach investors to raise up to $250 million to finance the initial stages of its satellite service. It was also planning to buy as many of the MDS licences that it could when these licences finally were due to be auctioned in mid-year. It was expected to lose $7 million that year on its limited narrowcast service,[11] the $19 million in cash it had at the time of its float was nearly exhausted,[12] and yet it was about to embark on a $500 million investment program to build its satellite service. The MDS auctions were the most pressing expense, however. Strategically, Australis could not afford to allow a competitor to buy any of the licences and set up a cheap rival subscription service, the type of service that Steve Cosser had originally conceived to out-manoeuvre the satellite licence owners. After having secured the main satellite licence, Australis was now the industry incumbent which was vulnerable to an MDS attack. Its main fear was that PMT would use its financial muscle to buy up the MDS licences and undermine its efforts to secure programming.

The legal actions also threatened to delay any fund-raising by Australis. No investor would put in money if Australis's licence was in jeopardy because of the legal challenge. An action like this from such well-heeled opponents could take a year or more to resolve. Although the documents lodged with the Federal Court late on Friday night received very little attention in the media at the time, they had the potential to seriously delay Australis's plans. With Optus and Telstra preparing to begin a cable roll-out, the two or three-year lead time Australis believed it had with its satellite service would be lost. It would have little hope trying to compete with rich pay TV consortiums based around Optus and Telstra for movie programming in Hollywood. Australis' survival depended on it being able to gain the first-mover advantage, to secure the best programming, and have a substantial subscriber base well before the cable groups got started. If it was slowed for any reason, then it would be swamped by the cable-based competition.

This is precisely what the legal actions were designed to achieve. The two claims were meant to harry and disrupt Australis, rather than mount a serious case for hurt and damages. PMT had correctly identified a sensitive link between the two licence holders. Century had not repaid the Lenfest loan for its licence deposit, and the relationship between the two licence holders was far closer through their infrastructure sharing arrangement than the legislation ever envisaged. PMT was on firm ground, and Australis knew it. The satellite operator responded feistily the following Monday, declaring that it would seek expedited hearings so the court would deal with them 'as they deserve'. Australis intended 'to move forward with its stated intention of introducing subscriber broadcast television to the Australian viewing public by the fourth quarter of this year'.[13]

The ABA said it would 'look at the terms of the action in the light of any new information and the *Broadcasting Services Act*'.[14]

Rod Price happened to be in Australia at the time PMT made its move in the courts. Price was effectively a tax exile in London, flying in and out of Australia staying a few days at most. The only time Price spent any period of time in the country was at Christmas, when he stayed for a week or two at his grazing property Tahara near Wagga Wagga. Even then, he spent almost the entire time on the phone.

Price flew to Canberra on the Monday to see Lee, who gave him ready entry to the ministerial suite. 'Our group has just paid the Government $117 million for a satellite licence and we're being prevented from raising the money we need to get our service going,' Price told Lee. 'We'll be creating jobs and giving the majority of the population a new service. What is PMT going to do for the country? They've failed to get a satellite licence, and now they're indulging in sour grapes and trying to stop the people who paid the Government a lot of money. Does the Government want yet another pay TV fiasco on its hands?'

The last point touched a nerve. Lee was also unhappy that a government-owned business, Telstra, was taking legal action against a government regulatory authority. He phoned Blount. Lee was angry and accused the Telstra chief of subverting government pay TV policy. Blount replied that PMT's advice was that the two licences may be in breach of the *Broadcasting Act*. 'Well, it's back in the hands of the ABA now, so perhaps they are the best people to determine that,' Lee said. 'I don't want Telstra suing a government regulator.' The Minister followed up his phone call with a stiff 'please explain' letter to Hoare.

Lee also rang Peter Barron at Consolidated Press and the PMT chairman, Malcolm Colless at News, urging them to call off the action. Price had been very persuasive. The actions were withdrawn within a week. True to form, Lenfest and Continental-Century pulled the wool over the ABA's eyes again. The watchdog saw no irregularities in the fact that Lenfest had effectively paid the deposit for the other satellite licence and for two months controlled both licences. The horse had bolted.

Another sensitive issue Lee had to tackle was the demand by the free-to-air networks that the best sporting programs be reserved for them. Lee didn't need much convincing and remembered the words of Michael Duffy, John Button and Graham Richardson around the Cabinet table warning of a backlash among Labor voters if they couldn't see the football and cricket free on television. The commercial networks, of course, bombarded viewers with advertising on their sporting coverage and had a habit, too, of tying up the rights to some sports such as test cricket, particularly matches played in the West Indies and the sub-continent, and then declining to air them. In these cases, no-one got to see them.

Lee asked the ABA in February to assess which events should be declared out of bounds for pay TV to 'siphon' from the free-to-air networks. After a three-month process, the ABA recommended that the Minister keep an anti-siphoning list to a minimum and that it only include material of national importance or cultural significance. It put three options to Lee. The first, rather sarcastically, was that he draw up a list of all those events nominated by the free-to-air broadcasters; the second, a list of major events; and third, a 'short list' of events such as the Melbourne Cup, football finals and test cricket played in Australia. The ABA also suggested a watch list of potentially sensitive programs and an activating mechanism which would allow the Minister to ban pay TV from buying the rights, presumably if lobbying from the commercial networks was strong enough.

A senior minister would later concede that of all the lobbying by the networks to date, their ability to deny pay TV any sports programming was 'the big one'. Their main ally in Canberra, Graham Richardson, had resigned as Health Minister in late March just as a scandal over his associations with two Gold Coast businessmen and a prostitution ring were about to become public through a Queensland Criminal Justice Commission investigation. But Michael Lee was just as willing to give the networks what they wanted.

Having been told by Peter Barron that Lee was to make a decision soon on the proposed anti-siphoning list, Nine Network head David Leckie and his counterpart at Seven, Bob Campbell, headed for Canberra with Barron. They waited in a small, windowless ante-room near Lee's office to help the Minister add the finishing touches to his list. Waiting in Lee's office while he moved between his suite and the ante-room where Leckie and Campbell were waiting, were department head Michael Hutchinson and senior policy adviser Chris North. After two or three trips to the nearby ante-room, Lee had completed his list. Of the ABA's original list of about 10 sporting events, they had added at least another 20. Lee himself was concerned about golf, and added the British Open and the US Masters and PGA. He also included international netball, in which the commercial networks have never shown any interest and which remains the preserve of the ABC.

During this time, Lee called the Sydney Organising Committee for the Olympic Games (SOCOG) chairman, Gary Pemberton, to seek his advice. Pemberton asked that the list not include the Olympic Games events and opening and closing ceremonies, lest it jeopardise potential sponsorship deals. Remarkably, the most popular sporting event of all was excluded from the list of events which would be declared the exclusive preserve of the commercial networks. The final list represented the 'comprehensive list nominated by the free-to-air broadcasters', that is, the ABA's first, sarcastic, option, plus some more events inserted by Lee. It included all Australian Football League and Australian Rugby League games, Australian Rugby Union Tests, the Rugby World Cup and Hong Kong Sevens, all cricket Tests and one-day games, the National

Soccer League finals series, the English FA Cup final, and the Football World Cup, all the grand slam tennis opens, Davis Cup, the NSW and men's and women's hardcourt championships, international netball, the National Basketball League finals, the six top world golf tournaments, the formula one car and motorcycle grands prix, and the Bathurst 1000.

There was nothing else left. To add salt to the wounds, the networks insisted on a 10-year protection period, until 2004. At least the agreement had an anti-hoarding mechanism to stop the networks winning sporting rights then not airing the events, as they often did. Pay TV would have access to those sports the networks didn't want, and it could also broadcast sporting events which had been previously aired on the networks. Pay TV simply could not have exclusive rights to any of the sports on Lee's list. Richardson and Barron had previously assured Lee that 'the punters will support you on this' and that he would get no opposition in Parliament.

Lee gazetted the list on May 31. Neil Gamble reacted immediately and described the list as 'ridiculous'.[15] Chris North resigned as a result. He had had enough of the cynical greed of the networks, dressing up their demands as public interest, and the readiness of the politicians to appease them. North had warned the Minister that if the Government collaborated with the networks to lock up all of the best sports programming, then subscription TV would develop its own sporting events. Even North could not have imagined how true his warning was to be, and the impact on rugby league and to a lesser extent rugby union that Lee's anti-siphoning list would have.

The perversity of the situation was that the only pay TV operator on the horizon, Australis, had very little money and was losing on its modest narrowcast operations. It lost $3.8 million in the six months to December 31, 1993, and Rodney Price predicted that the company would lose $10 million for the full year.[16] The networks, by contrast, were making combined operating profits of close to $400 million on advertising revenues of more than $2 billion a year. By this stage they had fully recovered from the traumas of the early 1990s and were powerful commercial organisations once again. They didn't need any charity. Australis couldn't hope to compete with the networks in buying sporting rights. It was no contest, but the networks were backed to the hilt by Lee.

Australia's competition watchdog, the Trade Practices Commission, had declared the anti-siphoning rules 'an artificial constraint on competition' in its submission to the earlier ABA inquiry. The commercial networks had the capacity to out-bid pay TV for sporting rights and the networks' need to protect their advertising revenue would oblige them to do so.[17]

Leckie and Campbell could see potential harm to their businesses sometime in the next century, but they knew they were safe for the foreseeable future. They had learned from the dramatic boost that Rupert Murdoch's BSkyB received in Britain when Sam Chisholm bought the five-year rights to the Premier League soccer in 1992 for £304 million, outbidding the commercial ITV network.[18] The football increased BSkyB's subscribers by 400,000 in the first year. Leckie and Campbell would make sure the same wouldn't happen in Australia – not until 2004 at least.

Rupert Murdoch took his family on a spring skiing holiday in 1994 to Aspen, where he keeps an apartment. One evening in February, he sat with his children Elisabeth, Lachlan and James to ask them what they wanted to do. Elisabeth said she would like to work at BSkyB in London. Lachlan, who at 22 had just graduated in philosophy at Princeton, wasn't sure. His father asked him if he wanted to work in Australia for a while. Ken Cowley had suggested earlier to the News Corp chairman that a newspaper like the Townsville *Bulletin*, or somewhere he would avoid the glare of the spotlight that would be on him in Sydney, would provide Lachlan with good grounding in the business. 'Sure, why not,' he replied. Over the ensuing weeks there was a change of plan. Lachlan would be appointed publisher of the *Courier Mail* in Brisbane, instead. This newspaper had the additional attraction for the Murdochs in that it was 56 per cent owned by the family company, Cruden Investments. During the heat of the takeover battle for Herald and Weekly Times in 1986–87, Murdoch had bid personally for the Brisbane paper and after winning it and selling 44 per cent to his listed News Corporation, had retained a personal interest. At the *Courier Mail*, Lachlan would work with Ken Cowley's brother, John. It would be the ideal introduction to the media business for the heir to the Murdoch crown.

After his highly effective lobbying of Michael Lee to head off the potentially damaging legal actions by PMT against Australis, Rod Price returned to London. He was chairman of the Thistle Hotels chain, which was acquired by Brierley in 1991 in a takeover strategy which went terribly wrong. Brierley had bought into Mount Charlotte group, as it was known then, and launched a takeover. It had expected to flush out another buyer, thus making a tidy profit when accepting the counter bid. Unfortunately, no white knight appeared, and Brierley was forced to proceed with a $1 billion takeover which nearly broke the New Zealand group. The hotels were run down and, as mostly three-star establishments, were badly positioned in the market. Recession in the UK and falling property values exacerbated the problems at Mount Charlotte, which Brierley later re-named Thistle. Through Price, Brierley invested heavily in lifting the hotel ratings to four star to attract better-heeled customers. It was a long and expensive business.

As Thistle was Brierley's single largest investment, Price was carrying a heavy responsibility for the group. Despite his pressing commitments in the UK and also with Brierley's interests in the US, Price was being drawn increasingly into the unfolding Australis drama. He flew back to Australia early in May on a crucial mission, to persuade investors to tip in at least $200 million to allow Australis to begin the huge investment in its satellite service. Australis's first major outlay, however, would be on taking a stranglehold over the MDS licences which the Government announced in March it would auction the following July. Price and Neil Gamble knew well that unless Australis bought most, if not all, of them, it would expose Australis's underbelly to opportunistic intruders.

Wayne Burt had arranged meetings and conference calls with most of Australis's shareholders. These were the people he and Price expected would be most receptive to their requests for more money. On the evening of May 12, Price and Burt, in a series of presentations to fund managers in Sydney and by video link to investors in Melbourne and London, drove home the line that Australis was the best placed of any pay TV aspirant to deliver a service to more than 90 per cent of the population. As a result it could be confident of securing the best movie and sports programming. Fortunately, Lee hadn't announced his anti-siphoning list at this stage. Australis's satellite service, Burt and Price claimed, had a one-to-two-year break on cable. It expected to secure most of the MDS licences on offer in July. If the fund managers were going to back anyone in pay TV in Australia, then it had to be Australis.

The investment groups knew it would be a bit of a gamble, but Price was very persuasive. If the business was to take off, then

Australis looked to be the player to which they should hitch their fortunes. Yet he and Burt fell well short of their target of $200 million. By the time they had finished their pitches, they had pledges to buy 135 million shares at $1.30, or a 10 cent discount on the current share price. The stock had continued its appreciation and remained at levels above even the bullish predictions of analysts such as Alex Pollak, since the purchase of the satellite licence six months before.

Although Australis and sections of the media promoted the $175.5 million raised by Burt and Price as a vote of confidence by the markets in Australis's strategy,[19] Burt had taken some insurance just in case the shareholders baulked as the hat was being passed around. He wasn't expecting the placement to be easy. Australis didn't have any programming and there was still the threat of PMT buying up MDS licences.

After the souring of his relations with Albert Hadid and Hadid's angry complaints to Burt's superiors at Bain and Co, Ken Borda and Maurice Newman, Burt resigned from his directorship at the end of December and went to work with Steve Cosser and Richard Wiesener in France. He wanted to move eventually to the UK, but in the meantime Cosser and Wiesener had some tidying up to do with Australis and Burt would help them. One of these loose ends was to help in the fund-raising effort ahead of the MDS auctions. The morning before Burt and Price did their call-around of the investors, he phoned a friend of his and Cosser's, a Monaco-based Irish-Australian lawyer and merchant banker named Michael Fitzgerald. Burt was not confident he would raise as much as Australis required and asked Fitzgerald if he had clients who could take up to $80 million worth of Australis shares in the forthcoming fund-raising if it fell short. Fitzgerald said he would be able to cover that amount. The arrangement was entirely verbal. Burt recalled later: 'Placement was extremely difficult and until the last moment when a very large institution came in surprisingly and took $45 million worth of stock in one two-minute phone call, placement was in a lot of trouble and six institutions between them . . . took over $110 million, $120 million worth of stock. All those people were hanging in the balance until the last moment, so it was a very, very difficult placement.'[20]

A lot of the stock, which was a mixture of ordinary shares and convertible notes, was taken up by stockbrokers and other intermediaries and took days to find its final buyers. In the end, Fitzgerald's offer to take up the $80 million worth was not called upon. Burt was saved by the last-minute intervention of a large institutional buyer, believed to have been AMP. But Fitzgerald still demanded a fee for having taken on the risk, and this fee would have to be paid by Burt personally out of the $2.58 million to which he was entitled from the $5.68 million which Australis had agreed to pay him and Bains for raising the money.

Burt's $2.58 million share was lodged by Bain with the Hong Kong Bank in Australia on August 22, 1994. The bank then transferred the money to Guyerzeller Bank AG in Zurich.[21]

Burt claimed later that he paid $1.72 million to Fitzgerald and kept $860,000 under the oral agreement he struck with the Monaco-based investment banker. Fitzgerald later re-invested the money on behalf of Burt.[22] After completing the fund-raising, Burt stayed on in Australia until just before the end of the tax year, then left permanently to live in Europe. Burt admitted later that his share of the fee was not declared in his final tax return for the year to June 30, 1994.[23]


Although the $175.5 million seemed a lot of money to a cash-strapped company like Australis, it was not nearly enough. In a little over a month's time, Australis would need to spend about half of the proceeds buying most of the 190 metropolitan MDS licences due to be sold in a fresh round of auctions starting on July 1. It would need to make another large, long-term cash raising before the end of the year. Despite its looming cash shortage, Gamble and Price knew it was imperative that Australis move quickly to secure rights to Hollywood movies which would form the backbone of any pay TV service. For all of the manoeuvrings and drama over the previous 12 months with the MDS and satellite auctions, neither Australis nor any of the other potential players had any programming of significance. As the likely first operator, Australis still faced the unenviable task of having to deal with the Hollywood studios. In the wake of its fund-raising, Australis claimed it was positioned to deliver a pay TV service by the end of the year.[24] With Optus and Telstra starting to move on their cable roll-outs, Australis knew they too would be looking to tie up programming, and they had a lot more money than Australis. Time was running out quickly. The last thing Gamble and Price wanted was a set-piece auction for movie product in Hollywood.

Sport was the other key ingredient. TCI's programming arm, Liberty Media, had already suggested – or, more to the point, insisted – that Australis use its Prime Sports channel. Although Price and Gamble wanted to sign up with the rival sports programmer, ESPN, which was in the Time Warner stable, TCI/Liberty/Lenfest used the weight of their dominant share-holding. Soon after TCI imposed Prime Sports on Australis, it proved its worth by buying up the international rights to the Australia v West Indies Test cricket series in the Caribbean the following March. The Nine Network had the Australian free-to-air rights. Australis now had access to Prime's parallel international rights. It would be an interesting test of Michael Lee's new anti-siphoning rule when Australis went to broadcast the game.

Movies, however, were the key to pay TV programming and they remained elusive. TCI provided one of its key programmers, a man named George Stein, who in turn hired a short, cigar-chomping lawyer in his mid-50s named Ken Ziffren. He was regarded as one of Hollywood's 10 most powerful people, and operated out of the glass-walled 'Die Hard' building on Century Boulevard, which overlooked the Twentieth Century Fox studio lot. Ironically, many of Fox's executives worked out of the same building, but Ziffren had a policy of never acting for Fox. He was always on the other side. If anyone could open doors, it was Ziffren. His clients included the National Football League and a host of film stars. Despite his pulling power, the studios were holding back, although discussions appeared to be cordial. TCI had not appreci-ated that negotiating for Australian subscription TV would be an entirely different proposition to dealing on behalf of its cable affiliates, which all held regional monopolies. There was no programming competition at the regional level in the US.

The studios had seen the commercial networks in Australia break ranks occasionally and spark a bidding war for movie rights, which proved to be richly rewarding. It happened in 1987 when Frank Lowy tried to out-manoeuvre the Seven and Nine networks and went alone to Hollywood to try to grab the best movie deals. The studios bankrupted Ten and extracted heavy price increases from Seven and Nine. They did likewise with BSB in the UK when it tried to lock up the best movies ahead of Sky TV. Hollywood could sense a similar situation developing again. Rather than rush in to do a deal with Australis, the studios decided to hold back and see what developed. Although they were normally fierce competi-tors, when it came to signing up overseas rights, they could reap far greater benefits if they stuck together. By mid-1994, they already had some soundings from a potential rival based around a phone company called Optus.

After meeting Albert Hadid at the San Francisco cable trade fair in April the previous year, the head of Denver-based United International Holdings (UIH), Mike Fries, had kept a close eye on developments in Australia. He told Hadid at the time he was interested in investing in the Australian industry, but only as a franchisee of a primary operator. Gamble and Price had decided by now that by selling the rights to the Australis signal to franchisees outside the metropolitan areas (where Australis intended to focus), it could set in place some fresh revenue streams on which Australis could count before it went into the MDS auctions. It was crucial, too, that if Australis was to set up a franchise system, that the franchisees acquire the MDS licences in their regions. Gamble didn't want to have to buy all 540 licences to be auctioned around the country.

Wayne Burt remembered Hadid talking about Fries and UIH and suggested to Neil Gamble that he get in contact with the American. When he took the call from Gamble, Fries said he would despatch two of his most senior executives out to Australia to talk about a franchise deal. Gamble suggested he instead send them to London to see Price. A few days later, Price received two visitors from the US, Don Hagans and Mark Booth.

The other obvious franchise holder for Australis was the A licence owner, the Continental Century partnership, which was still unstable because of the poisonous relationship between the partners following the boat-board argument back in February. Continental Century had also been shaken out to the tune of $19.75 million, which the partners had agreed in March to pay Albert Hadid to buy him out of his 8.5 per cent of the A licence. The catch for Hadid was that he would be paid in the form of Australis shares, about 19 million of them at just over a $1 each as a result of a contra deal between Continental Century and Australis. If Hadid was unsure about how close were the A and B licences, he wasn't now. Australis was effectively controlling both.

Price did most of the negotiations with Hagans and Booth and the terms of the franchise agreement were not finalised until the night before the MDS auctions were due to begin in Sydney on Monday July 11. He was under time pressure to strike a deal which would both bring in more money and share the cost of buying as many licences as possible, before the auctions started.

The Australis camp was very nervous at the flurry of media speculation that PMT was planning to be an aggressive bidder at the MDS auctions,[25] and that it would set up a cheap rival service to undermine Australis's more expensive satellite business. PMT was being portrayed as bent on revenge for missing out on the satellite licence. Such was the financial power being marshalled by PMT for the MDS auctions, that its poorest shareholder, the Ten Network, pulled out of the consortium four days earlier.[26] It shied away from what was shaping as an expensive fight, preferring to explore its own low-cost options. Ten's parent, CanWest, was negotiating separately with Telstra for access to some of the 64 channels Telstra would soon have available on its cable. Ten chief executive Peter Viner said at the time, 'Ten can achieve its objectives without being a shareholder in PMT.'[27]

Under such pressure and fearing the worst at the auctions, Price made a fundamental mistake in his discussions with Hagans and Booth. He made assumptions about programming costs which turned out to be well below the cost levels that Australis would incur. Price may have negotiated what appeared to be an attractive fixed percentage of their net revenue, plus a share of the cost of Australis's subscriber management system, but Australis would end up paying more for the programming that it provided UIH than it received back in fees from its franchisee. It would lose money on every subscriber UIH signed up. What was worse, UIH was by far the larger of the two franchisees, covering 1.6 million households in the Northern Territory, all of Queensland except Brisbane, inland NSW, and regional Victoria and South Australia. Continental Century, which used the name East Coast Television for its franchisee business, had coastal NSW (except Sydney) and Tasmania, or about 717,000 households. The deal had the capacity to bleed Australis to death.

A regular visitor at this time to Paul Keating in his offices in Canberra and Sydney was Ken Cowley, the News Limited chairman. Because of News's extensive commercial interests in media and aviation, Cowley had plenty to discuss with the Prime Minister. Keating enjoyed talking to Cowley and Murdoch, to hear their views on international developments and have a gossip about Australian corporate figures. At one such meeting early in July,

Cowley had a number of issues to talk over with Keating. As Cowley was about to leave, Keating said to him:

'Rupert and News have got a lot out of Australia. They've had one or two decisions go their way which have helped them. I'd like you to consider putting something back. Australia has a boutique film industry, an art-house industry, but it's got all the wherewithal to do better. It could be a producer of major English language films. It's got the actors, producers, directors. If we could get some interest from anyone with film interests we can do very well.

'If News was of a mind to do something along this line, we would facilitate the development of a set of world-class studios here in Australia. It would be a matter of choice which city, but one site you could consider is the Sydney Showground site. It could be a movie studio and theme park.'

Cowley listened intently and realised this was something News could deliver. Keating had watched as the NSW Liberal Government under Nick Greiner and his successor John Fahey had wanted to turn the Showground over to high density unit development. The Royal Agricultural Society was about to move the Easter Show to new showgrounds at Homebush near the Olympics site. If News agreed to build a Fox studio on the old Showground arena, Keating would kill two birds with one stone. He would foil the State Liberal Government's short-sighted plans for the area and score a big political win with the arts community.

Cowley told Keating 'it would cost a fair bit' but he was soon to fly to Los Angeles for one of his regular meetings with Murdoch and would take it up with him.

On the morning of Monday July 11, the worst fears of Neil Gamble, Gary Weiss and Wayne Burt were realised as they walked down into the Wesley Centre, a large meeting room with blue seats tiered back from a raised stage. There, seated in the front row were Nick Falloon, Malcolm Colless and the Nine Network's legal counsel, James McLaughlin. The Wesley Centre was in the basement of the Piccadilly Centre, one of Westpac's showcase developments of the late 1980s, which the bank was forced to complete after the developer, Girvan Ltd, went broke. It had been the scene of some fiery company annual meetings over the years, but Gamble could see Australis and its bold plans for a pay TV service going down in flames that morning amid a bidding duel with the combined might of Kerry Packer, Rupert Murdoch and Telstra.

He also saw Albert Hadid with the merchant banker Nick Whitlam, who had put together a plan for Hadid to set up a low-cost, three to six channel national pay TV service using MDS to compete with Australis. Gamble was too preoccupied to ask Hadid what he was doing there, given that he had just acquired over 8 per cent of Australis. There were also a number of other be-suited men sitting around who Gamble did not recognise. The three Australis people took their seats a few rows back from the front. Gamble used his mobile phone to ring Rodney Price in his office in London, where it was 1am. With Price was Steve Cosser. Gamble told them that PMT was in the room and that he feared they only needed to bid up the prices of the first two of the six licences to be auctioned that morning to levels beyond Australis's reach to destabilise Australis's business.

When the auction got underway Gamble was surprised to see Albert Hadid bidding against a man using a mobile phone who looked like a lawyer. It was too early for him to enter the bidding at that stage, and he was keeping an eye on the three PMT men. With the bids rising in $100,000 increments, the lawyer dropped out at $1.7 million, and Gamble entered the auction. To his amazement he was bidding against Albert Hadid, who was angry that he had still not been paid for his A licence interest. Neither Nick Falloon nor Malcolm Colless lifted a finger. When the bidding reached $2.5 million, the auctioneer knocked the licence down to Gamble. He realised Australis wouldn't be able to stand much more of that. There were another 189 licences to go.

Gamble was puzzled but enormously relieved that the PMT people didn't bid, but Hadid was going to cost them a lot of money. He turned to Burt to ask him what he thought Hadid was up to. Burt said he had no idea. The Australis people didn't know, either, that the lawyer bidding in the early stages was Bill Spain, a partner with law firm Gilbert and Tobin, who was there on behalf of Martin Hannes. Continental Cablevision was looking to get two licences in each capital city if it could win them for a reasonable price. It also wanted to ensure that Australis didn't get its licences too cheaply.

Falloon and Colless kept their hands in their pockets because Telstra had vigorously opposed the notion of buying any MDS licences. From London, Sam Chisholm had advised that if PMT bid for MDS and lost, then it would give enormous credibility to

Australis and its strategy. But Falloon had wanted to bid. His view was that PMT only needed to put in a few bids to force up the price that Australis would pay. As it turned out, Martin Hannes did the job for him, and PMT was not seen to have given MDS the credibility it would have conferred had it joined the auction.

Bidding for the second licence followed an almost identical pattern. Burt walked over to Hadid and asked to speak to him outside. In a corridor outside one of the entrances to the theatre, Hadid and Burt engaged in a heated exchange. Burt asked him to stop bidding because he was pushing the price too high. The two disagree as to what was settled: Hadid claims he agreed to stop bidding in exchange for two licences in each capital city, but Burt claims Hadid wanted just two licences in Sydney for ethnic programming, and that he'd phoned Price in London to confirm it. Hadid did not bid for the next licence and the rest went to Gamble relatively cheaply, with Bill Spain dropping out early.

After the auction finished, Gamble, Burt and Weiss repaired across the road for lunch in the San Francisco bar at the Hilton. 'What was all that about?' Gamble asked Burt of Hadid's furious bidding for the first two licences and his sudden withdrawal. Gamble was unaware of the drama in the corridor. Burt said he had offered Hadid two licences in Sydney, with Rod Price's permission.

The three enjoyed their lunch and the subject was not raised again. In two days' time, the auction process moved to Melbourne. Gamble took the flight to Melbourne the next evening and after dinner went to bed early. He was awoken by a phone call in his room at the Park Royal Hotel at 1am. It was Price calling from London. 'Where's Wayne Burt?' he asked a dazed Gamble. Burt was not in his room. 'We've got a problem with Hadid. He's threatening to sue us.' Gamble tracked Burt down to another room in the hotel, where he was with John Lever and Vanda Gould, still working on the A licence holder's franchise agreement.

Burt told Gamble that Hadid was staying in the same hotel. They should meet him before the auctions started and try to work something out.

Gamble and Burt met Hadid and Nick Whitlam at 8am in a meeting room in the hotel. 'What is the problem?' Gamble asked Hadid, who replied that he had done a nationwide two-channel deal with Burt two days earlier and that was why he stopped bidding. Burt disputed his version of events. The two started arguing again. Gamble intervened. 'Rod Price is the one who is supposed to have agreed to the Burt version. I'll call him and settle it.' Gamble used his mobile to phone Price at his Belgravia home. It was about midnight London time. Time zones and the usual courtesies about international phone calls were being ignored now. Price had been asleep, but confirmed Burt's story. Gamble turned to Hadid, 'Price says the licences were only for Sydney. If you want licences in Melbourne you'll have to bid for them.' Hadid stormed out with Whitlam in tow.

At 10am, Hadid fronted the Melbourne round and started bidding very aggressively. He had a point to make now. Gamble ended up paying $4 million for the first licence. Melbourne was a smaller market than Sydney, yet Australis would be paying nearly twice as much for the six licences. He rang Price. 'What shall I do? He's bidding us out of the park.' Price suggested Gamble let Hadid win the next licence. Next time, once the bidding hit $4 million, Gamble pulled out, leaving the bid with Hadid, who had to write a cheque on the spot for a 10 per cent deposit, or $400,000.

Hadid didn't bid again. Gamble let Bill Spain, who Australis knew by then was representing Continental Cablevision, get the next two. Australis got the final two for under $1 million each.

After the auctions were over Hadid called a press conference and on national television accused Australis of backtracking and Burt of breaking his word. He would sue Australis for hundreds of millions of dollars.

The auctions rolled around to Canberra, Adelaide, Perth and Brisbane and then into the regions. Australis ended up with 136 licences and UIH and Continental Century most of the rest. Continental Cablevision picked up 10, all in the capital cities. The regional licences were purchased cheaply because UIH's Don Hagans, who bought most of these non-metropolitan licences, faced no competition.

During the round of regional auctions, Hagans' offsider Mark Booth disappeared for a few days. He had been contacted by Sam Chisholm, who told him Rupert Murdoch would call. An hour or so later, Murdoch called and asked him to fly to New York for a meeting. News was planning to go into the pay TV business in Australia and it needed someone with attitude to run the operation. Booth had learned the game with Warner Bros in the early 1980s when he worked with the MTV Network before being sent to London in 1986 to set up MTV Europe. In 1989 he moved across to Robert Maxwell's Mirror Group when it was looking at entering the television content business, and before the Maxwell empire collapsed amid the scandal of hundreds of millions of pounds in missing superannuation money, Booth had skipped back across the Atlantic to Los Angeles to head UIH's program negotiating team.

Booth told Murdoch he was interested, but wanted to think about it. Then he flew back to help Hagans buy the rest of the regional licences UIH needed.

At Telstra, Gerry Moriarty and the head of his strategy and commercial group, David Pitt, found that there might be more demand for capacity on their cable than they could accommodate with just 64 analogue channels. In early 1994, digital technology was at least 12 to 18 months away, when it might be in a position to offer up to 200 channels using compression techniques. Still, this was too far off for Telstra's immediate plans. It wanted to secure a number of program providers for its cable to effectively pay for the cable roll-out. Moriarty and Pitt had yet to work out what they would charge for their network. They were still in the process of deciding what they really wanted to do with the cable they were about to start rolling out from their metropolitan fibre optic loop to the suburbs. A number of potential players had indicated their willingness to take up channels on the cable, but Moriarty cautioned his colleague that the speculative nature of the satellite bidding process indicated there may be a gold rush mentality setting in for the premium low number channels on Telstra's cable. He suggested to Pitt, however, that if genuine interest remained strong, then Telstra might consider putting down two cables rather than one.

Apart from CanWest, for which Moriarty had great respect, another group calling itself Cable Television Services (CTS) was also bidding for space on the Telstra cable. CTS was founded in 1991 by a group of relative unknowns in the media industry, including George Frame, a former promotions manager for NBN-3 in Newcastle, and a former Citibank executive, Andrew Randall. Just as the pay TV battle was starting to heat up in early 1994, the pair recruited Lynton Taylor, Kerry Packer's former executive assistant, who quit late in 1993 to pursue new opportunities. (It had become increasingly apparent to Taylor, who had been with Packer for 21 years, that he was meeting growing resistance from the new breed of senior executives in the Packer organisation, including Brian Powers and Nick Falloon.)

CTS launched itself with great fanfare on March 1, 1994, promising 10 channels which would include pay-per-view, and 'a wide variety of internationally renowned news and sports programs, recent release and classic movies, children's programs and cartoons, music videos, documentaries and family programs'.[28] CTS promised to be the first multi-channel cable television provider on Telstra's 'common carrier' cable network. It would offer its array of programs for about $10 a week.

Moriarty was inclined to treat Taylor with some seriousness given his 21 years as a senior figure in the Packer organisation, his role in setting up World Series Cricket in 1977 and as the former chairman of the PMT consortium. The Telstra head of multimedia agreed to sign an agreement late in February providing CTS with the 10 channels it wanted on Telstra's cable even before Telstra had worked out its charges and before it had selected its main subcontractors to build its network. CTS wanted to be seen as the standard-bearer for cable. Its announcement also knocked Australis's share price down a few notches. No-one was expecting cable to bounce out of the starting gate quite so quickly. Australis's claim to be the first player in the multi-channel market was suddenly under challenge. CTS chairman Taylor claimed at its launch that his new service would be available in just five months.[29] Typically for this incubating industry, Taylor's estimate was wildly optimistic.

Fortunately for Australis and Neil Gamble, CTS proved to be more hype than substance. Had it been backed by serious investors, it could have delivered a fatal knock-out to Australis long before it could establish its satellite service. But CTS's Achilles' heel was its complex and rather flimsy corporate structure. Frame and Randall chose an obscure company called Chelsea Securities Ltd as the vehicle through which to raise between $30 million and $40 million to establish CTS's service. Perth-based Chelsea was part of the Transcontinental Resources group of entrepreneur Tony Trevisian. Another director was Peter Jermyn, a name synonymous with Perth's entrepreneurial miners of the 1980s and a former colleague of the Sydney businessman Ian Joye, who left Australia in 1994 ahead of a liquidators' examination into the collapse of the Coronet group of companies he once controlled.

CTS gradually faded from the scene after the fanfare of its launch. Telstra eventually bought CTS out of its agreement, delivering a large, but undisclosed, amount of money to Frame, Randall, Chelsea and Trevisian. It was a decision which further fuelled Communications Minister Michael Lee's anger with Telstra.[30]

On June 15, 1994 rumours swirled through the investment community when stockbroker J.B. Were waded into the market to buy 12 million John Fairfax shares, three to four times normal daily turnover. The next morning the Fairfax press speculated that the buying was by institutional investors. *The Australian* newspaper, owned by Rupert Murdoch's News Limited, was unable to identify the buyer, but declared that the Were purchase bore the hallmarks of a raid by a serious corporate player. The shares bought by Were represented about 1.5 per cent of Fairfax. Because it was below the 5 per cent threshold at which buyers must reveal themselves, there was no obligation on the purchaser to declare its hand. The Fairfax board, chaired by retired former NSW Chief Justice Sir Laurence Street, didn't believe the coverage of its own newspapers, and feared a predator. Fairfax's managing director, a bellicose South African named Steve Mulholland, served formal section 719 (3) notices under the Corporations Law on Were, requiring the broker to reveal the identity of the ultimate buyer. After a delay of several weeks, and before Were was able to inform the Australian Stock Exchange, a two-sentence press release from News Limited revealed that News was in fact the buyer, and that the purchase was 'a passive investment'.

Rupert Murdoch was, and still is, perhaps the world's most aggressive media investor. He is not known for taking 'passive investment' positions. No-one believed a word of the second sentence. For Fairfax, no more determined and formidable foe could suddenly appear in its share register.

Although Fairfax had recovered well since its 12 months in receivership in 1991, its controlling shareholder, Conrad Black, was faring badly. Not only had the Labor Government in Australia capped his Fairfax shareholding at 25 per cent, but the Canadian's *Daily Telegraph* newspaper in the UK was being torn to shreds in a Fleet Street discounting war started by Murdoch's *The Times* in September 1993. Murdoch had cut the *Times'* cover price from 45p to 30p, and by mid-1994 the *Telegraph's* circulation started to tumble below the critical one million threshold. *The Times*, in the meantime, had nearly doubled its circulation to over 600,000 and climbing. Black's biggest mistake was to sell 12.8 million of his shares in Telegraph Plc to UK institutions at 570p just four weeks before he cut the *Daily Telegraph's* cover price from 48p to 30p to match *The Times*. Murdoch replied by cutting his price to 20p. The Telegraph Plc's share price plummeted immediately to around 400p, leaving those investment groups which had bought the shares from Black's Canadian-based Hollinger Inc holding unrealised losses of over £27 million. Although the London Stock Exchange later cleared Black of any improper behaviour, his name was mud in London. He would never be able to raise money in the city again, and what was worse, the discounting war had reduced the once rich stream of profits from his *Daily Telegraph* and its *Sunday Telegraph* stablemate to barely break even. His empire was in trouble, and the 25 per cent of Fairfax owned by Telegraph Plc looked destined to go on to the market.

Murdoch's raid on the Fairfax register came at a time of great unease and uncertainty for the group. Just days before News Limited declared its hand, Kerry Packer announced that he would merge his two main operating divisions, Nine Network Ltd (which held the television stations) and Australian Consolidated Press, publisher of his numerous magazine titles, including *Australian Women's Weekly*, *Woman's Day*, *Cleo*, and *The Bulletin*. Nine Network was the re-named Bond Media, which Packer aggressively acquired from the embattled Bond Corporation in 1991. The merger would require the approval of outside shareholders, who owned about 55 per cent of each company. Packer and Brian Powers planned to create a $2.3 billion media and communications business easily capable of acquiring Fairfax. Packer's private company, Consolidated Press Holdings (CPH), owned 45 per cent of the companies and would emerge with a similar holding in the merged company.

Packer had long wanted to buy Fairfax for complex personal reasons. Fairfax's *The National Times* newspaper had published in 1984 case histories prepared by the Costigan Royal Commission in the early 1980s which included allegations against one figure – codenamed Goanna in the articles, but Squirrel by Costigan – of drug dealing, money laundering and tax evasion. Packer confronted the swirling rumours by identifying himself as the person in question. He denied the allegations strenuously. He was never charged and the allegations were never tested in the courts. Three years later he was cleared of any wrongdoing by Labor Attorney-General Lionel Bowen, but the humiliation caused by the articles – for which Fairfax apologised – and damage to his reputation were so great that Packer nursed a lingering desire to own the newspapers and one day punish those responsible. Paul Keating's cross-media ownership rules stopped him in 1986, but by 1994 there was anticipation that the law might be changed or watered down. Packer was preparing to make a run at Fairfax using as a launching pad the

15 per cent stake he had built since early 1993. News Limited's unexpected appearance meant he was suddenly being challenged by Rupert Murdoch, who controlled a company 10 times bigger than even the enlarged Packer empire.

Murdoch's desire for Fairfax was no less than Packer's, but his motivation was the rich classified advertising columns, the 'rivers of gold' which made the Fairfax papers more profitable than his own. News Limited faced trade practices and foreign ownership hurdles getting to Fairfax. News may have been deemed foreign because of Rupert Murdoch's US citizenship, but Paul Keating personally regarded the company as Australian because its proprietor was undisputedly Australian-born and the group incorporated in Australia. As Treasurer in 1987, Keating had no hesitation approving News's takeover of Herald and Weekly Times. While Murdoch and Ken Cowley were hopeful that their relationship with the Prime Minister might deliver them the legislative changes necessary to also go for Fairfax, Keating had rebuffed them. Still, Murdoch was not prepared to stand by and allow Packer a clear run at Fairfax. He wanted a seat at the table and would move to 5 per cent over the ensuing months. If Murdoch and News could not have Fairfax, then neither would Packer. A 5 per cent stake would take the combined 'foreign' interests of News and Conrad Black to the maximum permissible 30 per cent. This represented a formidable block to Packer's ambitions. The looming battle for Fairfax was being dragged into the wider manoeuvring for positions ahead of an even mightier clash over pay TV.

In this highly volatile environment in Australia's media and communications sectors, Michael Lee decided he should make a grand tour of overseas media and pay TV interests to familiarise himself with the latest developments. His predecessor Graham Richardson had done the same two years earlier. This was the primary reason for the trip, but Michael Lee was also the bearer of a special request from Paul Keating to Rupert Murdoch in Los Angeles.

Lee travelled against the spin of the globe, flying first to France to see Canal+ in Paris, then to BSkyB's headquarters in Isleworth near London to visit Sam Chisholm. After these straightforward briefings, he and his staff took a trans-Atlantic flight to New York, where he was due to visit Gerry Lenfest. The pair met in Lee's Manhattan hotel foyer. Lee wanted to gain some assurances that Lenfest was in the Australian pay TV industry for the long haul.

Lenfest promised Lee he was. Lee was impressed by Lenfest's cool demeanour. The Australis share price had fallen heavily from a peak of $1.60 in January to around the $1 mark because of growing expectations in the market that cable would challenge satellite much sooner than originally expected. The CTS announcement in March knocked 10 cents off the Australis share price and the stock kept sliding as first Telstra and then Optus unveiled their cable roll-out plans.

Lee then flew to Los Angeles and a meeting arranged with Murdoch by Tom Mockridge, a former press secretary to Keating who was now working on special projects at News in Sydney. The first question Lee asked Murdoch after the ministerial party filed into Murdoch's office on the Fox studio lot concerned his intentions regarding Fairfax. 'It's just an interest,' Murdoch assured Lee. 'Fairfax is really of little interest and our Australian newspapers are only 5 per cent of our global assets.' Lee and his two minders, a lawyer and adviser Samantha 'Sam' Mostyn, press secretary Bob Bowden, and a departmental official, Bob Palfreyman, listened while Murdoch gave a detailed briefing on News's US film and television interests in a meeting room adjoining his office.

When it was time for Lee's party to leave, Murdoch asked them, 'What are you guys doing tonight?' Lee said they had nothing planned. 'We've got this new movie called *True Lies* which has had some cost blow-outs and we're not sure how it's going to go, but the premiere is tonight. Would you like to see it?' Half an hour before the film and associated entertainment was due to start, two long limousines pulled up outside the Hollywood hotel in which Lee and his staff were staying. Murdoch was seated in the front car and Lee joined him. The three staff climbed into the rear vehicle. As they drove the 10 minutes or so to the theatre, Murdoch asked Lee if he would join him for dinner. They only needed to catch the first few minutes of the film.

Lee agreed. When the cars arrived, the theatre and sky above was lit up by searchlights and a red carpet led to the theatre doors. Before getting out of the car, Murdoch asked the driver to wait around the corner, because he wouldn't be long. He led the others up the carpet and explained to one of the security guards at the door who he was and that he was bringing in some friends. The guard didn't believe him and was about to order him away when he turned to a be-suited but well-built overseer nearby and said, 'This guy reckons he's Rupert Murdoch!' The well-dressed man grovelled, 'Mr Murdoch, please come this way.' Murdoch led the group through and he and Lee stood at the rear of the theatre while Lee's staff sat down. An attendant walked up to the two men while they stood and ordered them to sit down or get out of the theatre. Murdoch politely explained that he and his companion were about to go to dinner. Ten minutes into the film, the two walked back to the car, which drove them to a nearby restaurant.

After the pair laughed about the treatment Murdoch received at the theatre, Lee asked him: 'Rupert, have you had a chance to think about the studio proposal?' Murdoch said he had. He had raised it with some of the senior Fox executives and they were dead against it. 'But I'm the boss, and I think it's a good idea. We'd like to do it.'

Bob Mansfield called a press conference on July 27 to confirm the industry rumours mounting since Optus and Continental Cablevision announced their joint venture in May. His board had just approved plans to build an advanced cable network which would deliver local phone calls, a multi-channel pay TV service and, eventually, interactive entertainment and information services. He wouldn't say how much this would cost, but indicated it would be 'in the billions' of dollars. The most important component of the cable service would be local phone calls. 'It now looks as though true competition to the phone market is on the horizon for local phone calls, as our network will have that capacity,' said Mansfield.[31]

Although Telstra had already announced plans in April to build a network passing 1.1 million homes in two-and-a-half years, the Optus plan was far more expansive. It would put its cable past two million homes within four years. In the wake of the Optus announcement, Telstra gave off-the-record briefings to journalists suggesting that its roll-out had been extended to 1.7 million homes and that it would achieve this new target by the end of 1997, a little over three years away.[32]

Neither Mansfield nor his partner Martin Hannes was 100 per cent certain that the technology being developed by Continental Cablevision in the US to put voice and video down the same cable would be ready for commercial application when it would be called upon, sometime in 1996. This was still two years away and, meanwhile, Optus knew that its protected duopoly with Telstra would expire on July 1, 1997 when new competitors could come into the market with deregulation. If it did nothing, it would be dependent on the Telstra network and would eventually be marginalised when the new players flooded in to the market. Mansfield had thrown down the gauntlet to Telstra. The race to put cable into the suburbs was now well and truly on.

After having secured the capital city MDS licences by early August, Neil Gamble felt reasonably confident that no competitor could set up a cheap rival pay TV service and undermine Australis's business in the very short term. Australis had paid $64 million for another 57 capital city licences. The auctions were still being held around the regional centres, and when they finished, the Spectrum Management Agency, on behalf of the Government, had raised a total of $90 million for the 190 licences. Most of the regional licences went to the Australis franchisees, UIH through its Australian operating arm CTV, and the Continental-Century partnership through its franchise company, East Coast Pay Television.[33]

Despite locking up the key MDS licences to add to its satellite, Australis remained highly vulnerable to attack. Gamble wanted to shore up its defences by forming a partnership with one of the phone companies, which were both preparing for an assault on the pay TV market. Meanwhile, he had George Stein and Ken Ziffren in Los Angeles attempting to reach arrangements with the studios, but they still appeared to be getting nowhere. The studios were watching developments in Australia and were delighted to hear that Optus was in fact going to launch a full phone and pay TV service in competition with Telstra and Australis. They could feel an auction coming on.

Gamble was climbing one hurdle after another for Australis, but getting the studio agreements loomed like a mountain. Also, the Optus announcement realised his worst fears – that cable was emerging as a threat, years before it had earlier been expected. He phoned Gerry Moriarty to see whether Telstra would take Australis's proposed 10 channels on its common cable. Moriarty was close to setting the charges for the Telstra cable and was open to the offer, but Australis would have to pay Telstra to take space. In order to fund its cable roll-out by charging access to its cable, Telstra was talking about a channel allocation fee of $500,000 plus further fees of $50,000 per channel, plus yet another fee of 50 cents per channel per home passed.[34] This wasn't what Gamble wanted to hear. He wanted Telstra to pay him for the movies and sport he would soon have on offer. He asked Moriarty whether

Telstra would be prepared to consider a closer relationship, and suggested he make a presentation on what Australis planned to do and how it could complement Telstra's plans. In mid-August, Gamble took his slide show over to Telstra and gave one of his regular presentations to the Telstra executive committee, which included Moriarty, Frank Blount, Harvey Parker, who ran the main Telstra business of commercial and consumer telephony, the finance and administration head, Paul Rizzo, and Craig Cameron, an Australian hired by Blount from NCR in Japan to run strategic marketing and development.

Gamble's main message was that Telstra clearly faced a well-telegraphed threat from Optus, and that in the end programming was the key to any response from Telstra. Australis would use its own satellite and MDS resources, but would also distribute the same 10-channel package down Telstra's cable. It was negotiating in Hollywood and through its connections to TCI had access already to a range of programming, including Prime Sports and the Discovery channel. As Blount listened, he thought that perhaps TCI were the people Telstra should be talking to.

Gamble then called his old Wormald International colleague Bob Mansfield at Optus and suggested they have a talk. They were both early starters, and the pair agreed to talk over a McDonald's hamburger in Mansfield's North Sydney office at 6.30am. The Australis chief executive told his friend that he was about to go to the US 'to go shopping' for programs. 'You guys are about to lay some cable, why don't we do a deal?' Gamble put to him. 'From a strategic point of view I've got a blank piece of paper. I've got these licences, and it's your satellite, so why don't we work together?'

Mansfield said it sounded good. He'd talk to his board and call Gamble back. When he rang two days later he told Gamble: 'As far as my board is concerned, Australis doesn't have enough credibility and we'd prefer to do our own thing.' Gamble was stunned. Mansfield didn't even want to talk any further. Telstra didn't appear to be much interested and now Gamble had been given the brush-off by his former colleague. Australis was on its own. What would happen when the two phone companies started competing against each other? Australis wouldn't stand a chance.

Gamble did not have to wait long for the answer to his questions. Three weeks later, on September 20, Optus and Continental Cablevision announced that they were bringing two new members into their consortium, along with an ambitious extension of the roll-out plans for their cable network. If Gamble had been worried about their earlier announcement of an intention to build a network to enter the local call market and pay TV business, this latest move was a direct threat to his business. Joining Optus and Continental Cablevision were the Seven and Nine networks. The partners had decided to call the consortium Optus Vision, after the two main shareholders. Optus's cable roll-out plans would be extended to pass half of Australia's six million homes, and cost $3 billion. Nine and Seven would bring with them a rich array of film and sporting rights, and studio contacts, to add to Optus's and Continental Cablevision's phone expertise.

According to the very up-beat press release the four partners issued on the day, 'Construction of the network will commence next month. Over the next five years the network will be deployed rapidly in key urban markets around Australia, including Sydney, Melbourne, Brisbane, Adelaide and Perth offering customers unprecedented choice in local and overseas television as well as local phone calls.' With the benefit of hindsight, the claim was highly optimistic. But it had the desired effect, and sent Telstra into a panic. The Australis share price, which had been trading for most of the year above $1.20, plunged below the $1 threshold and headed towards 80 cents.

A consortium as ambitious as this could only have been made possible by the break-up of the PMT group, which freed the partners to go their own way. Nine and Seven opted to align themselves with the rival of their former PMT associate, Telstra.

Three weeks earlier, about the same time as Neil Gamble was waiting on Bob Mansfield's answer to his late August suggestion that Australis and Optus work together, Frank Blount called a meeting of the PMT principals in the 15th-floor boardroom of Telstra's Sydney tower. This was the first time since PMT had been formed by Kerry Packer in April 1993 that the heads of the member companies had come together. Blount had been concerned for some time that this high-powered group had not been able to achieve anything. After the conclusion of the MDS licence auctions, there seemed little point in the group continuing.

At the meeting, Blount put a question to Kerry Packer, Ken Cowley, and Ivan Deveson and Bob Campbell from Seven. 'Is there anything here?' he asked. 'We've been at this for a year-and-a-half and we don't seem to be getting any traction. It seems we are only trying to protect turf, as opposed to doing anything.' All the men in the room knew PMT was dead. Blount was right. No-one was doing anything. PMT had become a blocking operation.

After the meeting, Blount called Ken Cowley aside. The two agreed that they had to dissolve the consortium or remain paralysed. The members were all potential competitors but by sitting around in the same room, no-one was prepared to move. On September 9, Blount and Cowley issued a joint statement. They announced, 'on behalf of all members the dissolution by consent of the Australian Pay Television Consortium (also known as the PMT consortium). The members of the consortium agreed they should now be free to pursue other opportunities.'

Once this decision was made, these opportunities flowed remarkably quickly. Blount received a phone call out of the blue from Fred Vierra, head of TCI International. Vierra had been tipped off by Neil Gamble after the Australis chief made his presentation, and had detected a glimmer of interest in TCI among the Telstra people. Vierra said TCI was keen to do something in the Asian region and saw Australia as an ideal jumping-off point. This had become a bit of a well-worn phrase among some US and European companies in the early 1990s, but in Vierra's case he appeared to mean it. This would be a direct investment rather than the indirect exposure the group had to Australia through Australis.

Blount offered to send a team of his senior people to Denver to talk to Vierra and the TCI chairman, John Malone. Within a day or two, Moriarty, Craig Cameron, David Pitt and Telstra's senior legal officer, David Krasnostein, were on a plane to the Colorado capital. Blount, however, had a nagging desire to strike a partnership deal with News. He and Cowley had become good friends by this time and he had been impressed with the film and television businesses News had acquired or built in the US, the UK and in Asia. Once he and Ken Cowley dissolved PMT, Blount decided he wanted to bring in News as Telstra's partner.

Brian Powers and Nick Falloon started their discussions with Bob Mansfield even before Blount and Cowley's September 9 announcement. The Publishing and Broadcasting Ltd (PBL) men knew PMT was dead when the consortium backed away from bidding for MDS licences in Sydney's Wesley Centre on July 7.

PBL had taken the option in April to buy 15 per cent of Optus Communications, so it was a good excuse for Mansfield to get Falloon and Powers into a room to start talking about financing the

Optus cable. In the weeks leading up to and following the unveiling of the Optus-Continental Cablevision joint venture on July 27, the discussions between Optus and PBL were intense. If they were to form a consortium based around the proposed Optus cable, then a pay TV service with the very best sport and movie programs was essential to ensure its success. Kerry Packer had the view, going back to early 1993, that it was better to have everyone inside the tent 'pissing out', as he would say, rather than anyone outside returning the favour. Speed was paramount. Telstra was slowly shaping its plans to roll out a cable, but was still working out how much it would charge outside program suppliers and what it wanted on the cable. The Optus consortium would be far more focused in where it was going. Packer warned during one of the early meetings in July that the country could not afford two cables and that it was essential to bring in News as well, to close off programming opportunities for Telstra.

Once Falloon and Powers had worked the numbers, they asked Mansfield to invite News in. A crucial element of the Optus plan, insisted upon by the PBL pair, was that revenues from the proposed telephone service provided via the cable go into the joint venture company. In their discussions earlier with Telstra, the government carrier wouldn't hear of this. The Telstra cable wasn't designed to carry phone traffic in the early years anyway, so sharing of phone revenues wasn't on the agenda. Pay TV alone would pay for the cable. This was why Powers and Packer walked away from Telstra.

If Optus, Continental Cablevision and PBL were to entice News into their consortium they would have to present a compelling case. First they needed to get the ownership structure right. The three groups toyed with a 25 per cent share for each of them plus News in the early stages. This implied a four-way sharing of the $1.5 billion they believed the partnership should contribute, with the remaining $1.5 billion to be borrowed or financed from the cash flows of the business once it got started. Packer made the point that, added to their own resources and programming capabilities, the Murdoch group would be the key to forming a dominant pay TV consortium. Not only was it financially well endowed, it had its own Hollywood studio and had more experience in satellite pay TV than any other organisation globally. Packer's worst fear, and there was no indication at this stage that it would occur, was that News would join Telstra. Packer and Powers agreed that they should court News seriously and that they should sell the concept to Rupert Murdoch personally.

Brian Powers turned on an enthusiastic salesman's performance in the fourth floor boardroom at News Limited for Ken Cowley. Although he had brought James Packer and Bob Mansfield with him for the presentation to News's Australian head, Powers did most of the talking. Kerry Packer had yet to stump up any money for his proposed investment in Optus Communications, but he was already becoming proprietorial about the company. The Packer camp was having a major influence on Optus and was pressing very hard to put together a consortium which would bring dominant programming for Optus's proposed phone and pay TV cable service.

Powers recapped PBL's discussions with Telstra and the fact that the talks had gone nowhere because Telstra wanted too much from the program suppliers to use its cable. Also Telstra would not countenance sharing its telephone revenues with any joint venturers in a pay TV business. So PBL had gone to Optus. 'We should think about this,' Powers suggested to Cowley. The proposed $3 billion cost of the Optus cable would be shared among four consortium members. After losses in the initial years while the pay TV and telephone business got on its feet, the pay-back period would be far quicker than the pay TV business Telstra was contemplating because of the addition of the telephone revenues. Even if Optus could achieve 10 per cent of the local call market after five years, it could mean around $500 million in revenue on the phone service alone. It would be a great opportunity for News, he said, to get into the telephony business for a modest initial outlay. By putting together the programming resources of Nine, News and the Seven Network which, he said, was also interested in joining, they could create a formidable combination.

Cowley wasn't so sure. He was thinking about his friend Frank Blount and the possibility of doing something with Telstra rather than Optus. He was also less than keen on News having to outlay nearly $400 million for a share of just a quarter. Yet he gave the impression to Powers that he and News were interested. Cowley said he was due to see Rupert Murdoch in London in a fortnight and would raise the Optus proposal with him.

Powers also was hoping to see Murdoch a short time after that. He was encouraged by Cowley's initial response. He was starting to sense that the Optus consortium idea was gaining some momentum. If he persuaded News to come in, there would be nothing left for Telstra and it would leave the marketplace wide open for the new partnership.

When Cowley saw Murdoch in his Wapping office two weeks later, they were joined by BSkyB chief executive Sam Chisholm and News's chief legal counsel, Bruce McWilliam. Chisholm and McWilliam had become close friends and working associates since they were on opposing sides during Kerry Packer's hostile takeover of Bond Media in 1991. McWilliam had been Packer's legal adviser then, and Chisholm was Bond's television boss. When Chisholm was hired by Murdoch later that year and moved to London, Chisholm brought McWilliam across with him to News.

Cowley outlined to Murdoch, Chisholm and McWilliam the proposal Powers had put to him a fortnight earlier and concluded by making some negative comments about getting only 25 per cent for a $400 million outlay. The negativity rubbed off a little on Murdoch, but he seemed willing to listen further. 'Brian Powers is coming to see me in Los Angeles in a week, so we'll see if he's prepared to sweeten the deal,' Murdoch said. 'We'd want at least 30 per cent.'

Powers came from a different angle in his pitch to Murdoch when the two met in Murdoch's office on the Fox studio lot. He emphasised the necessity for the consortium to snare the choicest movie rights in Hollywood and sports programming, which would leave no room for Telstra. Continental Cablevision, he said, was close to tying up ESPN Inc to provide one sports channel for the Optus service. If News would commit its Fox studio, then PBL could use its connections with Warner Brothers to bring it in as well. Once the other studios sensed that the Optus consortium was the dominant group, others would follow, Powers argued. Murdoch agreed, but told Powers News would want at least 30 per cent of the group. It wasn't interested in being a minor investor. Powers said he would discuss it with Packer and Mansfield when he returned to Australia. It was a matter only of meeting Murdoch's terms. Powers was supremely confident that News would join.

News's demand for more than 25 per cent forced a re-arrangement of the shareholdings among the other members of the Optus Vision consortium

Bob Mansfield didn't want Optus to sidelined into a minority position, either. It had more at stake with this venture than anyone. He wanted at least 35 per cent. His partner, Martin Hannes at Continental Cablevision – which would be providing much of the technology for the new system, as well as programming – believed it should have an interest at least as large as News. Over the ensuing weeks, the three parties worked on permutations of shareholdings to accommodate News. Bob Campbell was as keen for Seven to be in the consortium as Optus Vision was to have Seven's rights to Australian football and the 1996 Olympics.

Through September, Ken Cowley could feel the growing pressure on News to sign up, and started to dig in his heels. He wanted to go with Telstra, but sensed that Murdoch was tempted to go with Optus if the terms were agreeable. Brian Powers and Nick Falloon were concentrating their lobbying efforts on Murdoch, who would ultimately make the decision. Cowley realised what was going on and started to resent the fact that Powers was trying to go over his head. Powers regarded Cowley as being out of touch and obstinate in not appreciating a good business opportunity. Relations between the two men had never been particularly warm, but they were starting to deteriorate.

A few days after formally announcing the dissolution of PMT, Ken Cowley flew to London for the September News Corporation board meeting. Cowley wanted to go into a partnership with Telstra after his conversation with Frank Blount in the wake of the winding up of PMT, and was determined to stop News rushing into Optus Vision. At the meeting, he urged the group not to commit to the Optus plan. Telstra was also putting down a cable and it would be unwise for News to lock itself in at this stage. 'We should wait until all the cards are on the table and have the freedom to move later,' he told his fellow directors. He added that Paul Keating would see News joining Optus Vision as a direct attack on Telstra. 'It would not go down well for us in Canberra,' Cowley warned.

The next day News announced, along with a profit for the year of $1.21 billion, that it was putting its pay TV plans in Australia 'on hold'. Cowley called Powers and told him News wanted to 'sit it out' for a few weeks. He expressed a fear that if News went into partnership with PBL then it might cause problems in Canberra. Powers assumed he was referring to potentially poor perceptions of News and PBL collaborating in the same consortium. Cowley's real concern was his relationship with Keating.

A week later, Optus Vision unveiled its ambitious plans. Optus Communications would be the dominant shareholder with 35 per cent, Continental Cablevision would take 30 per cent, Nine Network 20 per cent and Seven 15 per cent. News had appeared merely to back away from joining, and Bob Mansfield and Brian Powers were still hopeful of bringing it in.

As Neil Gamble settled into seat 3B on the Qantas jumbo flight to Los Angeles, he was taken aback when he saw Nick Falloon and the Seven Network's legal officer, Sean O'Halloran, walk into the first-class cabin and take their seats two rows ahead of him. The three men exchanged pleasantries, with Gamble asking, 'And what are you going to be doing in LA?' Falloon laughed as he replied, 'Probably the same as you.' He wasn't joking. Gamble was joining Rodney Price and Ken Ziffren for what he expected would be final negotiations to tie up three or even four of the Hollywood studios for Australis's movie channels. The appearance of the Nine and Seven men could only mean one thing, that they might try to open up a bidding war between Australis and the consortium that Kerry Packer had been trying to group around the Optus phone network.

As the cabin lights dimmed after dinner, Gamble took his briefcase from the overhead locker to do some paper work. Two rows ahead of him, Falloon and O'Halloran were ordering champagne. To Gamble, they looked very confident.

# 9

# When friends fall out

Rod Price had been living in the downmarket Beverly Prescott Hotel on the corner of Rodeo Drive and Pico Boulevard for several weeks by the time Gamble arrived in mid-September. Price stayed at the hotel, despite its rather shabby appearance compared with the others in this very expensive part of Los Angeles, because it was owned by Brierley Investments. To the New Zealand company it was a piece of real estate. Price, along with the TCI programmer George Stein and the lawyer Ken Ziffren, had been starting to make some progress with most of the studios, who seemed reasonably happy with the sort of rates per subscriber and minimum subscription rates Australis was promising. Warner Bros, which had long-standing connections with Kerry Packer and the Nine Network, was not cooperating, and Australis knew it had little hope of signing it. Twentieth Century Fox was also out of bounds. Rupert Murdoch had kept it on ice until he decided whether News Corp was going into pay TV or not.

Price had been able to keep the attention of the studios because he could claim without fear of rebuttal that Australis was the only pay TV operator which had a delivery system; that is, satellite and MDS in place and only two to three months way from operation. Although Optus and Telstra had big plans for cable networks, the studios knew that even if they started immediately they were years away from reaching a significant audience.

The warming relationship that Price, Stein and Ziffren believed they had developed with the studios came to an abrupt end on September 20, the day the Optus Vision consortium unveiled itself. Falloon and O'Halloran had been doing the rounds for a few days already and were indicating they would offer better rates per subscriber and high minimum subscriber guarantees. The weeks of effort by the Australis team in moderating the studio demands were being rapidly blown away.

At one meeting in Ziffren's office overlooking the Fox studio lot, a day or two after Optus Vision launched, the Australis team was presenting the studio chiefs with their latest offer on rates per subscriber, and minimum subscription guarantees, when a senior Paramount executive, Jack Waterman, started complaining that the rates 'aren't rich enough for us' and that 'we've got a better deal'. As the studio chiefs were picking the deal to pieces, Gamble had to leave the room for a few minutes to go to the toilet. As he walked back into the room, the studio heads were walking towards the door shouting that the deal wasn't good enough. They were 'out of here'.

Gamble stood in the door and wouldn't let them out. 'There is something wrong here . . . I've only been here a couple of days, so just give us a chance to reassess everything . . . ' Waterman and his colleagues from Columbia, MGM and Universal backed off for a moment. The atmosphere was electric. 'OK,' said Waterman. 'We'll be back in 40 minutes. We're going to have some lunch.'

In 40 minutes the meeting reconvened. Ziffren suggested another approach. Why not add another element in which the studios and Australis would form a partnership and the studios would share the profits as well as taking a fee by supplying the movies? The concept needed more work, but Ziffren invited them to think about it. Waterman and his colleague quite liked the idea. By the time the meeting broke up later that afternoon, they appeared to be back on side again.

When he got back to his hotel, Gamble rang Price, who had left town briefly to go to Hong Kong on Brierley Investments business. 'Rod, the studio negotiations have gone off the rails. I think we've settled them down for the moment, but I'd say we've got a lot more work ahead of us if we want to sign them on. I've got to get back to Sydney. The company isn't being run and we've got negotiations on the digital standard and deciding on hardware for the satellite service.' Price said he would take a plane back to Los Angeles the next day.

Over the ensuing weeks, Price and Ziffren refined the movie partnership proposal and continued to sweeten the fee arrangements as Falloon, O'Halloran and the PBL counsel James McLaughlin, who joined his colleagues in LA from time to time, also chipped away at the studios as the bidding war intensified.

In the second week of October, Falloon flew back to Sydney for talks with Mansfield and Powers. Optus Vision needed a circuit breaker. It was trench warfare back in LA with the studios gradually forcing up the bidding by the Australian pay TV hopefuls, but not committing themselves. Unless Optus Vision was able to sign up at least two other studios on top of Warner, it would jeopardise the whole local call strategy of Optus Communications. Powers suggested it might be worthwhile making one last attempt to persuade Rupert Murdoch to put News into Optus Vision first. Murdoch had kept News's Fox studios out of the negotiations to date and it would be a coup if News came in and brought Fox with it. If News declined to move to Optus Vision, then Falloon would have to raise the ante in the bidding race for the other studios so high that it would knock the poorer Australis out of contention.

Over the weekend of October 8–9, Falloon returned to LA to see Murdoch for an early meeting on the Monday. If he was able to persuade Murdoch to bring News and its studio into Optus Vision, then the timing would allow Murdoch to make an announcement at the News annual meeting in Adelaide early the following week.

When Falloon arrived at Murdoch's office, Sam Chisholm and Bruce McWilliam were with him. He was struck by the ordinariness of the pale wood furniture and white carpet of the office, compared with some of the extravagant working environments of other studio bosses, such as Paramount's Jack Waterman. Murdoch had moved into Barry Diller's old office suite on the ground floor of the 1920s administration building on the studio lot. Adjoining the office was a small conference room and a permanent display board divided into half-hour time slots showing the four US networks' weekly programs and their ratings from the previous week. To get to Murdoch, Falloon had to go past a receptionist and then the small office of Dot Wyandoe, a tall, elegant woman in her 50s who had been his personal assistant for many years. Falloon went over the Optus Vision proposal in detail, outlining the permutations of shareholdings and the size of the investment required if News decided to join. He showed Murdoch five years of projected revenues leading to break-even between revenue and outgoings in two years, and profit by the fourth year.

The Optus Vision plan was attractive on the surface because it included the telephone business which Telstra could not, or would not, match. As Falloon hammered home the benefits of the phone revenues to the partnership, Murdoch appeared to be slightly preoccupied, moving his eyes sideways to a screen on his desk as e-mail messages came up almost constantly.

Falloon argued that if everything worked out as projected, Optus Vision looked to be a good and profitable investment. He fielded a few questions from Murdoch, Chisholm and McWilliam, mostly relating to the limited size of the shareholdings on offer and the seemingly high investment levels involved in paying for the cost of the cable. Falloon asked them to think about what they had talked about and offered to meet again the next day. He met Murdoch alone the next day for an hour or so of discussions in which Falloon pressed the point that it was essential if the business was to be profitable that Australia have one dominant provider. If two or three operators started competing for content and subscribers, pay TV would become a train wreck. Murdoch's media empire may have been considerably larger and more diverse than Packer's, but he was constantly warned by Sam Chisholm that Kerry Packer was a ferocious competitor on his home turf. Murdoch didn't have to be told. Falloon's numbers and the prospect of heavy losses in a competitive situation persuaded Murdoch that it might be a good idea. He got up, shook Falloon's hand and, much to Falloon's surprise, said, 'Tell Kerry we're in.'

Ken Cowley was in Melbourne in the Ansett Airlines offices when he received the call from Murdoch early on Tuesday morning to tell him News would be joining Optus Vision. He accepted Murdoch's decision and was forced to hide his bitter disappointment. Cowley waited for half an hour or so, then called Frank Blount. 'Frank, I'm sorry, but News has decided to go to the other camp,' he said. Blount took the news well. It wasn't the end of the world. Telstra was still talking to TCI and there was a chance they may do a joint venture deal, although TCI was still insisting on a share of phone revenues. 'Ken, I understand,' Blount said.

Through the day, Blount became increasingly despondent about losing the opportunity to do a deal with News. That evening he took the lift to the ground floor of Telstra's Melbourne headquarters in Exhibition Street and walked across the road to Marquetti's, a small Italian restaurant. The only vacant table was in the doorway, but Blount took it anyway. He was just finishing his meal of pasta and white wine when Harvey Parker, Telstra's head of commercial and consumer division responsible for the cable roll-out, walked passed with News's Malcolm Colless.

'Can we join you?' Parker asked Blount. 'Sure, pull up a couple of chairs,' the American replied. He was glad to have some company. Colless ordered a bottle of expensive red wine. Blount told the pair what had happened. 'Yes, we know,' Colless said. 'The Optus thing can be unwound, you know. I know Ken is very keen to do something with Telstra. If I sent a signal that you (Blount) would listen, I'm sure he'd come and see you.'

The next morning Colless called Cowley, who was in the Ansett building a short cab ride away. Cowley phoned Murdoch first in Los Angeles and told him the Optus Vision option was not the right one. Telstra was building its own cable, and News would-n't have to pay the huge infrastructure costs of the Optus Vision network. News could do a joint venture with Telstra on a programming company, and leave the major costs to the carrier. Cowley, once again invoking Paul Keating's name, added that this was what the Prime Minister also wanted. He was able to sow seeds of doubt in Murdoch's mind which had been so firm only a few days earlier. Murdoch told Cowley to handle it. 'I'll back your judgment on this one,' he said.

Cowley then took a cab around to see Blount in Exhibition Street. 'News can unwind the Optus Vision deal. We haven't signed anything. I want to go with Telstra,' Cowley told a delighted Blount. Cowley's view was that even in the face of an onslaught on its dominant market share in telephony, Telstra had the financial resources to fight back. It simply could not be knocked over, par-ticularly if it was being backed by a group the size of News Corp.

In Sydney, Kerry Packer and Brian Powers were preparing to fly to LA for a signing ceremony with Rupert Murdoch and his Fox studio chiefs to bring News into Optus Vision. Powers wasn't expecting to get a call from Ken Cowley to say that News had changed its mind. It wasn't going into Optus Vision after all. Packer was stunned. He thought the deal was in the bag. Four days earlier, Murdoch had said he was in, now he wasn't.

Powers phoned Falloon in LA straight away. 'We've lost News. Bob Mansfield's given you the go-ahead to offer $10 million sign-on fees to the studios, you'd better do it, quickly,' he ordered

At least it seemed Optus Vision's main competitor was Australis, which the Packer people also believed lacked the finan-cial muscle to be a serious long-term player in a business which would lose many hundreds of millions of dollars before giving a return to its investors. Packer and Powers were comforted when Rupert Murdoch told reporters after the News Corp annual meeting a few days later that News had 'no plans' to go into the pay TV industry, 'maybe nothing at all'.[1]

Falloon rang around the studios to seek yet another meeting. When he and O'Halloran did the tour, offering them individually a big sign-on fee, they all thought Christmas had arrived early. But instincts developed over years of grinding down the buyers of their movie products aren't surrendered easily. The studios would milk this once-in-a-decade opportunity for all it was worth. One by one, as they were approached by the Optus Vision negotiators, they turned around and demanded $20 million.

Then they went back to Price and Ziffren and demanded $20 million from Australis, too. All the patient and delicate negotiating by the Australis team, which seemed close to securing a five-year supply deal, with options to extend for further five-year periods with Columbia, Disney, MGM, Paramount and Universal, suddenly blew up in their faces. It took Price and Ziffren nearly three weeks to settle the studios' greed, but in the end they had to match the $10 million sign-on fee offered by Falloon. The Australis negotiators refused to pay the fee to MGM, because it was not a producing studio and had only a library of aging movies, but with some classics such as *Gone with the Wind*. MGM, desperate for any cash it could get, moved straight across to Optus Vision.

This left Columbia-TriStar, Disney, Paramount, and Universal. Suddenly, Disney moved across to Optus Vision. The Australis people didn't know why, but Falloon had offered Disney a minimum subscriber guarantee the studio could not refuse. It would pay the studio on the basis of a minimum of 600,000 subscribers for the 1998 year, rising to 850,000 in 1999, 900,000 in 2000 and a whopping 1.2 million in 2001. Even on Optus's most optimistic projections, it could never hope to get near these levels. The Disney deal with Optus Vision was by far the most lucrative of the arrangements struck with the other studios. By comparison, Optus would pay MGM fees based on a guaranteed subscriber level of 700,000 for the year 2001, and Warner 800,000 by the same year. Although the subscriber rates offered by Australis were generally lower, the agreements were struck in US dollars, whereas the Optus deals were in Australian currency, at Packer's insistence.

On the weekend of November 19–20, Price and Ziffren were ready to formally sign the remaining three studios to Australis. Neil Gamble was a guest of the South Australian Government at the Grand Prix in Adelaide, where Australis had undertaken to build its subscriber management system using an interest-free $7.5 million loan from the State Government. All three studios were due to sign on Saturday Australian time, or late Friday evening LA time. As had been the experience right through the difficult and exhaustive dealings with the studios, even this formality dragged on longer than expected. Gamble spent most of the weekend in the South Australian Government's hospitality tent waiting to be kept up to date from LA via his mobile phone. Every time Rod Price rang to inform him of yet another unforeseen delay, another pack of screaming formula one racers in practice session would drown out the conversation. The movie partnership agreement was finally signed in Ziffren's office on Saturday night, LA time, while at the same time half way round the world the Adelaide grand prix race was in full cry. Gamble could hardly hear a word Price was saying, but he picked up enough to know that Australis had finally secured three studios, two of which, Paramount and Universal, were the hottest in Hollywood at the time.

Nick Falloon and Sean O'Halloran mopped up the others over the ensuing days, with Warner their 'hot' studio. Optus also signed up the smaller New Regency studio, in which PBL had a 30 per cent stake. Still uncommitted was News's Fox. Its parent was still deciding whether or not it would commit to pay TV, and then whether it would go with Optus Vision or Telstra.

News had lost crucial time over the previous six weeks after having frozen its pay TV plans in September, then going close to signing with Optus Vision in late October, before finally switching across to Telstra. In the meantime, its two rivals were consolidating the core elements of their programming. While Australis and Optus Vision were counting their prizes, News's chief negotiators, Sam Chisholm and Bruce McWilliam, were in Chisholm's London apartment with Telstra's general counsel, David Krasnostein, and head of business development, Craig Cameron, working out the mechanics of their alliance.

Once News and Telstra got down to the nitty-gritty, as opposed to the warm statements of intent by Ken Cowley and Frank Blount, it very quickly became apparent that the cultural gap between News and Telstra was a wide one. Telstra was determined to maintain full control of its cable and keep News at arm's length as a provider of material for the cable. It offered Chisholm a guaranteed return for providing the content. Chisholm wanted a genuine joint venture and management control for News. Cameron and Krasnostein weren't sure about this. Both parties realised this arrangement was going to take time to settle, and time was not a commodity News and Telstra possessed at this stage.

Back in Australia, Frank Blount, Harvey Parker and Gerry Moriarty were persuading the Telstra board that it was essential in preserving the value of the corporation to respond vigorously to the Optus Vision proposal. They prepared plans for an even bigger network roll-out to four million homes at a cost of $3.5 billion. Drawing from the 'black box' model devised by Hambros' Chris Beare, the Telstra board were persuaded that failure to respond to Optus Vision would result in a loss of $7 billion in shareholder value. By responding, Telstra was expected to reduce the net loss to $5 billion in value. Frank Blount and Telstra chairman David Hoare flew to Canberra to see Prime Minister Keating to brief him on Telstra's emerging strategy and their desire to bring in News as a partner. Keating told the Telstra pair without any equivocation that he supported the plan and the News involvement. 'A clever country needs a cable running through it,' he told Blount and Hoare.

Keating had been impressed with Murdoch's vision but also his modest, almost deferential, manner on the handful of occasions he had met the News chairman. Increasingly, he was contrasting in his own mind the ambitious global strategies of Murdoch's with the very domestic focus of Kerry Packer and the constant requests from the Packer camp for favours. Murdoch had put his hand out more than once, too – for Herald and Weekly Times and the government ban on Air New Zealand competing in the domestic market, which helped Ansett (and also the soon-to-be-privatised Qantas) – but Keating regarded the political hand-outs to be running heavily Packer's way.

In a document prepared for a Cabinet meeting on November 10, a committee of senior officials from the departments of Communications, Treasury, Finance and Prime Minister and Cabinet, concluded further:

> Telstra's estimates are based on Optus still fully rolling out its proposed network. This would lead to an unexpectedly early and comprehensive roll-out of broadband telecommunications service delivery capacity. However, faced with Telstra's competitive response, Optus may modify its own plans. If Telstra's response led to a reduction in Optus's roll-out plans, this would further improve the benefits of Telstra's plans.

Telstra assesses that the implications for its earnings before interest and tax ($million):

|  | 1994/95 | 1995/96 | 1996/97 |
|---|---|---|---|
| Corporate plan | 3306 | 3552 | 3778 |
| No Telstra response | 3223 | 2842 | 2807 |
| Telstra response | 3173 | 2998 | 2551 |

In an accompanying four-page document also prepared for Cabinet, Telstra sought to justify its choice of News Corporation as its preferred partner. First, the document outlined reasons such as the need to add content components to its phone network, and that pay TV was the first significant revenue service that could begin to fund the upgrading of its 'carriage business' to a broadband infrastructure (ie, cable). 'We need a strong partner,' the submission argued. 'Optus Vision poses serious threats to the value of our telephony local and access business.' The submission then argued why News Corp was a suitable partner, based on its ownership of the Fox studio and television networks and Fox Video and its interests in pay TV in the UK, Latin America, Germany and in Asia. The final page of the document listed all the potential partners, then gives a number of ticks depending on their capacity to deliver certain benefits to a partnership. Not surprisingly, News topped the list with a maximum three ticks on three of the five categories. These were: content ownership and buying power; programming, packaging, and marketing expertise; subscriber management expertise; proprietary technology ownership; additional distribution channels; and financial resources. Number two was Australis/TCI, followed by Nine Network/Australian Consolidated Press, Seven Network, Time Warner and Viacom.

Cabinet discussed the proposed joint venture at its meeting in Canberra on November 10, but made no decision. Communications Minister Michael Lee, with Paul Keating's support, said it was a matter for the Telstra board, which was doing its shareholder the courtesy of keeping it informed.

The next day Ken Cowley and Frank Blount announced the joint venture. Telstra would increase the scope and accelerate its cable roll-out to pass four million homes at a cost of $3.5 billion. The carrier would own the cable, and the Telstra-News joint venture programming company would be responsible for providing a multi-channel pay TV service on the cable. Cowley said, 'The diversity of programming offered by this venture will be second to none and will cover premium, first run and classic movies, news, sports and music channels, games, children's entertainment and ethnic community channels.'[2]

The launch of the News-Telstra joint venture was hailed as 'a battle to the death' between the interests of Rupert Murdoch and Kerry Packer.[3] It was certainly shaping as a battle, but Ken Cowley's pledge of a 'diversity of programming' was a very bold and adventurous statement. The joint venture company had at best a small fraction of the quantity or quality of programming it would need for a fully-fledged pay TV service. News and Telstra at that point could count only on getting access to movies from the News group's Fox studio which, in 1994, was a middle-ranking production house. Its huge box office hits of the late 1990s, such as *Titanic*, were not even in the planning stages. Also, News Corp was only just starting to put together a Fox Sports service to sell to US cable groups. This programming stream was still in its infancy. And that was it. Australis and Optus Vision had locked up all the other studios, along with the top sports programmers, ESPN and Prime Sports, plus general programmers such as TCI's Discovery channel and TV1.

Without a strong portfolio of programs to show on the new Telstra cable, the grand plan would fall in a heap and leave a clear path for Optus to win the pay TV and multi-media race and carve out large chunks of Telstra's telephone business. But as Telstra was putting up the money for the cable, it was up to News to find the content. The task of finding those programs now fell entirely on to the shoulders of Ken Cowley, who quickly flicked the job on to his BSkyB head, Sam Chisholm.

Apart from suddenly focusing the partners' minds on the fact that they had no programs, the announcement of the News-Telstra pay TV joint venture severely jolted the relationship between Rupert Murdoch and Kerry Packer. After having been disappointed by News's decision to pull out of Optus Vision almost at the point of signing up four weeks earlier, Packer and Powers were flabbergasted by this latest shock. PBL had no idea News had been talking to Telstra at this late stage. On the contrary, Packer and Powers were under the clear impression from Cowley and News that they wouldn't be buying into pay TV at all. They felt betrayed.

Yet Packer was filled with grudging admiration for Murdoch, for striking what appeared to be such an attractive deal, at taxpayer expense. When he heard the news about the News-Telstra alliance, Packer was in Argentina, playing polo. He rang Paul Keating to express his dismay that News should be given such apparently favourable treatment. After listening for a minute or so to Packer's complaint, Keating snapped. He poured a stream of invective down the phone at the bewildered billionaire. Relations between Keating and Packer had come to an abrupt end. The feud would last for years and occasionally flare up in public, the latest instance being a series of revelations in 1999 by Nine Network's *60 Minutes* program over Keating's past interest in a Hunter Valley piggery.

While Rupert Murdoch was addressing the News Corp annual meeting in Adelaide on October 18, 1994, promising to put his signals into two-thirds of the homes in the world that have televisions,[4] Paul Keating stepped onto a stage in front of a huge tapestry covering a wall of one of the soaring main galleries of Canberra's National Gallery. The tapestry was a metaphor for the canvas that Keating was about to paint in his cultural policy speech to a large gathering of Labor supporters, artists, actors and arts and indigenous leaders. With an election he knew would be very hard to win less than 18 months away, Keating was shoring up a vital and influential constituency within Labor's electorate. It was also an opportunity to contrast his more visionary approach to cultural issues with the almost complete lack of interest on the subject by his political opponents. After stirring performances by the Australian Opera's Cheryl Barker and David Hobson, singing extracts from Pucini's *La Boheme*, and the Bangarra dance company, Keating walked to the microphone.

'This is a very great pleasure,' Keating began. 'No government has ever delivered a national cultural policy for Australia on anything like these dimensions.' It was a classic Keating delivery, harking back to the early colonial years when arts was polarised between 'evening dress and the opera' at one extreme, and the 'wattle and the bottle' at the other. Farewelling the old manifestations of Australian cultural insecurity, and the days when Australia's best artists were forced to live overseas because there was so little in their own country, Keating said his government would attempt to bring cultural issues into life's mainstream. 'We are putting cultural issues at the centre because the more we succeed in encouraging a creative spirit and the flow of creative ideas, the more we will succeed as an economy and a society,' Keating told his audience.

He then went on to nominate specific initiatives, such as the formation of a National Academy of Music, a National Indigenous

Performing Arts Centre, further funding for new gateways for the National Museum in the old Parliament House and at Sydney's old Customs House, extra assistance for the Australian Chamber Orchestra and the Sydney Symphony Orchestra, the formation of a special television production fund worth $20 million a year, and so on. The promises totalled over $250 million.

Then Keating dropped the totally unexpected news 'that after negotiations with the Commonwealth Government and subject to the settlement of some final details, the News Corporation Limited and its film production company 20th Century Fox have agreed to establish a movie studio in Australia to produce major international feature length films'. Keating had negotiated the broad terms of the studio arrangements with Rupert Murdoch and Ken Cowley five days earlier at the News Limited house in Canberra's Red Hill, a large, 1950s bungalow with pool, tennis court and library. It had housed Herald and Weekly Times bureau chiefs until News bought it along with H&WT in the 1987 takeover.

Although News would invest $20 million in start-up costs, the company would expect some State and Federal Government concessions and no tendering process to win the studio for Sydney. With the populist Victorian Premier Jeff Kennett keen to bid for any high-profile event or investment, Keating was confident the conservative NSW State Government of John Fahey would accept the deal.

After his annual pilgrimage to Adelaide, where News Corp had its roots in the modestly circulating tabloid, the *News*, Murdoch flew to Sydney. As always, he had innumerable matters to attend to while keeping up his intense interest in the progress of the US network ratings, but perhaps the most pressing was the final negotiations for his group's pay TV joint venture with Telstra. Cowley suggested it would be a good idea for him to meet his new partner, Telstra chief executive Frank Blount. The two met in Cowley's fourth-floor office at Holt Street. Murdoch had with him his son Lachlan, who was 22, recently graduated from Princeton and working with Cowley's brother, John, at the *Courier Mail* in Brisbane.

Rupert Murdoch and Blount talked generally about their new pay TV venture, opportunities they might pursue with the cable, and the different cultures of the two organisations, which they agreed needed to be worked on. Blount also raised the issue of the News Corp succession. 'As we're going into a partnership, I always like to know who I'm doing business with,' Blount said as he touched on a highly sensitive issue at News. Murdoch pointed to Ken Cowley. 'We've got Ken, we've got lots of people. We're in great shape for the succession,' he replied.


Bob Mansfield spread the map of Sydney across his lap and in front of Michael Lee, sitting next to him in the government executive jet for the half-hour flight from Canberra to Sydney. The Optus chief had been waiting outside Lee's Parliament House office for most of the afternoon to see him, and this was his only chance to put a new plan involving Optus's proposed cable roll-out. Running his finger around post code boundaries on the map, Mansfield put to Lee the solution to the looming problem of having two national cable roll-outs: each carrier should be allocated an area to cable and if one carrier did not take up its rights after a certain time, then the rival could move in and cable the zone. The carriers would have access to each other's networks. By dividing the cities into cable regions held by one carrier or the other, it would halve the overall cost of the roll-out for each company, resulting in a faster and fuller roll-out. It was a powerful argument. Lee listened, but felt as uneasy about the idea as Frank Blount had done 19 months earlier, when Kerry Packer suggested a similar plan.

Lee was already starting to have doubts about the Optus Vision strategy. What began for him as a promising breakthrough in new competition in the Australian telephone market was becoming more complicated as the partners insisted that their cable be for their exclusive use. Lee and Keating had envisaged that the Optus and Telstra cables would be accessible to all legitimate providers of content, be it pay TV or commercial services like home shopping. Bob Mansfield and Brian Powers insisted now that Optus Vision have full control and be the sole provider of content for its cable. This was not made clear in the days after September's launch of Optus Vision. Mansfield argued that outside content providers would confuse subscribers and weaken the Optus marketing effort. It was essential to the Optus strategy that it package its pay TV and telephone services and sell them together. Pay TV would act as an incentive to 'pull through' customers to the Optus telephone service.

Now Mansfield had thrown in yet another complication with his regional monopolies proposal. As Lee got into his government car for the 20-minute drive to his city office, with his staff members

Sam Mostyn and Bob Bowden, he commented, 'Mansfield will try on anything.' But he was still open to Mansfield's suggestion.

When Lee rang Keating, the Prime Minister was furious, blaming Kerry Packer for the latest development. 'It's not on,' Keating declared. 'It'll only entrench a duopoly forever.' Keating also realised on reflection after his brief conversation with Lee that it would also give Optus a huge one-off leg-up alongside Telstra and potentially strip billions of dollars in value from the government-owned carrier. Keating was planning to begin a sell-down of Telstra after the next election and had already held discussions with BHP and National Australia Bank to test their interest in buying strategic stakes of about 15 per cent each. If Lee was unsure about the Mansfield plan after it was put to him, he was in no doubt after his conversation with Keating. He hardened his stance towards the Optus plan accordingly.

A week after his aircraft meeting with Mansfield, Lee was due to give a speech on the subject of the telecommunications industry after deregulation in July 1997. On November 23, the day before he was to deliver the speech, Lee provided a copy to Kerry Packer's adviser, Peter Barron. The next morning, Barron rang Lee. 'If you make that speech, Optus Vision will cancel its cable roll-out within an hour,' he warned Lee.

When he took the podium at the conference in a hotel in Sydney's Chinatown, Lee outlined the case for duplication, the benefits including reduced prices and increased investment and competition in telecommunications, banking and retailing. 'Duplication of infrastructure, or the threat that it may develop, is essential for competition,' he told his audience. Further, 'In recent weeks some have argued that I should intervene to prevent duplication between Telstra and Optus . . . that in response the Optus Vision consortium has advocated splitting the country into regional monopolies for cable operators. I see no merit in either myself or any regulator drawing lines on maps to give carriers monopolies over this infrastructure.' Lee went on to say that the Government would insist on open access to the two cables after July 1997, but if competition was sufficient, may extend the period for closed cables until mid-1999.

After he left the conference, Lee went to the ABC studios for a live interview on the current affairs program, *PM*. He was settling into his chair when the program's producer brought in a faxed news release. It was Optus Vision threatening to cancel its cable roll-out. In it, Mansfield said, 'If the changes announced by the minister are passed into law, then Optus Vision will withdraw from the race, the monopoly powers of Telstra will be greatly enhanced and the prospect of local phone calls becoming cheaper will effectively disappear.' The consortium would seek to become a service provider of movies, sport and other available pay TV programs on 'the taxpayer-funded' Telstra network, according to the statement.[5] Bob Campbell and Ivan Deveson immediately pulled Seven Network out of the consortium, a move which threatened to implode Optus Vision. The following week, Seven's Sean O'Halloran called Sam Chisholm to see whether News-Telstra was prepared to take over Optus Vision's contracts with the studios. Eight days later, on December 2, PBL said it would not proceed with its proposed $318 million investment in Optus Communications. Kerry Packer and Brian Powers didn't expect Optus Vision to collapse, but believed that as the parent company was one step removed from the telephone revenues, it was more vulnerable in a drawn-out struggle with News-Telstra in a pay TV war. PBL's potential exposure to the Optus Vision pay TV consortium involved significantly less money and the investment would be staged over a three-year period.

From this point on, Kerry Packer insisted that his investments in pay TV would be kept to the minimum necessary to remain a player. PBL switched its focus to the embryonic, but suddenly troubled, Optus Vision. The promise and ambition of the consortium's September launch was suddenly darkened with uncertainty. Yet Bob Mansfield had kept the door open. His carefully worded threat to withdraw depended on Michael Lee enshrining the elements of his seminar speech in legislation, something which was never likely to occur.

Amos Hostetter junior, chairman and chief executive of Continental Cablevision, had been meaning to get out to Australia again for some time to meet the partners in Optus Vision and get a feel for the industry in which his company was about to invest close to $US500 million. On his first night in Australia he had dinner at Kerry Packer's Bellevue Hill home with James Packer, Bob Mansfield, Martin Hannes and Brian Powers and their partners. Three weeks earlier, News and Telstra had announced their joint venture and Packer senior and Powers were telling Hostetter about how close they had come to bringing News into Optus Vision and what a great deal it appeared to have done using the Telstra cable.

Hostetter – a well-dressed man in his mid-50s with grey hair combed over his ears who was one of the founders of Continental Cablevision in the small town of Tiffin, Ohio, in 1963 – seemed quite concerned about this. He had been briefed about the News-Telstra alliance, but wasn't aware of the background. 'This is going to be a free-for-all,' he warned his dinner companions. 'Don't expect normal rules here.' Packer, Powers and Mansfield thought Hostetter was exaggerating a little to make his point. Hostetter could see a stoush coming, but the scale of the conflict and the toll it would reap would be well beyond even his dire predictions.

The Sam and Bruce act rolled into Sydney on the first weekend of December 1994, the day after PBL's decision to pull out of its Optus Communications investment. Sam Chisholm and Bruce McWilliam were in the antipodes on their annual Christmas holiday to escape the freezing mists of London. Despite the fact that their main opposition was in turmoil, it turned out to be the holiday from hell. The two men had been good friends since 1983 when Kerry Packer adopted McWilliam's legal partnership, with Malcolm Turnbull as the main legal adviser to the Consolidated Press companies. These included the Nine Network, where Chisholm was managing director. Over the years Sam and Bruce became good friends, and when Chisholm was hired by Rupert Murdoch to run Sky TV (which later merged with BSB to form BSkyB), he asked Murdoch to take on McWilliam as well. McWilliam was tall, cultured and urbane, quite a contrast to Chisholm, who was short and pugnacious. Whenever Chisholm travelled, and it was often, he insisted McWilliam go with him. Chisholm liked the company. He trusted McWilliam and would constantly bounce ideas off him.

They were barely back when Mark Booth, whom they had hired a few weeks earlier from the US cable group UIH, sought an urgent meeting with them. Chisholm invited Booth to his house in Douglas Street, St Ives, surrounded typically in this verdant suburb with large trees. The three sat in Chisholm's large and comfortably appointed lounge room, dominated by a huge television set in one corner. Booth had officially started his job as chief executive of the News-Telstra joint venture the day before. He had 64 channels on the Telstra cable, but nothing to put on it. 'Guys, I've got no programming,' Booth wailed to Chisholm and McWilliam.

Sam and Bruce could see this coming. They had spent a week talking to the studios at the height of the Australis-Optus Vision duel in late October in an attempt to lure them to yet another Australian operator. The News pair were hampered by the fact that they were unable to tell the studios whether their service was cable or satellite. In fact, they had specifically been instructed by Telstra not to mention the carrier's name. They were quickly shown the door. The lawyer and investment banker Malcolm Turnbull also flew to Los Angeles on spec, but with News's knowledge, to try to open negotiations with the studios on a new front in a last-gasp effort to turn them away from Australis or Optus Vision. Turnbull had very little authority, only the force of his argument, in particular his view that Australis was not strong enough financially to be a viable long-term operator.

It was too late. Australis's ability to deliver six million homes with its satellite and Nick Falloon's $10 million sign-on fees for Optus Vision, meant that Chisholm, McWilliam and Turnbull didn't stand a chance. Also, the appearance of TCI's George Stein at many of the negotiating sessions gave the studios confidence that the largest cable group in the US was standing behind Australis. News and Telstra suddenly found themselves out-manoeuvred, empty-handed and staring at the prospect of a multi-billion-dollar information superhighway without any traffic.

While they were in Los Angeles, after having been rebuffed by the studios, Chisholm and McWilliam contacted Rodney Price at the Beverly Prescott, and offered him a deal. News-Telstra would pay Australis its own program costs per subscriber plus 10 per cent to put the Australis program package down the Telstra cable. Australis had struck an arrangement in September to buy space on the Telstra cable when it was envisaged as a common carrier. Now that News and Telstra had formed their joint venture, the Telstra cable, like Optus Vision's, would be exclusively for the use of the programs supplied by the partnership. As Frank Blount recalled later, 'I had to spend so much time in Canberra trying to under-stand the policy. We were going to have an open system, they would have a closed one. I couldn't see how the two could co-exist.'[6]

The new deal Chisholm and McWilliam were putting to Price was quite a different one to the earlier proposal for Telstra's open cable. The Australis programming would represent the major portion of the News-Telstra package and clearly would be worth potentially big dollars to Australis. Price initially was receptive to the idea. It represented a steady cash flow to Australis while it built up its own satellite and MDS subscriber base. Telstra's cable, Price believed, was years away from being a threat. He also wanted Australis to have an option to buy 20 per cent of the News-Telstra joint venture.

Frank Blount at Telstra and News's Ken Cowley didn't like the idea of diluting their respective interests at all, but as they became increasingly nervous about the joint venture's dearth of programs, Chisholm and McWilliam weren't ready to say no to Price at this delicate stage. Then, suddenly, Price disappeared. Anxious to keep the line open with the Australis chairman, Chisholm and McWilliam tried desperately to find him. They tried his various Australian contact numbers, and in the UK, New Zealand, the US and Hong Kong, but to no avail.

After several days of calling and hearing nothing from Price, Chisholm discovered he was recovering in Jakarta after becoming very ill with food poisoning. When Chisholm phoned Murdoch to inform him that Price had been tracked down to a hospital in Indonesia, Murdoch quipped, 'Nothing too mild, I hope.' Although this was clearly an unplanned disappearance, even Murdoch was becoming irritated by Price's inclination to be out of contact, sometimes for days on end.

His colleagues at Australis, too, were unable to get in touch with him sometimes, as he travelled extensively on Australis and Brierley Investments business. Price and Neil Gamble had a deal that when they needed to talk they would ring, no matter what the time. Gamble was the big loser from this arrangement. He was the one invariably woken by calls at 2 or 3am.

Chisholm and McWilliam were on a very tight deadline. They were being pressed by Telstra to find content for the cable and they had only one source for the bulk of their programs. and that was Australis. From a negotiating point of view, it was a most uncomfortable position. They had no leverage, but neither did they have time for Price's idiosyncrasies.

It was Monday and, with less than a week to go until Christmas, Nick Falloon wanted to take some time to recover from the three months of relentless negotiations with the Hollywood studios and travelling between Sydney and LA. He booked four nights for his family at the Hyatt at Coolum on Queensland's Sunshine Coast and planned to return to Sydney on Friday, the day before

Christmas Eve. He would spend the next few days relaxing around the pool, playing some golf on the resort's beautiful 18-hole course and eating at the hotel's numerous restaurants. But he had barely walked into his unit and put down his bags when the phone rang. It was Kerry Packer. 'Something's just come up. You'd better get back to Sydney. A plane's on its way to collect you,' Packer barked down the phone to the bewildered Falloon.

The 'something' flowed from a phone call earlier that day from Bob Mansfield to his old friend Neil Gamble at Australis. Mansfield had rebuffed Gamble back in August when the Australis head had suggested joining together to buy studio rights. Now Mansfield wanted to do that deal. Unfortunately the bidding between the two groups during October had pushed the cost of the studio product to heights they couldn't have imagined when the two men first talked. Optus Vision was not as dead as the media had portrayed it a few weeks earlier. Despite the rhetoric of his response to the Lee speech, Mansfield and his Optus Communications board were determined that the pay TV consortium would survive. Suddenly, they were being presented with an opportunity to put it back onto the front foot by dramatically out-manoeuvring Telstra. The arrival in Sydney of such high-profile operators as Sam Chisholm and Bruce McWilliam became common knowledge within a few days, along with the fact that they would be trying to do a deal with Rod Price to buy the Australis package for the News-Telstra cable. Mansfield also wanted to buy the Australis package, and he knew that if he moved quickly he could leave Telstra empty-handed.

'Neil, bring your people around, we should talk,' Mansfield said to his old Wormald colleague. Neil Gamble was only too happy to oblige.

Gamble and Price knew they had an auction now. After the initial discussions with the Optus Vision people, the Australis board met in the Brierley Investments board room in Sydney's Gateway building, a blue-green glass tower which rises sharply behind Circular Quay and its row of ferry wharves. Australis had moved finally from the condemned Castlereagh St building and was based in an old warehouse in Bulwarra Rd in the decaying inner city suburb of Ultimo. The building was in the process of being redeveloped into a special-purpose building for the pay TV company. The dust and sound of hammer drills and jackhammers was driving Gamble and his executives mad. In the calm of the Brierley boardroom, the Australis board was able to contemplate how it would navigate its way between the two phone company consortiums.

During the meeting, programming director Peter Rose said he had been phoned by the head of Universal, Blair Westlake, with the news that Sam Chisholm had been calling the studios trying to persuade them to deal directly with News-Telstra rather than through Australis. Chisholm had suspected that Australis's arrangements with the studios did not include exclusive rights over cable as well, which appears to have been the case. However, knowing that Chisholm had been trying to woo the studios back in October, Price had been able to convince Westlake, Waterman and the other bosses not to deal with anybody else but Australis. It was a perceptive move by Price, who was helped, too, by the studios' resentment towards Chisholm after he had slashed about $2 billion from the fees that would have gone to them under the original contracts with the old Sky and BSB. It was said to be the most money ever taken out of Hollywood outside the courts. The studios were keen to exact revenge on the BSkyB boss. Westlake had just handed Price enormous leverage in the negotiations he was about to have with Chisholm, and the Australis chairman would immediately use it.

Price's blood visibly boiled when he heard about Chisholm's approaches. He picked up the handpiece of the large speaker phone at the centre of the table and dialled Chisholm's home number in St Ives. 'Rod Price here, Sam. Don't fuck with my studios.' Those in the room could not hear a voice at the other end of the line for several seconds. Then Chisholm responded. 'Rod, how do we sort this thing out? How do we work together?' Price terminated the conversation by repeating his warning. Then he turned to his colleagues and insisted that Australis pursue its talks with Optus Vision.

On Friday morning at 8am the Australis and Optus Vision people gathered in the Optus boardroom in North Sydney for the final round of negotiations. The aim was for Optus Vision to buy the Australis movie and sports channels for broadcasting on its cable, a similar arrangement to the one Chisholm and McWilliam had also been attempting to reach with Australis.

The complication in the negotiations, apart from price, was that Optus had already signed up Disney, MGM and Warner Bros and there would be contractual problems adding more studios. The Optus studios were providing their content exclusively for Optus's cable and would resist having their programming and fees being diluted by the inclusion of other studios. Australis could expect to meet similar resistance from its studios. Still, the Australis and Optus Vision executives and their lawyers believed they could find a way around this potential hurdle and negotiated through the day and into the night. The Australis delegation, Neil Gamble and lawyer Robert Mangioni, also pressed for and got a 5 per cent 'free carry' in Optus Vision. For the Optus Vision partners this was a critical deal. In their enthusiasm to do the deal they were prepared to give a bit away. On the Optus side, there was Kerry and James Packer, Nick Falloon, Continental Cablevision's Martin Hannes and Seven's Sean O'Halloran. The Seven executive was in a particularly sensitive position. Not only had his network officially pulled out of the consortium, but his two largest shareholders, News and Telstra, would have reacted sharply if they found out that he was involved in discussions with a rival pay TV group to strike a deal designed to thwart a multi-billion-dollar strategy. Chisholm and Ken Cowley were planning to soon start exerting pressure on Seven to cross over to News-Telstra and bring its rich portfolio of sporting rights with it.

On the day before Christmas Eve, however, Optus Vision was moving to tie up Australis's programming by offering to pay the satellite operator its costs, plus a margin. The combined service would be divided into two, with Optus Vision customers all receiving the Optus package and the Australis channels constituting another tier for which the subscriber would pay extra. Once the arrangement was implemented, it would block Australis from supplying its channels to News-Telstra. The two parties hoped that by keeping the packages separate, they would also meet any concerns from their respective studios. Negotiations continued through the night with the agreement being documented, then signed, by Bob Mansfield and Neil Gamble at 4am on Christmas Eve morning. Rod Price wasn't there for the signing. He had left the previous morning to spend Christmas at his pastoral spread near Wagga Wagga. While Gamble and Mangioni were slugging it out in the Optus boardroom, he was spending most of the Friday on the phone, keeping his other deal alive with Sam Chisholm and News-Telstra.

Australis was keeping its options open, but moving into dangerous territory at the same time. If one of the deals fell over for any reason, then it could always fall back on the other. But if they both remained intact, then Australis would be forced to walk away from one of the cable consortiums and risk legal action. Because it was financially much weaker than the rival Optus and Telstra consortiums, Price believed Australis's best chance of staying alive was to use its valuable movie rights to play its larger competitors off against each other. Eventually, it would be bought out by one of them, hopefully for a large profit.

The Optus Vision program supply arrangement was conditional on the approval of the Australis studios, Columbia Tri-Star, Paramount and Universal. Studio reaction to the pact would take several days at least. Once it was signed, however, Gamble and Mangioni then turned their attention to negotiations with Chisholm and McWilliam in the hope of getting an even better deal from News-Telstra. The News pair had heard that Australis was also speaking to Optus Vision, but were unaware of how far their discussions had gone. It added another element of uncertainty to their negotiating position.

That evening, Chisholm and his wife Rhonda were hosting some St Ives neighbours and good friends of theirs, Dick and Sue Warburton, for Christmas Eve drinks. Chisholm had a good stock of chilled, non-vintage, Louis Roederer Cristal on ice for his guests, but the evening was not going well. The phone kept on ringing. Chisholm, McWilliam and Mark Booth were constantly having to gather around a small table with a speaker phone, sweating on a draft contract they had negotiated with Price and Gamble over the previous few days, but talks had been sporadic. Gamble was difficult to contact and Price had returned to his farm the previous day. Chisholm and McWilliam were also finalising negotiations with Reuters in London to take over the Sky News bureaus around the world in a move which would save Sky £12 million in yearly running costs.

By evening too, after a long day of negotiations over the phone with Price at his farm, Chisholm had secured a package consisting of the eight channels of programs from Australis and its A licence partner, XYZ Entertainment. The package was marketed under the name of Galaxy by the A and B licence holders, but it was controlled very much by Australis, which had grabbed the best programming for its four channels. It had the two movie channels, a 'premium' entertainment channel from the television arms of the three studios called TV1, and Premier Sports. The A licence holder, the troubled Continental Century partnership, contributed a music channel called Red, the Nickelodeon general entertainment channel, the Discovery channel and a cartoon channel.

As Chisholm suspected that Australis was also negotiating with Optus Vision, he was intent on reaching an unconditional agreement with Price; that is, one that Australis could not back away from. This also weakened his bargaining position. To strike a deal from which Australis could not escape, Chisholm would probably have to give on some key points. That Saturday morning he rang Rupert Murdoch in LA to explain the situation. Murdoch told him to get the Australis channels, 'whatever it takes'. News could always re-negotiate the terms later, or even buy Australis out to negate what was shaping as a harsh deal for News-Telstra.

Chisholm and Price negotiated point by point issues such as cooperation over the sports channel (Australis had TCI's Prime and News had Fox Sports) and over the two channels owned, but not used, by the ABC, and best endeavours to consolidate customer service centres, and cooperation to produce on-line services. Chisholm agreed that News and Telstra would each take up 25.5 million shares at $1.40, a total of $71.4 million when Australis was trading around the $1.10 mark. He accepted, too, Price's demand that Australis would have an option to acquire up to 20 per cent of the News-Telstra partnership, but on Chisholm's insistence at a price at least equal to News and Telstra's costs. In return, Australis would grant News-Telstra exclusive rights to carry its channels on cable. Finally, Chisholm and Price had to settle on a margin that News-Telstra would pay Australis and the A licence holder, Continental Century, on top of their program costs, which totalled $US17 per subscriber a month. Australis took the lion's share of this total, $US12.85, compared with $US4.15 for the XYZ Entertainment package of the A licence partnership. This reflected the high cost of the two movie channels from the Hollywood studios, which accounted for about $US8 per subscriber, per month. By comparison, BSkyB's movie and sports channels were paying an average of 15p each for the material they broadcast, thanks to Chisholm's negotiating skills with the studios. Australis was paying a world industry record for its content, and News-Telstra would be forced to pay even more than that.

Price wanted $US6 for the margin, on top of Australis's costs. Chisholm offered half that and they settled on $US4.70. Price insisted that the contract run for 50 years, the full length of the movie partnership agreement he had struck with the studios. Chisholm choked and declared this was preposterous. It would be a world record for a commercial supply contract, when five or 10 years in total is the norm. Price held firm. He had Chisholm over a barrel. The BSkyB chief feared that if he didn't give way on some of these points that Price might do a deal with Optus Vision instead and News-Telstra would have nothing. From Price's point of view, he wanted a contract which would imply a very high nominal value to boost Australis's asset base. The longer the contract period, the larger the grossed-up figure. To multiply any number by 50 produces a big number. When Neil Gamble and Robert Mangioni – who had been working at Mangioni's law firm's offices in the city documenting the negotiated points – started to calculate the overall value of the contract they were staggered at the numbers. Working off the minimum subscriber guarantees, which rose from 10,000 in 1995 to 550,000 by 2001, the value of the contract would compound to several billion dollars over the period. This included Australis's own costs, which would pass straight through to the studios, but the gross number would sound very enticing to potential investors and shareholders.

By 6pm, as Chisholm's guests started to arrive, he was still waiting for a draft agreement to be faxed to him from Mangioni and Gamble. The air-conditioning had broken down in the offices of Mangioni's firm, Tress Cocks and Maddox, and the pair were in extreme discomfort.

Chisholm and Price were talking every 15 minutes or so on the phone, both bemoaning the delay. Price had just struck the deal of his corporate life at the expense of the world's most feared media tycoon, but he had friends at his farm, too, and had to join his guests.

As the night dragged on, Chisholm's guests came and went, while Mangioni made the heads of agreement as tight as possible legally. Finally, the document chugged out of Chisholm's fax machine at 2am on Christmas morning. He and McWilliam signed it and faxed it through to Price, and also to Murdoch. The News negotiators realised they would have to take their medicine. They were very confident, however, that the situation would not last, and that they would end up on top sooner or later.

Gamble and Mangioni had put together two major deals over the previous 42 hours with hardly a break. Over the ensuing days they would have to walk away from one of them, but they were confident that the arrangement they had struck with Sam Chisholm on Christmas morning would ensure Australis's survival for some time to come. The Tuesday after the weekend Christmas break, Gamble and Price sat in the temporary Australis boardroom in the company's renovation-ravaged offices to check the reaction of their three studios to the Optus Vision deal they had struck the previous Friday. Jack Waterman's voice came through the speaker phone: 'Nice deal Rod, but we don't like it. We don't like riding second class.' That was that. The studios had vetoed the deal with Optus Vision. Price and Gamble had their escape clause.

On the same Tuesday, Bruce McWilliam had to front up to Craig Cameron and David Krasnostein at Telstra to brief them on the programming deal he and Sam Chisholm had just done with Australis. Telstra had played no part in the negotiations at all, leaving the matter entirely to News. The two men read the document. Then Cameron said, 'We can't agree to this. There is no way the board will agree to it.' They went to see Frank Blount, who also took a sharp intake of breath when he realised the size of the contingent liability aggregated over the 50-year period of the agreement, created largely by the compounding increases each year on the channel payments. He called Ken Cowley. 'We can't sign this. I can't take this to the board and say this is the best we can do. I need to do my own due diligence with Rod Price,' he told the News chairman. Cowley urged Blount to do that, if he could improve the terms.

Blount then attempted to contact Price. After getting the runaround for two or three days, he traced him to the Canadian winter resort at Whistler Mountain, where Price had just flown in to do some helicopter skiing with his wife Loeen. Blount was about to fly to London on another matter, and asked Price if he could meet him there. Price said he'd have marriage problems if he left his family and asked the Telstra chief to meet him in Vancouver instead. Blount reluctantly agreed. His need to have the meeting was greater than Price's. The Australis chairman had a signed agreement. On January 3 after the New Year long weekend, Blount boarded a plane with Cameron and Krasnostein bound for the Canadian west coast.

That Tuesday, too, Neil Gamble finally gave Bob Mansfield the bad news about the studio veto. Mansfield had been ringing two or three times a day through the previous week wanting to know what the Australis studios thought of the deal with Optus Vision. Gamble had been putting him off just to be sure there would be no last-minute hitches with the News–Telstra agreement. When Gamble took Mansfield's call and told him the studios had said no, the Optus boss knew he had lost what he thought was a good chance of delivering a knock-out blow to Telstra. The one consolation Mansfield could take from the exercise was that it demonstrated Optus Vision clearly was not dead.

PR man Murray Williams had just walked back after lunch into the office of his firm, Investor Relations, when he received an unexpected phone call. It was from Grant Snowdon, a director at the Australian Securities Commission (ASC). Snowdon came straight to the point. He was calling in relation to section 1002 of the Corporations Law. He asked to see Williams that day. 'What would that section be?' Williams asked nervously. It related to dealing in shares with inside knowledge, Snowdon replied. 'That sounds serious. Does it involve me?' Williams inquired. 'Yes, it does,' Snowdon said.

At 4.30pm that afternoon Williams, accompanied by his lawyer, Stephen Menzies, met Snowdon and two other ASC investigators, called Flynn and Riordan, at the modish art deco offices of Menzies' firm Allen Allen and Hemsley. Menzies, a nervous, hyperactive lawyer, had worked with the ASC on secondment in the early 1990s running its growing list of prosecutions with limited success, and was specialising now in defending ASC targets. It was a case of gamekeeper turned poacher.

Menzies asked them why they wanted to talk to his client. 'We want to talk to him as part of a wider investigation into trading in Australis Media shares,' Snowdon said. Then Riordan chipped in. 'If Mr Williams would like to assist the commission with its wider inquiries then it might be helpful to him.' Williams and Menzies looked at each other, and Williams said he wasn't in a position to help. He didn't know enough about anybody else's activities. But he had the clear impression that the ASC was going after much bigger fish than him. It had been more than 12 months since he bought his 125,000 shares on the afternoon of Australis's satellite announcement, and he still had them. The shares were held in a family company called Issuebay Pty Ltd, of which he was a director. The Australis share price had since surged from time to time on heavy volumes before announcements such as the studio deal, so there were clearly well-informed buyers trading the stock. He could guess, but didn't know for sure, who they were. One thing he did know was that the ASC had him cold. Despite the fact that the ASC clearly had far more significant targets in its sights, Williams' main concern, given the ASC's poor success rate in prosecuting corporate crime, was that it would try to make an example of him.

When Frank Blount and his Telstra team arrived in Vancouver, he rang Rod Price, who had already booked into a hotel on the city's waterfront. Blount suggested they have an initial discussion about the issues ahead of them over dinner that night. The Telstra chief was waiting at their table in the hotel's restaurant when Price arrived a few minutes late. Blount was cradling a martini as Price was led to the table by a waiter, who asked him whether he wanted a drink too. 'I'll have the same as my friend, a vodka martini on the rocks with a twist,' he told the waiter. Price went on. 'Frank, we have two things in common. Vodka martini is my favourite drink . . . ' he paused. Blount encouraged him to recall the second. 'And we've both slept with the same woman!' Then followed another pause while Blount searched his memory, before Price broke the tension by telling Blount he had sat next to his wife on a trans-Pacific flight a year earlier.

Over the next two days, Blount, Cameron and Krasnostein chipped away at Price to win some concessions in the agreement which was so punishing for News and Telstra. There was so much fat in the deal for Price he could afford to give way on some of the terms and still have a potentially very lucrative arrangement. Price conceded to drop the full term of the agreement from 50 years down to 25 years, to reduce what Blount regarded as a frightening contingent liability. They also negotiated down the payments to Australis, which rose with subscriber numbers.

When the Telstra team flew on to London they were still not happy with the deal. It was significantly better than the first deal struck by Sam Chisholm, but would still be the global industry's most expensive pay television program supply arrangement. Chisholm could at least take some consolation from the fact that he had secured the content News-Telstra needed, when they were staring at the prospect of having nothing. Had Chisholm known that the Australis deal with Optus Vision was never a goer, then his hand would have been strengthened enormously in his dealings with Price.

'Welcome to the future,' intoned Ron Casey as he was transmitted out of Australis's Melbourne studios in Australia's first pay TV broadcast, of Galaxy's Premier Sports Network, on Australia Day, 1995. Steve Cosser must have appreciated the irony given that in 1986 he had taken Casey – when he ran Melbourne's HSV7 – to the cleaners over the Victorian Football League rights. Now Casey was launching Cosser's pay TV service. Casey's greeting to the 1,500-or-so subscribers and freeloaders taking the Galaxy service was a steal from Bruce Gyngell's opening line on black and white television in September 1956, when he greeted viewers with the words, 'Welcome to television.' Australis was broadcasting only with its MDS service to an audience probably no bigger at this stage than Gyngell's. Its use of the Optus satellite was being delayed by continuing negotiations over an international standard for a digital service, which in turn was holding up production of suitable set-top receiver boxes. Casey introduced a US sedan car race as the first event on Premier Sports Network. He also promised netball and women's golf, along with soccer, rugby league, rugby union, cricket, basketball, skiing, parachuting, hang-gliding and more car and motor bike racing – all ad-free.

Among those watching the first Galaxy broadcast from the Melbourne studio was Casey himself.[7] His introduction had been pre-recorded. At least Gyngell went live.

Now that Australis was broadcasting, however, the pressure to obtain quality sports coverage – as opposed to the interminable flow of limited interest events such as stock cars and speedboat racing being force-fed to Australis from TCI's Prime Sports – would only get greater if Australis wanted to lift its subscriptions. On March 9, 1995, Australia would begin a Test cricket series against the West Indies which would decide the cricket world's top team. There was enormous interest among cricket supporters in Australia in the series, but there would be no television coverage. Nine Network had the rights, but it had no plans to show it, apart from highlights during its news programs. Prime held the international pay TV rights to the Test series, which it could pass on to Australis in Australia. Within six weeks of the launch of its Premier Sports Network, Australis had an opportunity to air a serious sporting event, but it was prevented from doing so by Michael Lee's anti-siphoning list. Under Lee's rules Australis could only cover the Test if one of the commercial networks was also showing it. Nine said it had no intention of covering the series. As the public outcry grew, Nine boss David Leckie said his network would only show the games if Australis agreed to a 12-hour delay. Nine was reluctant to go to the expense of sending a commentary team to the West Indies, but it wasn't going to let anyone else cover it either. As a result, the series which would decide world cricket's best team would not be seen in Australia. Play started at midnight Australian time and ended at 8am, so the broadcasts would not interfere with the network's prime time programming. 'Sports fans want action sports, but Nine's insistence that we delay our telecasts is detrimental to the interests of cricket lovers who want to watch this series live and commercial free on Prime Sports,' Australis's head of sports, Rick Jemison, declared in response to the Nine stand.[8] His boss, Neil Gamble, was determined to demonstrate just how hypocritical, inconsistent and slavishly pandering to the networks Lee's policy was.

As January rolled into February, Nine's David Leckie continued to dig in his heels. The start of the Test series drew closer, and it was becoming increasingly apparent, even to the architect of Labor's anti-siphoning policy, that he had allowed himself to be manipulated by the networks a year earlier when he framed his list. Lee attempted to salvage a sensible outcome from the growing farce. In mid-February, he approached Seven and the ABC to ask them if they were prepared to broadcast the Test series. Both refused. They were part of the 'keep off the grass' culture, under which the networks tacitly agreed not to compete against each other for sporting rights. Lee had one more avenue, and that was Ten which, under its new owner CanWest, was outside this cosy club. CanWest was also under scrutiny from the Australian Broadcasting Authority, which was still having difficulty coming to grips with the reality of the CanWest control structure. When Lee walked into Ten chief executive Peter Viner's office to ask him to broadcast the Test matches, Viner readily agreed. Ten would take the same Prime Sports feed as Australis and broadcast it overnight. The only difference between Ten's and Galaxy's broadcast was that Ten would be showing advertisements. At least those cricket fans keen enough to sit up all night to watch the play would see it. David Leckie at Nine couldn't have cared less. The audience was minimal. Australis's determination to take on Lee and Leckie meant that it was able to broadcast a sporting event that would not normally have been seen live in Australia. It was an early strategic and public relations win for pay TV.


At 10am on Monday, February 6, Ken Cowley and News executive David Smith walked up the stairs of the Australian Rugby League headquarters in the heart of Sydney's legal precinct in Phillip Street. On the first floor of the building, representatives of the ARL's 20 clubs were waiting to hear their argument for forming a 12-club Super League. What Cowley and Smith wanted was the pay TV rights to the new competition. They argued that reducing the 20 clubs to 12 through mergers or dissipation would create a stronger, more televisual, competition.

Cowley knew that rugby league's pay TV rights were held by Kerry Packer and the Nine Network, rights they had held since early 1993 when the ARL was approached by the US ESPN group with an offer to buy them. The ARL's directors, Ken Arthurson and John Quayle, went straight to Packer at the time and put it to him that they had an approach for the pay TV rights. Would he like to buy them for the same price? Packer accepted. When the issue had arisen at PMT meetings, Packer's people had made it clear that this was one of the assets that Nine would bring to the consortium.

The News chairman was making a direct approach to the game's executive and clubs in a move reminiscent of the way that Packer and Lynton Taylor out-manoeuvred the ABC and won the television rights to the 1977 Ashes series in the UK, when they flew to London to lobby the Test and County Cricket Board. Packer won the rights and then took control of the game later that year when he set up his rebel World Series Cricket. Cowley was embarking on a very similar course with rugby league 18 years later. The difference between Packer's cricket hijack and Cowley's attempt to grab the pay TV rights for rugby league was that in 1995 the establishment administrators were waiting for him. Rumours of a News move on the clubs had swirled around the sport since mid-1994. News was talking to the ARL about sponsorship of the game after the Winfield cigarette brand's contract expired that year. Arthurson sought a meeting with Cowley on November 10, the day before the News-Telstra cable venture was announced. Cowley admitted that News was exploring the possibility of starting a Super League with a competition of just 12 'super' teams, compared to the 20 teams which would contest the 1995 season.[9] The News Limited chairman said he was planning to make a presentation to the ARL at a future date. Arthurson pointed out that Kerry Packer held the television rights. 'We're looking for the pay TV rights,' Cowley said. 'Why don't you go and see Kerry Packer and sit down and talk to him,' Arthurson suggested. 'If he's happy about it, well we can have further talks.'

Later that day, Cowley rang back to tell Arthurson he had seen Kerry Packer and had almost been thrown out of his office. Arthurson and Quayle took out some insurance by asking all 20 clubs to sign loyalty agreements with the ARL at the end of November. Two weeks later, when Cowley met Mark Booth on his first day in the job as managing director of the News-Telstra pay TV venture, Cowley asked Booth if he thought it would be helpful to have rugby league. 'Too right it would be,' Booth replied.

The day before Cowley and Smith were due to address the clubs on February 6, the ARL chairman phoned Cowley at home to tell him that he would not be offering any support for the Super League proposal. Although Cowley knew some of the clubs present at the meeting were favourable to the News proposal – Brisbane and Canberra in particular – the majority were not, because the News plan meant the end of at least eight clubs. He assured the group that Super League was not a corporate attack on the game, but that News had a different vision to the establishment. 'It is not intended for News to own the game. Whatever happens we will not start up a rebel league,' he said.[10]

David Smith did not go over well with the clubs, according to Arthurson in his account of the meeting. 'Cowley spoke well with apparent sincerity. David Smith, however, didn't do anywhere near as well . . . Smith came across as arrogant and dogmatic.'[11] During lunch, the North Sydney club delegate, Bob Saunders, suggested to Arthurson that he invite Kerry Packer to also address the clubs. In view of the fact that Packer stood to lose his grip on rugby league program rights if News got its Super League started, Packer did not take much convincing. He told the ARL executives he would be over shortly. At 2.30 he and Brian Powers strode up the same steps into ARL headquarters that Cowley and Smith had climbed a few hours earlier. Packer was typically unambiguous with his delivery to the clubs. 'If you want to sell the business, I'll buy it off you,' he said to them, challenging the notion of doing a deal with any outside organisation. But perhaps his most memorable line was: 'I just want you all to know that I've got a legally binding contract with you people and if any of the clubs go against it, I'll sue the arse off you.'[12]

At the end of the afternoon, the clubs voted to stay with the establishment ARL. Arthurson handed out fresh loyalty agreements to supplement the November document they had signed. The clubs were given 48 hours to sign and return the new agreement. But that wasn't the end of it, and Arthurson knew it. He rang Cowley that evening to tell him of the vote. Cowley thanked Arthurson, whom he was sarcastically referring to privately as 'Askerson', and said, 'We are certainly not discarding the idea and we will be pursuing it in the future.' Any further approaches, Cowley told Arthurson, would be made 'through the front door' of the ARL.[13] The 'front door' reference had a ring of similarity with the strategy News used to put its foot on the Seven Network in 1993.

At the annual World Economic Forum in Davos, Switzerland, where the globe's most prominent business tycoons gather each year to discuss the ills of the world, Rupert Murdoch bumped into Conrad Black. The two engaged in light-hearted banter about world events, the relentless newspaper price war in the UK that Murdoch's *The Times* was waging against Black's *Telegraph* newspaper, and John Fairfax.

A group of journalists sprung the two in conversation and gathered around. Murdoch put on a bit of a show and told Black he might buy some shares in Fairfax. He revealed to Black and the assembled throng that News had built its stake to just under the 5 per cent permissible at the time. He might go to 10 per cent but thought he could go as high as 20 per cent. Black lightheartedly welcomed Murdoch to buy. 'As far as I'm concerned you're welcome. I would rather have a shareholder like you than an imbecile institution,' he told Murdoch and the reporters.[14] With Black on 25 per cent and foreign interests capped at 30 per cent by former Labor Treasurer John Dawkins, News ostensibly could not go higher, but the rule could be changed at any time at the discretion of the Treasurer of the day. Murdoch, however, was intending to buy more Fairfax shares. He was hopeful that the seed he had planted in Keating's mind on Hayman Island 18 months earlier and Ken Cowley's good friendship with the Prime Minister may start to bear fruit.

Kerry Packer fumed when the next day's newspapers reported the exchange in Davos. He was stuck on 15 per cent, while Black was at 25 per cent, and now Rupert Murdoch was threatening to go higher. Packer was an Australian, yet the laws of the day were discriminating against him. On Friday morning, February 10, Packer rang his friend Neville Miles, who by now had moved to set up a Sydney office of the old Melbourne brokerage firm EL&C Baillieu, and told him to buy Fairfax shares. Packer had been given legal advice some months earlier that the *Broadcasting Services Act* did not prevent him from going above 15 per cent in Fairfax. So long as he did not control the group or have directors on the board, he could go to a level just below Black's 25 per cent. It was bold advice, and probably correct as the wording of the law stood. Miles waded into the market the following Monday and bought 17 million shares, lifting Packer's interest to 16.4 per cent. The same day, News Limited's Newspoll reported that in opinion testing over the weekend the conservative Liberal Party leader, John Howard, had taken a decisive lead over Paul Keating as preferred leader.[15] Packer was gambling with some confidence that the conservative parties would win the next election and abolish the cross-media rule which prevented him from buying Fairfax.

EL&C Baillieu's buying immediately identified the purchaser as Packer. The next day, Packer revealed his hand and Lee promptly referred his share buying to the Australian Broadcasting Authority. Two days later, Miles bought another 5.8 million shares, taking Packer's interest to 17.2 per cent. Packer was clever enough to keep his shareholding in ordinary voting shares just below 15 per cent. His interest was in excess of this threshold because he also held 29.5 million non-voting convertible notes, which he had bought from Hellman and Friedman some time earlier. The notes could easily be converted into voting shares in the hands of an Australian, but Packer had chosen to keep them in their non-voting form. The night of his second raid, Packer asked to appear on his own network's *A Current Affair* program, presented by long-term Nine journalist Ray Martin. He wanted to publicly defend his decision to test the cross-media ownership rules. In an electrifying 30-minute interview (including ads), Packer defended his share purchase as 'absolutely legal'. He said, 'I see in the paper that Rupert Murdoch thinks he might buy a bit more than 5 per cent and I see Conrad Black saying he wants to go to 35 per cent. And I'm not going to be stuck here at 15 per cent with everyone moving around me.'[16]

Packer went on to assert that Conrad Black had no right to control John Fairfax. 'Why is he entitled to have more? I'm not entitled to go to Canada and buy his newspapers. Why is he entitled to come to Australia and buy newspapers Australians want to buy?' When reminded about the cross-media rules and his ownership of Channel Nine, Packer said with chilling intent, 'I've always had the choice of selling Channel Nine and buying Fairfax. If I was as preoccupied with buying Fairfax as all the Fairfax journalists would have you believe, I would already own Fairfax. There is no way in the world that I can be stopped from acquiring Fairfax if I sold Channel Nine.'

On his own pay TV plans, Packer said, 'We have gone very gingerly with Optus. I don't think there is any profit in it whatsoever for a considerable period of time. I doubt that there will be any profit for many, many years.' The mention of the subject prompted Packer to reveal his sensitivity to what he believed had been better treatment by Canberra of his media rivals. 'You have Rupert sitting there with Telecom, Rupert who is a ferocious competitor at the best of times, but imagine him spending the taxpayers' money instead of his own. What a competitor he will be, sitting there spending Telecom's money and buying his programming.'

The interview had not been rehearsed, and Martin asked out of the blue what Packer thought of John Howard. Packer replied, 'He's been around a long time. I think he's a decent man. I think he's an honest man. And I think he's a man who has seen the mistakes made and I don't think will make them again.'

Michael Lee's anger grew as he watched the interview. He thought of all the favours the Government had given Packer, in particular the anti-siphoning rule, which was giving him enormous grief at that moment. Lee was trying to persuade a network to show the West Indies Test tour, which Packer's Nine had refused to broadcast despite having the rights. He tried to call Paul Keating, who was in Perth, which was three hours behind the east coast. When he reached him he warned Keating about the interview. 'You'd better watch it,' Lee told him. Just before 10pm eastern time, Lee rang Keating in his hotel room. Keating was watching the last few minutes of the interview and was incandescent with rage. 'I'll get that bastard,' Keating said venomously down the phone.

The next day, Keating asked his press secretary Greg Turnbull to ring Nine's head of news and current affairs, Peter Meakin, and accept the standing invitation to appear on the network. Keating wanted to go on the *Sunday* program, where he would have a bit of time to say what he wanted to say and it would make good reading in the normally news-starved Monday morning newspapers.

Keating flew back to Canberra on Friday and asked Michael Lee to join him the next day to discuss tactics for his appearance the next day. The two met in Keating's office in Parliament and agreed that Packer's comments about John Howard were a pay back for Labor's decision to reject Optus's regional monopoly proposal. They thought the best way they could worry Packer would be for Keating to float the notion of a fourth television network, which would represent a threat to Packer's Nine.

The next day, Keating went a little further than planned. He raised the possibility of a fourth network, but when his interviewer, Laurie Oakes, asked him what he thought of Packer's criticisms of

Government policy, Keating's temper began to fray. Kerry Packer, Keating told Oakes, was a hard-headed businessman who had built his empire with great certainty, but this fracas over Fairfax 'has got a history to it'. It was to do with Optus and its request for regional cable monopolies. 'Now I said this to them: the last scam I had run past me that was ever this large, to transfer seven or eight billion from the Commonwealth purse to an industrial company . . . was when I saw reported Murray Farquhar's reported attempts to take gold reserves from the Philippines National Bank. That is the last scam that large . . . That is the sort of weight put on us by the Packer camp and Optus,' Keating told a stunned Oakes.[17] He was referring to the jailed former chief magistrate of NSW, Murray Farquhar, who died during his trial in December 1993 on charges of passport fraud in connection with a racket to remove $7 billion worth of gold from the Philippines National Bank.

Keating's remark was provocative and inflammatory. The Prime Minister clearly had no time any more for Kerry Packer. It was just as clear that the feeling was mutual, and that Packer was lining up behind John Howard in the expectation that he would win the next federal election.

By early February, Mark Booth, head of the News-Telstra pay TV venture, and Neil Lawrence – a creative director at advertising agency Young and Rubicam, which was handling the News-Telstra pay TV account – had picked the name Foxtel as the joint venture's brand name. Like Optus Vision, it was an amalgam. But with the Fox name at the front, Booth was able to rework and exploit the well-known 20th Century Fox studio logo, with its circling search-lights, to heavily associate Foxtel with entertainment. As the two phone companies were offering similar pay TV products, differentiating the offerings with clever marketing would be the key to this contest. Optus already had one of the top five best-known brand names in the country and therefore enjoyed a big start in this aspect of the battle.

Booth and Foxtel had a lot of catching up to do, but Booth chose to focus on promoting the brand rather than the prospective content. He was able to draw on one particular Fox character, Bart Simpson, to present Foxtel as a television company with attitude, as a 'must-have' product. Optus, by contrast, gave off confusing signals with its advertising, mixing a pitch for phone business as well as pay TV. It was also well behind Telstra with its cable roll-out.

Telstra had begun running its cable through its underground ducts the previous July, and by the time Optus Vision began stringing its cable from electricity poles in Sydney's Blacktown on February 13, Telstra already had its cable past 100,000 homes in Sydney, Melbourne and Brisbane. Because Optus had chosen the cheaper but unsightly aerial cable, it could roll out cable more quickly than Telstra, but would be unlikely to catch it. Telstra expected to have passed 400,000 homes by June 1995, whereas Optus Vision was looking to have passed 100,000 by the end of the year. The best marketing effort would fail if there was no cable, and therefore no service to satisfy demand. Speed in rolling out its cable was now the essential objective for Optus.

Ken Cowley's aggressive bid on February 6 to win the rugby league pay TV rights for Foxtel widened the battle to a new front. If Optus Vision and its partner PBL – which was supplying the sport to the cable operator's content package – failed to defend their ground, they would lose a critical skirmish in the marketing war.

Optus Vision had another challenge. It did not have a chief executive. Bob Mansfield and Martin Hannes looked at a number of candidates, mostly Americans, but decided they needed an Australian chief executive with a strong marketing background. At one of their meetings, Brian Powers raised the name of Geoffrey Cousins, a former chairman of Australia's largest advertising agency, George Patterson, and a member of the PBL board. Cousins was a tough, highly competitive and combative person with a dry sense of humour. He was in his early fifties and looking for another challenge. The Optus Vision partners decided he would be ideal for the job. Cousins accepted their offer and was due to start the job on Monday, April 3, 1995.

In the weeks after they were rebuffed by the ARL on February 6, Cowley, Smith and John Ribot, manager of the pro-Super League club Brisbane, offered players and clubs huge sums to bring them across to the new competition. The News Limited foyer in Holt Street saw a steady stream of players like Canberra's Ricky Stuart, Laurie Daley and Bradley Clyde and Cronulla's Andrew Ettinghausen, as they signed up for Super League on contracts worth $700,000 a year. Staff at News started to joke that they should wear a Canberra Raiders shirt into the office one day and see if Ken Cowley or David Smith would rush up to them with a big offer.

Another stream of players and club officials had also had been coming and going from the Goldfields House offices of News's lawyers, Atanaskovic Hartnell. Cowley had convinced Rupert Murdoch that he could buy enough players and clubs to start a competition for $20 million. Murdoch, who was heavily preoccupied with matters in the US and Europe at this stage, thought it to be a reasonable outlay and left it to Cowley to handle.

By early 1995, Cowley had become enormously powerful in the News organisation. Not only had he put News into alliance with Telstra, but he was the architect of the Super League strategy and was also running News's half-owned Australian domestic airline, Ansett. His colleagues were beginning to think he had too much on his plate. But buoyed by the independence and authority Murdoch was giving him, and his continuing close friendship with Paul Keating, Cowley was starting to believe he could perform miracles. By Friday, March 31, his Super League campaign was complete. Brisbane, Canberra, Canterbury, Cronulla, Penrith, and the three clubs which had only joined the competition that year, Auckland, Perth and Townsville, all had moved across to the News competition. Super League would create another four clubs based in Adelaide, south Queensland, Newcastle, and Melbourne to make up the number to 12. News had a football competition for its pay TV service. It appeared to be a remarkably clinical exercise. The ARL and Kerry Packer had been out-manoeuvred and the establishment competition looked to be in trouble, with some of its best teams having defected.

Cousins' first day in his new job as head of Optus Vision came two days earlier than he expected. Brian Powers called him into Packer's Park Street headquarters on Saturday to discuss Optus Vision's response to the News raids on rugby league clubs and players. Unless Optus Vision started matching the huge payer payments and club sponsorships that were on offer, the ARL would be reduced to a peripheral competition and the television rights similarly debased. Kerry Packer opened the discussion. He said a defence of the ARL could cost the consortium anything up to $100 million. 'How serious are we?' he asked as he pointed his finger at those around the table: his son James, Brian Powers, Bob Mansfield, Martin Hannes and Cousins. 'This is not free television, it is pay television.' Those at the meeting realised that they not only needed to put up some serious money, but they had to move quickly – that is, that day – to shore up the ARL. And their broadcasting rights.

Packer offered to put $10 million from PBL into a fighting fund. Mansfield appreciated the seriousness of the situation and offered $40 million from Optus Communications. He and Geoff Cousins would need to ring the other Optus shareholders, Cable and Wireless and Bell South, to test their resolve to defend their position. Rugby league was the major winter sport in NSW and Queensland, two States which could not be ignored in any marketing campaign. If News was able to achieve ascendancy in its coverage of the sport, it would threaten Optus's telephony ambitions. Over the week starting April 3, Optus Vision and PBL started handing out some staggering payments to clubs, players and key coaches like Manly's Bob Fulton, Easts' Phil Gould and Newcastle's Malcolm Reilly – $47.5 million in the first few days of the bidding war between the two competitions.[18] The money was flowing like water. Players and coaches suddenly became wealthy men.

The next wave of people to walk through the ARL's offices in Phillip Street were serious-looking men in dark suits. They looked very much out of place. 'Who are these blokes?' Arthurson asked his offsider, Quayle. 'Lawyers,' Quayle answered.[19]

As Arthurson and Quayle were fending off News's attack on their rugby league competition, the pay TV war between Telstra and Optus was opening up on a new front. Both Optus Vision and Foxtel were preparing to woo the Seven Network, or more particularly the network's array of pay and free-to-air sporting rights over the Australian Football League (AFL), rugby union, the Australian and NSW Open tennis, the Australian Masters and Open golf, the Bathurst 1000 touring car race and the Atlanta and Sydney Olympics. Seven chairman Ivan Deveson and managing director Bob Campbell had pulled the network out of Optus Vision in November and were determined to be a program supplier and play off the two pay TV groups for the best deal. This may have been a good strategy for Seven, but it suited neither Optus nor Foxtel. Both wanted to lock up Seven's programming and, just as importantly, deny the rival pay TV group access to the coverage. Ken Cowley was confident – as News and Telstra held 25 per cent of Seven between them – that the network would come across to Foxtel without too much prodding. This was a serious miscalculation.

Optus Vision's Geoff Cousins wasn't at all fazed by the pressure mounting in Seven's register and was preparing to make an offer Seven's board would not be able to refuse.

Then, on April 11, stockbroker Bain and Co snapped up 4.3 million call options over Seven shares, followed by a buy order for physical stock at $3.15, or 10 per cent above its previous day's close, which netted another five million shares. The buyer had put its foot on just under 4 per cent of the network. Although there was no legal requirement for the buyers to declare themselves below the 5 per cent threshold, Kerry Stokes and executives of his privately-held Australian Capital Equity group confirmed off the record that they were the buyers. For the record, Stokes would make 'no comment'.

Stokes was a knock-about type who was orphaned as a baby and raised in poor circumstances in Melbourne by foster parents. After trying his hand at jobs ranging from television repairs to cane cutting and trucking, he moved to Perth in the late 1960s and took up selling real estate and property development. He resisted the easy credit of the 1980s and emerged at the end of the decade in good shape financially, picking off some choice assets of some of the more adventurous entrepreneurs of the decade. His smartest move was to buy the old Bell Bros caterpillar dealership from Robert Holmes a Court after he got into severe problems in the wake of the 1987 stockmarket crash. Stokes had made his name more recently as a close friend and business associate of Ken Cowley. In 1993 he and Cowley extended a financial lifeline to the collapsed Adelaide investment company Bennett and Fisher, which owned the famous RM Williams outback shoe and clothing company. In the 1991 print media inquiry, Cowley admitted that News had financed Stokes' purchase of the *Canberra Times* newspaper from Kerry Packer in 1989. Stokes had been warehousing the paper for News, pending a change of the law which would allow News to take it off his hands.

Not surprisingly, the market believed Stokes was again acting as a stalking horse for News, a suggestion vigorously denied by Stokes.[20] Cowley said later that Stokes went into Seven on his own initiative, but once in there 'he got some encouragement, verbally' from News to press on.[21] PBL and Optus Vision were spreading the word privately that Stokes was being supported financially by News, a suggestion also vehemently rejected by Stokes.

Campbell and Deveson could not have been surprised by Stokes' dramatic appearance in the Seven register. After all, they had blocked his determined efforts to take an interest in the network in the 1993 float and would have realised he might return. The Seven share price had fallen sharply in late March after the network broke its advertising agreements and lifted ad rates 10 per cent, damaging Seven's credibility and triggering a short-term evaporation of advertising support. The network was then forced to offer discounts to bring advertisers back. It was a mammoth bungle. Stokes seized the opportunity to buy the stock at a three-month low.

Day after day, Stokes soaked up more shares in Seven and by April 20, when he had reached 13 per cent, he demanded publicly that he replace Deveson as chairman.[22]

As the pressure mounted on Deveson with each day's buying by Stokes, the Seven chairman was displaying far too much independence for the taste of its two major shareholders. In a strongly worded statement to the Australian Stock Exchange, the Seven board said, 'To date the company has received an attractive proposal to participate in the Optus Vision venture. The company has not yet received an acceptable proposal from Foxtel. However, Foxtel has indicated it would make an improved proposal to Seven Network Ltd in the immediate future.'[23]

Foxtel chief Mark Booth had submitted a one-page only proposal to Seven, confident that the board would feel obliged to join the News-Telstra alliance. By contrast, Optus Vision had presented a comprehensive document of 100 pages. Still, Seven gave Foxtel more time to come up with a better offer, although the News and Telstra board representatives, Dulcie Boling (*New Idea* magazine publisher for News) and Paul Rizzo (Telstra) were excluded from discussions on the pay TV issue. On April 25, as Stokes was pushing towards the 20 per cent takeover threshold where he would be in a position to walk into the board room and demand the chair, Seven's directors agreed to meet Geoff Cousins in the network's Melbourne studio boardroom. Cousins had only recently stepped down as a director of Seven and knew Deveson and Campbell very well and the right psychological buttons to push. He also had an ally in Sean O'Halloran, the network's legal counsel, who had worked closely with Nick Falloon negotiating the movie contracts for Optus Vision.

Cousins went into full sales mode, reiterating the terms outlined in the Optus Vision offer document given to the board two weeks earlier. These included a 2 per cent share in Optus Vision costing the network $26 million, a 30 per cent interest in the two sports channels (another $20 million) alongside the US ESPN group, 8.33 per cent of the two movie channels ($8 million) and a money back guarantee with interest if performance benchmarks were not met to July 1998. The stake in the sports partnership would enable Seven to draw fees as a supplier of content to the partnership, and also take a share of profit at the other end from the partnership's sale of programming to Optus Vision. Cousins then stole the night by offering Seven a $10 million sign-on fee. It was reminiscent of Falloon and O'Halloran's offer to the Hollywood studios which snatched Disney and MGM from under Australis's nose.

That night Seven's board signed up with Cousins and Optus Vision. It was a last-gasp decision by the Seven board, taken in the absence of the News and Telstra directors and with Stokes' threats and aggressive buying of Seven shares forming a noisy backdrop. Foxtel's Mark Booth did not make another offer. Sam Chisholm and Ken Cowley told him the playing field was tilted against them and that it looked like Deveson and Campbell were determined to take Seven into Optus Vision regardless. Chisholm also assured Booth that the AFL rights weren't pivotal, that Nine used to beat Seven without them. Booth wasn't so sure. All his instincts told him he needed the Australian rules football.

Seven's decision to join caused yet another reconfiguration of the consortium's shareholding. Both Optus Communications and Continental Cablevision held 46.5 per cent, PBL 5 per cent and Seven 2 per cent. The decision to join Optus Vision did nothing to stop the turmoil in its share register and Stokes telegraphing daily through the media that he was after the chairman's position. The pressure on Deveson to step down was intense, but he toughed it out for another fortnight . . . and then jumped before he was pushed. The board elected Ian Holmes, a long-term chief executive of the Grundy Organisation who had been invited on to the board only a few days earlier to the hot seat as chairman. Holmes was highly regarded in the programming industry, but was without a job after Reg Grundy sold his business to Pearson International in late March for $378 million.[24]

Holmes attempted to meet some of Stokes' criticisms of the network, and announced a cost-cutting program less than a week after he was elected chairman. On May 30, as Stokes kept up his buying, Holmes bowed to the inevitable and invited the Perth businessman and one of his senior executives, Bill Rayner, on to the board.

Stokes was not going to be an easy person to live with for the independent directors Peter Ritchie and lawyer Michael Robinson, and of course, the object of much of his criticism, managing director Bob Campbell. Within days of Stokes moving to the takeover threshold he asked for Campbell's resignation, but not before Campbell had extended the network's AFL rights to 2001, starting at $20 million a year and escalating to $50 million in the final year. Stokes was furious. Three days later, on June 26, Holmes quit, citing the next day at a press conference, after Stokes had been elected to the chairmanship, lack of time and commitment to do the job.[25]

In his first meeting with directors Stokes asked them one by one whether they had read the lengthy Optus Vision agreement. They had all read the 15-page executive summary, but none had read the whole document. Stokes' lawyers had already been through the agreement, but it looked watertight. Despite his declared intention of taking Seven out of Optus Vision as quickly as it had gone in, Stokes and Seven's program portfolio looked to be bound to Optus Vision. The only possible escape clause now was the performance guarantee that Cousins had given.

The loss of Seven had been a major blow to Foxtel, although amazingly it had not tried hard to win it. Cousins crowed after his victory, '(Winning Seven) was not essential for us. For Foxtel, on the other hand, it was absolutely vital. They have very little programming, frankly, to offer the Australian people now in terms of pay TV. They are in a tough spot.'[26] By bringing Seven into the same consortium as Nine, Cousins had introduced a highly volatile element into the Optus Vision ownership structure. Seven and Nine had been bitter rivals since the late 1950s and with Kerry Stokes looking for any opportunity to pull Seven out of the consortium, Cousins' short-term strategic win would turn into a destructive force in the longer term.

As of late April 1995, however, Optus Vision had the two major winter codes, AFL and rugby league, and a major marketing advantage over its rival.

Before the football season started, News Limited sued the ARL in the Federal Court, alleging that the February 1995 loyalty agreements breached the *Trade Practices Act*. It also sought court permission to have talks with a number of clubs. The ARL counter-sued News, claiming News had tried to induce players and clubs to break the agreements. Justice Burchett set a hearing date of September 25, immediately after that year's grand final, for the hearing date. While both sides awaited the court hearing, all 20 teams played the 1995 season under the auspices of the ARL. There was considerable ill-feeling between the teams that had chosen to stay with the establishment and those which had opted to move to

Super League. The season ended with Super League club Canterbury beating ARL club Manly 17–4 in the grand final. At half time in the match, Optus Vision attempted a tricky piece of entertainment which involved film characters running in and out of a large wooden container designed to look like a television set, suspended from a crane a few feet above the ground. But a wire holding the 'set' snapped, and it lurched sideways and on to the ground. The advertising for Optus Vision dressed up as entertainment looked very amateurish. Fortunately none of the actors running in and out of the 'set' was hurt. Cousins admitted later the performance had not gone well, but appreciated that he had got plenty of attention for his brand.

The so-called Telstra-News Corporation (TNC) agreement with Australis wasn't settled until March 1995. Frank Blount's renegotiation of some of the more painful terms that Rod Price had inflicted on Sam Chisholm on Christmas Eve, and Telstra's own bureaucratic processes, contributed to the delay. By the time Blount and Ken Cowley launched Foxtel on March 9, Telstra had lifted its construction program to the point that it was passing 3,000 homes a day, all through its underground ducts. Telstra was contemplating installing part of its cable overhead, because it was far cheaper, but held back in the early stages as Optus Vision attracted much adverse publicity and considerable flak from a number of suburban councils in Sydney and Melbourne which resisted the erection of the overhead cable. The councils demanded a lease fee from Optus for using above-ground space with a view to setting up a fund to eventually place all cables and wires underground. At the March 9 launch, Blount also gave an updated estimate of Telstra's expected expenditure on cable construction of $3.9 billion, $400 million more than the initial projected cost in November the previous year.

It was now a full-scale race between the two phone companies. The quicker the cable went out, the faster the phone company could start signing up pay TV customers. This was critical for Optus, because it hoped to turn pay TV subscribers into phone users when it had its telephony technology in place. For Telstra, the more homes it signed up for pay TV, the harder it would make it for Optus to win the customers. As a result, it became imperative for each company to get its cable into target areas before the other. Once a rival put its cable down a street and its sales force canvassed the homes, then the second arrival faced the prospect of having doors closed in its face.

Blount had told his board he expected an 'overbuild' – that is, Telstra and Optus cables going down the same street – of about 20 per cent. Telstra was concentrating its roll-out in the more affluent eastern suburbs of Sydney and Melbourne initially, while Optus focused on the newer suburbs in the west, where it believed disposable incomes were higher. As the roll-out pace quickened and the phone companies started to adapt their strategies to the fast-changing situation, they began to follow each other down the same streets. By the end of the 1995, it was becoming apparent that the 'overbuild' was going to be considerably more than Blount's initial estimate.

The accelerating roll-out by the cable groups started to ring alarm bells at Australis. In the early days Cosser, and then Price and Gamble, believed they had a two-year window to build a subscriber base for their satellite business before they would be troubled by cable. The experience in every other country was that cable construction was a slow and expensive process.

Australis also needed more money. The $175.5 million that Wayne Burt and Price had raised the previous May was running low until Australis's coffers were topped up by the $71.4 million injection from News and Telstra, courtesy of the TNC agreement.

Australis would need another $200 million to complete development of its satellite service and fund the company's costs until it started to break even, expected to be in 1999. Australis would be the first satellite operator in the world to adopt the Motion Picture Experts' Group's MPEG-2 digital standard, agreed at a meeting in Singapore late in 1994 to ensure a worldwide standard for equipment and broadcasting quality. The wide variation in standards in colour television as it was introduced progressively around the world and the VHS v Beta video technology struggle in the 1980s – which eventually proved so disastrous for Beta and the Sony Corporation – would not be repeated in digital satellite broadcasting.

Being the world's guinea pig was proving to be expensive for Australis. As it was an untried business with profits years away, Australis could not simply go to a bank and borrow money. There was an established source of funds for subscription broadcasters, and that was in the US, where cable companies had been raising money for decades by issuing bonds to investors who understood the business. Typically, the investors, such as mutual funds and life companies, would buy the bonds and not expect to be repaid the money, plus compound interest, for another five or 10 years. It gave the company issuing the securities time to make enough money to be able to at least pay the interest. The principal amount could be refinanced through a further issue of bonds or notes.

In May, Neil Gamble and Australis's newly-hired finance director, Geoff Kleeman, flew to New York with Kevin Skelton, an Australia-based media financing specialist with the US investment bank Merrill Lynch. Gamble, Kleeman and Price wanted to raise at least $US150 million ($A205 million), but were hoping to get as much as $US175 million. Kleeman had been Price's finance director at building materials group Pioneer International before Price retired and took up the chairman's job at Australis. Kleeman had trained as a chartered accountant after matriculating from Adelaide's Unley High School and was company secretary at Southern Farmers when it was run by Price in 1983. Price moved to Sydney in 1986 when he was hired by Ron Brierley to run IEL, and Kleeman joined him in 1989 when IEL was selling assets and struggling to survive in the wake of the 1987 stock market crash. When the management buyout of IEL backed by Abe Goldberg fell on its face with the collapse of Goldberg's Linter Group in late 1989, Price moved across to Pioneer and took Kleeman with him. A short, skinny man with greying hair, Kleeman remained composed and available for clearly thought out advice in pressure-filled situations.

The three Australis executives did a series of 'roadshow' presentations to mutual fund managers in New York, Boston, Chicago and San Francisco and in larger regional centres like Denver, Kansas City and Minneapolis, trying to persuade the funds to invest in a satellite broadcaster on the other side of the world. In the US, satellite groups like Echo Star and Prime Star were still in their infancy. Cable dominated the industry. Gamble and Kleeman had to convince these knowledgable but hard-headed fund managers that a new technology in another country was worth backing. They had one very important card to play, and that was their 25↑year agreement to supply their channels to the cable-based Foxtel partnership of News Corp and Telstra. The mutual funds had heard of these companies.

After their two-week tour of the US, the three returned to New York to ring the funds they had approached to ask them whether they were willing to invest in Australis's notes. The notes were not secured, but were subject to hundreds of clauses in a 257-page indenture document. Australis could not even sell an asset without giving the bond-holders 25 days notice. Because of the relatively high risk attached to Australis's business, the notes carried an interest return of 14 per cent, high even for 1995. High-yield bonds like these were commonly referred to in the US as 'junk bonds'. The Australis team received positive responses from Alliance Capital and Fidelity in New York, Oppenheimer in Boston, Janus Capital in Denver, Kemper in Chicago, Lutheran Brotherhood in Minneapolis, the State of Wisconsin and Reed Waddell in Kansas City. New York-based Merrill Lynch, a specialist in high-yield investments, also agreed to take some of the notes. In the end, Australis raised $US175 million from the investors; sufficient, they hoped, to see the company through its testing early years.

In the wake of losing Seven to Optus Vision, Mark Booth was keen for Foxtel to strengthen its program line-up by closing long-running negotiations with potential program suppliers for a news and current affairs channel. The leading contender was a joint venture between the ABC, John Fairfax and US cable group Cox Communications, called Australian Information Media. AIM would work with Turner International on its News Channel and with Viacom's Nickelodeon division to produce a children's entertainment package for the second channel.

The ABC was the pivotal player in this group and, to reflect its importance, held 51 per cent of the AIM partnership. It had more domestic news and broadcasting resources than the other partners, and a brand new special-purpose digitally equipped pay TV studio at its Gore Hill complex, courtesy of a one-off $12.5 million grant from the Federal Government. It also had two channels on the Optus satellite, but not the money to develop a satellite pay TV service. Instead, it had embarked on a course of being a program provider. ABC's head of pay TV, Kim Williams, had committed very substantial funds and people to AIM, but remarkably, 12 months or so into the project, did not have a distribution platform. Williams approached Neil Gamble to ask if he could add the ABC channels to Australis's package and to use Australis's subscriber management system. The arrangement would need Trade Practices Commission approval, as the ABC was supposed to be a competitor to the commercial operators.

The ABC's progress in getting into pay TV was interrupted when Williams left in mid-May to set up and manage the Fox studio at the Sydney showgrounds. He was replaced by the ABC's head of enterprises, Julie Steiner. Gamble finally told her that the price AIM wanted for the channels was far too high. It was a Rolls Royce when a Holden Commodore was more than adequate.

Mark Booth was an easier touch for Steiner. Foxtel needed the content. After some intense all-night negotiating sessions on price, shareholding arrangements and an agreement on distribution and minimum subscriber guarantees, the contract was ready to be signed in Foxtel's temporary offices in George Street, Sydney, in early July. Rupert Murdoch was in Australia for News's annual budget and planning talks and had read in the *Australian Financial Review* on a flight to Melbourne that the proposed deal was imminent. The *AFR* journalist, Mark Furness, had picked up the story the previous day and had sought confirmation from Fairfax's deputy chief executive, Michael Hoy, who called him to his office for a briefing. When he arrived, there were also journalists from Fairfax's *Sydney Morning Herald* and *The Age*, who had no idea what they were there for. Furness was not impressed. He thought he had a scoop. At the end of the briefing, Hoy told the journalists to get a comment from Steiner, who said it was a breakthrough for AIM and that it would be a good partnership.

The next morning – the day the deal was due to be signed at 9.30am – Murdoch noticed the story wasn't in any of the News Limited papers. It appeared to have been selectively leaked to the Fairfax press before the deal was signed, and he was the mug paying the high price for the two channels. On landing in Melbourne at 8am, he immediately rang Mark Booth and told him not to sign the agreement. Booth attempted to reason with him, but Murdoch was firm. There were cheaper and better alternatives available. In an hour-and-a-half, delegations from the ABC, Nickelodeon and Australis and their lawyers were due in his office to sign the deal. Booth tried to call him back, but Murdoch was out of contact. He left a message at Murdoch's Melbourne office to call as soon as possible. Just before 9.30, Julie Steiner, Neil Gamble and Peter Rose from Australis, and News's lawyer Ian Phillip from the firm Allen Allen and Hemsley, started to arrive. The phone rang in Booth's office and he walked over to take the call. It was Murdoch. Booth pleaded with him to allow the deal to go ahead, but Murdoch was adamant. The deal was off. Booth walked ashen-faced from his office to tell Steiner the bad news. She was devastated. It could be the end of the ABC's ambitions in pay TV. Talks with Optus Vision were going nowhere, for largely the same reason the Foxtel deal had just fallen over. The service was too expensive. AIM was insisting on 33 per cent more than similar news and entertainment material available from overseas or a package on offer from the free-to-air networks.[27]

Unless she could get Optus Vision back to the negotiating table, Steiner would have to sack the 100 staff she and Kim Williams had recruited and find another use for a state-of-the-art studio complex purpose-built for a satellite pay TV service. The staff were only just beginning to move in. The $12.5 million Keating had begrudgingly given ABC chief David Hill two-and-a-half years earlier, and Hill's bold plans to take on Murdoch and Packer in pay TV, were evaporating before Steiner's horrified eyes.

One of Neil Gamble's best friends was fellow South African John Greaves, finance director of Optus Communications. Greaves was Gamble's best man at his wedding and the two men and their wives travelled extensively together when they were in their 20s, before they all left South Africa in the late 1970s. Gamble and Greaves kept in close contact after they moved to Australia, and were colleagues in the dark days at Wormald International. Now Greaves was working with their old friend Bob Mansfield at Optus. At dinner parties and barbecues at each other's homes, the topic of conversation inevitably drifted on to the subject that was consuming their working lives – pay TV. Greaves warned his friend that he had to be careful what he said, but Gamble's intuition led him to believe that Optus Vision was going to be very aggressive on the pricing of its pay TV package. Greaves wouldn't be specific, but Gamble suddenly feared a looming price war developing between the two phone company consortiums.

Australis's projections of earning profits and having up to one million subscribers by the turn of the century were in tatters already now that the two cable-based pay TV groups were rolling out their cable far more rapidly than Australis had anticipated. A discounting war between these well-funded rivals would play further havoc with Australis's own forecasts. Australis in April 1995 reduced its $299 connection fee to $99 – compared to its average cost of over $1,000 – to accelerate its subscriber take-up. It kept its monthly subscription at $49.95 for the Galaxy package of eight channels. Unfortunately, its satellite was still several months away and Australis was having difficulty meeting early demand with its MDS service because of bottlenecks in equipment supplies.[28]

Australis's expectations of reaching even 200,000 subscribers by April 1996 were looking very optimistic.

The window of opportunity which seemed so wide when Australis launched its Premier Sports service with such optimism in January appeared to have closed by mid-year. If Gamble's information was correct – that Optus Vision would soon start a discounting war with its cable rival – then Australis would be shot to pieces in the crossfire. It would be forced to cut its connection rate still further and its monthly subscriber rates to below its own costs. For every new subscriber it signed, it would increase its losses. Australis would go broke within months.

In July, Rodney Price was in Australia and invited Gamble and Geoff Kleeman to his property, Tahara, to plan their next move. The Murrumbidgee River chugged by lazily only a few metres away as the three sat on the verandah of Price's homestead. Tahara, like its close namesake in the film, would have been more at home on the set of *Gone With the Wind*. Gamble told Price and Kleeman, 'I think the only way out for us is to start negotiations with Telstra and News to merge Foxtel and Australis.' Price was lukewarm to the idea, but didn't dismiss it. His relations with Sam Chisholm in London were still good and he said it might be worth pursuing. The alternative, of trying to slug it out against Foxtel and Optus Vision, was barely worth thinking about. Price agreed to speak to Chisholm when he returned to London in a week.

Sam Chisholm had been waiting for Rod Price to call him since Christmas Eve. That was when Price did him over in the negotiations over the Telstra-News Corporation agreement. Chisholm and Murdoch had been prepared to give way to Price's demands on the night because they were desperate for programming, but also because they knew that eventually they would claw back their concessions by merging with, or buying, Australis. Chisholm felt right through the months of humiliation after he had been forced to accept such harsh terms that Australis would not have the financial capacity to survive in a high-cost contest between Telstra and Optus. The satellite operator had only one place to go when it got into trouble, and that was to Foxtel. The TNC agreement bound Australis's and Foxtel's futures together. Chisholm knew Price would always want to keep open the option of going to Optus Vision to strengthen his negotiating hand, but in reality this would always be difficult. To strengthen Optus Vision would weaken

Foxtel, and Australis's survival hopes depended on Foxtel doing as well as possible.

Also, Australis had just raised $US175 million from a number of US mutual funds. In their representations to the funds, Price, Gamble and Kleeman had painted a rosy picture for the company; its capacity to reach 90 per cent of the population, its attractive programming, and its agreement with Foxtel. Despite the fact that Australis was an unknown quantity, the funds backed it. If it were to suddenly stumble into financial trouble so soon after the raising, there was a strong possibility that the funds would sue.

'Yes Rodney, I think we should talk,' Chisholm told a relieved Price.

On July 19, Australis shares experienced heavy turnover, with more than seven million shares changing hands. One parcel of 6.56 million shares was bought through Macquarie Bank's London office at 80 cents a share for an unnamed client. *The Australian* newspaper reported that the trading had 'reopened speculation that Mr Steve Cosser, a key shareholder in Australis, may be behind the share activity'.[29]

Bob Mansfield rocked the Optus camp when he announced in August 1995 that he was resigning to become chief executive at newspaper publisher John Fairfax. Mansfield was tired of the constant travelling involved in running Optus Communications and dealing with its Optus Vision associate and wanted to spend more time with his family. He had five children. The Fairfax job was a highly regarded and powerful position. Mansfield was also becoming increasingly frustrated with having to deal with three 25 per cent shareholders with different views and agendas and with none of them in control. As the business risks and stakes increased through 1995 with the emergence of Optus Vision and its ambitious cable strategy, Mansfield felt that running an organisation by committee only increased the chances that wrong decisions or halfhearted compromises would be made. His resignation meant that the strong figure in the Optus organisation now was the Optus Vision chief Geoff Cousins.

Although he had already started merger talks with Sam Chisholm, Rod Price gave an up-beat assessment on August 21 of Australis's prospects when announcing a loss of $122 million for the year to June 30. Price described the year as one of 'great achievement'. Subscriptions had reached 31,000, and the 'ground-breaking' satellite direct-to-home service was expected to start 'in the coming weeks' to pick up the backlog of 50,000 households waiting to be connected.

Price said, 'The financial result . . . is in line with our expectations. This pattern of financial results is a well known and inevitable feature of the early years of new pay television operations and is reversed over time as subscriber numbers build up.'[30] Price's optimism about Australis was clouded that same week by fresh legal action from Albert Hadid, who was still smarting after having been out-manoeuvred over the B satellite licence in November 1993. He had sued initially in January 1995, claiming $220 million in damages from Australis, Rodney Price, Lenfest Communications and Wayne Burt for engaging in misleading or deceptive conduct. Seven months later, he changed his statement of claim and alleged that the respondents had conspired to cheat and defraud him. Hadid claimed that Lenfest owed to him a fiduciary duty, which it breached. In the revised statement of claim, Hadid raised his damages claim to $705 million.[31] Australis, Lenfest and Burt all denied the allegations and vowed to contest the claim vigorously. It would be a year or two before the claim got to the courts. Meanwhile, Australis had more pressing matters to resolve.

Australis was charging its MDS subscribers $49.95 a month for an eight-channel service. Price declined to nominate a rental for the satellite, which would probably be higher because its installation and delivery costs were significantly greater than MDS. The franchisees taking the Australis signal would set their own fee structure.

Until this time, Mark Booth had indicated Foxtel would price its service at about the same as the Australis fee. But a week after Price's announcement, Geoff Cousins stunned the industry and blew Australis's and Foxtel's finely tuned calculations away when he announced Optus Vision's pricing package. Connection would be $29.95; a core service of news, entertainment, education and music was just $25 a month; and a deluxe package with full sport and movies on top of the core channels $39.95. The service would begin on September 20, exactly a year after Optus Vision launched.

Australis spokesman Jim Hoggett reacted by saying, 'Optus Vision will go broke even more quickly than we originally thought.'[32] As combative as ever, Cousins described this claim as nonsense. 'We have always said we will be a low-cost producer.

People have just not realised what we meant.' Gamble and Price had been expecting something like this, but not quite as bad. Their main concern was that Foxtel would try to match Optus Vision.

Foxtel's Mark Booth, who had the highest costs of all three operators, was also staggered by the prices. He responded by saying his service would be 'competitive' when it launched on October 23 with the blockbuster movie *Jurassic Park*. Telstra's own connection costs for each subscriber (which were not borne by Foxtel) varied enormously depending on the age and condition of the 'pits' in front of each house, but averaged at least $1,200. Further, it paid Foxtel $150 for each connection. Foxtel was paying Australis $27 per subscriber per month for its eight channel package and had further costs for its own Fox entertainment, sports and news channels. Overall, its cost would be at least $40 per subscriber per month. Optus had pitched its price below Foxtel's costs and perhaps below Australis's as well. This was the unforeseen situation in which Australis's arrangements with its franchisees would lead to heavy losses.

It appeared that Australis's worst fear would be realised. Australis would struggle to gain subscribers in the main cities where the cable was being rolled out because households would always choose a cheaper service which offered more channels. This was cable. Before he left to live in France, Steve Cosser had set up Australis as the metropolitan service provider (where the cable companies were now threatening to take control between them) and the regional and rural areas had been sold to the franchisees, which were being subsidised by Australis. The lower the industry price structure fell, the greater the subsidy Australis gave its franchisees. The Australis share price tumbled 20 cents in the days following the Optus price announcement.

Rod Price, in London, was so nervous about developments in Australia he rang up Sam Chisholm at his apartment the day after Optus Vision set its prices and asked to see him. He insisted that Foxtel did not have to match Optus Vision, not at that stage. He impressed on Chisholm that if Foxtel did meet Optus Vision then Australis's Galaxy would also have to drop its rates.

Chisholm pointed out that Foxtel's main aim was to beat Optus Vision and it had no choice but to match the going rates. He told Price the cable roll-out was not sufficiently advanced to worry Australis, yet.

Price left with nothing but the hope that the merger would proceed. Australis was suddenly in deep trouble. If Optus Vision's price structure wasn't enough for him to worry about, four days later Cousins delivered another hammer blow to his two rivals. Optus Vision would double the rate of its roll-out and was aiming to pass 2.3 million homes and overtake Telstra by the end of 1996. Cousins had sensed that Australis was vulnerable and wanted to deliver a knock-out blow to Foxtel before Telstra could crank up its momentum. The acceleration of the roll-out by Optus was a hugely ambitious task and required the assembly of special purpose telescopic lift trucks in Australia. Cousins had scoured the world for as many of these types of truck as he could find, and would now have to make them himself. He was leaning on local suppliers such as BHP to lift output of the strand which goes into coaxial cables, and on the cable manufacturer Olex to double production.

The demands and objectives of Optus Vision were beginning to dominate the agenda, too, of its 46.5 per cent parent company, Optus Communications, which remained focused on offering long distance and mobile phone services. Optus Communications was experiencing strong growth in its revenues, which had reached $1.4 billion for the year to June 30, 1995, but its high development costs, including heavy expenditure on Optus Vision, meant that it was still losing money ($17 million in 1995), but moving into profit.[33] After the departure of Bob Mansfield in November, Optus Communications was briefly without a chief executive. The demands of Optus Vision were putting enormous strains on the young company. Cousins was becoming a driven man and appeared to be obsessed with winning this war against Telstra and News. He realised that if he did not strike swiftly and decisively to overwhelm Foxtel in the early stages of the battle, then Optus Vision would eventually be overcome by the superior commercial firepower of the Foxtel partners. Optus Vision had one chance, and Cousins was determined to seize it.

# 10
# Total war

Bob Ellicott QC stood at the lectern in front of Justice James Burchett in court 21A of the Federal Court. 'News Limited have knowingly plundered and pillaged property and benefits of property of the ARL and its clubs,' he told the judge in the Australian Rugby League's opening address of its counter-claim against News for trying induce clubs and players to break loyalty agreements with the ARL. Reaching deeper into his briefcase of metaphors, the former Federal Attorney-General continued in his typically pugnacious style, 'It was like the Visigoths coming in and wrecking something that was never theirs and pulling it apart.'[1]

Two days earlier, Roger Gyles QC had accused the Australian Rugby League, in his opening address in News's claim against the league, of using 'economic duress' to convince 20 clubs to sign loyalty agreements on February 6. 'Mr Arthurson and others have a view that they personify the game and that the game is capable of being a proprietary piece of property which is the property of the governing body,' he told Justice Burchett.[2]

After 51 days of hearings – during which the inner workings of the so-called Super League 'war room' and the ARL's defence of its interests from its Phillip St bunker were regurgitated in a courtroom battle of comparable scale to the cable war being fought between Optus and Telstra in the suburbs – Burchett retired to consider his verdict.

The judge's decision would decide at one extreme whether News could pursue its Super League ambitions or, at the other, whether Super League would be told to return its 300 contracted players and eight clubs to the ARL. If Super League won, the ARL would be relegated to a second division, mostly Sydney-based competition isolated from world competition because England and New Zealand had also signed with Super League. A win by the ARL would mean a humiliating retreat by Super League, which would be forced to decide whether to surrender its teams or continue to support them indefinitely while they remained off the field. There was little room for compromise in Burchett's finding. Surely, one would live, the other would die.

The public saw the appearance of the rival league and the bitter defence by the ARL as a narrow battle over sports programming, but the conflict carried far greater stakes than this. Because Foxtel had lost the Australian Football League, it was imperative for its marketing that it have a major winter ball sport in its programming. In June 1995, News had signed the three southern hemisphere rugby unions in a 10-year, $US550 million deal which would give Foxtel top-level international and Super 12 rugby rights. The deal was done in Sam Chisholm's London apartment. South African businessman Johann Rupert, the head of Rothmans and the M Net television group, tried to co-opt Kerry Packer into supporting a rival rugby union competition, but the establishment unions in this case snuffed out the challenge quickly and delivered their national and regional teams to News.

Although the exciting Super 12 competition gave union a huge boost in Australia, New Zealand and South Africa, union at this time was still a relatively minor sport in Australia. It didn't have the pulling power of Australian rules or rugby league. Without at least one of these, Foxtel feared that its subscriber numbers would slip behind Optus Vision's and that Telstra would quickly lose large slabs of its local call phone business. As Kerry Packer and Geoff Cousins were in no mood to share the ARL coverage with Foxtel, News as the prime supplier of programs to the partnership believed it had no choice but to attempt to form another competition, just as Packer had done with cricket in 1977. The phone companies had multi-billion dollar cable networks riding on the success of movie and sports channels on their pay TV services. ARL versus Super League was ultimately Optus versus Telstra and Kerry Packer versus Rupert Murdoch.

While Bob Ellicott and Roger Gyles slugged it out in the Federal Court, Ken Cowley and Brian Powers met privately a number of times to try to resolve the dispute outside the courtroom. Despite the public perception of fierce rivalry and a bitter falling out between the News and PBL camps, Murdoch and Packer were pragmatic people who could see beyond short-term ruptures. During one of their discussions in Cowley's office, Powers suggested out of the blue that perhaps they could also do a deal on their wider media interests, to carve up Australia's main media assets between them. Packer was worried about News's shareholding in Seven, he said, and feared it had the potential to make Seven into a more determined competitor to Nine. Although the Seven investment clearly was not working out as well for News as it had hoped, things could easily change. Powers thought Packer might be prepared to sell his Fairfax shareholding to News if News was prepared to get out of Seven and buy into Nine. Packer wanted Fairfax, but his main priority was always to protect his main business, Nine. And there was no way Paul Keating would allow Packer to buy Fairfax.

It was a sweeping and audacious proposal, and it surprised Cowley. There was no doubt, thought Cowley, that Murdoch wanted Fairfax. The two had talked about it over the years and had tried to persuade Paul Keating on Hayman Island in 1993 to accept a plan for Cowley to buy the News Limited papers using a low-interest loan from the parent, News Corporation. This would free Rupert Murdoch, they believed, to bid for Fairfax. Keating had been cool to the idea then, but he might change his mind. Keating faced another election before the end of May 1996 and might prefer to have people he trusted and respected running the country's major newspapers, rather than the journalists' collective which effectively controlled Fairfax.

Cowley told Powers about this long-running contingency plan. If Keating were to accept the idea, then Cowley would take News's Seven interest as well. The two decided to keep refining the proposal along with their negotiations over the rugby league.

By early November 1995, Cowley and Powers had settled on the re-shuffle of their media interests, but the unknown quantity was how Optus Vision and its combative chief executive, Geoff Cousins, would react to any settlement proposal for the rugby league dispute. Optus Vision had put up most of the $60 million spent so far in shoring up the ARL's clubs and players and was contemplating a longer-term financial support package. Powers could only offer his best efforts to persuade Optus Vision and Cousins to accept a deal. In an attempt to draw the polarised positions of the ARL and News closer, Powers had devised his own plan which the warring parties, initially, had been happy with, and that involved moving over two years towards a 14-team 'super' competition. The teams would be decided on the basis of their performance over the 1996 and 1997 seasons.[3]

On November 8, Cowley, Powers, Packer and Murdoch gathered in Murdoch's Wapping offices in London to work out final points and sign the agreement. Packer was in the UK for the polo season, which had just finished, and Cowley had flown across for a News Corporation board meeting. Powers regularly flew to London while Packer was in residence there, so the trip was not unusual.

The two-hour meeting was jovial and constructive, a stark contrast to the insults both sides were throwing at each other in the Federal Court 20,000 kilometres away in Sydney. Packer would sell News an option to buy PBL's 17.2 per cent stake in Fairfax at $3.20 a share. Before News could exercise the option, it would have to arrange to sell its own newspapers. News also agreed to sell its interest in Seven. Although it was not part of the London agreement, the likely buyer of these interests was Cowley.[4] News also agreed to buy 20 per cent of Nine Network. Cowley and Powers believed that if News tried to buy 20 per cent of the parent company, PBL, it would attract the attention of Allan Fels, chairman of the Australian Competition and Consumer Commission. The ACCC would be unlikely to allow News to own both Fairfax and 20 per cent of PBL, which was Australia's largest magazine publisher. Instead, they had to isolate the investment to Nine. News would buy a share of the PBL subsidiary which held the network. News also agreed to sell Nine the free-to-air rights to Super League, assuming it survived the court battle, and to supply new product from Fox in the US to Nine.

The deal was extraordinary for a number of reasons. First, it depended on Keating agreeing to allow Murdoch to sell his newspapers to his lieutenant of 33 years to enable him to bid for Fairfax; News would turn its back on Seven and its promise to supply Fox programs to the network, to sell them instead to Nine; and Nine would seriously dilute its support for the ARL by buying the rights to the rival Super League. Most of the deal was kept strictly confidential. But when Nine announced its purchase of the Fox product, it sent shockwaves through Seven. When it disclosed that it had bought the Super League rights, Nine stunned the ARL. In his memoirs, Ken Arthurson gave this forthright opinion of the deal: 'I regarded Channel Nine's decision to shake hands with Super League to the detriment of the ARL, after all that had gone on, as a breathtaking piece of corporate treachery. I knew such a decision wouldn't have been made without Kerry Packer giving the nod. And that hurt most of all.'⁵

From Packer's point of view, the deal was a matter of furthering his corporate interests. It was a commercial decision. PBL and Nine stood to gain far more from the rights to Super League and Fox programming and with News as a 20 per cent shareholder than from a sentimental attachment to the ARL.

After returning from London, Cowley and a senior News executive and former Keating press secretary, Tom Mockridge, travelled to Canberra to attempt to win the endorsement of the two political leaders. First, Cowley went alone to see Opposition leader John Howard. After explaining the scenario, Cowley asked Howard if he had any problems with it. Howard said he didn't and liked the idea of a new media company (Cowley's) emerging.⁶ Cowley then gathered Mockridge to visit Keating in the Prime Minister's office. Keating had with him his chief adviser, Don Russell. When Cowley outlined a similar proposal to the one he had put to Keating two-and-a-half years earlier, Keating said, 'No, mate, no. It's just not possible.' Keating had been contemplating calling an election for the end of the year, but the opinion polls were so bad for him he had decided to wait until the New Year. He thought it would be political suicide to be seen to be presiding over such a massive media carve-up in front of a cynical electorate.

The years of romancing Keating had come to a final 'no' on the favour Cowley and Murdoch most wanted to be granted. A major leg of the deal had just fallen away. Packer wouldn't have News as a shareholder in Nine, but News was bound to provide Nine with the Super League and Fox programming rights, although the football rights would hinge on the Federal Court's decision. Packer suspected, too, that News wouldn't remain a shareholder in Seven much longer.

On February 23, 1996 at 4pm, Justice Burchett re-entered court 21A to deliver his verdict to a room packed with about 250 barristers, solicitors, ARL and Super League officials, the public and media. The ARL loyalty agreements were 'commercially proper' and the evidence presented in the lengthy trial 'made it plain that News Limited and the Super League companies acted, in the relevant sense, with dishonesty,' Burchett told the court.[7] Worse for News, Burchett found that the rebel clubs had breached their fiduciary duties in releasing their players to Super League and transferring their trade marks to the rival competition. The trademarks belonged to the ARL and its clubs in a joint venture arrangement and were not the property of the clubs to transfer to Super League.

Further, Burchett found that the ARL had not monopolised the league market, which he declared was part of a broader market in competition with other sports for spectators. Super League chief John Ribot was 'apt to colour his evidence to suit the contentions he was supporting'.[8] Of Ken Cowley and David Smith, who did not appear in the witness box on legal advice, Burchett said, 'The evidence does not disclose whether they told him (Rupert Murdoch) all the details of their own duplicity.'[9]

Burchett found for the ARL on every point it claimed, and rejected all of Super League's arguments. The ARL could not have hoped for a more comprehensive victory. Outside the court, Arthurson and Quayle were elated, but conciliatory towards Super League and its players, inviting them to rejoin the ARL. Cousins was typically combative and needled his rivals: 'We have all the AFL, all the rugby league, all of the soccer, and the club rugby, and that's just our winter sports, so it's going to be a long cold winter for Foxtel. How are they going to sell subscriptions? Darned if I know.'[10]

Ribot and News's lawyer, John Atanaskovic, looked stunned as they sat in the body of the court studying the four-page brief to the 218-page judgment handed down by the judge. Both felt the judge had gone way over the top in his findings and were already thinking about an appeal. But Super League had sensed that the decision would go against it. A few hours before Burchett delivered his findings, David Smith resigned from News.

About an hour after the judgment, Ken Cowley, flanked by Lachlan Murdoch and John Ribot, faced a handful of reporters in a conference room at the Sheraton on the Park Hotel, where Rupert Murdoch three years earlier had outlined his vision for Australia's role in Asia. 'This is a setback, there can be no question about that,' Cowley said. 'But change for the better must always overcome the obstacles that are set in place by the interests entrenched in the past. If I may be so bold, in the sweep of the future of rugby league this will be viewed as a temporary, albeit painful, reversal. Our resolve . . . remains undiminished as is our commitment to Super League.' Later, Cowley released a statement saying that News would appeal against the decision, in particular the 'fundamental unsoundness' of Burchett's finding that the ARL and the clubs were a joint venture. 'Our legal advisers have examined the judgment carefully and believe there are substantial grounds for an appeal,' his statement said. Given the drubbing Super League had just taken at the hands of the judge, these were brave words. News and Foxtel were plunged into a mood of dark pessimism. By contrast, Optus Vision and Geoff Cousins had won a remarkable victory and were in a state of elation.

While Cowley, Ribot and about a dozen News and Super League executives drowned their sorrows in a room News had taken for the night, Lachlan Murdoch walked out onto a hotel landing overlooking Hyde Park. He had great respect for Cowley, but the long-serving News man had landed the group in terrible strife. His company and some of its senior executives would be mocked, humiliated and gloated over in the newspapers the next day. Murdoch had re-located to Sydney from Brisbane in July and had helped keep spirits alive in the Super League camp during the court case by getting to know some of the players, dining and drinking with them. His appearances at press conferences were more for the show of having a Murdoch at the table than substance. Super League was Cowley and Ribot's creation.

As the 25-year-old stared out over the thick leafy mass of Hyde Park at dusk, Murdoch believed he felt like his father did when he arrived in Adelaide in 1953 after leaving Oxford University to take over his inheritance, a struggling tabloid newspaper called the *News*. It was going to be up to him now to lead the group out of this mess, he thought to himself.

The next day, the coverage in the weekend newspapers was as damning as he expected. Lachlan Murdoch feared that the loss could cause serious morale problems at News. On Monday, he walked through the newsrooms of the *Telegraph* and *The Australian* greeting staff to show them he wasn't a remote figure sulking in an office upstairs.

Two days later, Justice Burchett gave even more joy to the ARL and Cousins when he brought down 36 orders flowing from his judgment of the previous week. He banned Super League for five years, instructed Super League players to return to their ARL clubs, or to another ARL club, and ordered the clubs to hand over all of their jerseys, socks, shorts, T-shirts, footballs, mascots and other promotional material to the ARL. Burchett's orders were designed to kill Super League stone dead.

Lachlan Murdoch rang James Packer when he heard the orders and asked if they could meet. Packer suggested Murdoch see him and his father at the Packers' compound in Bellevue Hill that afternoon. A News driver took the young Murdoch and Ken Cowley out to the Packer home, where Kerry and James and Brian Powers were waiting. The men all walked into a large lounge room where Lachlan put it to the Packers that PBL take all the free-to-air and pay TV broadcasting rights over Super League. They could have it, on one condition: that News manage the competition for a period, for three or five years, to recover some of the $100 million the group had invested so far.

Powers said he would call Geoff Cousins and ask him around right away. They shouldn't make a decision without him. The young Murdoch suggested that he and Cowley go for a walk around the garden for 15 minutes to give the PBL trio time to think about his offer. By the time they returned to the house, Cousins was already there. Murdoch and Cowley could tell from the look on their faces that they were going to reject the offer. 'Thanks, but no thanks,' Powers told them. Cousins had convinced his colleagues that Super League would collapse within days. There was no point doing a deal.

If it was possible to pick a high point for the ARL and Optus Vision, this was it. The ARL appeared to have seen off this threat to its control over the game and to the broadcasting rights, and Optus Vision had gained a clear edge over Foxtel in its winter sports programming. Their elation would be short-lived. Burchett had dug himself in so deeply with his decision and his subsequent orders that he had given News substantial grounds for an appeal. On March 13, the full bench of the Federal Court stayed, or lifted, six of the more extravagant of Burchett's orders, giving Super League a lifeline until the result of a full appeal, due to be heard in May, two months away. The three judges, Justices Davies, Lockhart and Hill, kept those orders in place that would allow the ARL to start its 1996 competition with its 20 teams from 1995. But Justice Davies said the News appeal would raise many important issues of public interest.[11] The tide of circumstances which had flowed so powerfully against News and Super League three weeks earlier suddenly started to turn.

Rod Price's approach to Sam Chisholm the previous August to explore the possibility of a merger quickly gained momentum over the ensuing weeks. Price's business was heading for the wall if he didn't merge, and Chisholm wanted to get control of the program supply agreement. There was plenty of willingness on both sides to do the deal. All that was required was to work out the terms. Neil Gamble and Mark Booth held a series of meetings over August and September to set the groundwork for a full-scale negotiating session between teams from Australis, News and Telstra at Sydney's Sheraton Menzies over the weekend of October 14–15, 1995.

Amazingly, dozens of executives and lawyers from the three companies were able to negotiate a complex merger over a two-day period in a hotel in central Sydney without anyone from Optus Vision, PBL, or the media, learning about it. The parties had chosen a floor of the hotel that was being renovated, to minimise the risk of being seen by a passing stockbroker or banker.

A major hurdle was Australis's agreements with its two franchisees, Continental Century and UIH. Because Australis had underestimated the cost of its programming and that it had not foreseen in July the previous year when it struck the deals that it would be forced to cut its monthly subscription fees, it was losing heavily on the arrangements. It wasn't until this late stage in the negotiations, however, that News and Telstra found out about the franchise issue. At one point Ken Cowley threatened to call the deal off. But by the end of the weekend, the three groups believed they had progressed enough to make an announcement and try to sort out some of the peripheral impediments later.

Price announced the merger on October 18. Australis would buy Foxtel in a reverse takeover by issuing News and Telstra 642 million Australis shares and convertible notes to give them each 28.75 per cent, or a total of 57.5 per cent, and control, between them. The issue of the shares at $1.33 each therefore valued the Foxtel business, which had yet to begin broadcasting, at $854 million. Australis shareholders, including Lenfest, would be watered down to a total of 42.5 per cent in the combined Australis/Foxtel. The deal would need their approval, but for them it was a case of having 42.5 per cent of a viable business rather than 100 per cent of a company that could not survive. The franchisee issue continued to be a problem, and News sought to have the terms toughened in its favour, fearing that the situation might be worse than Price was portraying. Cowley later insisted that the combined shareholding by News and Telstra be raised to 60 per cent, and at a later meeting in Los Angeles, Rupert Murdoch squeezed another 2.5 per cent out of Price, taking the News-Telstra interest to 62.5 per cent.

Stockbroker Burrows Ltd, which had been an underwriter to the Australis float in September 1993, recommended to its clients that they sell their Australis shares because of this dilution.[12] One shareholder to take the advice was Steve Cosser. He sold his entire holding of convertible notes (which became ordinary shares in the hands of Australian investors) for a total of $35 million. Bain and Co sold 25 million notes on October 30 at 97 cents and 10 million a week earlier at $1 each, as the Australis share price rose strongly in the wake of the merger announcement.

From the time of his first sale of shares to Ron Brierley's GPG Plc in January 1993, to this latest sale, Cosser and his partner Richard Wiesener crystallised about $70 million[13] from an initial investment of about $300,000 in the original MDS licences. They were the two single biggest winners from pay TV in Australia.

Another potential stumbling block for Australis and Foxtel was the Australian Competition and Consumer Commission (ACCC) and its chairman Allan Fels. Both companies had Queen's Counsel advice that the merger would not breach the *Trade Practices Act*. Their view was based on a Trade Practices Commission (the ACCC's predecessor, also chaired by Fels) report in 1993 which concluded that pay TV was part of an overall market with free-to-air television and video.[14] If the ACCC continued to hold that view, then the merger should be approved, Australis and News were told. Price, no doubt, was hoping Fels had forgotten his intemperate remark at the oil industry dinner in March 1993. Fortunately, as News had insisted that it handle negotiations with the ACCC, Price would probably not suffer the embarrassment of being reminded of it.

Fels was emerging as Canberra's most powerful bureaucrat in the mid-1990s as Federal and State governments progressively implemented the national competition policy outlined by Professor Fred Hilmer. With the privatisation of former government monopolies and enterprises and dismantling of old regulatory regimes in telecommunications, electricity, transport, oil, gas, and the professions, the old specific industry regulators became redundant. The competition policing role was handed over increasingly to Fels.

Added to this, the Labor Government tightened the *Trade Practices Act* in 1993 to empower Fels to challenge any merger which he felt might substantially reduce competition, as opposed to the previous test of stopping mergers which produced a dominant player. This gave him enormous power. In reality he only had to say 'no', giving rise to his nickname among the numerous corporations he had offended as 'Doctor No'. If merger partners chose to challenge his decision it could take 12 to 18 months to see it through the court and appeal process. Very few deals could stay in limbo for this long and survive. Most mergers ended the moment he said the word, no matter how wrong the companies wishing to merge felt he may have been. Alternatively, if a company believed a merger offered important national benefits which might outweigh any reduction in competition, Fels would normally invite them to apply for an authorisation. Few companies chose this path, because it meant revealing sensitive commercial information to the TPC/ACCC, whose officers in their 'market inquiries' would show the information to competitors to get their reaction.

So Australis and Foxtel would take the risk of having their merger decided on competition grounds. Booth, Gamble and News's lawyer, Ian Phillip, presented their merger plans for the first time to Fels in his Sydney office a few days after the merger announcement. They had further meetings with him in Canberra and Melbourne, answering any questions he had and stressing the point that in the overall television and media market, the merger would not have a significant impact on competition.

Fels appeared to be fairly receptive to the proposal initially. But by December as the talks continued, his attitude started to turn. Booth and Gamble were getting negative feedback. Fels would ask, what would be the impact on competition in the telephone market if he let the merger through? The Australis and Foxtel executives weren't sure how to answer the question. They had always thought this was a merger between two pay TV companies.

After leaving the Department of Communications, Chris North went into business as a Canberra-based consultant to companies in the telecommunications business. He was sitting in the ACCC's offices in the outer Canberra suburb of Belconnen discussing a matter with Terry Cassells, an ACCC officer looking after media industry issues, when they heard uproarious laughter coming from Fels' office a short distance away. The door opened and out came Fels, followed by Geoff Cousins, who was slapping the ACCC chairman on the back as they chuckled over a joke Cousins had just told.

Cousins regarded the Australis-Foxtel merger as a major threat to Optus Vision because it would immediately reduce Foxtel's program costs and strengthen its hand in the battle for pay TV subscribers. Foxtel would no longer pay the $6 per subscriber per month margin, and the merged company would have a strong, combined program package. News and Telstra, who would control the enlarged group, would also gain access to Australis's satellite licence to broaden their potential market.

Rather than trying to argue that the merger would concentrate power in this embryonic industry, Cousins focused his discussions with Fels on the telephone side of the consortium's business. Optus Vision would be seriously handicapped in its efforts to be an effective competitor to Telstra if the ACCC allowed the merger. In fact, Optus would consider stopping its roll-out and cancel its plans to offer telephony over its own network. Telstra would maintain its effective monopoly. Australians would continue to pay too much for their phone charges. Cousins was bluffing, but Fels fell for it. Optus had committed to the network and would roll it out regardless. It had no choice, if it wanted to be a serious player.

But Cousins had located the merger's Achilles heel. He was also able to play on Fels' desire to be seen as an architect of industry policy. Fels had used his power to force concessions from companies wanting to merge, or by blocking mergers, to shape the retail and oil industries. Now he would do the same with telephony. When Neil Gamble on one of his visits told Fels that Australis would collapse if the merger didn't go ahead, Fels didn't believe him. 'I get people coming to me every day saying their company's going broke,' he scoffed in a newspaper interview at this time. Gamble wasn't kidding. He was a straight talker who lacked Cousins' smooth, urbane manner, which won Fels over.

Over the Christmas break, Australis and News were coming to the conclusion that Fels would block the merger. In a last-ditch bid to try to persuade Fels to allow it, Ken Cowley asked Sam Chisholm and Bruce McWilliam, who were in Sydney, to fly to Melbourne to see Fels. Chisholm knew more about television and pay television than anyone in the country, even Fels. Cowley offered them the News Gulfstream jet to fly down.

Chisholm didn't talk about trade practices law or market definitions, but drew on his experience as head of Britain's biggest pay TV operator and former boss of Kerry Packer's Nine Network to forecast to Fels what would happen if he blocked the merger. 'It will be a bloody nightmare,' he told the ACCC chairman. He talked about the experience in the UK where BSB and Sky lost hundreds of millions of pounds before they merged. The experience had been similar in Australia, with huge losses looming for all three players, which had raised the stakes by bidding up the cost of programming, while two were in the process of rolling out multi-billion-dollar cable networks.

The ACCC should let the industry develop to the stage where it stabilised, and then it should regulate. Eventually there would have to be mergers. Why allow a tragedy to be played out in which the players would lose billions? Chisholm became very annoyed when Fels appeared unconvinced at this point. He was trying to tell the regulator the harsh realities of life in the business as opposed to the ACCC's narrow view of the matter through the prism of the *Trade Practices Act*.

Fels thanked Chisholm for his views and the News executives left. He had already made his decision to block the merger. In his mind it was more important for Australia to have competition in its telephone market than to preserve a pay TV operator which he believed had paid too much for its licence and programming. Australis had made mistakes. If it collapsed, too bad.

Neil Gamble was enjoying the light, relatively quiet and open spaces of his newly-built office in Pyrmont after more than two years of very trying conditions in Castlereagh Street and more recently in Pyrmont as the special-purpose building was constructed around the Australis operation. On the morning of February 7, 1996 the letter he had been half expecting arrived through his fax machine. It was from Allan Fels. While the content of the letter came as no surprise, it contained such bad news that it hardly lessened the blow. The ACCC chairman said he believed the merger would lessen competition in the pay TV market. He invited Australis and Foxtel to try again after the telecommunications market was deregulated after July 1, 1997. That was 18 months away. Gamble wondered whether Australis could last 18 weeks. Australis's losses were accelerating with the aggressive bid for subscribers after the launch of its satellite service in October, in anticipation that the merger with Foxtel would proceed. News and Telstra had pledged financial support of up to $400 million by way of short-term guarantees of Australis's borrowings, if the merger had been allowed to proceed.[15]

Australis had cut its connection fee, first from $299 to $99.95, and then to $19.95, and its monthly rental from $49.95 to $39.95 to stay competitive with the cable companies. On the installation costs alone it was losing at a rate of more than $1,000 per subscriber. With connections running at 30,000 a month at this stage, Australis was bleeding money at a rate of $30 million a month. Its money was running out fast. Australis had negotiated an emergency loan of $150 million with its bankers in October to finance the losses until the merger with Foxtel was completed. Once this money was exhausted, unless the merger proceeded, it was unlikely Australis would be able to raise any more money. It was at the end of its credit facilities and its capacity to raise more cash. Australis had wagered its existence on the merger proceeding. It was haemorrhaging and suddenly the means to stem the flow had been pulled away.

In an independent report dated December 29, 1995, prepared for a proposed meeting of Australis shareholders had the ACCC approved the merger, the merchant bank Grant Samuel and Associates stated:

> The Foxtel acquisition will transform Australis. The future of Australis if the Foxtel acquisition does not proceed is uncertain. Australis is vulnerable in the face of the intense competition between Optus Vision and Foxtel. This competition reflects the prospective competition between Optus Vision and Telstra in the far more valuable telephony market. In the light of the competitive pressures now evident in the market the ability of Australis to raise sufficient finance to fund operating losses and capital expenditure in the short term has become a serious issue.[16]

It was after midnight in London, where Rodney Price lived in an elegant Belgravia house that he had bought several years earlier from Basil Sellers, one of Steve Cosser's original backers. Price had been a regular caller at all hours of the night to Gamble's Mosman house, so Gamble had no hesitation breaking Price's sleep with the bad news. Price took the news calmly, despite the hour. He reminded Gamble that Australis might still be able to rely on the Infrastructure Sharing Agreement they had formalised with the A licence holder Continental Century on the deck of *Lionheart* in February 1994. Continental Century had agreed to make up 25 per cent of Australis's costs and losses until it moved into break-even in return for 25 per cent of the cash flow once Galaxy started making money. By February 1996, that 25 per cent figure had reached $150 million.[17] Also, Australis could wind back its subscriber drive and increase its installation and monthly rentals as a short-term measure. Right now, it needed cash. It was struggling to meet its wages bill. Price said he would ring Cowley to see if News could tip in some short-term money.

Even during the merger discussions with News in October, Australis had been experiencing liquidity problems. Price had asked News for a $50 million loan to top up the $150 million short-term facility that Australis had negotiated that month to replace a longer-term $300 million line of credit. Price and Gamble had taken the smaller loan because it was available immediately, whereas the $300 million facility was not available until Australis was generating positive earnings.[18] The Australis chairman had also leaned on Gerry Lenfest to tip in money and on January 19, before the Foxtel merger was rejected, Lenfest lent Australis $US18.53 million.[19]

Immediately after Fels' knock-back, Cowley told Price he would consider putting in $6 million to $10 million as a short-term bridge until Australis could work out its next step. After talking to Price, however, Cowley sensed the problem was far greater than Price was letting on. He called Sam Chisholm and told him to fly immediately to Sydney. News had to decide whether it should keep Australis afloat – along with its programming agreement with Foxtel – or whether it should let it go. When Chisholm arrived, he came to the view that Australis's problems were terminal. News should not put in any money because it would not get it back.

In the meantime, Price didn't stop at Lenfest and Cowley. He also called Fred Vierra, the head of TCI International, the division of John Malone's company which looked after its overseas interests, including its indirect investment in Australis. Australis had two valuable assets, its deals with the Hollywood studios, and its 25-year contract to on-sell its movie rights to Foxtel. Price and Neil Gamble were well aware that News as the buyer of the Australis program feed and Lenfest/TCI as partners with Australis would pay money to keep the relationships alive. Price would squeeze every bit of juice that he could from this advantageous position. The danger for Price was that News and TCI might start talking to each other behind his back. Rupert Murdoch and John Malone had been mutual admirers for many years. It was quite natural that Vierra and Chisholm would soon end up talking.

By this time, TCI and Lenfest had a total exposure to Australis of close to $250 million. Apart from the initial $138 million that Lenfest had paid for the B licence, and the $US18.53 million ($28 million) loan it had provided in late January, both Lenfest and TCI had guaranteed Australis's payments to the Hollywood studios as a result of the frantic dealmaking with the studios in October and November the previous year. These payment guarantees had blown out to $US67 million ($A103 million).[20]

Even John Malone, the remote and imposing chief executive of TCI, had become concerned about the situation in Australia. In late February 1996, he sent a team of half a dozen lawyers and accountants to Sydney to find out the precise position and prospects for his exposure to this troubled group.

Neil Gamble gave what he described later as the 'mother of all presentations' over the weekend of February 17–18 to this group of Americans.[21] He can't even remember their names, only that they sat stony faced through his description and analysis of Australis's strengths and its problems. The asset that Australis had, and which Gamble kept hammering home to the Americans, was a legally watertight, 25-year agreement to supply programs to News and Telstra. For this income stream alone, Australis was worth preserving, he argued. After talking to them through most of the Saturday, the TCI team spent Sunday poring over documents and financial details. On the Monday they flew back to the US, without giving any indication of their attitude, although their body language suggested it was far from positive.

About the middle of the next week, Price called Gamble in the middle of the night. He had just heard from Fred Vierra that TCI was prepared to invest another $US250 million. The terms of the loan were tough. Australis would have to slow its installations, lift its monthly rental charges back to $49.95 and not compete in the areas where cable was being rolled out. Price and Gamble were pleased about the money, but it meant that Australis was effectively giving up being an active player in the pay TV market. It was doomed to become a conduit for the Foxtel programming and its subscriber base would inevitably fall when households taking the Galaxy signal switched to cheaper cable as it rolled up their streets.

Geoff Kleeman flew to London to meet up with Price in the first weekend in March. They were due to sign the new funding agreement with Fred Vierra, who was Denver-based but spent time regularly in the UK on TCI's cable interests there. After some initial discussions with a TCI lawyer, Steve Brett, Vierra asked Price and Kleeman to come to see him the following morning, the Thursday. As Price and Kleeman were shown into Vierra's spartan office in Albemarle Street they saw Vierra behind his desk. But at the side of the room was Bruce McWilliam, Rupert Murdoch's lawyer.

Price took a step back. McWilliam was the last person he expected to see here. Vierra came straight to the point. 'Rod, we don't think this funding proposal is going to work. Australis looks to be in worse shape than we thought. We can't see a point when Australis is going to make money. It's up against the cable operators in the cities and has sold the regions to its franchisees. We have another proposal we'd like to make.' Vierra told Price and Kleeman that instead of a direct investment, TCI and News wanted to buy the Telstra-News Corporation (TNC) programming agreement. He made an initial offer of $175 million. Price and Kleeman were speechless. As the future of Australia's first pay TV operator was being discussed in this small and unadorned office, the four men couldn't help but notice that immediately across the road was the main shop floor of the DKNY retail store in Bond Street, with dozens of young women trying on the latest New York designers' fashions. Ignoring the distraction, Price said after several minutes of discussion, 'That's not the deal we were talking about . . . and the price is too low.' He turned to Kleeman and McWilliam and asked them to leave the room so he could speak to Vierra alone.

A few minutes later Price stormed out and took Kleeman with him. As they walked to the lift, Price said they were meeting again at his house on Saturday. They had been ambushed. But the problem for Price and Kleeman was that they needed money urgently, and this was the only deal on the table.

They both realised, too, that if they sold the TNC agreement, for whatever price, Australis was doomed to a slow but certain end. Vierra and McWilliam had them over a barrel. At Price's home in Chester Street, just behind Buckingham Palace, McWilliam started to extract some revenge for the drubbing Price handed to him and Chisholm on Christmas Eve, 1994. Now Price was the party with very little bargaining power, although at one point in the conversation he threatened to go to Optus Vision 'and fuck News'. With his back to wall, the Australis chairman agreed to sell the TNC agreement, but kept trying to push the price up. He wanted $200 million. Also, he wanted an option to buy half of it back again.

McWilliam sensed that the Australis pair were desperate, and was determined to drive home his advantage. News and TCI would pay 10 per cent up front, or $17.5 million, and the rest would follow after News had a chance to examine Australis more closely and pending regulatory approvals. Price and Kleeman knew this was nowhere near enough. Australis was being pressed for immediate payment of $75.9 million from its creditors, mainly the studios ($14.8 million), set-top box providers ($26.8 million) and sales tax owed ($16.7 million).[22]

Price and Kleeman didn't like the offer from McWilliam but shook hands, realising it was the only option at that stage. The next day they took a plane to the US to see Leonard Tow, head of Century Communications, New Canaan, Connecticut. Price and Kleeman wanted to see whether Tow was willing to pay the $150 million Century was due to provide under the infrastructure sharing agreement. He gave them short shrift. His group didn't intend to invest any more money in Australia.

While Price and Kleeman were flying on to Denver to try to persuade John Malone to keep to his earlier pledge to invest $US250 million, Malone called Murdoch, to enlist his help in deciding whether Australis was worth backing. Murdoch said News had very detailed information about Australis as a result of their merger discussions. He would have a look at it and get back to him.

Murdoch called Chisholm and sought his advice. Chisholm said News should retain Malcolm Turnbull and Cass O'Connor, who had good knowledge of the pay TV business and would be well-placed to analyse Australis. Turnbull had also dealt successfully with the Fairfax bond holders in 1991 and brought them in as members of the Tourang consortium, which eventually won Fairfax. Chisholm thought he had the required force of character to persuade the mutual funds which bought the $US175 million bond issue in April the previous year to support News's proposal. News was lining up some heavy artillery against Australis.

Chisholm and McWilliam provided O'Connor with as much financial detail on Australis as they had. O'Connor constructed a simple one-page spread sheet showing Australis's revenue, outgoings and the interest and final balloon payments on its bonds. The information on which she based her analysis was provided to News by Australis, so it was probably accurate. The spreadsheet showed that after costs were deducted from projected revenue, Australis would become cashflow positive to the tune of $19.4 million in the 1999–2000 year. After deducting interest on its bank loans plus regular repayments of the $8 million loan from the South Australian Government, the break-even year was pushed back to 2001–2002, when it would make $17.4 million. But the losses in the earlier years were so large that the cumulative negative cash flow simply kept mounting and in 2002–2003, when the first balloon interest payments were due on its bonds, Australis would be cash flow negative to the tune of $419.6 million for the year. Its cumulative negative cash flow that year was $1.15 billion, falling only slightly the next year to $1.023 billion.[23]

O'Connor told Turnbull Australis could not survive. It was a black hole. When he had been told by Turnbull about Australis's parlous position, Sam Chisholm called Fred Vierra in Denver. The news rattled Vierra, who was worried about being sued by the US bond holders. He resigned from the Australis board on March 28. The next day, Gerry Lenfest followed suit.

On April 10, McWilliam arranged a four-way conference call between himself in London, Malcolm Turnbull in Sydney, Sam Morris, the Lenfest Group general counsel in New York, and Fred Vierra, who was in Argentina at the time. Turnbull dominated the discussion. Using O'Connor's numbers, he confidently predicted that Australis was gone, that anyone who put money in would lose it. Morris was the hardest to convince. Despite Gerry Lenfest's resignation as a director, the Lenfest group had the largest exposure of anyone in Australis and therefore the most to lose. Over the course of the four-way conversation, News would assert later in court documents, McWilliam persuaded the other three to agree that their interests would be better protected by buying the TNC agreement than by pumping in money.

That evening, London time, McWilliam drew up draft offers to fax individually to all Australis directors, as Price had been uncontactable for several days. He gave the board five days to reply to the offer. In that time, Gerry Lenfest persuaded McWilliam and Chisholm to raise the offer to $200 million. Neil Gamble called McWilliam to report that there was disagreement among the Australis directors and asked if he could try to negotiate the price up a little. He pointed out that the sale would require minority shareholder approval and would need an experts' report to decide whether or not it was fair. On Friday, April 12, McWilliam received Murdoch's approval to go to $250 million.

That night, at the Castlecrag Montessori School wine and cheese night, Ross McCreath approached Nick Falloon to ask if PBL might be interested in putting rescue funds into Australis.

The following Monday, April 15, Gamble faxed a letter marked 'urgent' and 'private and confidential' to McWilliam. He said that the $250 million offer needed to be increased to $300 million. 'The higher figure would more fairly reflect the value of the assets being sold.'[24] Further, Gamble said the 10 per cent deposit needed to be increased to 30 per cent, and a necessary condition before securing any longer-term arrangement was to procure bridging finance of $75 million from News. Gamble also urged News and Telstra 'to give the Foxtel merger a final go' and freeze subscription growth, or even consider selling the satellite and MDS distribution platform to satisfy the ACCC.

McWilliam and Chisholm believed they had Price, Gamble and Australis where they wanted them. But Ian Phillip, News's lawyer, was taking a bit longer than expected to draw up the final legal agreement for signing. On Monday, too, after talking to McCreath, Gamble put in a call to Falloon. The PBL finance director waited a day before calling him back, but at lunchtime that day Gamble was in a taxi on his way to Park Street.

It wasn't until Thursday night London time that Sam Chisholm had a sense that something was going wrong, and finally got through to Gamble on his mobile phone. Chisholm was not to know that while they were talking, Gamble was in the PBL boardroom in Park Street, sitting next to Nick Falloon.

Australis had done a deal with Kerry Packer, but had given everything away to get Packer's signature on the piece of paper. Packer had also won another round in the wider battle with Rupert Murdoch. What was worse for Murdoch, the expensive program supply agreement with Foxtel was still in place, and Packer had taken effective control of it.

Lenfest had joined Packer's PBL, Ron Brierley's GPG Plc, and franchisee UIH to guarantee a six-month loan of $US125 million ($A162 million at the exchange rate of the day) from Lenfest's bank, Toronto Dominion[25] to Australis to give it time to raise more long-term finance, most probably another bond raising in the US. Lenfest also agreed to extend the $US18.5 million loan it had made in January to Australis. J.P. Morgan Investment Management Australia also bought 23.5 million convertible notes at 54.5 cents each, or $12.8 million. In all the financing package was worth $200 million to Australis. It was typically complex, with Australis also agreeing to offer the investors a total of 74 million options over shares with an exercise price of just 20 cents, a hefty discount on the 64 cents the shares were trading at just before Australis called a trading halt to its stock on March 27.

The Australian Stock Exchange asked Australis to provide more information about the options, and three days later the company responded with a breakdown of the options issued. The lion's share went to PBL and Lenfest – 31 million each – with the rest going to GPG and UIH.

The Australian Stock Exchange (ASX) and Australis share-holders were unaware of two of the most important elements of the deal, which the company had declined to disclose. Perhaps the most material in terms of its potential impact on Australis was its agreement to give PBL first and last right of refusal over any asset that Australis chose to sell, and consult with PBL before it sold anything.[26]

Gamble and Price also agreed to enter into a joint venture with PBL to deal with the satellite distribution rights of its programming. PBL also had a right of first refusal and last right to match any offer made to Australis to participate in a satellite joint venture. To protect its exposure to Australis, PBL had taken control over all of the company's assets and its ability to do future deals on its satellite transmission. Lenfest guaranteed $US75 million, or more than half of the facility, yet got nothing but the expectation that Australis had bought another six months survival. Packer, Powers and Falloon, however, had taken a mortgage over Australis in return for guaranteeing $US32 million worth of the facility. PBL hadn't put up a cent. Once again Packer had demonstrated his ability to gain maximum leverage with minimum outlay.

On the evening of April 23, 1996, Geoff Cousins appeared on the ABC's *Lateline* current affairs program, where he was interviewed by Quentin Dempster on the Australis rescue. He said, 'We're certainly very pleased to see that result, Quentin, because having fought that proposed merger between Foxtel and Australis very vigorously with the ACCC we didn't want to see Foxtel and News Ltd achieve a merger, a de facto merger if you will, by stealth and therefore we are pleased to see that this (News's attempt to buy the TNC agreement) has not been allowed to happen. I think, incidentally, it's a very good thing for the shareholders of Australis that it didn't happen.'[27]

When Dempster said that Foxtel was claiming 60,000 pay TV subscribers and asked Cousins how many Optus Vision had, Cousins replied, 'Well, we consistently said we are never going to release our subscriber figures. Why in God's name you'd run around giving your competitors information, I don't know . . . '

After the first and last right arrangement with PBL was revealed in the media,[28] Australis was forced to acknowledge it in the form of a two-line disclosure buried on page 12 of the explanatory memorandum for a shareholders meeting on June 11 to approve the rescue. It gave no indication at all of the extent of the control that PBL was exercising over their company. Despite continued prodding from the ASX to disclose all material matters, the Australis board steadfastly refused to reveal the full terms of the PBL Deed, despite making an undertaking to the exchange that it had fully disclosed.

On June 5, stockbroking analyst Peter Dobrijevic, of BZW Australia, issued a report valuing Australis shares at 34 cents, compared with their trading level of 42 cents at the time. He recommended to his clients that they sell the stock.[29] Brokers usually couch their recommendations in euphemisms like 'hold' or 'accumulate'. Rarely do they give such unambiguous advice. He was the only analyst to give a valuation this low. Most stockbrokers had valuations above 50 cents, reflecting the 54.5 cents that J.P. Morgan had paid for its shares in the rescue, and had greeted the rescue package as being good for Australis. To be fair, they had only the barest details of the so-called PBL Deed. The shares were being traded in an information vacuum. Dobrijevic also criticised Australis in his brief for not producing an independent report on the transaction for shareholders. Such a report would have had to reveal in full detail the PBL Deed and its implications for the company. It would also have had to value the program supply agreement with Foxtel, which Neil Gamble placed at $300 million in his negotiations with Sam Chisholm, but which he and Geoff Kleeman reckoned was worth $800 million in talks with US bond holders. Australis's financial position was far worse than the company was saying, even with the new loan money. The so-called Turnbull Report, prepared by Cass O'Connor and based on information and projections supplied by Australis to Foxtel, gave Australis no chance of survival.

With Rod Price becoming increasingly absorbed with his other interests by late 1996,[30] the pressure fell mostly on Neil Gamble and Geoff Kleeman to save Australis's deteriorating position. If they could raise the $US225 million they hoped to get through a new bond issue,[31] then Australis might survive. Once it had put in place the six-month loan guarantee from the PBL consortium, Australis was engaged in a race against time to raise these fresh, long-term funds.

The Toronto Dominion loan expired on October 31, so the new capital would have to be raised before then in order to repay it. Australis's task would not be easy, because if it had any hope at all of issuing new bonds it would have to offer the investors top-ranking security, a position already enjoyed by the holders of the $US175 million worth of senior subordinated discount notes the company had issued a year earlier. It would have to try to persuade the earlier investors to surrender some of their rights over the company, a formidable ask.

Neil Gamble and Geoff Kleeman flew to New York in the first week of May to brief those bond holders on Australis's position and to soften them up to take reduced security on their existing investment in the company. However they approached their next fund raising, Gamble and Kleeman would need the consent of the bond holders. An early blow was the withdrawal of the previous manager, Merrill Lynch, which was the acknowledged leader in high-yield financing of this type in the US and accounted for about 40 per cent of the funds raised for the cable industry. It was also a major investor in the industry. A senior Merrill executive, Gerry Kenny, explained that as it had arranged the previous placement, it would be in a conflict of interest with the next one, as it would involve the earlier investors making significant concessions. The Australis camp thought there was a conspiracy, and heard that Murdoch, whose News Corp was a major client of Merrills, had intervened personally to persuade the investment bank not to act for Australis. Their fears were fed by the fact that News appeared determined now to use its power to drive Australis to the wall so it could deal directly with the studios. Australis approached the next largest player in the high-yield market, Salomon Brothers, which agreed to work with them.

At the briefing were the largest of the bond holders, Merrill Lynch, Fidelity, Smith Barney and Oppenheimer, who had their lawyer, a bald, overweight, unshaven man named Chaim Fortgang, from the firm Wachtel Lipton Rosen and Katz. They wanted Gamble and Kleeman to tell them why Australis was back so soon for more money. Why not try to resurrect the merger? What was Australis's business plan? It was a torrid session, but Kleeman would say afterwards there was no ranting or raving, as these people were wont to do if their money was at risk.

The Australis pair explained that News Corp had offered them a fire sale price of $275 million for the Foxtel programming agreement, which they claimed was worth closer to $800 million, notwithstanding Gamble's earlier valuation of $300 million in his letter to Bruce McWilliam. Gamble said he believed Foxtel was losing between $3 and $5 on every subscriber a month because of their programming costs, and that was why News was so keen to buy out Australis.

The bond holders weren't interested in any problems that News may have had. Their concern was for their money in

Australis. Gamble and Kleeman were made aware that it was going to be very hard raising the money they needed. It would have to come from the same investors who took part in the previous year's raising. Would they put in good money after bad? Clearly the money they had invested a year earlier appeared to them to be at risk. Gamble and Kleeman would be forced to consider offering security over the company's assets (already mortgaged to PBL) to persuade the bond holders to increase their exposure to Australis.

Australis also struck a problem with its franchisees, who objected immediately to Australis's satellite joint venture with Optus Vision, which PBL had wrung out of Australis during negotiations over the rescue package. UIH and Continental Century believed correctly that Optus Vision would use the satellite to compete with them, and they had exclusive access to Australis's satellite technology in their regions. Cousins was pushing hard to launch a satellite service once Australis's licence monopoly expired in July 1997. Optus Vision had its eye on the regions where its cable would never reach and where it would be in direct competition with the Australis franchisees. They threatened to sue Australis. Foxtel feared the deal with Optus Vision would lock News-Telstra out of satellite forever, and threatened to sue also.

Thirdly, Neil Gamble wasn't going to hand over the satellite platform – which Australis had spent more than $200 million building – to Optus Vision for nothing. Australis wanted substantial compensation. Its digital broadcasting system was a world first and worth a premium on top of the investment costs. Cousins was pushing very hard. He wanted to get control of Australis as part of his wider campaign to deny Foxtel programming and distribution capabilities. Gamble found himself squeezed between some powerful and persistent forces. It soon became obvious that the satellite joint venture simply would never happen, no matter how demanding was Cousins.

Australis was already being fought over and its parts picked at by its rivals. Even if it succeeded in raising the fresh funds in New York, the money would only delay the inevitable. In the longer term, Australis could not survive in the fierce crossfire between the cable operators. Its only hope was to hang on as long as possible to its program supply arrangement with Foxtel.

In May 1996, Neil Gamble took a call from David Benn, a consultant with the executive search firm Korn Ferry. Benn had been hired by the US casino group Showboat to find a chief executive for the new Sydney casino, which was being built a short stroll away from Australis's Pyrmont headquarters. Showboat had the management contract for the casino after winning a bitter contest for the rights with Kerry Packer and the Circus Circus group.

Gamble had already been prepared to surrender his job as a result of the merger with Foxtel, and now PBL was effectively in control of Australis he was being forced into a secondary role once again. He was interested to hear what Benn had to offer. After some exploratory discussions with Benn, Showboat flew Gamble secretly to Las Vegas early in July to meet Showboat's board and chief executive, Kel Houssells III. He was offered the job.

After returning to Australia, he was thrust straight back into the turmoil engulfing Australis, but his attention was elsewhere. He had to complete extensive and searching questions on his background, finances and tax records for a probity test conducted by the Casino Control Authority. Four weeks later, after he lodged the papers, his name was linked to speculation in the media about the casino job. Gamble was horrified and embarrassed. Most of the staff at Australis had no idea, although he had confided in Geoff Kleeman and Rod Price. The word was out, so Gamble had no choice but to gather his senior management team together to tell them he was leaving.

Australis had come under siege at this point, after a draft prospectus for the company's proposed bond offering fell into the hands of journalists from *The Australian*, a News Limited newspaper.[32] A letter dated July 15 attached to the prospectus stated that 'the full amount of the interim credit facility (the Toronto Dominion loan guaranteed by the PBL consortium) will be drawn by July 31, 1996'. The letter and offer document also detailed PBL's first and last rights over the Australis assets, and that control of the company would be handed over to a business and finance committee of the board of directors made up of PBL managing director James Packer, Rod Price, Australis deputy chairman Mark Johnson and Gerry Lenfest. It also revealed that the disconnection (or 'churn') rate experienced by Australis had risen from 21 per cent in late 1995 to 31.7 per cent in the four months to June 30, 1996. This represented about 38,000 disconnections[33] and the rate was accelerating. None of this highly sensitive information had been released by the company in Australia.

The leaking of the draft prospectus provoked an aggressive query from the ASX, which demanded to know more about the recapitalisation plan. Under the ASX's continuous disclosure listing rule (rule 3.1), companies are obliged to disclose all material information once it becomes known to the company. In this case, potential investors in the US, where disclosure is far tougher still and legal action always a threat, were receiving information on the company denied to its shareholders in Australia. On July 29, Australis asked for trading in its shares to be suspended as a result of the leaking of the prospectus. In a reply to the ASX, Australis stated that it wanted to complete an unregistered offering and that release of the document would force it to do a registered offering, which would be far more costly and time-consuming.[34] Australis continued to insist that there was no information in the draft prospectus that had not been previously disclosed. The reply finally gave more details of the PBL Deed. Shareholders at the June 11 meeting had voted on the recapitalisation plan in almost complete ignorance of the implications of this arrangement.

At this time too, the Australis board had become so concerned that the company was insolvent, that it could not pay its debts when they were due, that directors were becoming worried about their own legal position. The board called in Price Waterhouse to advise it whether it could continue to trade or put the company into receivership. The advice the board received was that so long as the company was reasonably confident the money would come in before the Toronto Dominion loan expired, then it could continue to trade.

Three months after his landslide election win over Paul Keating in March 1996, Liberal Prime Minister John Howard was asked by his friend Geoff Cousins to open Optus Vision's local call service. In a heavily promoted and well-rehearsed launch at the Darling Harbour Convention Centre, Howard was to call an elderly couple, Bill and Verna Cocks, at their home in suburban Lindfield using an Optus phone. The new Prime Minister had to wait a few minutes for the arrival of James Packer, but once the heir to the Packer billions arrived and sat at the front of the audience, Howard was able to put his call though. 'Well, good morning Mrs Cocks, you are the very first customer,' he said. 'I certainly am, Prime Minister, and it is a great privilege for us to be the first customer of the Optus local telephone call service.'

In his introduction, Cousins had made much of the fact that a local call on the Optus network would cost just 20 cents, compared with a Telstra local call costing 25 cents. It was a new deal, he told his small but enthusiastic audience of Optus employees, media and politicians.

The launching of the phone service was the culmination of Cousins' stewardship at Optus Vision. Telephony was to be the main revenue earner for the consortium and pay TV only an inducement to secure the subscriber as a phone customer. Unfortunately, Optus's much-touted phone system didn't work. Once the high-tech, hybrid fibre optic-coaxial cable network relentlessly being strung out through the suburbs started to overload, it would simply crash. It would be another two years before Optus sorted out the software problems which prevented more than a handful of callers using the system.

Callers to Optus several months after the launch were still being told the service would not be available until 1997.[35] Cousins had launched far too early. He took a gamble that the Optus engineers could get it to work in time. Although the engineers were able to patch through a line from Howard to Bill and Verna Cocks, the system simply wasn't ready. He resigned in September from what he described as 'the toughest job in the country'. Provocative to the end, Cousins declared: 'The major battles are over. Optus Vision is absolutely in the winning position.'[36]

The same day Cousins resigned, Optus Vision announced that it had 100,000 subscribers. Foxtel revealed a few days earlier it had 115,000 and Australis was estimated to have 110,000.[37] The relative position of the three groups seemed a little more evenly poised than Cousins' fighting words suggested.

In early August 1996, as Australis was still being buffeted by the revelations contained in its draft prospectus, Geoff Kleeman returned to the US to try to win the consent of the bond holders to make a new bond placement. The July 15 letter to the noteholders had given them until August 12 to give their consent. Kleeman found that the mood of the US funds had hardened. The deadline meant nothing to them. They wanted certainty about the extent of cost savings Australis would make to ensure the company's survival and they wanted $US50 million, hurt money, invested upfront by other investors. Kleeman persuaded Lenfest, PBL, UIH and GPG to put in more money, and he found another willing investor in the AMP Society, which said it would invest $US10 million. This was not enough, however.

Kleeman called Gamble and told him that there was no chance of winning the bond holders over unless the company made some move to reduce costs or get in more money. Gamble told him that the franchisees had approached Australis with a low-priced takeover offer which he thought to be unacceptable. The franchisees, UIH and Century, were offering 22 cents a share, or about $130 million for the company. Most of this would be in the form of shares. It was highly conditional and dependent on obtaining finance. Optus Vision was continuing to press Australis on the satellite sharing arrangement. Both groups, Optus Vision and the franchisees, were looking to take advantage of Australis's critical financial position.

The August 12 deadline passed as the two groups negotiated with Australis. The board invited them to put their case formally on the evening of August 20. In the chaotic environment in which Australis was operating, the presentations did not start until 10pm. While they were waiting outside the boardroom for UIH's Don Hagans to give his spiel, Optus Vision's Nick Falloon and James McLaughlin and their legal adviser Gina Cass-Gottlieb, from the firm Gilbert and Tobin, whiled away the time watching Galaxy's new night-time entertainment channel.

After UIH and Optus Vision had finished, the Australis board reconvened at 1am and picked the Optus Vision joint venture proposal. Gamble and the other directors knew it would create problems with the franchisees and Foxtel, but they were rapidly running out of time. This plan would give the company a substantial cash injection which would reduce the amount it needed to raise in the US. Optus Vision would pay Australis $25 million to gain access to Australis's satellite platform in which it had invested so much to build, including development of the IREDETO encryption system used in the set-top boxes. By combining their installation and service divisions, customer service centres and subscriber management systems, which would all go into the joint venture, both groups would make substantial cost savings. Also as part of the deal, PBL and Lenfest would contribute an extra $US17.5 million in short-term funding to tide Australis over while it pursued the bond raising.[38]

The deal was finalised at 6am and announced at 9am. Gamble called Geoff Kleeman and gave him the details of the deal, which would allow him to go back to the bond holders with a tangible strategy which would cut costs and raise fresh money.

Gamble resigned that day. Now that PBL was going in even deeper, Nick Falloon prepared to fly to New York to help Kleeman win over the bond holders. Foxtel partners News and Telstra threatened to oppose the alliance between Optus Vision and Australis before the Australian Competition and Consumer Commission and gave notice that they would sue to unwind it on the grounds that it breached Australis's program supply deal with Foxtel.

Australis shares, which had plunged to just 12 cents in the wake of the forced disclosures from the draft prospectus, bounced back to 25 cents, touching an intra-day high of 34 cents in response to the Optus Vision deal.

Within days of the Optus Vision joint venture being announced, Malcolm Turnbull paid a visit to Chaim Fortgang in his Sixth Avenue office, which happened to be diagonally opposite News Corp's New York base. The Australian merchant banker asked Fortgang what the bond holders wanted to do. He also spelled out the deep financial trouble that Australis was in. Any further capital raising among Fortgang's clients would be a matter of pouring good money after bad, Turnbull told him.

Before he left, Turnbull put it to Fortgang that News and Telstra might be interested in making an offer to his clients for their bonds. The New York lawyer said the bond holders would want all of their money back, 100 cents in the dollar. Turnbull explained that if they weren't worthless then, they would be if the next bond raising went ahead, thus pushing them further back in terms of security. Fortgang stuck to his demand for full payment.

Kleeman had been based semi-permanently in New York since early August, moving every week or so to a new hotel, going for a walk for an hour or more in the late morning when he had a brief respite from the phone calls from Australia and Denver (where TCI and UIH were based). Even after he was joined by Falloon, they struggled to win over the bond holders, who had been spooked by Malcolm Turnbull. They were using their lingering concerns to screw Australis a little harder

Australis's business continued to bleed and on September 21, the company announced a loss for the financial year just gone of $221 million, but after a $30 million abnormal cost for the aborted Foxtel merger, this figure blew out to $251.7 million. The loss took Australis's accumulated losses to $393.8 million.[39]

It was having difficulty meeting day-to-day expenses, such as wages, and went to PBL for more cash. Brian Powers agreed to pay

Australis $18 million for 'certain surplus assets', probably excess set-top boxes, as a way of lending Australis money. The price of the loan was very high indeed. Powers wanted top-up security. In order to get this latest desperately needed cash, Australis was forced to amend the PBL Deed to include its satellite licence.[40] Now there was nothing of Australis which PBL did not control.

With little more than a week to go before the Toronto Dominion facility expired, Falloon and Kleeman were joined by Rod Price and the three travelled to Los Angeles, San Francisco and Chicago to make one more pitch to the large bond holders. The feedback wasn't very encouraging, but they thought they might just get enough money. As a result of the money that would go into Australis from the Optus Vision alliance, Australis needed to raise $US150 million from the US rather than the original $US225 million.

Falloon and Kleeman returned to Australia and Price to London after the mission and the three started on the follow-up calls to the bond holders to get commitments from them. Starting at 2am on the morning before the short-term bank facility expired, they managed to raise just $US75 million from the US bond holders. With a shortfall looming, Falloon was able to get Kerry Packer's and Brian Powers' agreement to put in another $US35.6 million and Gerry Lenfest dug deep into his pocket for $US40 million.[41] Kleeman was exhausted and had had enough of Australis when the financing was finished. He told Price he was leaving.

Australis was only buying time with this capital raising. It faced a formidable debt repayment schedule when the bonds matured that only the most optimistic followers of the company believed it could meet. Normally, a company would pay the interest component then refinance the principal amount. Given Australis's difficulties in attracting funds and its reliance on old friends Lenfest and PBL to take up half the issue, this was surely the last bond raising Australis would ever make. The new raising would involve a so-called balloon payment in 2002 of $US278 million, and the bond issue from 1995 which matured in 2003 involved a payment of $US383 million. In Australian dollars these two repayments totalled just over $1 billion.

By this time, too, cracks were appearing in the structure of Optus Vision. The Australis-Optus Vision deal had forced the new Optus Communications chief executive, Ziggy Switkowski, the former head of Kodak Australia, to disclose that the Optus Vision partners had done a deal behind Seven Network's back to allow PBL to increase its maximum stake, if it chose, to 33 per cent rather than the previously agreed limit of 20 per cent.

Now that Seven was under the control of Kerry Stokes, it was becoming increasingly paranoid in reaction to being obviously excluded from key decisions being made by the other consortium members, Optus, Continental Cablevision and Nine Network. It claimed it was not consulted on the decision in October to commit $160 million over five years to the Australian Rugby League. This was clearly a decision made under pressure from Nine's owner, PBL, to protect not only Optus Vision's rugby league rights, but also Nine's.

On October 6, in a surprise reversal of Justice Burchett's February judgment, the full bench of the Federal Court agreed with Super League that the loyalty agreements the ARL had pressured the league clubs into signing contained 'exclusionary provisions' and were therefore illegal under the *Trade Practices Act*. Justices Lockhart, Sackville and Von Doussa found that the contracts between the clubs and the ARL were for the 1995 season only. The ARL was entitled to claim damages against Super League for any losses for that season only. It was small compensation. The appeal judgment was an enormous blow to the ARL, and Super League immediately moved to complete its acquisitions of clubs and players. The Optus Vision commitment would hold the ARL together only for as long as it took to come to some agreement with Super League.

For Stokes the package which was offered without his knowledge was the final straw. Seven sued its own consortium. When he lured Seven into Optus Vision in April the previous year, Geoff Cousins was interested only in securing Seven's sports programming. He wasn't particularly mindful of the fact that Seven and Nine had been bitter network rivals for decades and that it would be difficult for the two of them to live in the same syndicate. The relationship between Stokes and Cousins was reportedly a very prickly one, too.[42]

If Stokes could prove that the consortium had breached the shareholders' agreement, then Seven had the option of buying the Optus Vision cable system and pay TV business for 85 per cent of the $1.6 billion cost of the network, or 85 per cent of the mean of valuations prepared by the warring parties. In an affidavit to the court Seven had estimated the network to be worth a net $3, whereas the non-Seven members valued it at the $1.6 billion cost to date.[43] Stokes made it known at the time he launched the action that he wanted to buy the network, then on-sell it for a profit to an international phone company.[44] Such were the uncertainties generated by Seven's legal action, that it forced Optus Communications' founding shareholder, Mayne Nickless, to abandon the proposed float of its 25 per cent stake in the parent company. Tensions in Optus Vision were starting to infect the shareholding structure of the Optus Communications parent company. By the end of 1996, both groups were becoming highly unstable.

Kerry Stokes was starting a game of very high stakes poker with Australia's most feared gambler, Kerry Packer. The Packer camp was more convinced than ever that Stokes was a stooge for Rupert Murdoch.


When acting Australis chairman Mark Johnson addressed the company's 1996 annual meeting, which was to be its last, he said with grand understatement that the year had been 'very difficult' for the company. Johnson, a director of Macquarie Bank and a veteran corporate adviser, told the meeting that the October 31 raising of $US250 million 'closes the financial liquidity crisis chapter and puts the company on a solid financial basis going forward'.[45] The money would finance the company through to a positive cash flow position, he said.

Johnson's outlook was highly optimistic, at best. Australis's first quarter results released six days earlier, showing a net loss of $51.1 million for the three months compared with $33 million in the same period in 1995, predicted that the company 'will have significant negative cash flow from operating activities and investing activities in each fiscal year through at least fiscal 1998'.[46]

Johnson was telling shareholders that the $88 million Australis had in the kitty after repaying its loans from the money raised in October would last for at least another 18 months. Australis suffered a negative cash flow of $29.6 million for the quarter, or just under $10 million a month. The $88 million would last nine, perhaps 10 months at most. In reality, Australis might just survive to the start of the 1998 financial year in July.


Kerry Stokes' determination to prosecute his legal action against Seven's fellow consortium members in Optus Vision was creating intense stresses and strains in the group, which was split between those who wanted to fight him and those, primarily PBL, which wanted to call his bluff and offer to sell the cable network and pay TV business to Seven. The figure settled upon as 85 per cent of the $680 million mean of the two valuations was $648.7 million.[47]

Despite the fact that this amount was about half the estimated net value of the network, PBL's chairman, Brian Powers, who was pushing to call Stokes' bluff, believed Seven and Stokes were both too highly geared to pay this much and would back away rather than collapse under the weight of debt needed to buy a loss-making asset. Optus chief executive Ziggy Switkowski wanted the cable network to add to Optus Communications' long-distance and mobile phone networks, so favoured a settlement in which the Optus parent would buy out the minorities in Optus Vision. This would also settle the debilitating row between Seven and Nine.

Optus Communications 25 per cent shareholder Mayne Nickless was desperate for any solution that would allow it to sell or float its interest in the parent company, a desire that was being thwarted by the poisonous relationship between the two networks and Stokes' legal action.

On March 28, 1997, Switkowski announced that Optus Communications would buy out its bickering Optus Vision partners by offering shares in the parent. Optus Vision had lost $170 million in the six months to December 31, 1996, and its losses appeared to be accelerating after it posted a loss of $160 million for the 12 months to June 30, 1996. Switkowski was aiming to make cost savings of about $60 million a year from the integration of Optus and Optus vision.[48]

Now all that was left was to resolve the instability in the parent company. The shareholder conflicts in Optus also claimed Switkowski, who was sacked in June and replaced by a Cable and Wireless executive, Peter Howell-Davies. Two months later, Switkowski, a trained nuclear physicist before joining Kodak and then Optus, turned up as the group managing director of business and international at Telstra, much to the horror of Howell-Davies.

In July, 24.5 per cent Optus Communications shareholder Britain's Cable and Wireless paid the other 24.5 per cent shareholder Bell South of the US $980 million for its interest, to effectively take control of the company.[49] President of Bell South International, Buddy Miller, hinted that the US and UK shareholders were pulling in different direction in Optus: 'The future success of Optus's complex business . . . requires speed and clarity of decision making that can only be achieved with a single telecommunications shareholder in control.'[50]

Any slim hope that Australis Media might survive was dashed on May 30, when the NSW Supreme Court blocked its joint venture with Optus Vision because it breached its exclusivity agreement with Foxtel. The decision came as a complete surprise to both Australis and Optus Vision, which expected to defeat the News Limited action. In its half year results announced in March, Australis said, 'Because the . . . satellite joint venture contemplates the sale of certain assets of the company for cash and is expected to reduce cash and operating costs, the failure to establish the venture could have a material adverse effect on liquidity and, therefore, a significant impact on the company's ability to continue as a going concern.'[51]

Australis said it would appeal against the decision, but this would take six to eight months at least and its cash reserves were already dwindling to perilously low levels. At the end of May, it had just $35.1 million left of the $88 million in net proceeds from the capital raising the previous November.[52] At its rate of losses it could last another three to four months at most. Had it beaten off News and been able to proceed with the Optus Vision alliance, Australis would have received its $25 million cash injection and shaved its costs by 10–15 per cent. Now, it was heading for oblivion. It could be saved only by trying to merge again with Foxtel, or with Optus Vision. Last time it tried to do a deal to supply programs to Optus Vision, in December 1994, the Australis studios vetoed the deal. They would do the same again. Australis in reality had one hope only, and that was to start talking to the Foxtel partners again.

Lachlan Murdoch and James Packer weren't going to wait for an appeal to decide what to do next. PBL had played its last card in trying to put together Australis and Optus Vision to frustrate Foxtel, News and Telstra, but after the Supreme Court decision the fight against the Murdochs was looking increasingly pointless. Murdoch and News were lucky to win that round. Australis won its appeal in December 1997.[53] But the initial court victory by Foxtel in May brought the Murdochs and the Packers back together again to quickly staunch the losses in the pay TV industry. Rodney Price in London knew the game was up too, and called Mark Booth in Sydney. Australis and Foxtel should start talking again to see if they could reignite the merger blocked in February the previous year by Alan Fels. Fels had invited them to apply again after deregulation of the telecommunications industry in July 1997, and it was getting close to that date.

By mid-1997, Foxtel was emerging as the clear winner in the pay TV race, with more than 200,000 subscribers.[54] The ructions in the Optus group had cost it valuable momentum and with an estimated 150,000–160,000 subscribers,[55] Optus was slipping behind the News-Telstra partnership.

Despite the apparent animosity between the families and the breakdown in the professional relationship between Ken Cowley and Brian Powers through the ARL-Super League fight, Lachlan Murdoch and James Packer talked most days. They were sensible enough to know that the flare-up between their fathers and between their commercial interests would die down sooner or later. The huge losses and commercial damage that had been caused by the contest between Optus and Telstra and between the Murdochs and the Packers over phones, pay TV and rugby league was a stark lesson to both families that they would both do far better if they co-existed peacefully.

James Packer called Lachlan Murdoch within a day or two of the May 30 Supreme Court judgment and suggested the two start talking about resolving the pay TV mess. They agreed that the key to any rationalisation of the industry was for Foxtel to acquire Australis and that PBL should come in to support Foxtel, to create a clear winner in the industry. PBL still held its right of first and last refusal over Australis's assets, both hardware and software, so its cooperation was essential. The re-joining of the Packers, the Murdochs and Telstra was the broad plan that Kerry Packer developed back in March 1993, when he invited Frank Blount and Ken Cowley to join him in the PMT consortium. Rod Price and Mark Booth were already talking, so there was little to stop the two groups trying to get together again. Allan Fels was the only unpredictable factor.

On June 20, News and PBL announced that they intended to work together towards the rationalisation of the pay TV industry 'for the benefit of Foxtel' and that they would 'equalise' their interests in pay TV.[56] The announcement came as a shock to both Australis and Optus Vision, which had been so strongly supported by the Packers in the past. Australis had lost its main bargaining chip now that it could no longer play off the Murdochs and the Packers. It was vulnerable to being absorbed by interests associated with one of the families.

Australis's new chief executive, Sean O'Halloran, the former Seven legal counsel who had been hired from Optus Vision the previous September, approached Optus to see if it would consider an alternative proposal. The merged Optus and Optus Vision was focusing its energies almost entirely on getting its telephone technology working properly. Pay TV was a bleeding headache.

On July 25, more than three weeks after telecommunications deregulation officially began, Australis and Foxtel announced once again that they planned to merge. It would bring together Foxtel's estimated 230,000 subscribers and Australis's 65,000 satellite and MDS customers, and eliminate Foxtel's costly program supply agreement.

By now, Australis was a limping corporate wreck and had no stomach for a fight such as it had in March and April the previous year. O'Halloran and Price wanted the merger to proceed and for Foxtel to become the marketing name of the merged companies. It would also reassure the US bond holders, who had invested $US325 million in Australis, that they would eventually be re-paid.

In the wake of Super League's dramatic courtroom win on October 6, 1996, and the hiring of former Cathay Pacific chief executive Rod Eddington to run Ansett in January 1997, Ken Cowley felt confident enough that News was back on track to talk to Rupert Murdoch about his son Lachlan's succession to the job as managing director at News Corp's Australian arm.[57] Lachlan Murdoch had been involved in key decisions on the group's core media business since moving to Sydney in July 1995 and was talking on a daily basis to his father. Cowley felt that this might start to affect his relationship with Rupert Murdoch. Lachlan was ready, Cowley assured Murdoch senior.

On Monday, April 14, Rupert Murdoch announced that Cowley would step down as executive chairman and that Lachlan Murdoch would assume overall responsibility for the company's Australian operations. 'In the 33 years Mr Cowley has spent with News I have worked with no finer executive,' stated Murdoch. 'It has been my privilege to rely absolutely on his integrity, business acumen, leadership and loyalty.'

While ACCC head Allan Fels was assessing the merger and its implications, the American chief executive of Cable and Wireless, Dick 'Dial a Deal' Brown, met Rupert Murdoch in his Wapping office in September 1997 to reach a broader understanding between their two groups in Australia. Brown was keen to gain some assurance from Murdoch that Foxtel and Optus would work towards program sharing to eliminate the costly nature of their exclusive studio and sports programming. Murdoch wanted an assurance from Brown that Optus would not try to stop the Australis-Foxtel merger. Brown agreed. Just before the two signed a one-page memorandum, Bruce McWilliam wrote a clause at the bottom to say that the document was not legally binding. Brown and Murdoch signed. It was a meaningless exercise. Almost within days, the new Optus chief executive, Chris Anderson, was lobbying Allan Fels to block the merger. He used the same argument that Geoff Cousins had used two years earlier: if this merger goes ahead, then Optus will have no hope of effectively competing against Telstra.

The ACCC once again accepted the argument, but it had to take a different approach to block the merger. In the deregulated environment it could not intervene to stop a merger before it happened but, rather, it had to wait until after the merger was announced and was being put in place before injuncting it. There is a subtle but perceptible difference between the two.

On October 14, Fels sought an injunction in the Federal Court to stop the merger, after Australis and Foxtel ignored a deadline of midday, October 13, to call the merger off. The challenge facing Australis and Foxtel – whose legal advice was that they would eventually win the case – was that the ACCC, once granted an injunction, could string the main hearing out for a few months. On the day the ACCC sought its injunction, Australis had $15 million left,[58] suggesting it might last another three to four weeks, given its rate of losses.

Although it was an option for News and Telstra to allow Australis to go into receivership and then try to re-negotiate supply arrangements with the studios, there was no certainty that Foxtel could achieve this. Lachlan Murdoch called Chris Anderson to ask him if Optus would supply its programs to Foxtel on a short-term emergency basis in the event Australis went into receivership and Foxtel was unable to reach a new arrangement with the old Australis studios.

Fels' eagerness to block the Australis-Foxtel merger this time was to get him and the ACCC into trouble. After winning an injunction to block the merger on October 14, the ACCC and its solicitor, the Australian Government Solicitor, decided to retain two lawyers from Gilbert and Tobin to help them fight the merger proposal. Gilbert and Tobin were long-standing legal advisers to

Optus Communications and PBL. It was because of Optus's vigorous lobbying against the Australis-Foxtel merger that the ACCC had decided to block it. Optus stood to be the main beneficiary if the merger did not proceed.

At directions hearings on October 24 and again three days later, counsel for the ACCC raised the matter of Gilbert and Tobin advising the ACCC and the AGS. Telstra's lawyers, Mallesons Stephen Jaques, objected strongly to the use of Gilbert and Tobin on the grounds that there was a conflict of interest.[59] However, both the ACCC in a statement on November 20 and Optus on the same day stated that no objection was raised to the use of the Optus solicitors as advisers to the ACCC in its case against Australis and Foxtel. These statements were clearly wrong.

The merger collapsed in the end because the ACCC sought time to prepare its case, and then Telstra asked for time once it was clear that Optus would raise issues of telephone competition. News and Australis on October 29 had sought a hearing before Christmas to decide the matter quickly, but were refused after the ACCC, advised by the Government Solicitor and Gilbert and Tobin, opposed the application.

Australis's situation was desperate now. It had run out of money and when it asked for backing from News and Telstra, they refused. The Foxtel partners were not prepared to pour money into Australis when they did not know how long it would take to resolve the court action. On November 10, Australis announced the merger was off, and that it expected to go into receivership at any time.

When word leaked that the ACCC had used Optus's legal advisers, it incensed David Hawker, the chairman of the House of Representative Standing Committee on Financial Institutions and Public Administration, and one of the committee members, Joe Hockey. They used a regular sitting of the committee to question Fels and one of his officers, Hank Spier. After persistently questioning Fels as to whether it was appropriate that the Government Solicitor and the ACCC use a law firm which had acted in the past for a beneficiary of an ACCC decision, Fels finally said, 'No, not in general, and it does not happen in general.'[60]

When Hockey asked Fels whether there had been other occasions when the ACCC had been in a similar situation, Spier intervened and said, 'Yes, there have.' He declined to name them. When another committee member, Ian Causley, asked Fels whether Foxtel was happy about the use of the Gilbert and Tobin lawyers, Fels said, 'They were told about it . . . It was totally disclosed. It was in court and everything.' At the committee's next sitting, the Deputy Government Solicitor, Bob Alexander, said that Telstra 'did object strenuously to the engagement of Gilbert and Tobin solicitors'.[61]

Fels was also challenged on the *Business Sunday* program on November 16 about the claim by Optus that it would pull out of telephones if the Australis-Foxtel merger went ahead. Presenter Michael Pascoe asked, 'Professor, you've been quite sceptical in the past about companies claiming they'd close if you didn't take certain action. Why have you bought the Optus story this time?'

Fels replied, 'Well we have powerful evidence that they would withdraw from both pay TV and the local telephone business, which we will be producing in court. They have to soon spend another billion to complete the cable roll-out and network and to finance the funding of the installation of it into homes. Now the directors have advised that they are not going to proceed with this investment if the merger goes ahead. They have sworn affidavits which will be produced in court and they will be available in court for cross-examination, and we find their evidence quite credible.'[62]

Fels blamed Australis for having chalked up losses of $700 million and having paid too much for its satellite licence and for its Hollywood films. He made no mention of the fact that the studio agreements were so expensive mainly because of counter-bidding from Optus, and that Optus had made crucial mistakes too, including creating the unstable Optus Vision shareholding structure, and setting the industry price structure at unsustainably low levels in September 1995. It was Geoff Cousins' $19.95 connection fee and $25 a month subscriber rate that forced Australis to try to merge with Foxtel the first time around.

When asked about Optus's inability to get its phone system working properly, Fels defended the company vigorously. 'Contrary to some claims, they are now selling local telephone services at the rate of 2,000 a week. They have 20,000 customers and the network is operating. There's nothing wrong with it. But it's not complete,' he said. Optus couldn't have put its case better.

Behind the public rhetoric of Fels and Anderson, the ACCC was briefed on the real situation by Christopher Weston, Optus's director of strategy and regulation, who was seconded to Optus from Cable and Wireless in June 1997. Weston told Fels that the merged Australis-Foxtel would have a 72 per cent market share and Optus Vision 28 per cent and this would place Optus Vision at a disadvantage in acquiring pay TV content, and therefore affect its ability to compete. Optus's strategy was to use the Optus Vision broadband cable network to supply local telephone services in competition with Telstra. Its ability to offer a competitive pay television service which it could bundle together and sell as a package with its telephone services was critical to the success of this strategy.

Weston also revealed to Fels that the Optus board had made a decision to run the business down to save costs. It had adopted a 'slow growth' policy to trim the losses it was sustaining on the network and the pay TV business. This had nothing to do with the Australis-Foxtel merger, but more to do with addressing Optus's internal cost problems.

Optus's modelling was based on an assumption that Optus Vision's pay television market share in 2004–2005 would be 15.8 per cent, well below its share as it stood in late 1997. The market share was expected to fall as a result of a strategy deliberately pursued by the Optus board, and nothing to do with a merger between Australis and Foxtel, yet Fels chose to parrot the public utterances of the Optus executives to justify his decision to fight the merger.

Fels accepted Optus' public posturing unquestioningly as a basis for blocking the merger. Optus had spent more than $2 billion building a cable network, had gone through a difficult restructuring of its shareholding, and Fels appeared to believe it would simply walk away.

In his evidence before the House Committee four days after his television appearance, Fels attempted to explain his dilemma in choosing between the survival of Australis or Optus. 'The Commission faced a very difficult issue, an unpleasant choice, between possible Australis Media failure and possible Optus failure. The Commission concluded in short . . . that Optus would withdraw from pay TV and, even more importantly, from local telephone competition.'

Fels had made his choice. He decided to let Australis go. But the experience appears to have affected him. Fels sought guidance at the St James Ethics Centre in the wake of the ACCC fiasco and the legal support from Optus. The centre is run by a former Oxford University academic, Simon Longstaff, who counsels individuals, mostly business executives, who find themselves in difficult ethical situations.

With Australis teetering, Lachlan Murdoch had to make a crucial decision on how Foxtel could gain control of the studio agreements or risk losing its key supply of programs if Australis went into liquidation. He needed a back-up deal with the studios. On Tuesday November 12, after News and Telstra had decided not to support Australis any longer and Allan Fels was defending his role in its imminent collapse, Lachlan was hosting an editorial conference at the new Fox studio at the old Sydney Showground.

It was a very hot day, and the young Murdoch had been dining at Lucio's restaurant in Paddington until 4am that morning. He had picked up a McDonald's on his way to the studio for the 10am conference. He wasn't feeling well. During a discussion on bureau staff numbers, his mobile phone rang. It was a call from the US with the news that the studios might be ready to talk to him. They weren't happy with what was happening at Australis. He excused himself for a few minutes, then returned to tell his editors he had to fly to the US. On his way back to the office he called Foxtel's new chief executive, Tom Mockridge, and Foxtel lawyer Richard Freudenstein and asked them to get ready for the 1.55pm flight to Los Angeles.

Before he left, he rang the studio programming chiefs, Jack Waterman from Paramount, Universal's Blair Westlake, Columbia Tri Star's Jack Ford (who was an Australian), and Fox's Mark Kaner and told them he needed to meet them in Vancouver the following day. Murdoch's timing was not good. All of them were preparing to take a few days off in the lead-up to Thanksgiving that Thursday. Murdoch could not approach them directly while they were in the US, because he was to put a proposal to them which would seek to have them transfer their supply contracts from Australis to Foxtel. In Canada, however, they could negotiate beyond the reach of US law, which forbade inducements to break a contract.

Murdoch would argue this was not the case, but the US bond holders would be desperate to sue anyone once Australis collapsed and they lost all of their $US325 million. The negotiation in a waterfront hotel in Vancouver went for three days. The sticking point was the studios' insistence that if Australis went under and News was to benefit, then the studios should share some of that benefit. They were still scarred from the experience at the hands of Sam Chisholm, who pocketed all of the benefits for BSkyB and News Corp. When Murdoch, Mockridge and Freudenstein returned to Australia that weekend, they had to keep the re-negotiation strictly confidential. If word had leaked, the deal would probably have been challenged by Australis and/or the bond holders.

Australis limped through the next few weeks as the owner of the Australis building in Pyrmont, Mike Boulos, attempted to negotiate a rescue deal in which he would invest $100 million, and had the newly-appointed acting chief executive, Peter Rose, negotiate with the bond holders to convert the money owed to them into equity in the business. It was a complex deal, which also needed the approval of the studios, which had just done a deal with Lachlan Murdoch for Foxtel.

Sean O'Halloran was sacked by the Australis board in late November after a series of bizarre events in New York where he was negotiating with the bond holders. O'Halloran was drained and exhausted by the experience. He had run up charge card expenses of more than $100,000 buying watches and jewellery for the Russian bodyguard he had hired, after claiming to have received death threats. Australis knocked back the bill, causing O'Halloran further discomfort in New York. Then, on a flight from New York to Los Angeles, he was taken off the aircraft and admitted to hospital, suffering what he later described as a 'medical seizure'.

O'Halloran had experienced a difficult personal life during 1996 after he separated from his de facto wife and child and then underwent a type of wedding ceremony with a male friend.

In the meantime, during several weeks of tense negotiations, the delicate framework of the rescue deal came under attack from both News and Telstra, who sued Australis over its attempts to issue yet another line of bonds to raise $US40 million from existing bond holders. News, which had bought $US26.75 million worth of the Australis senior notes from PBL in June, as part of the equalisation agreement, claimed in the Supreme Court in New York that the new issue was unauthorised and would rank ahead of the bonds issued by the company in October 1996. News also alleged that Australis, the issuer, was insolvent and unable to pay its obligations. Telstra sued Australis in the NSW Supreme Court, seeking winding up orders on the grounds that Australis was insolvent.

Telstra, which had bought $US18.6 million of the same senior notes issued in October 1996, was granted the orders on May 18, 1998. On May 20, Australis failed to make a scheduled monthly payment to the Movie Partnership, and the Hollywood studios switched their supply arrangements directly to Foxtel.[63] In the end,

News and Telstra decided to put Australis out of its misery rather than have it stagger on and risk disruption to program supplies.

The end came swiftly. The following day, receivers appointed by the US noteholders on May 1 placed Australis into liquidation and that night screens of its 12,000 MDS subscribers went black. Australis' 65,000 satellite subscribers were kept in the picture only because their service was taken over that night by the regional satellite operator UIH (now renamed Austar in Australia). The previous November as Australis faced imminent collapse, Austar and the satellite owner Optus struck a joint venture ostensibly to give Austar access to Optus' program package. But it also placed the two companies in a position to take over the Australis signal and supply its satellite subscribers once the inevitable occurred and Australis failed.

From midnight on May 21, Australis died. Kerry Packer's dream five years earlier of a dominant pay TV consortium became a reality.

# Epilogue

On December 21, 1999, Liberal Communications Minister Richard Alston faced a phalanx of television cameras and journalists in the ministerial offices in Phillip Street Sydney as he outlined the Federal Government's policy on the use of spectrum for the next broadcasting frontier, digital television.

The Federal Cabinet decision contained no surprises, as he had already announced the policy-in-principle 20 months earlier. Then, he really did shock the media and information technology industries, because it represented such a complete victory for the commercial networks, and was only partly diluted in the 1999 pre-Christmas announcement to deflect the political heat. The greatest surprise was the fact that Alston would give the three commercial networks, along with the ABC and SBS, sufficient spectrum to enable them to broadcast not only a digital signal, but the highest standard of digital, known as 1080i high definition. The Government would also restrict other users of digital spectrum mostly to datacasting of text, permitting just 10 minutes of video for each half an hour to ensure that no-one tries to compete with the networks. Longer video is allowed, so long as it doesn't have a host and requires the viewer to click on an icon to gain access. It's restrictive and prescriptive to the point of farce.

In contrast to the Howard Government's efforts to reform tax, deregulate industries and dismantle monopolies in business and labour, Alston confirmed the networks' protected status by declaring that the Government would not allow a fourth commercial network before the end of 2006. He had initially been persuaded to extend their market protection to 2008, but the lobbying campaign in Canberra in reaction to this overt protectionism was so ferocious he gave way a little on this issue.

After failing to win control of pay TV in 1992, the networks weren't going to be caught out or out-manoeuvred this time. Led by Nine and its main lobbyist, the former Liberal Party executive director Andrew Robb, the networks moved well ahead of other potential users of the spectrum to win spectacular concessions from the Government. The Liberal administration had learned none of the lessons of the pay TV lobbying campaigns of Labor in the early 1990s and attempted to dictate how valuable publicly-owned spectrum should be used, what information could be transmitted, and also to impose technical standards for reasons motivated more by politics than public benefit.

Alston and Prime Minister John Howard forgot, too, the investment distortions and losses totalling $2.5 billion from the early years of pay TV resulting from Labor's blunt use of policy to reward the media moguls in favour at the time, and punish those who had fallen foul of the Government. In 1995, Rupert Murdoch had the ear of Labor Prime Minister Paul Keating and the mogul out of favour was Kerry Packer. Four years later, Packer continued to enjoy the most-favoured-tycoon status that he won with the Howard Coalition Government's victory in March 1996.

While the government-owned networks, the ABC and SBS, will struggle, without special government assistance, to fully exploit the benefits of digital television, the gift of spectrum – estimated to be worth up to $2 billion at open auction – represented a massive transfer of wealth from taxpayer to the commercial networks.

Also, the insistence by the networks, Nine in particular, that the Government impose the highest of high-definition digital standards, guarantees that Australians will have the world's most expensive television sets, costing up to $10,000. This standard has been rejected, or has failed to attract industry favour, in other industrialised nations. Nine and Robb argued in Canberra that Australians deserved the best television, so-called cinemas in the lounge room. In the US, western Europe and Japan, high-definition television is regarded as too spectrum-hungry and less flexible than the standard definition digital signal, which uses one-fifth of the spectrum.

Had the networks conceded that standard definition would deliver a picture superior to the long-serving analogue, but with the addition of features like viewer choice of camera angles in sporting events and even multi-channelling, they risked the Government reducing the amount of spectrum being given away. By insisting on high definition, the networks ensured that the Government would give them the full seven megahertz of spectrum that it requires.

The networks had argued it would cost them hundreds of millions of dollars to develop digital television and therefore a gift of spectrum would be appropriate while they invested in digital and continued to provide their free-to-air services.

By the time other potential users of the spectrum woke up to what was happening in Canberra, it was too late. In a frantic last-gasp lobbying effort, new entrants such as Internet service provider OzEmail, news agency and datacaster Australian Associated Press, and John Fairfax attempted to persuade the Government of the folly of giving away spectrum, and also that it not be too restrictive on other commercial users.

The only concession Alston made to the arguments that he was simply giving away too much to the networks was that by December 1999 he decided to force them to transmit both high definition and standard definition signals along with continued broadcasting of their analogue signal until 2008.

This guarantees that high definition will be marginalised, but it will have served its purpose in winning the networks more spectrum than they need for their television broadcasts. High definition will have a tiny audience among those able to afford the sets and will be an advantage for blockbuster movies only. For 90 per cent of their broadcasting, the networks and their audiences will be happy with standard definition. The Government will come under pressure eventually to limit high-definition broadcasts to movies alone. This will leave the networks with plenty of the bandwidth they have been given for other commercial uses such as Internet, and interactive services like home shopping, banking and gambling – all products the networks wanted from pay TV.

OzEmail's head of corporate relations, Michael Ward, reflected the anger of non-network users of digital spectrum when he described the Howard Government's decision as 'betraying its ignorance, its incompetence or its corruption'.[1] The *Australian Financial Review* in its editorial in response to Alston's policy announcement said the decision lacked vision and merit and described his assertion that the decision was guided by consumer interest as 'convenient political rhetoric'. 'The lesson from the past decade in communications policy shows that governments which try to mandate certain technology outcomes, in the interests of consumers, invariably get it wrong,' the *AFR* chided.

The most aggrieved potential user, however, was Rupert Murdoch's News Corporation. News, along with most other potential datacasters, had hoped to persuade the Government to impose as few restrictions as possible on use of spectrum, to introduce new services and products enhanced with video. Unlike the networks, News, Fairfax and OzEmail would have to bid for spectrum at auction.

News clearly had ambitions to use the spectrum to datacast a broadcast-style commercial television service, but Alston ensured that this option was firmly closed off with the limit on the amount of video non-network service providers could show. Alston used a sledgehammer to punish News and the Murdochs, and reward the networks. He also hit a number of other unintended collateral targets such as AAP, Fairfax and OzEmail.

The digital decision was an early Christmas present for Kerry Packer, his Nine Network and its affiliated Internet service company, ecorp. Nine and ecorp will be able to provide an almost unlimited range of services using the digital spectrum given to the group. Packer could not have imagined, when he stuck his neck out in February 1995 and endorsed John Howard as a future prime minister, the dividends his commercial interests would later reap from Howard Government decisions.

As for Australis, its collapse in May 1998 allowed Foxtel to take its programming directly from the Hollywood movie and entertainment suppliers flowing from the deal Lachlan Murdoch struck the previous November. Foxtel also bought from the Australis liquidator 65,000 Galaxy set-top boxes, and the names of the subscribers, for an estimated $10 million. It was able to migrate 50,000 of those subscribers across to Foxtel. Remarkably, Optus passed up the opportunity to bid for these subscribers, despite the fact that it had them briefly in the wake of Australis' demise. Regional operator Austar was unable to exploit the collapse to add to its subscriber numbers, but picked up an additional 6,000 customers when it bought the Continental Century franchise for $US35 million from the Tow family using UIH shares as payment. Foxtel then moved quickly to negotiate access to transponder space on the Optus satellite to provide a satellite service to those former Galaxy subscribers out of reach of the Telstra cable.

Australis's pleas to Allan Fels and the Australian Competition and Consumer Commission – that it would collapse if its proposed mergers with Foxtel were blocked – were not bluff, but real. Ironically, its liquidation and Foxtel's purchase of most of the Australis subscriber base meant the merger effectively went ahead anyway, but at a fraction of the cost. Foxtel was not liable for the $1.08 billion Australis was due to repay the US bond holders between 2001 and 2004 as it would have been had the 1996 or 1997 merger proposals been passed.

More than $650 million had been invested in Australis since Steve Cosser raised the first $2.5 million in January 1993. The liquidator appointed in May 1998 was able to recover a total of just $15 million from the firesale of its assets. The biggest single loser from the collapse was Lenfest Communications, which lost all of the $200 million-plus it had invested in Cosser's company.

As 1999 came to a close, Foxtel had moved to a dominant position in the industry with about 550,000 subscribers, while Cable and Wireless Optus struggled to maintain the 200,000 it had reached by late 1998. Its subscriber base was static, although after two years of frustration, delays and system crashes Optus was enjoying growing success with its cable network for local calls and Internet services.

Kerry Packer's 1993 plan to bring together the most powerful players to form an unbeatable pay TV consortium had reached fruition with the equalisation agreement he struck with Rupert Murdoch in June 1997. From then on, Foxtel had the firepower to become the dominant pay TV provider Packer had always wanted. From Murdoch's point of view, the agreement took Packer out of contention as a potential financial supporter of Australis, but at high cost. It meant he would lose control of Foxtel.

Packer's PBL and News had 25 per cent each of Foxtel and Telstra held firmly on to its half share, despite attempts by Packer and Murdoch to persuade the telco to equalise their shareholdings at 33.3 per cent each. In one such attempt in March 1999, Packer and Murdoch met Telstra chief executive Ziggy Switkowski in Murdoch's Sydney office to put to him a deal: Foxtel would make an $800 million bid for regional operator Austar, then still wholly owned by UIH. As part of the deal, Telstra would sell 8.3 per cent of Foxtel each to News and PBL to bring all three partners into line on 33.3 per cent. A fortnight later, Telstra chief financial officer Paul Rizzo phoned Foxtel head Tom Mockridge to tell him Telstra wasn't prepared to water down its shareholding. The deal was off. Austar floated a few months later and by the end of the year its capitalisation had soared to $2.9 billion because it promised to offer high-speed Internet services. The market pushed it beyond the reach of the Foxtel partners if they ever wanted to revisit the acquisition option.

Foxtel will be the catalyst for further rationalisation of the industry, on its terms, until there is effectively one player. C&W Optus has given up trying to compete head on with Foxtel in pay TV. In late 1997 it subtlely changed its strategy from trying to 'pull-through' pay TV subscribers as phone customers to a new objective of 'bundling' together pay TV and fixed and mobile phone services to attract customers. Its programming increasingly will be non-exclusive to save costs, thus allowing Foxtel to offer a range of exclusive channels on top of programs it will share with Optus, such as news, entertainment, old movies, non-exclusive sport, and re-runs of US television.

No-one emerges very well from this short but very intense battle for supremacy in pay TV. Kerry Packer embellished his reputation for being a canny investor, having paid just $160 million for his quarter share of Foxtel, compared with Telstra's and News's far greater costs. Strategically, he is the biggest winner from the set-piece battle to establish pay TV. He has also retained his Nine Network's supremacy in free-to-air and can look forward to substantial advertising revenue increases with the arrival of digital television after January 2001.

Foxtel won the pay TV war, but at great cost. The Super League imbroglio is estimated to have cost News between $300 million and $400 million. Telstra and C&W Optus have completed only three-quarters of their $2 billion-plus cable roll-out and they have over-built to the extent of 80 per cent. C&W Optus must be content as a second player, with a less attractive suite of programs than Foxtel and a lower demographic.

Although the Howard Government has forbidden the networks to use digital television to multi-channel, this can never be ruled out given the favour the networks have received in Canberra. The Howard Government's decision to continue to protect the commercial networks will discourage the entry of new players into broadcasting and tend to entrench Australia's narrow media ownership.

One of those aspiring entrants, Albert Hadid, sued Australis, Bain and Co (now wholly owned by Deutsche Bank), Wayne Burt and Australis's former chairman Rodney Price over their disagreement as to who promised what during the first round of the MDS licence bidding. He sued them again claiming to have been conspired against and defrauded over the true value of the satellite licence he sold for $13 million to Don Heller at 4am in the Regent Hotel on November 17, 1993, only to learn that it was on-sold the next day to Australis for $138 million. He lost both actions, but is appealing against Justice Lehane's decision in the Federal Court on Christmas eve 1999 dismissing Hadid's allegations arising from the flick pass of the 'B' satellite licence by Lenfest to Australis.

Rupert Murdoch opted for a dramatic lifestyle change when he separated from his wife of 31 years, Anna, in mid-1998 and the following year married a 31-year-old executive with Star TV whom he had met in Hong Kong, Wendi Deng.

Neil Gamble resigned as chief executive of Sydney's Star City casino in December 1999 to work on his golf swing after the casino was acquired by the Melbourne-based Tabcorp.

Lenfest Communications was sold to US cable group Comcast in November 1999 for a mixture of cash and stock for a total of $US7 billion. Lenfest had been put into play the previous March when its 50 per cent owner, John Malone's TeleCommunications Inc, was acquired by US long-distance carrier AT&T. With cash and stock in Comcast valued at $US3.5 billion in the subsequent takeover of his half share, Gerry Lenfest will never have to work again.

Sean O'Halloran was found dead at the foot of a cliff at Cape Patton on Victoria's Great Ocean Road in October 1999. He had returned his daughter to her mother after O'Halloran and his daughter had been on a two-week holiday in Las Vegas.

Rodney Price resigned from Brierley Investments early in 1999 as the New Zealand investment group struggled with its portfolio of poorly performing assets. Its stock had plunged after the sale of its 46 per cent interest in the UK Thistle Hotel group had collapsed, focusing attention on its other holdings in profitless enterprises such as a property development on the Hawaiian island of Molokai. In December 1998 it sold its most-desired investment, the 25 per cent of John Fairfax that it had bought two years earlier from Conrad Black, and Price resigned from the Fairfax board, where he had been chairman until April that year.

A push by Fairfax's second largest investor, the FXF Trust controlled by Kerry Packer and Brian Powers, which holds 14.9 per cent of Fairfax, resulted in Powers being voted onto the board in April 1999 with the backing of key institutional shareholders. A week later, after Price stepped down as chairman, Powers was elevated to chairman. Although Price continues to live in London, he maintains various private investment interests, among them managing and expanding Tahara on the banks of the Murrumbidgee River at Wagga Wagga.

Steve Cosser's profitable exit from pay TV left him cashed up for his next investment foray, an attempt to corner the titanium market through a Dutch-registered company called Southern Mining Corp BV. The company held 80 per cent of a South African-based company, Southern Mining Corp, which owned the potentially rich Bothaville Deposit in South Africa and the Corridor Sands project in Mozambique.

Working from his Paris office, Cosser was also able to bring in some of his old partners and supporters from pay TV in Australia, including stockbroker Brent Potts and Peter Scanlon. His friend Wayne Burt was his representative on the board of Southern Mining Corp. The strategy came unstuck after a proposed joint venture with a former Anglo-American subsidiary, JCI, to develop the projects fell through and the share price collapsed, losing millions of dollars for Cosser and his backers. Cosser recently moved to London where his children will complete their education.

After leaving BSkyB in mid-1998, Sam Chisholm won the coveted job as chief negotiator for the UK Premier League in its talks with broadcasters present and potential, including his old company BSkyB.

Malcolm Turnbull's firm Turnbull and Partners was acquired by the US investment bank Goldman Sachs in August 1997 and he was appointed managing director in Australia and made a partner in November 1998. Goldman Sachs floated on the New York Stock Exchange in May 1999 and Turnbull rolled his partnership interest into shares. As a founding shareholder of OzEmail, he was one of major beneficiaries, taking about $59 million, when the US long-distance phone group MCI WorldCom bought the Internet service provider early in 1999.

Murray Williams eventually pleaded guilty to insider trading and was fined $50,000 and sentenced by Justice Kinchington in the NSW District Court in October 1996 to 18 months periodic detention, of which he served six months. Before the matter went to court, he also compensated the four investors from whom he bought the 125,000 Australis shares on the afternoon of November 18, 1993. After using a stockbroker to track them down, he sold the shares in January and February 1996 for between $1.15 and $1.20, near their peak of $1.30 a share during the merger negotiations with Foxtel, realising a profit of about $70,000 for the investors.

Bob Mansfield resigned from John Fairfax in 1996 after falling out with Conrad Black's right-hand man Daniel Colson and spent two years working with the Howard Government helping to fast-track through the government bureaucracy major infrastructure proposals. In August 1999, Richard Alston made him a surprise appointment as chairman of Telstra, where he joined a growing list of ex-Optus people in senior positions at the group, including Telstra's managing director, Ziggy Switkowski.

Although the commercial television networks have been given fresh impetus from the Howard Government's digital broadcasting decision, pay TV has changed forever the television viewing patterns of Australians. Only one-sixth of households subscribes to either Austar, Foxtel or Optus Vision, but the growth in subscriber numbers will continue to cut into the audience held by the networks. It will force the once-complacent networks to improve the quality of their programming, with its cacophony of crass advertising, or suffer accelerated drift to the multi-channel cable and satellite offerings of the three operators.

Pay TV faces an early test in 2001 when the cable services switch to digital technology and have more than 200 channels available. It will allow the pay TV industry to greatly widen its services to pay-per-view sporting coverage and near-video on-demand movies, as well as the home banking and shopping services the industry always wanted. Telstra and Optus, with digitalisation of their cables, may come under pressure from the Government to open their cable to outside service providers, as indicated by Labor's former Communications Minister, Michael Lee.

Both telephone companies will be thirsty for content, however. Once the restrictive anti-siphoning rules expire in 2004, pay TV will also be able to secure wider and more relevant sports coverage, the rights to which are largely controlled by the networks until then.

Telstra through 1999 struck a series of commercial alliances with software and Internet companies which will enable it to offer a range of services over its cable, potentially in competition with Foxtel. This will lead to renewed strains in the partnership.

Having won the costly pay TV wars of the mid-1990s, the main threat to Foxtel will come from within, as its three powerful and headstrong partners, Rupert Murdoch, Kerry Packer and Telstra wrestle amongst themselves and their sometimes diverging commercial interests to dictate Foxtel's future role.

# Notes

## 1 Out of the frying pan

1 *Dished*, by Peter Chippindale and Suzanne Franks, Simon & Schuster, 1992, p262.

## 2 Setting the stage

1 *Elliott*, by Peter Denton, Little Hills Press, 1987, p55.
2 *Keating*, by Edna Carew, Allen & Unwin, 1988.
3 *Keating*, p175.
4 *The Rise and Rise of Kerry Packer*, by Paul Barry, Bantam Books, 1993, p324.
5 *The Man Who Couldn't Wait*, by V.C. Carroll, William Heinemann Australia, 1990, p140.
6 *Mediaweek*, quoted in Grant Samuel's independent report for Australis/Foxtel merger, October 24, 1997.

## 3 Bushtrack to the superhighway

1 *The Fixer*, by Marian Wilkinson, William Heinemann Australia, 1996, pp326–329.
2 *The Hawke Memoirs*, by R.J.L Hawke, William Heinemann Australia, 1994, p489.
3 *Beazley*, by Peter FitzSimons, HarperCollins Publishers, 1998, p310.
4 *The Australian*, September 19, 1990.

## 4 The game gets serious

1 *Dished*, p321.
2 Interview with the author, February 17, 1999.
3 *The Fixer*, William Heinemann Australia, p347.
4 *Australian Pay TV News*, No 3, October 1992, p8.
5 *The Australian*, October 9, 1992.
6 *The Australian*, October 14, 1992.
7 *The Australian*, October 14, 1992.
8 *The Australian*, October 14, 1992.
9 *The Australian*, October 29, 1992.
10 Australian Broadcasting Authority, *Investigation into Control, CanWest Global Communications Corporation/The Ten Group Ltd*, November 1995, p9.
11 *The Bank that Broke the Bank*, by Edna Carew, Doubleday, 1997, p390.

## 5 Betrayal

1 *Murdoch*, by William Shawcross, Pan Books, 1992, p539.
2 *Mean Business*, by Albert J. Dunlap, Random House, 1996, p132.
3 *The Australian* magazine, March 18–19, 1995, pp16–17.
4 From file notes of the Department of Transport and Communications tendered as evidence in the Federal Court in April 1993 during an action by Australis against the order by the Minister for Communications to terminate the auction for MDS licences.
5 Ibid.
6 *Sydney Morning Herald*, April 21, 1993.
7 ibid.
8 *The Weekend Australian*, January 30, 1993, p4.
9 *The Australian*, January 30, 1993.

## 6 Satellite dawn

1 Interview with the author, October 14, 1993.
2 *The Rise and Rise of Kerry Packer*, p465.
3 *The Australian*, February 24, 1993.
4 *The Australian*, March 13 and 15, 1993.
5 Optus Financial Data Book, for half year ended December 31, 1995; May 1996.
6 *Sydney Morning Herald*, May 7, 1993.
7 ibid.
8 *Sydney Morning Herald*, May 6, 1993.
9 *Murdoch*, by William Shawcross, Pan Books, 1993, p544.

10   *Arko, My Game,* by Ken Arthurson, Pan Macmillan Australia, 1997, p242.
11   ibid.
12   *Australian Business Monthly,* December 1992.

### 7   Midsummer manoeuvres

1   Lenfest press release, September 1, 1993.
2   Australis Prospectus, p24.
3   Macquarie Bank research, September 1993, p9.
4   Wayne Burt evidence, Federal Court transcript, July 14, 1998, p25.
5   Wayne Burt evidence to Federal Court, July 15, 1998.
6   Gerry Lenfest evidence to Federal Court, May 27, 1998, p5898.
7   ibid, p5899.
8   Burt evidence to Federal Court, July 16, 1998, p8437.
9   Lenfest Communications Inc, Information Memorandum, prepared by Toronto Dominion Bank, November 1, 1993, p4.

### 8   The coming of cable

1   Interview with the author, October 15, 1993.
2   Harvest Books, 1998.
3   *Pay TV News,* November 1993, p7.
4   *Pay TV News,* March 1994, p4.
5   Optus Financial Data Book, May 1996, p13.
6   Interview with the author, August 7, 1998.
7   Interview with author, February 23, 1999.
8   *Australian Financial Review,* October 18, 1993.
9   Letter from Peter Frame to various Time Warner executives including Art Barron, Lee De Boer and Steven Rosenberg, November 30, 1993.
10   ibid.
11   Macquarie Equities, report on Australis Media, September 1993, p23.
12   Australis Media prospectus, August 1993, p7.
13   Australis Media, release to Australian Stock Exchange, February 28, 1994.
14   Australian Broadcasting Authority, news release, February 25, 1994.
15   *Pay TV News,* April-May-June 1994, p3.
16   *Sydney Morning Herald,* March 17, 1994.
17   *The Australian,* April 4, 1994.
18   *Dished,* pp322–323.
19   *Sydney Morning Herald,* May 13, 1994, p21.

20 Wayne Burt, cross examination, in Hadid v Lenfest, Bain, Burt, Australis, Rodney Price, July 20, 1998.
21 Burt evidence, July 20, 1998.
22 ibid.
23 ibid.
24 *Sydney Morning Herald*, May 13, 1994.
25 For example, 'PMT Ups the Heat in Pay TV Scramble', by Mark Furness, *The Australian*, March 16, 1994.
26 *Australian Financial Review*, July 8, 1994, p27.
27 ibid.
28 CTS, press release, March 1, 1994.
29 ibid.
30 Interview with the author, July 17, 1998.
31 *Australian Financial Review*, July 28, 1994, p4.
32 *Sydney Morning Herald*, July 28, 1994, p5.
33 *Australian Pay TV News*, September 1994.
34 *Australian Pay TV News*, September 2, 1994.

## 9  When friends fall out

1 *Pay TV News*, October 19, 1994.
2 Joint News-Telstra press release, November 11, 1994.
3 Media consultant Peter Cox, quoted on Bloomberg financial news service, November 11, 1994.
4 *Sydney Morning Herald*, October 19, 1994.
5 Optus Vision media release, November 24, 1994.
6 Interview with author, December 15, 1998.
7 *Australian Pay TV News*, January 27, 1995.
8 *Australian Pay TV News*, February 24, 1995.
9 *Arko, My Game*, by Ken Arthurson, Pan Macmillan, 1997, p196.
10 ibid, p200.
11 ibid, pp200–201.
12 ibid, p202.
13 ibid, p206.
14 Bloomberg News, February 1, 1995.
15 *The Australian*, February 14, 1995.
16 *A Current Affair*, transcript, February 16, 1995.
17 *The Australian*, February 20, 1995, p1.
18 *Daily Telegraph*, December 20, 1997, p124.
19 *Arko, My Game*, p224.
20 *Australian Financial Review*, April 21, 1995, p1.
21 Ken Cowley, interview with the author, July 29, 1998.

22  *Sydney Morning Herald*, April 21, 1995, p21.
23  Seven Network statement to Australian Stock Exchange, April 19, 1995.
24  *Australian Pay TV News*, April 7, 1995.
25  *The Australian*, June 28, 1995.
26  *Australian Pay TV News*, May 5, 1995, p1.
27  *Australian Pay TV News*, July 14, 1995.
28  *Australian Pay TV News*, June 2, 1995, p2.
29  *The Australian*, July 20, 1995.
30  Australis Media, results for year to June 30, 1995, announced August 24.
31  Lenfest Communications Inc, prospectus for offer of $US300 million in 10.5 per cent senior subordinated notes, page f-31.
32  *The Australian*, September 1, 1995.
33  Optus Communications, Financial Data Book, May 1996.

**10  Total war**

1  *The Australian*, September 28, 1995.
2  *The Australian*, September 26, 1995.
3  *Arko, My Game*, by Ken Arthurson, Pan Macmillan, 1997, p239.
4  Brian Powers, interview with the author, October 19, 1998.
5  *Arko, My Game*, p11.
6  *Australian Financial Review*, September 6, 1997.
7  *The Australian*, February 24, 1996.
8  *Daily Telegraph*, February 24, 1996.
9  *Sydney Morning Herald*, February 24, 1996.
10  *The Australian*, February 24, 1996.
11  *The Australian*, March 14, 1996.
12  Peter Gray, interview with author, July 9, 1998.
13  *Australian Financial Review*, October 31, 1995 p23.
14  Report by Trade Practices Commission on allocation of subscription broadcasting licence B to Hi Vision, June 16, 1993.
15  Grant Samuel & Associates, independent report on Australis-Foxtel merger, December 29, 1995 (not released).
16  ibid.
17  ibid.
18  ibid.
19  Lenfest Communications Inc, prospectus for raising of $US300 million in 10.5 per cent senior subordinated notes, September 6, 1996.
20  Lenfest prospectus, page f-30.
21  Interview with the author, November 12, 1997.
22  Australis Media, Trade Creditors Estimate as at April 11, 1996.

23   Turnbull and Partners, financial report on Australis Media, March 1996.
24   Letter from Neil Gamble to Bruce McWilliam, April 15, 1996.
25   Australis Media, press release announcing funding package, April 19, 1996.
26   Draft prospectus for offer of $US225 million in senior, subordinated discount notes, July 15, 1996, p23.
27   Transcript, *Lateline* interview with Geoffrey Cousins, April 23, 1996.
28   *The Australian*, May 16, 1996, p27.
29   BZW report, June 5, 1996.
30   Neil Gamble, interview with the author, January 16, 1998.
31   Australis Media, statement to ASX, July 30, 1996.
32   Articles published July 26, 1996, headed 'Australis Denies Funds Gone' and 'ASX Must Ask for Promised Prospectus'.
33   Draft prospectus, p20.
34   Australis Media, letter to ASX, July 31, 1996.
35   *Australian Financial Review*, November 12, 1996.
36   *The Australian*, September 20, 1996, p23.
37   *Sydney Morning Herald*, September 20, 1996, p5.
38   *The Australian*, August 21, 1996.
39   Australis Media announcement, September 12, 1996.
40   Australis Media, results for year to June 30, 1996, subsequent events.
41   Australis Media announcement, November 1, 1996.
42   *Sydney Morning Herald*, December 2, 1996, p35.
43   *The Australian*, February 24, 1997.
44   *Sydney Morning Herald*, December 2, 1996.
45   Australis Media 1996 annual general meeting, chairman's speech.
46   Australis Media, September quarter results, December 5, 1996.
47   *The Australian*, February 24, 1997.
48   *The Australian*, April 25, 1997.
49   *The Australian*, July 2, 1997.
50   ibid.
51   *The Australian*, May 31, 1997, p53.
52   Report on March quarter result, *Sydney Morning Herald*, June 18, 1997.
53   *Australian Financial Review*, December 24, 1997, p11.
54   Foxtel media release, June 19, 1997.
55   *Sydney Morning Herald*, February 9, 1998.
56   News Limited announcement, June 20, 1997.
57   *Australian Financial Review*, September 6, 1997, p23.
58   *Sydney Morning Herald*, October 14, 1997, p25.
59   Evidence of Bob Alexander, Deputy Government Solicitor, to House

of Representatives Standing Committee on Financial Institutions and Public Administration, December 4, 1997.

60  House of Representatives Standing Committee on Financial Institutions and Public Administration, transcript, November 20, 1997.

61  House of Representatives Standing Committee on Financial Institutions and Public Administration, transcript, December 4, 1997.

62  Transcript, *Business Sunday*, November 16, 1997.

63  *Australian Financial Review*, May 22, 1998.

**Epilogue**

1  *Australian Financial Review*, December 22, 1999, p17.

# Index

# Other titles by Comerford and Miller

**Jobs of Our Own** *by Race Mathews*
Building a Stake-holder Society: Alternatives to the Market and the State.
*The case for distributism — the philosophy that ownership and economic power should belong to the people, not to the State or wealthy minorities.* £12.99

**The Armour Plated Ostrich** *by Tim Webb*
The Hidden Costs of Britain's Addiction to the Arms Business.
*A witty and well researched expose of Britain's addiction to the arms trade.* £9.99

**White Nation** *by Ghassan Hage*
Fantasies of White Supremacy in a Multicultural Society.
*Essential reading for everyone anxious to understand the basis of modern racism.* £12.99

**Celebrities, Culture and Cyberpace** *by McKenzie Wark*
Britain's New Labour has Echoes of the Australian Experience.
*The author, a media expert, examines the Cultural Revolution of Australia's 13 years of Labor rule – a time when policies very similar to Britain's New Labour were being applied.* £12.99

**Comrades and Capitalists** *by Rowan Callick*
Hong Kong since the Handover.
*Much has been written about Hong Kong before the handover. Of more historic importance was the first year under Chinese rule. Nothing turned out as expected. Capitalism, not communism, caused the problems that nearly wrecked the economy.* £9.99

Available from all good booksellers, or
in the United Kingdom from Central Books
99 Wallis Rd. Lodon E11 5LN Tel: 018 986 4854
(Visa and Master cards accepted)

COMERFORD

AND MILLER